The American Revolution
A Historical Guidebook

The American Revolution

A Historical Guidebook

The Conservation Fund

Frances H. Kennedy

EDITOR

OXFORD

UNIVERSITY PRESS

OXFORD
UNIVERSITY PRESS

Oxford University Press is a department of the
University of Oxford. It furthers the University's objective
of excellence in research, scholarship, and education
by publishing worldwide.

Oxford   New York

Auckland   Cape Town   Dar es Salaam   Hong Kong   Karachi
Kuala Lumpur   Madrid   Melbourne   Mexico City   Nairobi
New Delhi   Shanghai   Taipei   Toronto

With offices in

Argentina   Austria   Brazil   Chile   Czech Republic   France   Greece
Guatemala   Hungary   Italy   Japan   Poland   Portugal   Singapore
South Korea   Switzerland   Thailand   Turkey   Ukraine   Vietnam

Oxford is a registered trade mark of Oxford University Press
in the UK and certain other countries.

Published in the United States of America by
Oxford University Press
198 Madison Avenue, New York, NY 10016

Library of Congress Cataloging-in-Publication Data
The American Revolution : a historical guidebook
/ Frances H. Kennedy, editor.
pages   cm
Includes bibliographical references and indexes.
ISBN 978-0-19-932422-4 (hardback)
1. United States—History—Revolution, 1775–1783—Battlefields—Guidebooks.
2. United States—History—Revolution, 1775–1783—Monuments—Guidebooks.
3. United States—History—Revolution, 1775–1783—Museums—Guidebooks.
4. Historic sites—United States—Guidebooks.
5. United States—Guidebooks.   I. Kennedy, Frances H.
E230.A43 2014
973.3—dc23   2013040019

1 3 5 7 9 8 6 4 2
Printed in the United States of America
on acid-free paper

FOREWORD

Today, you can still walk in the footsteps of the Revolutionary War soldiers, visiting the meadows and farmland where lives were lost and families changed forever, in the name of freedom. That is only possible because conservationists across the country have banded together, collaborating to protect these places.

The Conservation Fund is proud to be part of this legacy. Since 1985, we have protected more than seven million acres, across America and in all 50 states. More than 200 projects protected historic places, including American Revolution lands in Massachusetts, Delaware, and Pennsylvania, among other states. We've also conserved dozens of Civil War battlefield sites, among other historic lands nationwide that have witnessed bravery, tragedy, and triumph.

Our American story begins outdoors. We invite you to join us as partners in conservation. Together, we can celebrate our outdoor heritage—and protect it for future generations to discover all over again.

Lawrence A. Selzer
President and CEO
The Conservation Fund

The Conservation Fund
1655 N. Fort Myer Drive, Suite 1300
Arlington, VA 22209
www.conservationfund.org

CONTENTS

MAPS AND ILLUSTRATIONS

TO THE READER

The United States of America began with a revolution. British subjects broke away from the empire, declared their independence, and established the United States of America. Thanks to the courage and vision of patriotic Revolutionaries, our nation was founded on an enduring commitment to the principles of equality and liberty. Thanks to wise preservation efforts by Americans over the centuries, we can learn about our history in the places where this commitment was first made and defended.

In these places we can discover anew the remarkable people who founded our nation and the relevance of their words and struggles for us today. In 1783, at the end of the Revolutionary War, General George Washington wrote in his final Circular to State Governments that there were four things "essential to the well being, I may even venture to say, to the existence of the United States as an Independent Power," including "the prevalence of that pacific and friendly Disposition, among the People of the United States, which will induce them to forget their local prejudices and policies, to make those mutual concessions which are requisite to the general prosperity, and in some instances, to sacrifice their individual advantages to the interest of the Community."

The American Revolution: A Historical Guidebook seeks to evoke this community, offering an overview of the Revolution by focusing on 147 historic places that are critical to our understanding of it, set in a roughly chronological narrative of the Revolution. Several of these numbered places are repeated, such as Independence Hall, because significant events occurred at each at different times. To illuminate these places and their historical context, the Guidebook incorporates excerpts from some of the most outstanding books written on the Revolution. These excerpts are also guides for further reading about the places—as well as the people, documents, and events of the Revolution. The page numbers of the excerpts are listed in the Bibliography, Permissions, and Copyright Information with the books from which they are drawn. The excerpts do not include the authors' notes and footnotes or ellipses to denote deletions. Several excerpts are from websites and National

Park Service brochures listed in the Bibliography, Permissions, and Copyright Information. The Conservation Fund and I are very grateful to the authors and their publishers for their generous permissions to reprint these excerpts. Our thanks also to the Gilder Lehrman Collection, the Library of Congress, and the National Archives, for permission to include images of historic documents from their collections, and to the National Museum of American History for permission to include images of objects from its collections.

The 147 places discussed in these pages are drawn from the *Report to Congress on the Historic Preservation of Revolutionary War and War of 1812 Sites in the United States* prepared by the National Park Service in 2007. All of the historic buildings and many of the battlefields are open to the public. Most have websites that provide information for visitors. This guide includes with each numbered place its current name, location, and information about any historical markers and nearby museums. The battles fought on land that is not open to the public are described without specific location information. Some important battles, including Long Island in August of 1776, are described but the sites are not among the 147 numbered places because they have been lost to development.

The six state maps at the end of the front matter show the general location of each place by its number. Three places are not on the maps because the historic area is not open to the public and there are no historical markers. The legend for each map shows the name and number of each place, the nearest town, and the page number in this book.

The book's appendices include the Declaration of Independence and an excerpt from the 2007 National Park Service Report to Congress. The Timeline includes the main events between 1763, when the Treaty of Paris ended the Seven Years' War, and 1791, when three-fourths of the states ratified the Bill of Rights. The About the Authors section includes information about the authors of the excerpts and their books. Further Resources includes the full addresses for the websites referenced; the names and locations of additional historic places; and the National Park Service websites for the national historical parks, sites, monuments, memorials, and battlefields included in this book. The Bibliography, Permissions, and Copyright Information provides full details of the retained copyrights.

ACKNOWLEDGMENTS

I am very grateful to the Gilder Lehrman Institute of American History and to Sandra Trenholm, Curator and Director of the Gilder Lehman Collection, and to Tom Mullusky, Special Collections Librarian at The Gilder Lehrman Institute of American History, for reproductions of the historic documents from the Collection. My thanks to Edward Redmond, Curator in the Geography and Map Division of the Library of Congress, for the digitized images of historic maps from the Collections of the Library of Congress. My thanks to Sam Anthony, Special Assistant to the Archivist of the United States, for digitized images of documents from the collections of the National Archives and Records Administration. My thanks to Harry R. Rubenstein, Chair and Curator, and Debra Hashim, Associate Curator, in the Division of Political History, for providing images of objects from the collections of the National Museum of American History. My thanks to Will Allen, Director of Strategic Conservation Planning at The Conservation Fund, for designing the six maps showing the 147 places.

Many authorities on the Revolution, in addition to the authors of the excerpts, and on the historic places were generous with their help, information, and wise counsel. Those in the National Park Service include: Marty Blatt, Erin Broadbent, Jonathan Burpee, Paul Carson, Cassius Cash, Debbie Conway, Joe Craig, Charles Cranfield, Dawn Davis, Frances Delmar, Diane Depew, Jeanne DeVito, Joe DiBello, Bert Dunkerly, Joe Finan, Leo Finnerty, Barbara Goodman, Tanya Gossett, Rick Hatcher, Paul Hawke, Jason Howell, Louis Hutchins, Peter Iris-Williams, Gina Johnson, Mary Laura Lamont, David Lowe, Cynthia MacLeod, Brian McCutchen, Linda Meyers, Terry Mitchell, Nancy Nelson, Leslie Obleschuk, Eric Olson, Karen Rehm, Chris Revels, Eric Schnitzer, Edie Shean-Hammond, Timothy Stone, Robert Sutton, Coxey Toogood, Bill Troppman, Mary Beth Wester, and John Whitehurst.

My thanks, also, to: Mike Aikey, Rachel Bliven, Keith Bohannon, Michael D. Coker, Linda Cordell, Joanna Craig, William deBuys, Jeanne DeVito, Arthur C. Edgar, Jr., George Fields, Christopher Fox, Elsa Gilbertson, Richard Greenwood, Elizabeth Hagood, Nathan Hale, Jason Harpe, Al Hester, Timothy Ives, Kirk Johnston, Jennifer L. Jones, Randall Jones, Rick Kanaski, Betsy Kuster, Laura McCarty, Lin Olsen, Nancy O'Malley, Dwight Pitcaithley, Douglas Powell, Becky M. Riddle, Brian Robson, Darlene Rogers, Stuart Sanders, Caren Schumacher, Michael J. Schwendau, Daniel Shafer, Roger Stapleton, Jonathan Stayer, Carol Tanzola, Wade Wells, and Eric Williams. My special thanks to Timothy Bent, Editor at Oxford University Press, to Assistant Editor Keely Latcham, and to Joellyn Ausanka, Senior Production Editor, for their wise counsel and for guiding it to publication.

Frances H. Kennedy
Washington, DC

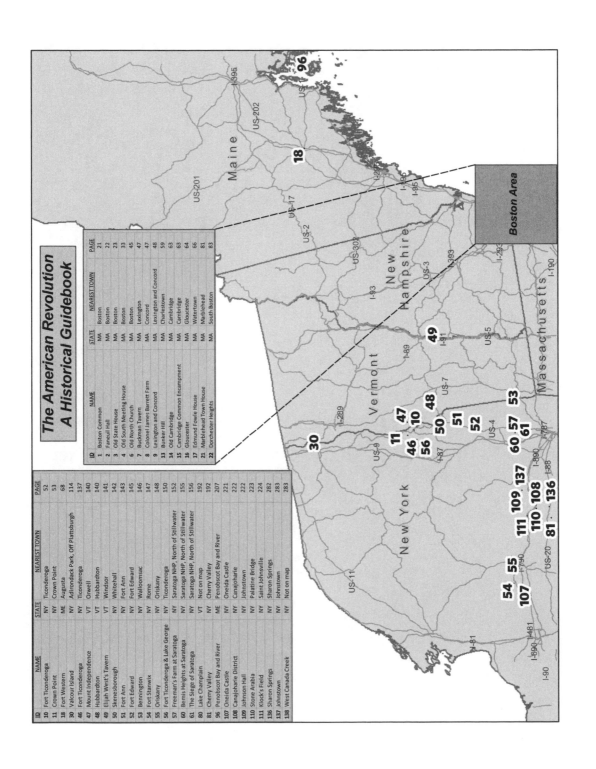

The American Revolution
A Historical Guidebook

Boston Area

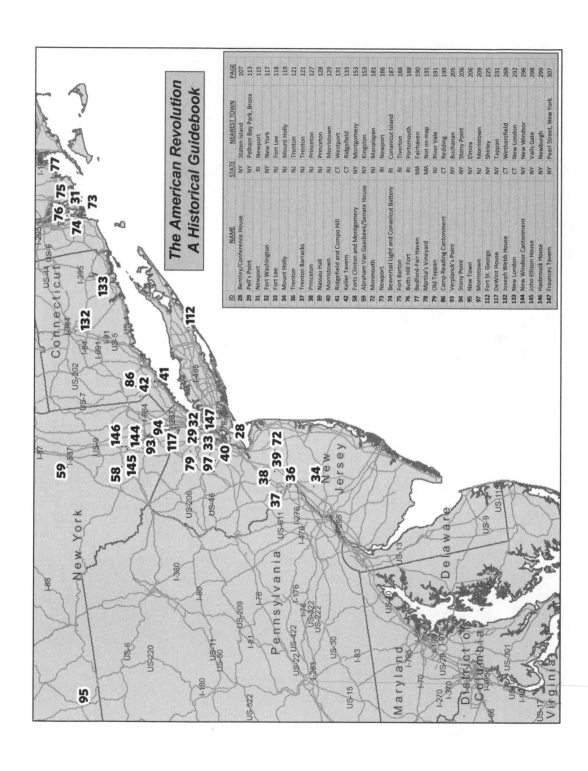

The American Revolution
A Historical Guidebook

ID	NAME	STATE	NEAREST TOWN	PAGE
28	Bentley/Conference House	NY	Staten Island	107
29	Pell's Point	NY	Pelham Bay Park, Bronx	113
31	Newport	RI	Newport	115
32	Fort Washington	NY	New York	117
33	Fort Lee	NJ	Fort Lee	118
34	Mount Holly	NJ	Mount Holly	119
36	Trenton	NJ	Trenton	121
37	Trenton Barracks	NJ	Trenton	121
38	Princeton	NJ	Princeton	127
39	Nassau Hall	NJ	Princeton	128
40	Morristown	NJ	Morristown	129
41	Ridgefield and Compo Hill	CT	Westport	131
42	Keller Tavern	CT	Ridgefield	133
58	Forts Clinton and Montgomery	NY	Montgomery	153
59	Abraham Van Gaasbeek/Senate House	NY	Kingston	153
72	Monmouth	NJ	Manalapan	181
73	Newport	RI	Newport	186
74	Beavertail Light and Conanicut Battery	RI	Conanicut Island	187
75	Fort Barton	RI	Tiverton	188
76	Butts Hill Fort	RI	Portsmouth	188
77	Bedford-Fair Haven	MA	Fairhaven	190
78	Martha's Vineyard	MA	Not on map	191
79	Old Tappan	NJ	River Vale	191
86	Camp Reading Cantonment	CT	Redding	199
93	Verplanck's Point	NY	Buchanan	205
94	Stony Point	NY	Stony Point	206
95	New Town	NY	Elmira	206
97	Morristown	NJ	Morristown	209
112	Fort St. George	NY	Shirley	225
117	DeWint House	NY	Tappan	231
132	Joseph Webb House	CT	Wethersfield	269
133	New London	CT	New London	292
144	New Windsor Cantonment	NY	New Windsor	296
145	John Ellison House	NY	Vails Gate	298
146	Hasbrouck House	NY	Newburgh	299
147	Fraunces Tavern	NY	Pearl Street, New York	307

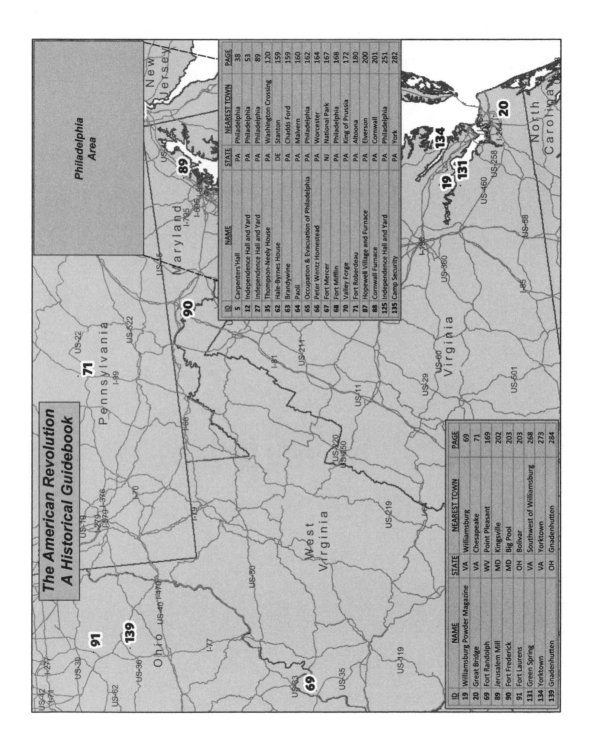

The American Revolution
A Historical Guidebook

Philadelphia Area

ID	NAME	STATE	NEAREST TOWN	PAGE
5	Carpenters' Hall	PA	Philadelphia	38
12	Independence Hall and Yard	PA	Philadelphia	53
27	Independence Hall and Yard	PA	Philadelphia	89
35	Thompson-Neely House	PA	Washington Crossing	120
62	Hale-Byrnes House	DE	Stanton	159
63	Brandywine	PA	Chadds Ford	159
64	Paoli	PA	Malvern	160
65	Occupation & Evacuation of Philadelphia	PA	Philadelphia	162
66	Peter Wentz Homestead	PA	Worcester	164
67	Fort Mercer	NJ	National Park	167
68	Fort Mifflin	PA	Philadelphia	168
70	Valley Forge	PA	King of Prussia	172
71	Fort Roberdeau	PA	Altoona	180
87	Hopewell Village and Furnace	PA	Elverson	200
88	Cornwall Furnace	PA	Cornwall	201
125	Independence Hall and Yard	PA	Philadelphia	251
135	Camp Security	PA	York	282

ID	NAME	STATE	NEAREST TOWN	PAGE
19	Williamsburg Powder Magazine	VA	Williamsburg	69
20	Great Bridge	VA	Chesapeake	71
69	Fort Randolph	WV	Point Pleasant	169
89	Jerusalem Mill	MD	Kingsville	202
90	Fort Frederick	MD	Big Pool	203
91	Fort Laurens	OH	Bolivar	203
131	Green Spring	VA	Southwest of Williamsburg	268
134	Yorktown	VA	Yorktown	273
139	Gnadenhutten	OH	Gnadenhutten	284

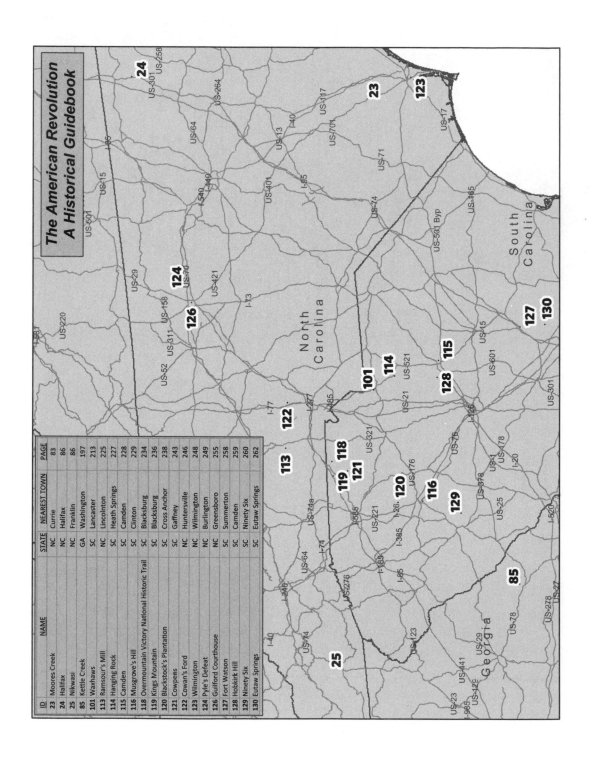

The American Revolution
A Historical Guidebook

ID	NAME	STATE	NEAREST TOWN	PAGE
23	Moores Creek	NC	Currie	83
24	Halifax	NC	Halifax	86
25	Nikwasi	NC	Franklin	86
85	Kettle Creek	GA	Washington	197
101	Waxhaws	SC	Lancaster	213
113	Ramsour's Mill	NC	Lincolnton	225
114	Hanging Rock	SC	Heath Springs	227
115	Camden	SC	Camden	228
116	Musgrove's Hill	SC	Clinton	229
118	Overmountain Victory National Historic Trail	SC	Blacksburg	234
119	Kings Mountain	SC	Blacksburg	236
120	Blackstock's Plantation	SC	Cross Anchor	238
121	Cowpens	SC	Gaffney	243
122	Cowan's Ford	NC	Huntersville	246
123	Wilmington	NC	Wilmington	248
124	Pyle's Defeat	NC	Burlington	249
126	Guilford Courthouse	NC	Greensboro	255
127	Fort Watson	SC	Summerton	258
128	Hobkirk Hill	SC	Camden	259
129	Ninety Six	SC	Ninety Six	260
130	Eutaw Springs	SC	Eutaw Springs	262

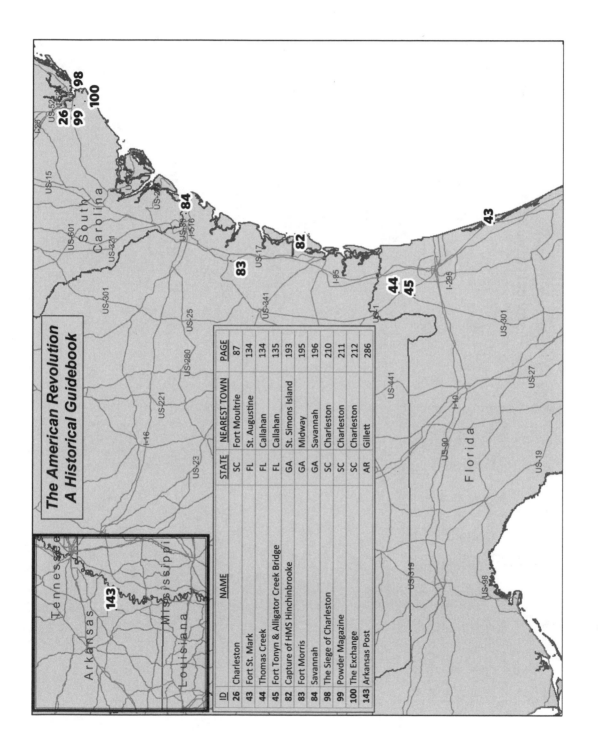

The American Revolution
A Historical Guidebook

ID	NAME	STATE	NEAREST TOWN	PAGE
26	Charleston	SC	Fort Moultrie	87
43	Fort St. Mark	FL	St. Augustine	134
44	Thomas Creek	FL	Callahan	134
45	Fort Tonyn & Alligator Creek Bridge	FL	Callahan	135
82	Capture of HMS Hinchinbrooke	GA	St. Simons Island	193
83	Fort Morris	GA	Midway	195
84	Savannah	GA	Savannah	196
98	The Siege of Charleston	SC	Charleston	210
99	Powder Magazine	SC	Charleston	211
100	The Exchange	SC	Charleston	212
143	Arkansas Post	AR	Gillett	286

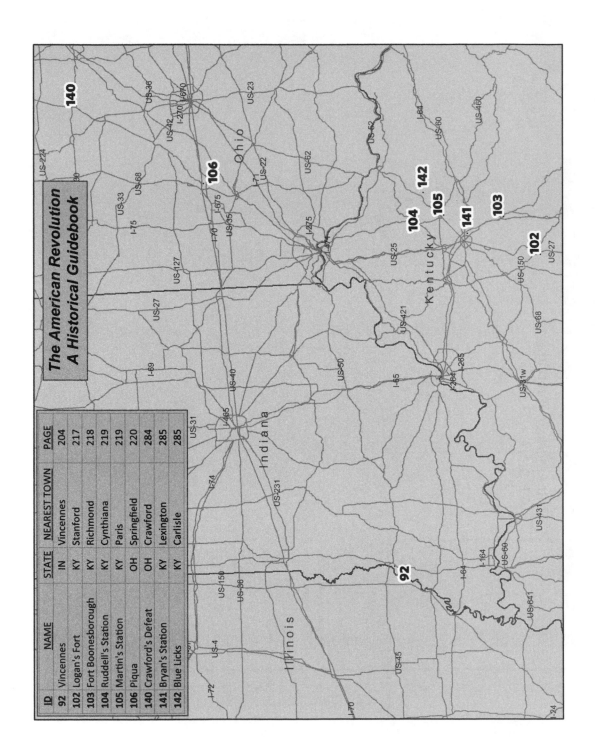

The American Revolution
A Historical Guidebook

ID	NAME	STATE	NEAREST TOWN	PAGE
92	Vincennes	IN	Vincennes	204
102	Logan's Fort	KY	Stanford	217
103	Fort Boonesborough	KY	Richmond	218
104	Ruddell's Station	KY	Cynthiana	219
105	Martin's Station	KY	Paris	219
106	Piqua	OH	Springfield	220
140	Crawford's Defeat	OH	Crawford	284
141	Bryan's Station	KY	Lexington	285
142	Blue Licks	KY	Carlisle	285

The American Revolution
A Historical Guidebook

The Coming of the American Revolution

The American Revolution began years before the British regiments arrived in 1768 to occupy the Boston Common (see #1). After the end of the Seven Years' War in 1763, the acts of Parliament and the colonists' reactions to them set events into motion that altered the relationship between Britain and its American colonies, leading to the occupation. The following excerpts from leading books on the Revolution provide an overview of the people and the events of those years, beginning with Gary B. Nash in *The Unknown American Revolution* on the importance of history.

> Only a history that gives play to all the constituent parts of society can overcome the defeatist notion that the past was inevitably determined. Historical inevitability is a winner's story, excusing mistakes of the past and relegating the loser's story to a footnote. If history did not unfold inevitably in the American Revolution, then surely a great many people must have been significant actors in its unfolding. Conscious of a complex past, readers today can embrace the idea that they, too, can contribute to a different future. Honest history can impart a sense of how the lone individual counts, how the possibilities of choice are infinite, how human capacity for both good and evil is ever present, and how dreams of a better society are in the hands of the dispossessed as much as in the possession of the putative brokers of our society's future.

The history of the American Revolution begins with Britain's relationship to its American colonies, which David Hackett Fischer outlines in *Albion's Seed: Four British Folkways in America.*

> The growth of regional folk cultures in British America was fostered by a unique political environment which was very different from other European colonies. New France and New Spain were more closely controlled by imperial authorities than were England's American provinces, which had more freedom to manage their own affairs.

This condition did not develop by design. English statesmen looked upon the empires of France and Spain with admiration, and even with envy. The authorities in London often tried to impose similar controls upon their own colonies. But for many years these efforts failed and regional cultures of British America were left to go their own way.

After the glorious Revolution, the new Protestant regime of William and Mary also tried to bring the colonies to heel, and at last succeeded in doing so. It created a new body called the Board of Trade, and a complex machinery of imperial government. But the delicate relationship between King and Parliament prevented either from asserting itself as forcefully as did imperial authorities in France and Spain. After 1714, Britain was ruled by German kings who cared little about America, and English ministers who knew less. One of them believed that Massachusetts was an island. There was in London a profound ignorance of American conditions.

Throughout the empire, colonial assemblies continued to claim parliamentary status, even though officials in London regarded them as comparable to municipal councils. This constitutional question was not resolved before 1775. While it continued, England's American provinces remained more nearly autonomous than other European colonies, and regional cultures developed with less interference from above.

While Americans were becoming increasingly autonomous, Britain was fighting France in a long war that would determine the control of North America. In *Crucible of War,* Fred Anderson documents the effects on America of the Seven Years' War—called the French and Indian War by the colonists—which ended with the 1763 Treaty of Paris.

The war was a violent imperial competition that resulted first in a decisive victory and then in a troubled attempt by metropolitan authorities to construct a new British empire along lines that would permit them to exercise effective control over colonies and conquests alike. The birth of an American republic was not anywhere in view. The war began when the diplomatic miscalculations of the Six Nations of the Iroquois allowed the French and British empires to confront each other over the control of the Ohio Valley. The ensuing conflict spread from North America to Europe, the Caribbean basin, West Africa, India, and the Philippine archipelago: in a real although more limited sense than we intend when we apply the words to twentieth-century conflicts, a world war. While the Seven Years' War resolved none of Europe's internecine conflicts, so far as North America and the British Empire were concerned, this immense conflict changed everything, and by no means only for the better. The war's progression, from its early years of French predominance to its climax in the Anglo-American conquest of Canada, and particularly in its protraction beyond 1760, set in motion the forces that created a hollow British empire. That outcome neither foretold nor necessitated the American Revolution; as any student of Spanish or Ottoman history can testify, empires can endure for centuries on end as mere shells of cultural affiliation and institutional form. Only the conflicted attempt to infuse meaning and efficacy into the imperial connection made the Revolution a possibility.

The Seven Years' War was above all a theater of intercultural interaction, an event by which the colonists of New France and British North America came into intimate contact both with metropolitan authorities—men who spoke their languages but who did not share their views of the war or the character of the imperial relationship—and with Indian peoples, whose participation as allies, enemies, negotiators, and neutrals so critically shaped the war's outcome. Its narrative logic suggests that the early experience of the war convinced British government officials (more mindful of colonial recalcitrance in the disastrous years of 1754–57 than of their enthusiasm in the years of victory, 1758–60) that the only rational way to deal with the American colonists was to exert control from Whitehall. Thus the war's lessons prompted a series of ministries to seek revenue from the colonies, even as they struggled to stabilize relations with the Indians and stem the outrush of settlers to regions that the war had made accessible. None of it worked.

The native peoples of the interior were the first to react negatively to changes imposed from above. They did it by launching the attacks that grew into the most successful pan-Indian resistance movement in American history, the war misleadingly called Pontiac's Rebellion. At almost precisely the same time, ministerial efforts to reform the administration of the colonies, raise modest revenues for their defense, and make the colonists more responsive to metropolitan authority precipitated violent civil disobedience in the Stamp Act crisis. Both Pontiac's Rebellion and the riotous resistance to the Stamp Act marked efforts of groups distant from the formal center of imperial power to "shape, challenge, [and] resist colonialism"—*not* with any intention to destroy the empire, but rather to define it in terms acceptable to themselves. Of course, no one in the British government saw the Indian insurrection or the Stamp Act riots in that way; nor did they appreciate the significance of the fact that both the Indians and the colonists, groups always more disposed to compete internally than to find common ground among themselves, had shown a sudden, unexpected capacity to achieve consensus.

The chaotic competition of two empires to control the Ohio Valley ended with the losing empire in ruins and the victor seeking to control its fabulous gains—and seemingly being repaid for its pains with ingratitude and resistance. The British authorities had no intention of letting either Indians or colonists define the character of empire. The future of Indian relations could, for the time being, be set aside; the question of the colonists' submission could not. Britain's subsequent efforts to specify the terms of the imperial relationship, and the reactions of the colonial populations to them, would begin a new chapter in the story of an Atlantic world transformed by war.

While Britain tried to control its relationship with its colonies, the Ottawa Indian leader Pontiac organized an anti-British uprising known as Pontiac's Rebellion, which began with the siege of Fort Detroit in May of 1763. This and other acts of violence on the frontier resulted in a new British policy declared by King George III. In *The People: A History of Native America*, R. David Edmunds, Frederick E. Hoxie, and Neal Salisbury describe the King's proclamation.

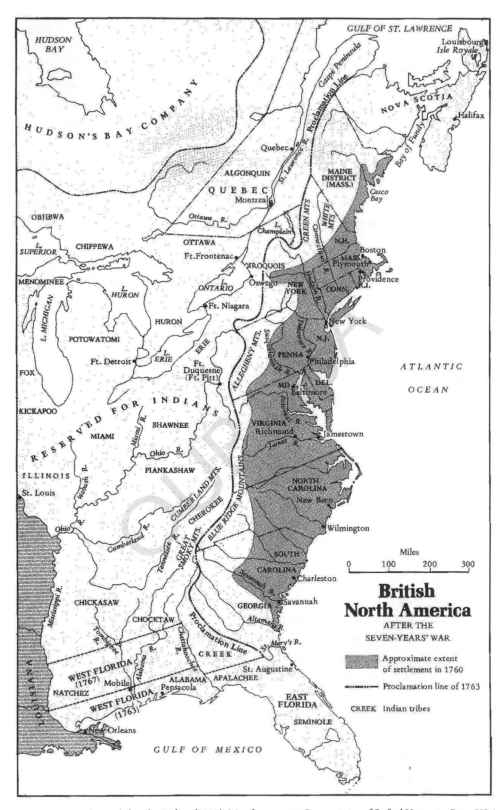

From: A Leap in the Dark *by John Ferling (2003). Map from p. xviii. By permission of Oxford University Press, USA*

The heart of the new British policy was set forth in the Proclamation of 1763, issued by King George III in October. A "Proclamation Line" along the crest of the Appalachian Mountains set limits to the colonies' western land claims. The proclamation recognized tribes' title to their unceded lands west of the line, although their sovereignty remained subordinate to that of the British and required that any sales of that land by Indians be approved by one of two Superintendents of Indian Affairs. The proclamation also empowered the superintendents to license traders west of the line and barred other non-Indians from crossing the line without the superintendents' permission. In other words, British officials would directly oversee all Anglo-Indian transactions, thereby avoiding the abuses of Native Americans by colonial agents and private individuals that had fueled Indians' anti-British sentiments.

The new regulations incurred the wrath of colonists who resented British authority, whether exerted in the form of taxes or of constraints on colonial expansion. From 1763 until colonists' resentments exploded in revolution twelve years later, British policymakers walked a tightrope between the conflicting interests of Native Americans and expansion-minded Anglo-Americans.

After the Seven Years' War, Britain controlled North America. In *1777: The Year of the Hangman,* John S. Pancake points to the costs of that control, Britain's enormous national debt, and Parliament's decision to pass the Stamp Act as a source of revenue.

If George Washington and his contemporaries had been told the American history books would have contained sections entitled: "The American Revolution: 1763–1789" they would have been amazed. Washington remarked on his return to his farm at the end of the Seven Years' War that "we are much rejoiced at the prospect of peace which 'tis hoped will be of long continuance." For the frame of the colonial mind had as yet conceived of no serious quarrels with the mother country, much less the notion of American Independence.

Yet what Professor Lawrence Gipson has called the Great War for Empire had given England a preponderance of power which ultimately proved her undoing. France and her allies were dismayed at the drastic shift in the balance of power and anxious for an opportunity to redress it. As Benjamin Franklin noted, "Every nation in Europe wishes to see Britain humbled, having all in turn been offended by her insolence." When her American colonies revolted England's enemies welcomed the opportunity, and their aid was crucial to the success of the War of Independence.

For the Americans in 1763, there was relief that the threat of New France which had hovered over the Northern horizon for more than a century was finally gone, although they did not perhaps perceive that they thereby became less dependent on the mother country. Loyalty is rooted in mutual needs and common hopes and fears. At the beginning of the eighteenth century 200,000 colonists were strung along the Atlantic littoral from Massachusetts to the Carolinas, a thin rim of Britain's empire. Their existence was vitally dependent on support from England. By 1763 the population had exploded to two million and the colonies were not only prosperous but remarkably self-reliant.

It might be noted in passing that their self-confidence generated a myth: that they, not the redcoats, had won this war, and the veterans' tales of Louisbourg and the Plains of Abraham lost nothing in the telling in the years after 1763. For such men of valor British regulars posed no serious problem when it came time to assert American rights by force of arms.

In fact, at the beginning of the French war, Americans had been extremely reluctant to aid the British army. Not a single colony came near meeting the quotas of men and supplies which the home government requested. Pleas and threats alike fell on deaf ears, for colonial assemblies controlled taxes and appropriations, including the salaries of the governors. Many a faithful servant of the crown, faced with royal displeasure 3,000 miles away or the wrath of the colonial assembly just across the street, was bludgeoned into submission by the power of the legislative purse. General Edward Braddock, on the eve of his fateful march to the forks of the Ohio, complained that Pennsylvania and Virginia "promised great matters and have done nothing, whereby instead of forwarding they have obstructed services." Only when the war government of William Pitt, driven to desperate measures, agreed to reimburse the colonies for wartime expenses, did colonial patriotism become as swollen as colonial purses. Royal officials had the uneasy feeling that one of the badly wounded casualties of the war was British authority in America.

England emerged from the war staggering under an enormous national debt, and a program of imperial retrenchment was inaugurated. George Grenville, a capable administrator but sadly lacking in imperial statesmanship, was the first of a series of ministers who attempted to set Britain's economic house in order. He began by instructing customs officers to begin enforcing the trade laws, a proposal which was not only startling but financially disastrous to crown officials who had been thriving off the bribes of colonial merchants. Under Grenville's whip they had no choice but to turn on their erstwhile benefactors and recover their former affluence by zealous—and often fraudulent—enforcement of intricate and complicated customs laws. Customs officials were entitled to a percentage of confiscated goods and cargoes, and their legal racketeering outraged colonial merchants.

Lord Grenville also began to cast up the accounts on the colonial books. He discovered that the administrative cost of the American colonies was several times as great as the revenue which they contributed. To Grenville's orderly mind this was an untidy situation and he set about to remedy it through taxation. To his credit, he asked for advice, even consulting that foremost expert in American affairs, Benjamin Franklin. The solution which Grenville hit upon was the Stamp Act of 1765 which levied a tax on all kinds of legal and commercial paper—newspapers, contracts, invoices, wills, and the like.

Parliament passed the Currency Act and the Sugar Act in 1764, and the Stamp Act and the Quartering Act in 1765. Colonists began vigorous protests, and in October 1765, delegates from nine colonies met in the Stamp Act Congress in New York and passed resolutions against the act. Edward Countryman details the act, the protests, and the Congress in *The American Revolution*.

The Stamp Act differed in important ways from all previous imperial legislation. One was its pervasiveness. Any colonist who bought or sold land, became an apprentice, went to church, married, read a newspaper, drank in a tavern, gambled, took public office, shipped goods elsewhere, or went to court would feel its effects. A second was its mode of collection: the taxes would be constantly evident, not paid once at a port of entry and then hidden in the overall price. A third was its requirement that payment be in sterling, with the threat of forfeiture if payment was not made. For people who rarely saw hard British coin, that threat was real. The act was part of a general assault on provincial paper money. Since 1752 New England colonies had been forbidden to make their money legal tender, and in 1764 that prohibition was extended to all the colonies. The Stamp Act managed to offend everyone. The revenues raised would remain in the colonies, paying the salaries of officials and the costs of troops. But neither troops nor officials would be subject to colonial control.

American writers came to see the political world in terms of an unending struggle between liberty and its enemies. Sometimes they called the enemy of liberty power. By that, they usually meant a government's ability and desire to make people do what it wanted. Sometimes they called it oppression. By that, they meant the use of inordinate strength to take away the property of free men and turn them into cringing dependents. Sometimes they described it as corruption. This was not simple bribe taking or embezzlement. It was their shorthand for all the social entanglements and all the dependency that came with any way of life much more complex than simple farming.

When Virginia's planters responded to the Stamp Act, they brought their own experience and this language together. Spurred by the anger of a young member named Patrick Henry, they passed a series of resolutions against the act. Widely and not always accurately reported, these resolutions declared Virginia's opposition to the act on four separate grounds. First, Virginia's founders had lost none of their English "Liberties, Privileges, Franchises, and Immunities" when they emigrated. Second, two royal charters had confirmed their rights. Third, the right to tax themselves by consent of their own representatives was "the distinguishing Characteristick" of their *British* freedom." Fourth, they had always controlled their own "internal Polity and Taxation." As the Burgesses knew, the Stamp Act challenged them in two ways. First, it threatened the property of all colonials, for if Parliament could take anything, it could take everything. Second, it threatened the Burgesses' own position as privileged men, for if Parliament could tax Virginians, their own house would quickly fade to inconsequence. The Irish gentry had seen exactly that fate befall their Parliament in Dublin, and no Burgess wanted it to happen in Williamsburg.

Assemblies elsewhere followed the Virginians' lead. By the end of 1765, Rhode Island, Pennsylvania, Maryland, Connecticut, Massachusetts, South Carolina, New Jersey, and New York all had adopted similar resolves. In October a Stamp Act Congress with delegates from nine colonies gathered in New York City. The congress adopted fourteen resolutions against the act. Making all the points the Virginians had made, it went on to defend jury trials, to protest the act's burdens, and to assert that America already contributed enormously to Britain's well-being. It finished its work with petitions to Parliament and an address to the king. Clearly, the leaders of the colonies were alarmed.

The movement that nullified the Stamp Act and forced its repeal was the first great drama of the Revolution. The movement itself changed the issues. Colonial writers attacked the rationales that British spokesmen offered. They forced inconsistencies into the open; they made Parliament search for new ways to achieve its goals. Direct colonial action made whole policies unworkable. Despite the number of times the British backed down, colonial resistance stiffened England's determination to finally resolve the issue its way.

Some aspects of the new British policy were clearly acts of government. The Proclamation Line that was intended to keep whites and Indians apart and thus prevent frontier warfare was one. So, too, was the decision to establish an American Board of Customs Commissioners and site it in Boston, and the decision in 1768 to deploy troops there for the commissioners' protection.

These acts caused more than simple debate because they became closely bound to the problem of taxation. Parliament itself made the confusion worse at a number of points. The first came in the spring of 1766, in the form of the Declaratory Act. Parliament enacted this law as a gesture to its own self-image. The Declaratory Act asserted that Parliament had power "to make laws and statutes...to bind the colonies and people of *America*...in all cases whatsoever." It seemed straightforward, but it was a masterpiece of doublespeak. An Englishman could take "all cases whatsoever" to include taxation. A colonial could take it that "laws and statutes" and taxation were not the same thing. But however one read it, it appeared at the time to be little more than a blustering afterthought, a gesture to Parliament's wounded pride at having had to repeal the Stamp Act.

By 1765 acts of Parliament had brought Americans together in a consensus, described by John Ferling in *A Leap in the Dark: The Struggle to Create the American Republic.*

The crowd actions in 1765 were accompanied by an astonishing intellectual ferment. Between May and November, town meetings in New England, as well as essayists and assemblies from one end of America to the other, took pains to define the rights of the colonists within the empire. The impact on some colonists was electrifying. John Adams believed that he and many others had been transformed by the events of that frantic year. The people in all social classes, he ruminated, had become "more attentive to their liberties, more inquisitive about them, and more determined to defend them." Many years later, he reflected that the "child Independence" was born in the minds of the colonists during the Stamp Act crisis.

Nonetheless, Americans did not advocate independence in 1765, and indeed they were not yet revolutionaries. Many were not yet even radicals, but as never before they had begun to contemplate their position within the empire. During that year a consensus crystallized that Parliament's power over the colonies was limited and did not include the authority to tax the provinces. But few Americans, and still fewer public officials—by and large pragmatic men who dealt in the hard realities of governance—were willing to explore just how far Parliament's authority stretched. Their object was the repeal of the Stamp Act, not the promulgation of treatises on political theory.

There was a growing consensus among the colonists in their desire to see the Stamp Act repealed, and there were also conflicts, pointed out by David Brion Davis and Steven Mintz in *The Boisterous Sea of Liberty: A Documentary History of America from Discovery through the Civil War.*

Few in Britain or its colonies could have imagined in 1763 that a war for independence would erupt within a dozen years. The American colonists had a long history of squabbling with one another, and, before 1765, relations among the colonists were much more quarrelsome than their relations with Great Britain.

Rapid population growth within the colonies was a source of many intercolonial disputes, including conflicts over colonial boundaries. New York clashed with Connecticut and Massachusetts; Pennsylvania with Connecticut and Virginia; and New York and New Hampshire over claims to present-day Vermont.

Westerners and Easterners within individual colonies also fought over issues of representation, taxation, Indian policy, and the slow establishment of governmental institutions in frontier areas. In 1764 the Paxton Boys, a group of Scotch-Irish frontier settlers from western Pennsylvania, marched on Philadelphia, and withdrew only after they were promised a greater representation in the Quaker-dominated provincial assembly and greater protection against Indians. In the late 1760s in backcountry South Carolina, where local government was largely nonexistent, frontier settlers organized themselves into vigilante groups known as Regulators to maintain order. Only extension of a new court system into the backcountry kept the Regulators from attacking Charleston. In North Carolina in the early 1770s, the eastern militia had to suppress conflict in the backcountry, where settlers complained about underrepresentation in the colonial assembly, high taxes, exorbitant legal fees, and manipulation of debt laws by lawyers, merchants, and officials backed by eastern planters.

These regional conflicts often coincided with ethnic lines. Many backwoods residents were Scotch-Irish or German in descent, and they deeply resented the Anglo-American establishment of the more settled parts of the colonies. Conflict also surged periodically in areas where wealthy proprietors owned substantial amounts of land. In eastern New Jersey during the 1740s, and New York's Hudson River valley in 1757 and 1766, tenant farmers refused to pay rents and staged insurrections against landlords.

Yet for all their squabbles, the colonists did share certain characteristics in common, which became increasingly apparent during the years leading up to the Revolution. These included the absence of a titled, hereditary aristocracy; a widespread distribution of land; an unprecedented degree of ethnic and religious diversity; and broad eligibility to vote—50 to 75 percent of adult white males, compared to only about 20 percent in England. In contrast to the way Britons conceived of Parliament, the colonists thought of the members of the colonial assemblies as representatives of the people, accountable to their constituents and obligated to follow public instructions.

Certain shared economic grievances also gave a degree of common identity to the colonists, such as dependence on British and Scottish financial agents. The sharing of Protestant religious revivals as well as anti-Catholicism, too, proved to be important elements in an emerging American identity.

During the 1760s and 1770s all of these conditions, trends, and experiences contributed to a distinctive sense of American identity. Many colonists began to conceive of America as a truly "republican" society. By a republican society they meant something more than a government based on popular elections. Such a society emphasized personal independence, public virtue, and above all a suspicion of concentrated power as essential ingredients of a free society. Increasingly, Americans contrasted their society with Britain, with its landed aristocracy, political corruption, patronage, and bloated governmental bureaucracy. For decades, various European writers had idealized Americans as an industrious, egalitarian people, content with the simple joys of life. In the years preceding the Revolution, many Americans began to self-consciously reflect on this distinctive republican identity.

One important characteristic of the Americans was an interest in working with others to create associations that united their belief in individual rights and their concern for community. In *Benjamin Franklin: An American Life,* Walter Isaacson points to Franklin's leadership in weaving the two together.

Franklin picked up his penchant for forming do-good associations from Cotton Mather and others, but his organizational fervor and galvanizing personality made him the most influential force in instilling this as an enduring part of American life. "Americans of all ages, all stations in life, and all types of dispositions are forever forming associations," Tocqueville famously marveled. "Hospitals, prisons and schools take shape this way."

Tocqueville came to the conclusion that there was an inherent struggle in America between two opposing impulses: the spirit of rugged individualism versus the conflicting spirit of community and association building. Franklin would have disagreed. A fundamental aspect of Franklin's life, and of the American society he helped to create, was that individualism and communitarianism, so seemingly contradictory, were interwoven. The frontier attracted barn-raising pioneers who were ruggedly individualistic as well as fiercely supportive of their community. Franklin was the epitome of this admixture of self-reliance and civic involvement, and what he exemplified became part of the American character.

Franklin's subscription library, which was the first of its type in America, began when he suggested to his Junto that each member bring books to the clubhouse so that the others could use them. It worked well enough, but money was needed to supplement and care for the collection. So he decided to recruit subscribers who would pay dues for the right to borrow books, most of which would be imported from London.

The Library Company of Philadelphia was incorporated in 1731, when Franklin was 27. Its motto, written by Franklin, reflected the connection he made between goodness and godliness: *Communiter Bona profundere Deum est* (To pour forth benefits for the common good is divine).

While Americans were organizing associations, they were also coming together through their governments to declare their rights. In May 1765, the democratically elected legislative body in Virginia, the House of Burgesses, passed the Virginia Resolves. Introduced by Patrick Henry, a young and well known member of the House, the resolves asserted that only the colonists' elected representatives had the right to impose taxes. George Washington was among the opponents of the taxes Parliament levied on the colonies. John Rhodehamel describes Washington's early political views in *The Great Experiment: George Washington and the American Republic.*

The militancy of George Washington's political views has not always been recognized. If Washington moved reluctantly toward rebellion and independence, his ideas were more advanced than those of most colonials. As early as 1769 he predicted in a letter to a friend that "our lordly Masters in Great Britain will be satisfied with nothing less than the deprivation of American freedom." He declared that "no man shou'd scruple, or hesitate a moment to use a[r]ms in defense of so valuable a blessing." To speak of war with Britain at that early date was radical indeed. And certainly no man in America better understood how dangerous such a war must be.

The fierce denunciation of "our lordly Masters" was drawn from Washington's pen by taxes levied on the colonies by the British Parliament. Americans were outraged anew by the passage of the Townshend Acts in 1767. The bill was intended to raise revenues for the Crown by collecting duties on imports. Colonials countered with "nonimportation," the boycott of trade with Britain. By 1769, Washington had emerged as a leader of the nonimportation movement in Fairfax County, the most radical county in Virginia, a colony that was itself among the most outspoken in opposition to British authority.

The boycott of trade with Britain that Washington supported was one of the colonies' nonviolent protests. In *From Resistance to Revolution: Colonial Radicals and the Development of American Opposition to Britain, 1765–1776,* Pauline Maier describes the colonists' views on resistance and restraint.

The colonist's attitudes toward civil uprisings were part of a broader Anglo-American political tradition. In the course of the eighteenth century, colonists became increasingly interested in the idea of seventeenth-century English revolutionaries such as John Milton, Algernon Sidney, John Locke, and the later writers who carried on and developed this tradition— Robert Molesworth; John, Lord Somers; the Anglican bishop Benjamin Hoadly; John Trenchard and Thomas Gordon, whose essays, published together as *Cato's Letters,* were a classic for many Americans; the Scottish philosopher Francis Hutcheson; and the celebrated English historian of the 1760's and 1770's, Catharine Macaulay. By the 1760's, this "Real Whig" or "Commonwealthman" tradition provided a strong unifying element between colonists North and South. It offered, too, a corpus of ideas about public authority and popular political responsibilities that shaped the American revolutionary movement.

Spokesmen for this English revolutionary tradition were distinguished in the eighteenth century above all by their outspoken defense of the people's right to rise up against their rulers, which they supported in traditional contractual terms. Government was created by the people to promote the public welfare. If magistrates failed to honor that trust, they automatically forfeited their powers back to the people, who were free and even obliged to reclaim political authority. The people could do so, moreover, in acts of limited resistance, intended to nullify only isolated wrongful acts of the magistrates, or ultimately in revolution, which denied the continued legitimacy of the established government as a whole.

To stress the potential for revolution and disorder in these ideas, however, distorts not only the structure of late-seventeenth- and eighteenth-century Radical Whig thought, but also its influence on America. More than ever by the 1760's, Whig arguments for resistance and revolution rested on a firm commitment to an idealized version of the British regime and embodied an almost conservative desire to prevent it from further change or decay. The fundamental values of the Radical Whigs were realized most fully in a well-ordered free society, such that obedience to the law was stressed as much or more than occasional resistance to it. Moreover, while eighteenth-century Whig writers stood ready to challenge anyone who denied the people's right of revolution, they still sought to limit and even defer violence by a series of preconditions that were ever more carefully defined between Milton and mid-eighteenth-century writers like Hutcheson.

Naturally, the Real Whigs' justification of resistance could reinforce the colonists' tendency to condone uprisings where authorities were unresponsive to public needs. In fact, however, the Whigs' contrary emphasis on order and restraint counteracted any tendency toward a too-ready resort to force. In this way, Whiggism tempered the use of violence in the colonies, particularly during the eleven years before independence. The need to reconcile the impulse toward resistance with the injunction to restraint became, in fact, one of the central intellectual and practical problems of the American revolutionary movement.

Benjamin Franklin was living in London and serving as a colonial agent when the Stamp Act Congress passed resolutions against the act in October 1765. He was called before the House of Commons in February, 1776. In *The Marketplace of Revolution: How Consumer Politics Shaped American Independence,* T. H. Breen describes the proceedings.

Whatever his qualifications, Franklin experienced rough handling from the House of Commons. Over several grueling hours, he endured some 174 questions, 89 of which he classified as antagonistic. Try as they would, however, his interrogators could not control the proceedings. The nimble witness painted before their skeptical eyes a portrait of an expansive commercial empire, unprecedented in world history. Franklin warned Britain's rulers that unless they reconsidered taxing the colonists without representation and reformed new coercive modes of enforcement, they risked destroying the American goose that had laid so many golden eggs.

After an initial period of sparring, Franklin took charge of the exchange. The House of Commons wanted to know, for example, whether the colonists had merely used the passage of the Stamp Act as a convenient excuse to challenge imperial authority. Perhaps the Americans had long contemplated steering an independent political course. Perhaps recent revenue policies had only exacerbated tensions already present. Franklin dismissed that line of thought as nonsense. Before 1763, he insisted, the "temper" of the colonists toward Great Britain had been "the best in the world." What made their loyalty all the more impressive in his opinion was that it cost the Exchequer so little. Obedience never depended on "forts, citadels, garrisons or armies." The mere communication of command generated swift results in distant provinces, for, as the members of Parliament had obviously forgotten, the Americans "were governed by this country at the expense only of a little pen, ink and paper. They were led by a thread."

The image of imperial authority as a mere thread was inspired. This most gentle form of social and political control—English threads, not Spanish or French chains—explained the extraordinary might of the British Empire. The entire system drew strength not from military force but rather from shared values. The colonists, Franklin confessed, had "an affection, for Great-Britain, for its laws, its customs and manners, and even a fondness for its fashions, that greatly increased the commerce." And then, in a flash of rhetorical legerdemain, Franklin leapt from metaphorical "threads" of authority to the real manufactured threads that sustained the Atlantic economy, to the wool and cotton fibers woven into fashionable cloth which for a generation or more had transformed the very bodies of ordinary Americans into colorful emblems of a flourishing commercial empire. Statistics told a story of success. "I think the inhabitants of all the provinces together, taken at a medium, double in about 25 years," he explained. Stunning demographic growth only began to suggest the true potential of colonial trade. American demand, Franklin assured the members of Parliament, "increases much faster, as the consumption is not merely in proportion to their numbers, but grows with the growing abilities of the same numbers to pay for them. In 1723, the whole importation from Britain to Pennsylvania was but about 15,000 Pounds Sterling; it is now near Half a Million."

Commercial figures of this sort were, of course, old news. But Franklin interpreted the numbers in a strikingly innovative manner, pushing the political logic of everyday consumer demand in a direction that suggested that colonial buyers were neither as vulnerable nor as dependent as their British rulers may have imagined. In fact, the Stamp Act crisis had cast relations between Great Britain and the American colonies, between colonial consumers and English producers, in an entirely new light. No one had planned such a dramatic shift in political perspective. Reassessment of imperial identity simply evolved out of a confrontation with an aggressive House of Commons, an unintended consequence of an ill-conceived policy. And now, as a result of these events, the Americans began to appreciate that Britain's extraordinary commercial success in the New World had given them a voice in imperial affairs.

As the colonies were recognizing their value to the British economy, Parliament was focusing upon taxing and controlling them. In *From Resistance to Revolution,* Pauline Maier points to Britain's role in driving the American colonies toward independence.

For the radical movement to become revolutionary, more extreme conclusions were necessary. The Americans must become convinced, as John Dickinson put it, that "mistake or passion" could not explain Britain's wrong-headed actions. It had to appear "UNDOUBTED that an inveterate resolution is formed to annihilate the liberties of the governed," one that involved the King, Parliament, and ministry as centrally as their servants in the colonies. And to arrive at such a conclusion, colonists had to turn their eyes from their own continent to London, to examine the actions of King, Parliament, and ministry. In that fact lay the truth of a statement continually repeated by colonists during the frenetic days of the Stamp Act crisis—that only Great Britain could force America toward independence.

The movement toward independence was expanding and intensifying as Parliament threatened, and Americans defended, the universal rights and responsibilities held by all people. T. H. Breen details these in *American Insurgents, American Patriots: The Revolution of the People.*

The ideas that gave meaning to the American insurgency possess a simple elegance. The central element in popular political thought was a set of rights that God gave every man and woman long before they established civil government. These rights were universal; every human being could claim them. But rights carried responsibilities. God expected the people to preserve their rights. However burdensome this duty may have been in theory, it served to empower ordinary people in the contest against tyranny. As vigilant defenders of rights, they became judges of those who held authority, and in the imagined compact that bound rulers to subjects, it was the subjects who determined whether their magistrates were in fact working for the common good.

"Whig" was the name of one of the two political parties in Britain and an early term in America for the patriots. As Pauline Maier points out in *From Resistance to Revolution,* the Whig injunction was central to the Revolution, which was looming as British soldiers occupied Boston.

The challenge was imposing—more difficult than the young John Adams could realize in 1765 when he rejoiced in the opportunities given Americans by oppression. They could become "Brookes, Hampdens, Vanes, Seldens, Miltons, Nedhams, Harringtons, Nevilles, Sidneys, Lockes." Still, in the period of conflict the Americans' success as revolutionaries compared favorably with Adams's heroes largely because of their full response to both sides of the Whig injunction: to resist and to restrain disorder, to revolt but to prevent anarchy.

In 1766 Lieutenant Daniel Patterson prepared the map on the opposite page showing the British troop strengths and locations in the colonies. It also shows the colonies' competing land claims and the Proclamation Line of 1763 along the Appalachian Mountains, west of which were the "Lands Reserved for the Indians."

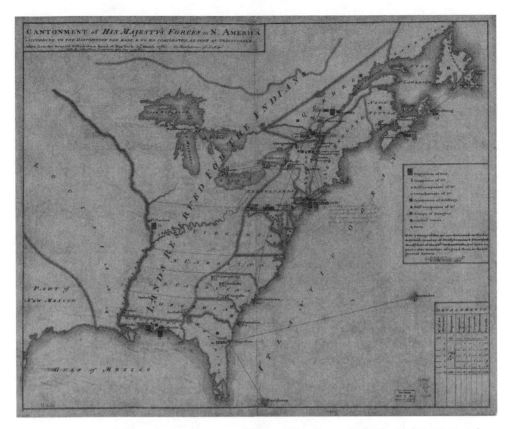

Distribution of British Troops in North America, 1766. Daniel Patterson. *Cantonment of His Majesty's forces in N. America according to the disposition now made & to be compleated as soon as practicable taken from the general distribution dated at New York 29th. March 1766* [1767]. *(Courtesy, Library of Congress, Geography and Map Division. http://hdl.loc.gov/loc.gmd/g3301r.ar011800)*

After Parliament repealed the Stamp Act in March 1766 and passed the Declaratory Act, it enacted import duties—the Townshend Acts—in 1767. Charles Townshend was Chancellor of the Exchequer. The protests against the duties resulted in the British occupation of Boston the following year, 1768.

PLACES OF THE

American Revolution

1. Boston Common, Massachusetts

Tremont, Beacon, Charles, Park, and Boylston Streets
Boston, Massachusetts

Boston Common was the site of Britain's first military action against the colonies. After Parliament repealed the Stamp Act in March 1766 and passed the Declaratory Act, it enacted import duties in 1767, the Townshend Acts. As a result of the strong protests against the Acts, four British regiments were ordered to occupy Boston to protect the customs commissioners. One of the regiments encamped on the Common during October 1768. During the occupation, which ended in March 1770, there were clashes between townspeople and soldiers on the Common. It was particularly dangerous after dark.

The Common, a fifty-acre park, is the oldest park in the nation. It was initially set aside in 1634 as a training ground for soldiers and as a grazing pasture for cattle.

Richard Archer describes Boston at the time of the occupation in *As If an Enemy's Country*.

Boston in 1768 was a much smaller city than we know it today. Its entire circumference was merely four miles, and it was less than three miles from the neck that linked the town to the mainland to the northeastern corner, where the Charlestown ferry landing stood. The bulk of the population resided either in the North End or the South End, which together composed two-thirds of the peninsula. Taking a brisk walk, in about an hour a person could see most of Boston, with its three hills, wood buildings and residences, church spires, and wharfs. No sidewalks aided the pedestrian, nor were there streetlamps providing light after dark.

The British troops upon landing may have been pleased with what they saw. Three years earlier Lord Adam Gordon had described Boston as "more like an English Old Town than any in America." But they would have been foolish to assume that familiarity meant welcome. Though they had not experienced the violent confrontation that had been rumored, for the most part they were met with sullen stares and silence. More overt opposition would come soon enough. "All is at present quiet," Andrew Eliot wrote in mid-October, "but there is a general gloom and uneasiness." He portrayed Boston as a garrisoned town, a recurring characterization used by town residents. Over time, the resentment grew.

The placing of four regiments in Boston as a police force to support British officials rather than as an army to protect the population certified that the town was being occupied as a hostile country and that Bostonians were viewed as an enemy people. That certainly was the impression of the citizens of Boston. Just like a bayonet, the standing army was thrust at them. In their minds they became not a subordinate but a separate people. They increasingly perceived themselves as Americans rather than British. The first American revolution was in Bostonians' sense of their identity.

On April 15, 1769, the Massachusetts Council, writing the Earl of Hillsborough, secretary of state for the American colonies, complained that the secrecy and circumstances attending the landing of troops in Boston were "as if in an Enemy's Country." The ministry was treating American colonies, Boston in particular, as alien land, and colonists, Bostonians in particular, recognized the change. Their loyalty to England was shaken. The immediate issue facing them was how to remove the occupying force. The larger issue was the colonies' place within the empire, and indeed whether there should be a place for them within the empire.

The second occupation of Boston began with the arrival in 1774 of eleven regiments to enforce the Coercive Acts. Washington's artillery on Dorchester Heights forced the British to evacuate Boston on March 17, 1776.

2. Faneuil Hall, Massachusetts

FANEUIL HALL, OWNED BY THE CITY OF BOSTON, IN
BOSTON NATIONAL HISTORICAL PARK
VISITOR CENTER FANEUIL HALL SQUARE
BOSTON, MASSACHUSETTS

Faneuil Hall, a market building and meeting hall, was built in 1742 and named for the merchant Peter Faneuil. It was the site of many protest meetings between 1764 and 1774, held as a result of the increased control Britain was exercising over its colonies compared with the years before 1763.

In October 1768 Lieutenant Colonel William Dalrymple, the commanding officer of the regiments occupying Boston, received permission from Boston officials for the 14th Regiment to billet in Faneuil Hall for two days. They stayed for a month. By 1769 the British had stationed nearly 4,000 troops in Boston, about one for every four Bostonians. After the Boston Massacre in 1770 (see #3), a town meeting held in the Hall resulted in the selection of a committee to call on Thomas Hutchinson, the acting royal governor, to remove the regiments from Boston. By mid-March 1770, the regiments had been moved from Boston to Castle Island in Boston Harbor.

3. Old State House, Massachusetts

OLD STATE HOUSE IN BOSTON NATIONAL HISTORICAL PARK
OPERATED BY THE BOSTONIAN SOCIETY
STATE AND WASHINGTON STREETS
BOSTON, MASSACHUSETTS

The occupation of Boston created tensions that resulted in crisis: the Boston Massacre near the Old State House, the oldest public building in Boston. Completed in 1713, it included a merchant's exchange on the first floor, and on the second, the Council Chamber of the royal governor and the meeting places for the Massachusetts Assembly, the Courts of Suffolk County, and the Massachusetts Supreme Judicial Court.

On March 5, 1770, a mob confronted British soldiers near the Old State House. When the men began to throw snowballs and sticks at Captain Thomas Preston and the eight soldiers with him, the soldiers fired, killing five colonists and wounding six. In their trial in a Boston court, the captain and the soldiers were defended by John Adams, a prominent lawyer. David McCullough describes the trials in *John Adams*.

There were to be two conspicuously fair trials held in the new courthouse on Queen Street. The first was of the British captain, Thomas Preston, the opening of the trial being delayed until October when passions had cooled. The second was of the soldiers. In the first trial John Adams was assisted by young Josiah Quincy, Jr., while the court-appointed lawyer trying the case was Josiah's brother, Samuel, assisted by Robert Treat Paine. Whether Captain Preston had given an order to fire, as was charged, could never be proven. Adams's argument for the defense, though unrecorded, was considered a virtuoso performance. Captain Preston was found not guilty.

Adams's closing for the second and longer trial, which was recorded, did not come until December 3, and lasted two days. The effect on the crowded courtroom was described as "electrical." Close study of the facts had convinced Adams of the innocence of the soldiers. The tragedy was not brought on by the soldiers, but by the mob, and the mob, it must be understood, was the inevitable result of the flawed policy of quartering troops in a city on the pretext of keeping the peace.

"Facts are stubborn things," he told the jury, "and whatever may be our wishes, our inclinations, or the dictums of our passions, they cannot alter the state of facts and evidence."

The jury remained out two and a half hours. Of the eight soldiers, six were acquitted and two found guilty of manslaughter, for which they were branded on their thumbs.

There were angry reactions to the decision. Adams was taken to task in the *Gazette* and claimed later to have suffered the loss of more than half of his practice. As time would show, John Adams's part in the drama did increase his public standing, making him in the long run more respected than ever.

Richard Archer describes the annual commemoration of the Massacre in *As If an Enemy's Country*.

Each year from 1771 to 1783 a commemoration of the Massacre on King Street was held. The annual tribute was a reminder of the perils of a standing army, the violations of colonial rights, the arrogance and perfidy of the royal government, and the existence of Bostonians and other colonists as a people apart, a population with unraveling ties to the British empire. Beginning at noon on March 5, 1771, church bells rang for an hour in Boston. In the evening Thomas Young gave an oration at the Manufactory. The next year Joseph Warren gave the oration in the afternoon at the Old South Church.

That was the pattern until 1776, when British troops again occupied Boston. By necessity, Peter Thacher of Malden gave the oration at the meetinghouse in nearby Watertown. In 1777, with the end of the second military occupation, the oration returned to Boston. There still was a political and psychological need for the citizens to remember. And so it went through 1783, until the Treaty of Paris recognized the United States as an independent country. The realization that had come with the landing of the occupying soldiers on October 1, 1768—that Bostonians and their countrymen were a separate people—had become a reality.

The expanding Revolution included leaders such as John Adams as well as artisans and other people from "out of doors," who increased the impact of the protests in Massachusetts and in other colonies. Alfred F. Young focuses on the leather apron men in "Ebenezer Mackintosh: Boston's Captain General of the Liberty Tree," in *Revolutionary Founders: Rebels, Radicals, and Reformers in the Making of the Nation*, edited by Alfred F. Young, Gary B. Nash, and Ray Raphael.

Historians weighing the sources of the American Revolution have rarely found a place for Ebenezer Mackintosh. But he had a measurable impact. He helped make political action by "leather apron" men acceptable and by shoemakers in particular. The "gentry" often singled them out for derision, invoking the proverb "Shoemaker, stick to thy last." A patriot aristocrat in Charleston offered the condescending rationale: men who knew little more than "to cobble an old shoe in a decent manner or to build a necessary house" lacked the education or leisure to participate in government.

Not so Boston's patriot leaders. In 1772 "Crispin"—the name of the patron saint of shoemakers—began an anti-Loyalist article in *The Massachusetts Spy* (a paper aimed at working people) by avowing, "I am a shoemaker, a citizen, a free man and a freeholder." The printer Isaiah Thomas added a postscript justifying "Crispin's" performance: "it should be known what common people, even *coblers* think and feel under the present administration." The rise to active citizenship by mechanics was also the theme of another Boston shoemaker, George Robert Twelves Hewes, whose memoirs recounted one episode after another in which he cast off deference to his betters. "We are all from the cobbler up to the senator become politicians," a Bostonian could claim in 1774.

Mackintosh also influenced the leaders who emerged in the Stamp Act–crisis, more perhaps than they could afford to say. It was a time when John Adams, Samuel Adams, and John Hancock, the three men who became Massachusetts's principal figures in the Revolution, learned different strategies for accommodating "the people out of doors" who were challenging those "within doors" with power in legislative chambers. "The year," John Adams confided to his diary at the end of 1765, "has been the most remarkable year of my Life." He was moved that "the People, even to the lowest ranks have become more attentive to their Liberties"—but he was also furious at the threats to individuals and property, and he undertook a lifelong commitment to maintain a due sense of "rank and subordination" in "the lowest ranks." For Samuel Adams, 1765 was the year he learned the importance of associations, committees, and the town meeting as a means of organizing ordinary people. John Hancock—twenty-seven, newly rich, and new to politics—learned in 1765 how he might use his fortune to advance both a cause and himself. His entertaining and outfitting Pope's Day officers while displaying all the trappings of great wealth began a style of patrician patronage that over time would make him the most popular politician in Massachusetts. He also discovered how crucial it was to keep the allegiance of his fellow merchants in the patriot coalition. In the final crisis, in 1775–76, a large proportion of the town's merchants and most of its men of greatest wealth would favor independence. This presence of merchants in the patriot coalition helps explain why in Boston the class feeling of the poor against the rich was more or less absorbed within the conflict with Britain.

All three leaders subscribed to the strategy expressed by the two rallying cries posted on the Liberty Tree late in 1765: "Vox populi, vox dei" and "Good Order and Steady" (which would reappear later as the slogan "No violence or you will hurt the cause"). The large, more or less peaceful demonstrations Mackintosh led gave them the confidence to claim "The Voice of the People is the Voice of God." At the same time they learned that the mere threat of violence to property and the symbolic violence to people implicit in hanging effigies could effectively intimidate enemies. Mackintosh's success lay in organizing the people "out of doors" to a sense of their potential, drawing on rituals of popular culture familiar to them. The success of the Sons of Liberty leaders lay in bringing such people, newly aroused, literally indoors and into a political system that would be enlarged by their presence. The Revolution in Boston owes much to both.

While Mackintosh was expanding the political system in Boston, other artisans were active in New York. One of the documents in *The Boisterous Sea of Liberty* by David Brion Davis and Steven Mintz is a public statement about artisans.

The revolutionary era greatly increased popular participation in politics. Political pamphlets proliferated, and newspapers were transformed from business organs into vehicles for political discussion. Not only did the number of subscribers multiply, but so, too, did the number of letters to the editor, as did circulation outside of cities. Popular demonstrations, many of which were initially and traditionally orchestrated from top down, grew more frequent and

To the FREE and LOYAL INHABITANTS of the CITY and COLONY of NEW-YORK.

Friends, fellow Citizens, fellow Countrymen, and fellow Freemen,

NOTHING can be more flagrantly wrong than the Assertion of some of our mercantile Dons, that the Mechanics have no Right to give their Sentiments about the Importation of *British* Commodities. For who, I would ask, is the Member of Community, that is absolutely independent of the rest? Or what particular Class among us, has an exclusive Right to decide a Question of general Concern? When the Non-Importation Agreement took Place, what End was it designed to answer? Not surely the private Emolument of Merchants, but the universal Weal of the Continent. It was to redeem from Perdition, from total Perdition, that Stock of *English* Liberty, to which every Subject, whatever may be his Rank, is equally intitled. Amidst all the Disparity of Fortune and Honours, there is one Lot as common to all *Englishmen*, as Death. It is, that we are all equally free. Sufficient is it therefore, to shew the matchless Absurdity of the exclusive Claim, of which a few interested Merchants have lately attempted, in a most assuming Manner, to avail themselves, in determining on the Question, whether the Non-Importation Agreement shall be rescinded, to observe, that it was not solemnly entered into for the Good of the Merchants alone, but for the Salvation of the Liberties of us all. Of this the trading Interest of this City were convinced, when, after forming themselves into a Society for executing that Agreement, they not only requested a similar Association of the Mechanics, but by frequent Meetings, conspired with them in Support of the important Compact. When the Parties engaged in it, none doubted the Necessity of so salutary a Measure: Every Man saw, that between an Importation of Goods, which stern Virtue ought ever to despise as a Means to encourage Luxury, and the Sacrifice of our inestimable Rights as Englishmen, there was no Medium. This View of the Subject begat and brought to Perfection, the important Resolution, which has inspired the Enemies of our Liberty on the other Side of the Atlantic, with Fear and Astonishment. We have seen the salutary Effects of this ever memorable Compact, in the Resolution to repeal all the odious Duties, but that on Tea; and this remains unrepealed for no other Reason than that a tyrannical Ministry will not stoop to it unasked; and the *East-India* Company scorn to request it of that tyrannical Ministry. Has not our Mother Country, by solemn Act of Legislation, declared that she has a Right to impose internal Taxes on us? And is not such an Imposition incompatible with our Liberty? But this Law is a meer dead Letter, unless it be carried into Exercise by some future Act. For this Purpose was the Law devised, imposing a Duty upon Tea, Paper, Glass, Painters Colours, &c. the very Articles which our *Egyptian* Task-Masters thought were most essential to us, as being not hitherto the Produce of this Country. And shall we not, for our own Sakes, shew that we can live without them? What are all the Riches, the Luxuries, and even the Conveniences of Life, compared with that Liberty wherewith God and Nature have set us free, with that inestimable Jewel which is the Basis of all other Enjoyments? They are Dross, vile contemptible Dross, unworthy the Notice of Men. Rouse then my fellow Citizens, fellow Countrymen, and fellow Freemen, of all Ranks, from the Man of Wealth, to the Man whose only Portion is Liberty: Suffer not a few interested, parricidical and treacherous Inhabitants, to gratify their Avarice at the Expence of our common Interests. Spurn at the assuming Upstart, who dares to assert, that in a Question of such universal Concern, none but the Merchants have a Right to decide. For shame! will you, can you believe that you are their Beasts of Burthen, that you must toil and sweat, that they may be filled? I know that there are many Merchants whose patriotic Hearts abhor the accursed Thought; but still of that Profession, there are some base and vile enough to estimate their private Gain above the public Weal. These are the Miscreants who dare to affirm, with an Assurance that merits public Chastisement, that the Mechanics, or in other Words, the Majority of the Community, are not to be consulted on a Point of universal, of dreadful Concern. But who has made those Wretches as Gods among us? Curse on the vile, the arrogant Usurpation. In fine, let the patriotic Merchants, the respectable Body of Mechanics, and the virtuous of all other Ranks, conspire; let them, I say, conspire, as it were with an Oath, to brand with public Infamy, and public Punishment, the Miscreants who, while the odious Power of Taxation by parliamentary Authority, is in one single Instance exercised, even dare to speak in Favour of the least Infraction of the Non-Importation Agreement, and who like accursed Villains,—would owe their Greatness to their Country's Ruin.

O! ye Betrayers of the glorious Cause, remember the *Boston* Importer, ROGERS, I say, remember him and tremble.

BRUTUS.

Alexander McDougall, To the free and loyal inhabitants…[Defense of non-importation agreements], May 16, 1770. *(Courtesy of The Gilder Lehrman Institute of American History, GLC02552)* more independent of elite control. And the number of examples of people acting independently of government through conventions and voluntary committees also increased.

In this document, a colonist who identifies himself as "Brutus" defends the right of ordinary mechanics and artisans to take an active political role over the objections of gentlemen.

Brutus [attributed to Alexander McDougall], To the Free and Loyal Inhabitants of the City and Colony of New-York, May 16, 1770 GLC 2552

> Nothing can be more flagrantly wrong than the Assertion of some of our mercantile Dons [leading merchants], that the: Mechanics have no Right to give their Sentiments about the Importation of British Commodities. For who, I would ask, is the Member of Community, that is absolutely independent of the rest? Or what particular Class among us, has an exclusive Right to decide a Question of general Concern? When the Non-Importation Agreement took Place, what End was it designed to answer? Not surely the private Emolument of Merchants, but the universal Weal [well-being] of the Continent. It was to redeem from Perdition, from total Perdition, the Stock of English Liberty, to which every Subject, whatever may be his Rank, is equally entitled. Amidst all the Disparity of fortune and Honours, there is one right as common to all Englishmen as Death. It is that we are all equally free. Sufficient it is therefore to shew the matchless Absurdity of the exclusive Claim, of which a few interested Merchants have lately attempted, in a most assuming Manner, to avail themselves, in determining on the Question, whether the Non-Importation Agreement shall be rescinded, to observe, that it was not solemnly entered into for the Good of the Merchants alone, but for the Salvation of the Liberties of us all. Of this the trading Interest of this City were convinced, when, after forming themselves into a Society for executing that Agreement, they not only requested a similar Association of the Mechanics, but by frequent Meetings conspired with them in support of the important Compact.... Every Man saw, that between an Importation of Goods, which stern Virtue ought ever to despise as a Means to encourage Luxury, and the Sacrifice of our inestimable Rights as Englishmen, there was no Medium. This view of the Subject began and brought to Perfection, the important Resolution to repeal all the odious Duties, but that on Tea; and this remains unrepealed for no other Reason than that a tyrannical Ministry will not stoop to it unasked; and the East-India Company scorn to request it of that tyrannical Ministry. Has not our Mother Country, by solemn Act of Legislation, declared that she has a right to impose internal Taxes on us? And is not such an Imposition incompatible with our Liberty?...And shall we not, for our own Sakes, shew that we can live without them? What are all the Riches, the Luxuries, and even the Conveniences of Life compared with that Liberty where with God and Nature have set us free, with that inestimable Jewel which is the Basis of all other Enjoyments?...

As T. H. Breen points out in *The Marketplace of Revolution,* the expansion of the protests to include Americans in many walks of life was made possible because colonists were coming to trust each other and work together on their common cause.

Over a decade of continuous experimentation, American colonists discovered a means to communicate aspirations and grievances to each other through a language of shared experience. Between 1764 and 1775, they built a sense of mutuality slowly and tentatively, and in the process of reaching out beyond familiar boundaries of class and gender, they developed radically inclusive structures of resistance. They created brilliant forms of collective and extra-legal political action, overcoming discouraging moments of alleged betrayal to bring forth an imagined national community unanticipated at the start of the revolutionary crisis.

Like revolutionaries throughout the world, they had to learn to trust each other. Simply mouthing a vocabulary of rights and freedom was not sufficient to persuade people that they could rely on others about whom they knew very little. Trust was the product of mutual education. It required the free flow of information; it could not be coerced. Although in the early days trust proved distressingly fragile, Americans persuaded themselves by 1774 that other Americans could be counted on to do what they had actually promised to do, quite simply, to make genuine sacrifices for a common cause.

Trust-building involved more than strategic considerations. As ordinary Americans affirmed their trust-worthiness through revolutionary acts that were then quickly reported in the popular press, they discovered that the language of rights and liberty was more than rhetoric. Within a framework of local groups that came to identify with similar groups in distant places, people translated personal sacrifice into revolutionary ideology. The point here is that if we begin an investigation of revolution with ideology—as many historians have done—we inevitably discount the social conditions that energized these ideas for the men and women who stood to lose the most in a conflict with Great Britain.

In this extraordinary political environment it quickly became apparent that if efforts to restrict the sale of imported goods were to have any chance of success, they would need the support of *all* consumers, women as well as men, poorer sorts as well as wealthy lawyers and merchants. Focusing attention almost exclusively on formal electoral politics, on the response of the various colonial legislatures to the demands of royal governors and British administrators, for example, obscures the development of a new kind of popular politics, one that encouraged ordinary consumers—precisely because they were consumers—to take a public stand on the pressing issues of the day.

The creation of so many committees to enforce the boycotts also raised hard questions about the constitution of political authority in a liberal society. These were for the most part voluntary bodies functioning outside the structures of formal government, and during the early stages of the protest against parliamentary taxation the colonists expected the merchant community to organize the non-importation effort. By the late 1760s, however, ordinary men and women were taking a more active role in controlling the consumer market, and as they came forward in ever larger numbers they triggered a far-reaching debate about democratic procedure. How could a movement that claimed to speak for the "people" demonstrate persuasively that it did in fact enjoy popular support? Elections sponsored by colonial officials were out of the question. Crown appointees would never have sanctioned such potentially treasonable organizations. The answer turned out to be the simple but ultimately deeply radical act of signing subscription rolls. Signing one's name to subscription lists was not in itself a new phenomenon; documents of this sort had a long history in England and colonial America. In this context, however, expressions of support for economic resistance of British policy amounted to a plebiscite, a bold, even courageous recording of the popular will. People who were ineligible to vote in colony elections affixed their names and marks on papers carried from house to house or posted in public gathering places. Numbers, of course, mattered, for the lists of signatures collected in Charleston, New York, and Boston legitimated the rhetoric of protest leaders who insisted that they spoke for the "people." As anyone who has ever signed a petition knows, adding one's name to a list that will be scrutinized by friends and neighbors is not an act lightly taken. Indeed, it amounts to a declaration of ideological commitment, and for ordinary people, who were seldom asked to sign political documents, participation in the subscription drives—in communal pledges of self-denial—facilitated the transition from private unhappiness to public resistance. With a stroke of the pen they exchanged the comfort of anonymity for identification with the common good.

After 1773 such lists circulated in small country towns and at rural county courthouses, as new converts joined the boycott movement in the name of the rights and liberties of the American people. Their decision to sign a piece of paper gave the non-consumption movement a transforming force that no one could have predicted during the Stamp Act crisis. Signers became enforcers, and the first major order of the Continental Congress of 1774 was the establishment of the Association, a huge network of local committees charged with halting once and for all the purchase of England's "Baubles." Comparisons with other eighteenth-century revolutions immediately suggest themselves. Citizen groups in America did not assassinate prominent loyalists. Nor did they incite angry farmers to destroy the homes of the ruling gentry. In this distinctively bourgeois rebellion, the ideological police ferreted out hidden canisters of tea and suspicious pieces of cloth.

Out of these collective experiences colonial Americans forged new political identities. The process was always about to come undone, but the people who joined the boycott movement gradually expanded their personal horizons. In the rhetoric accompanying non-importation, one encounters ever bolder self-descriptions as organizers and participants addressed their "Brethren of the Continent" and announced in local statements that they spoke in the authentic "voice of all America" or for the "whole body of the people." If these sentiments were not yet the stuff of full-blown nationalism, they forcefully reveal that the process of mobilization involved a rethinking of political self-identity, something that occurred well before the winning of national independence." Put another way, the spirit of nationalism was as much a cause as a result of revolution.

Only a people who had come to take "galloping consumption" for granted could fully have comprehended the revolutionary implications of an organized disruption of the imperial market. As we shall discover, Americans like the writer who signed his essay Colonus would turn the language of commerce on its head, reminding an unhappy generation, "When therefore the Americans consider their situation, in all its circumstance, and know themselves to be the best customers Great-Britain has, for her wares: When, instead of that protection, they reasonably expected from her, as a return for the custom they find themselves most grievously oppressed … [w]hat more natural, more justifiable method could they pursue, than to resolve to set about manufacturing themselves and not to import a farthing of British goods they can possibly do without?"

When the colonists finally and reluctantly decided that they could do without the "Baubles of Britain," they destroyed a vital cultural bond with the mother country. "The country," explained James Lovell to his friend Joseph Trumbull in December 1774 "seems determined to let England know that in the present struggle, commerce has lost all the temptations of a bait to catch the American farmer." Lovell may have exaggerated, but he helps us to understand why in 1774 the countryside supported the cities. Consumer goods had made it possible for the colonists to imagine a nation; the Association made it easier for Americans to imagine independence.

By 1772 the protestors in Boston were organizing and uniting with patriots in many Massachusetts towns. Barbara Clark Smith describes these protestors in "A Revolutionary Era" in *Boston and the American Revolution*.

Bostonians discovered common ground with planters in Virginia, farmers in Connecticut, and traders in Philadelphia, New York, and Charleston. From that discovery colonists took a new vision of themselves. They began to shape an identity less English, more American.

When a new challenge to their rights appeared, the Boston patriots relied on unity with others. In 1772, Thomas Hutchinson, now governor of the province, announced that the Royal Treasury, fed by customs revenue, would pay his own salary and the salaries of the judges of the superior court. It was a break for taxpayers but also a threat to liberty. Royal officers had depended on the elected Assembly for salaries. Armed with economic independence, those officers could execute unpopular policies without hesitation.

Alarmed, the Boston town meeting adopted a proposal by Samuel Adams. It named a Committee of Correspondence to compose an account of colonial rights and grievances and sent it to other Massachusetts towns, asking for "a free communication of their Sentiments" in return. As a way to mobilize unified resistance, the idea was a master stroke. Thousands gathered in town meetings to consider Boston's message. More than 100 towns appointed corresponding committees and sent replies to the capital. Most opposed the salary law. "All civil officers are or ought to be servants to the people and dependent upon them for their official Support," wrote Braintree's committee. Whatever their precise language in this case, the committees stood ready to protest all future provocation. Boston, whose ties to England now seemed a source of oppression, found security in new ties with inland communities.

Virginia, which had protested taxes by passing the Virginia Resolves in 1765, responded to Samuel Adams's idea and established a committee of correspondence in 1773. By early 1774 all of the colonies had committees except Pennsylvania and North Carolina. These committees' protests increased after all of the Townshend Acts were repealed in

1770, except one fateful duty. In *The American Revolution,* Gordon S. Wood details the decision of the prime minister, Lord North, to require a duty on tea.

> The financial returns to the British government from the customs reforms seemed in no way worth the costs. By 1770 less than £21,000 had been collected from the Townshend duties, while the loss to British business because of American nonimportation movements during the previous year was put at £700,000. It was therefore not surprising that the British government now abandoned the hope of securing revenue from the duties and labeled the Townshend program, in Lord Hillsborough's words, "contrary to the true principles of commerce." In 1770, after years of chaos in the British government, the reorganization of the king's ministry under Lord North prepared the way for repeal of the Townshend duties. Only the duty on tea was retained, to serve, as Lord North said, "as a mark of the supremacy of Parliament, and an efficient declaration of their right to govern the colonies."

Colonies were coming together through their committees of correspondence when Parliament passed the Tea Act in 1773. Edward Countryman in *The American Revolution* explains how one company's failures resulted in the Act.

> Like the chartered companies that began American colonization, the East India Company tried to carry out both the private function of making a profit and the public task of governing a society. Like the colonization companies, it mixed these in a way that made it impossible to do either. Thanks to its ramshackle structure and to the ineptitude, or worse, of its servants, the company was failing either to return a profit to its shareholders or to consolidate Britain's hold on India. But the company's survival was important, both for British purposes of state and for the fortunes of the many well-placed investors who had money in it. Parliament decided to rescue it—the result was the Tea Act of 1773.
>
> The act gave the East India Company two benefits. One was to allow it to market its tea directly to America, using its own agents there. Now it could bypass the network of auctions, wholesalers, and colonial merchants through which its tea previously had been sold. This was a straightforward rationalization of its business. It would give the company the same efficiency and economies of scale that global corporations seek in our own time. The other benefit was to free the company of the duty on tea that it imported to Britain and then reshipped to America. Only the Townshend tax of three pence a pound would remain. The combination, ministers foresaw, would make taxed tea sold by the company so cheap that it could undercut both tea that was traded legitimately by American merchants and tea that was smuggled in, usually by the same merchants. The consumer would benefit, for tea would drop in price. The company would benefit, for it would find the revenue in America that it could not raise in Britain or the East. The treasury would benefit, for taxes would be raised.
>
> Parliament's pride would benefit, for at last the colonies would have accepted a tax that Parliament had imposed. No one in London thought very much about the American merchants who might be crushed by the East India Company's newfound strength.

Boston Decr 11. 1773

Madam

The last ministerial Manœuvre, has excited a more open and determined Resistance than ever has been made before — The Tea Ships are all to return, whatever may be the Consequences — I suppose your wise Ministers will put the Nation to the expence of a few Millions to quell this Spirit by another Fleet and Army —

The Nation is so independent, So clear of Debt and so rich in Funds & Resources as yet untried, that there is no doubt to be made, She can well afford it —

But let me tell those wise Ministers, I would not advise them to try many more such Experiments —

a few more such Experiments will throw the most of the Trade of the Colonies, into the Hands of the Dutch, or will erect an independent Empire in America — perhaps both —

Nothing but equal Liberty and kind Treatment can secure the Attachment of the Colonies to Britain —

We are much concerned here at the unhappy Diversions among the Friends of the Constitution in the City of London — We hope to see a Reconciliation, as much depends on their Union, and Exertions —

I am much obliged to you for your Favour by Mr Clark — your most obedient Servant

John Adams

John Adams to Catharine Macaulay, December 11, 1773. *(Courtesy of The Gilder Lehrman Institute of American History, GLCO1787)*

The Tea Act galvanized the colonists. On December 11, 1773, John Adams wrote a letter to Catharine Macaulay, the author of a multivolume history of England who was sympathetic to the colonists, about the Tea Act. It included a prediction:

> But let me tell those wise Ministers, I would not advise them to try many more such Experiments.—a few more such Experiments will throw the most of the Trade of the Colonies, into the Hands of the Dutch, or will erect an independent Empire in America—perhaps both.

4. Old South Meeting House, Massachusetts

OLD SOUTH MEETING HOUSE IN BOSTON NATIONAL HISTORICAL PARK
OPERATED BY THE OLD SOUTH ASSOCIATION
WASHINGTON AND MILK STREETS
BOSTON, MASSACHUSETTS

In 1729, a Puritan congregation built the Old South Meeting House, the largest building in colonial Boston. It could hold 6,000 people and was the site of protest meetings after Parliament passed the Stamp Act. Bostonians also gathered in the Meeting House in 1768 to protest the British impressment of American sailors, in 1770 after the Boston Massacre to demand the removal of the occupying soldiers, and in 1772–1775 for the annual commemoration of the Massacre. During the British occupation of Boston, soldiers stripped the wood from its interior to burn for firewood and turned the space into an arena where they rode their horses.

On December 16, 1773, 5,000 men packed the Meeting House, to protest the May 1773 Tea Act. The colonists learned that the royal governor would not give his permission for the three ships, *Beaver*, *Dartmouth*, and *Eleanor*, to return to England without unloading the tea. In *Defiance of the Patriots: The Boston Tea Party and the Making of America*, Benjamin L. Carp describes the colonists' response.

> On December 16, 1773, at a crowded meeting in the largest church in Boston, the leather-dresser Adam Collson supposedly shouted, "Boston Harbor a tea-pot this night!" Collson then marched down to the water's edge at Griffin's Wharf to make his metaphor come true. If "a tempest in a teapot" describes a big disturbance about a small matter, Boston—in the midst of a turbulent political crisis over the authority of the British Empire—was in this moment a "teapot in a tempest." Collson and his companions staged an act of rebellion that would have worldwide significance.
>
> About a hundred men boarded the three trading ships that were riding at Griffin's Wharf in Boston harbor. They hoisted 340 chests onto the decks. These chests contained

more than 46 tons of tea. The men smashed open the chests, releasing the leaves' bittersweet aroma into the air. It was the intoxicating smell of exotic luxury, and a couple of men were so unable to resist it that they stuffed some of the leaves in their pockets. The rest of the men remembered that there were principles at stake. They dumped the tea into the saltwater below.

The Boston Tea Party had revolutionary significance—it set the stage for an American rebellion and the war that followed. The Tea Party was an expression of political ideology about taxes, rights, and authority. Just as important, it was a window onto American culture and society of the time. Americans' consumer habits, including the colonists' love of tea, played a role in the way the resistance unfolded. Prevailing views of American Indians in colonial society help us to understand the disguises that the destroyers wore. Boston's colonial legacy of riotous parades, angry protest, and political organization provided the ingredients that made the Tea Party possible. These elements offer a fuller picture of why the Tea Party happened. The disguises served partly as a warning, signifying that the boarders of the tea ships demanded anonymity on principle, whether or not they had achieved it in fact. If these disguises did not quite conceal, they still demanded concealment.

This warning was crucial to the plans of the Sons of Liberty on December 16, 1773. The town leaders such as Adams, Warren, and Young had been careful to ensure that the tea destroyers were seen as separate from the formal protests of the Town Meeting and the "Body of the People." By dressing as outsiders to the Boston community, each of the Tea Party men was effectively saying, *I am not one of the "Body of the People."* So long as the men's anonymity held, it would be impossible for the authorities or the East India Company to assign liability for the wasted wealth in the harbor. The leading Sons of Liberty hoped that the disguises would protect the town of Boston from blame.

In *John Adams: A Life,* John Ferling quotes Adams on the importance of the Boston Tea Party.

The following morning, a clear day, though one made bitterly cold by a howling northeast wind, John Adams rode back into Boston, returning from a week at court in Plymouth. He had barely reached town when he heard of the previous night's events. Adams knew at once that the popular party had burned its bridges. The destruction of the tea must have "important Consequences"; this was a watershed event, an "Epocha in History," as he put it. Nothing would be the same again in public affairs or, perhaps, in his private life as well. Despite the inevitability of British reprisals, Adams applauded the destruction of the tea. There had been no choice, he thought, and he called the defiant boarding of the vessels and the quick obliteration of the dutied beverage the "grandest Event" in the history of the colonial protest movement.

As for the future, the next move in this high-stakes game rested with the ministry.

In *Independence: The Struggle to Set America Free,* John Ferling describes Lord North and his response to the destruction of the tea.

Frederick North, Lord North, was into his fifth year as prime minister during the cool, damp London spring of 1774, a time when war or peace between Great Britain and its American colonies hung in the balance.

In 1770 the king, George III, had turned to Lord North, a political veteran with a background in finance, to form a government. North had entered Parliament in 1755, four years following his graduation from Oxford. After four more years he was brought into the Duke of Newcastle's cabinet as the Lord High Treasurer, a post he held for half a dozen years through several ministries. In 1767 the Duke of Grafton made North the chancellor of the exchequer, the official in charge of financial matters and the ministry's spokesman in the House of Commons, a position for which he was tailor-made, as he had few peers as a parliamentary debater. North still held that post three years later, when the government collapsed and the monarch asked him to head a new ministry. Despite his long service, North was only thirty-five years old when he became the "first minister"—he disliked the title "prime minister"—and moved into the cramped and as yet unnumbered residence on Downing Street that for a generation had been available for the head of the ministry.

North was pleasant, witty, charming, industrious, efficient, and bright. Sophisticated though never pompous, he had a knack for getting on with others, and his performance as chief financial minister had earned nearly universal praise. His appointment to head the ministry was widely applauded. Robert Walpole, the acid-tongued son of the former prime minister, thought North was "more able, more active, more assiduous, more resolute, and more fitted to deal with mankind" than any other possible choice.

With time and experience North's self-assurance had grown. One reason for his confidence was that the king remained steadfastly supportive. But the prime minister was also more poised because he felt that he saw the American problem with clarity, and he believed that there was but one choice that could be made. "As to America," he remarked in the spring of 1774,

> *there* is an unhappy necessity, but a great one. We must decide whether we will govern America or whether we will bid adieu to it, and give it that perfect liberty.... The dispute is now upon such ground, unless they see you are willing and able to maintain your authority, they will...totally throw it off. There is no man but must be conscious of the necessity to act with authority in that country in order to preserve the country as a subject country to Great Britain.

For North in 1774, the "unhappy necessity" could not have been more apparent. He must take the steps necessary to hold America or it would declare its independence.

The steps that Parliament took included passing the Coercive Acts in March 1774, primarily to punish Massachusetts for the Boston Tea Party. In May 1774 General Thomas Gage replaced Thomas Hutchinson as the royal governor of Massachusetts. Benjamin L. Carp details the Coercive Acts and the consequences in *Rebels Rising: Cities and the American Revolution*.

An outraged British ministry passed a series of acts in Parliament "for reestablishment of lawful authority" in Massachusetts, which the colonists called the "Intolerable Acts" of 1774. The Boston Port Act closed the city's harbor beginning June 1. The Massachusetts Government Act amended the colony's charter, giving the king greater powers to appoint several types of officials. The Administration of Justice Act allowed royal officials to stand trial outside of Massachusetts if accused of certain crimes. The Quartering Act, which applied to all the colonies, allowed governors to demand quarters for soldiers in uninhabited buildings. Though Parliament had aimed most of these acts at Massachusetts, colonists throughout North America saw them as dangerous precedents for the subversion of constitutional rights and liberties. Bostonians became martyrs suffering for the cause of all America. Americans sent aid to the blockaded city, and twelve colonies sent delegates to the first Continental Congress at Philadelphia in September 1774. These delegates proclaimed the Intolerable Acts unconstitutional and called for a boycott of British goods.

The objections, meetings, and disturbances that followed these imperial actions became impossible to ignore. During the years leading up to the Revolution, the mobilization of people from all social ranks was particularly intense in the urban centers. Because these populous polities were the loci of economic activity and government, they sharply felt the effects of imperial policies. As enforcement of the Navigation Acts and Quartering Acts became vital to the British Empire, American cities increasingly became the headquarters of the customs officials, vice-admiralty judges, naval and military officers, and governors who tried to ensure that city dwellers complied with imperial policies.

The cities also became the flash points for legislative protests, committee meetings, massive outdoor gatherings, intercolonial collaboration, newspaper harangues, boycotts, customs evasion, military-civilian violence, and riots. As centers for communication and social life, the cities were the hubs for the transmission of information and recruitment during times of crisis. Eighteenth-century urban political culture flowed through multiple avenues of communication, association, and social interaction—everything from the press to the streets, taverns, and churches. The cities provided places for people to interact, and the imperial crisis accelerated such interactions and stimulated a variety of revolutionary transformations. Americans faced choices about their identity, loyalty, and course of action, and they made their decisions about the revolutionary conflict in an environment of circulating ideas, arguments, and beliefs.

In *American Insurgents, American Patriots: The Revolution of the People,* T. H. Breen points to Americans' actions in response to the Coercive Acts as the start of the Revolution.

At the time, no one could plausibly have predicted such an abrupt intensification of popular resistance. The Boston Tea Party in December 1773 triggered the change. It did so, however, in a roundabout way. Dumping the tea into the harbor was a serious legal matter. About that, no one in Britain or America had the slightest doubts. The major concern—in Massachusetts, at least—was how Lord North and his allies in Parliament would react. Several months passed before the colonists learned the extent of their punishment. In a series of statutes known as the Coercive Acts, Parliament—like so many other uncertain imperial powers over the centuries—

decided that provocation of this sort justified an overwhelming show of toughness. The punitive legislation closed the port of Boston to all commerce except for coastal trade in basic supplies like firewood, restructured the Massachusetts government in ways that curtailed free speech in town meetings, and filled the colony's council with Crown appointees determined to restore law and order to the troubled commonwealth. To enforce the new system, the Crown dispatched to Boston an army of occupation under the command of General Thomas Gage.

Like news of the 9/11 attack, the destruction of Pearl Harbor, and the bombing of Fort Sumter, word of the Coercive Acts elicited outrage throughout the population. Colonists believed that the punishment for the Tea Party was totally out of proportion to the alleged crime. The legislation represented nothing less than an act of vengeance. Within the realm of public opinion, Britain's decision to employ the military to impose the hated policy demanded a response.

Not surprisingly, people who before this moment had not paid much attention to the imperial conflict suddenly did so. They experienced an awakening of political consciousness. In this electrified atmosphere Americans found ways to express their anger through actions that would forever destroy British authority beyond occupied Boston. Some individuals took tepid steps, small sacrifices in the name of a common cause; others followed more violent paths. However the Americans worked out the calculus of resistance, their actions represented the effectual start of the Revolution.

North and others who shared his assumptions expressed confidence that these reforms would soon return the colonists to a proper sense of obedience. Changing the structure of the Massachusetts government made good sense in a distant imperial capital, where democratic practices were often confused with public disorder. Considering how fiercely North and his friends defended the inviolability of ancient British institutions, however, it is striking how little regard they had for the constitutional traditions of Massachusetts. They never considered how deeply attached the colonists might be to familiar forms of local government or how angrily they would react to imperial planners for whom local political customs were just another irritant.

In response to the limitations on government in the Coercive Acts, the Massachusetts General Court resolved itself into the first Provincial Congress on October 7, 1774. It met in Concord, northwest of Boston, and began to plan for the defense of the colony.

Opposition to the acts spread from Massachusetts across the colonies, including to Virginia, where George Washington opposed them. Edward G. Lengel details the responses to the acts in Virginia in *General George Washington: A Military Life*.

The Coercive Acts radicalized colonial intellectuals and politicians, including Washington. The Virginia House of Burgesses condemned the acts even before they took effect, prompting Governor Dunmore, a loyal king's man, to order it dissolved. Washington reacted to the governor's move by becoming even more outspoken. Relieved from his responsibilities in the Burgesses, he openly decried Parliament's measures as a "Tyrannical System...a regular Plan at the expence of Law & justice, to overthrow our Constitutional Rights & liberties." He also helped organize and equip militia companies that formed in Fairfax and other Virginia counties, and reassured hesitant patriots that trained American soldiers could fight and even defeat British regulars. Armed rebellion, hitherto unthinkable, had become a very real prospect.

Yet independence was still "farthest of anything" from the thoughts of Washington and many other Americans. Most prominent Virginians refused even to consider it. In July 1774, Washington presided over the so-called Fairfax Resolves, in which he and other former Burgesses from the county rebuked the British government, promised that they would "use every Means which Heaven hath given Us to prevent our becoming it's Slaves," and laid out a plan for colonial resistance. All the same, they expressed their desire "to continue our Connection with, and Dependance upon the British Government." Few believed that in struggling for their liberties they were setting the stage for the birth of a new country.

Later that month in Williamsburg, the Virginia Convention adopted the Fairfax Resolves as a basis for its own platform and elected seven delegates, including Washington and Patrick Henry, to represent Virginia in the First Continental Congress.

~~~

5. Carpenters' Hall, Pennsylvania

CARPENTERS' HALL IN INDEPENDENCE NATIONAL HISTORICAL PARK
CHESTNUT STREET
PHILADELPHIA, PENNSYLVANIA

In the summer of 1774, the colonies began to consider meeting to decide how to respond to Parliament's threats to their liberties. Connecticut was the first to act; in June its committee of correspondence was instructed to choose delegates. On September 5 the First Continental Congress met in Carpenters' Hall in Philadelphia. There were fifty-six delegates from twelve colonies: Connecticut, Delaware, Maryland, Massachusetts, New Hampshire, New Jersey, New York, North Carolina, Pennsylvania, Rhode Island, South Carolina, and Virginia. Georgia, threatened by an uprising of Creek Indians, did not send delegates.

Robert Middlekauff describes the First Continental Congress in *The Glorious Cause: The American Revolution, 1763–1789.*

> In an environment heavy with mistrust, the proposal to convene a continental congress drew surprising agreement. The question was, as before, how to respond—not whether to respond.
>
> While Boston's leaders plotted, and arguments over this problem went on everywhere, colonial legislatures and unofficial bodies began to cut through the debate and to act. Connecticut's lower house was one of the first; early in June it instructed its committee of correspondence to

choose delegates to what became the first Continental Congress. Less than two weeks later Rhode Island's General Assembly chose its own delegates. Five colonies—Maryland, New Hampshire, New Jersey, Delaware, North Carolina—resorted to provincial assemblies, extraordinary bodies substituting for legislatures dissolved by peace-loving governors. A similar agency, the convention, chose Virginia's delegates in August; local committees made the choices in New York, and in South Carolina the Commons House of the assembly ratified the selections of the inhabitants. Georgia in 1774, badly frightened by an uprising of Creek Indians on the northern frontier, decided against sending delegates, lest it be deprived of British arms. Boston was distant, the Indians close by; danger may not have revived loyalty in Georgia but it subdued daring.

These local conflicts over the tactics to be used in responding to the Intolerable Acts were of great importance and affected the actions of the Congress itself. But they should not be overplayed. The fact is that a Continental Congress met and proved capable of making decisions crucial to the future of the empire. It did in part at least because the values and interests its delegates represented overrode the disagreements that marked its origins.

The delegates who rode into Philadelphia in late August and early September felt excitement and pride and even awe at what they were doing—not rage at Britain. Formal sessions began on September 5. From that day until the Congress dissolved itself on October 26, two major questions occupied it: what was the basis of American rights and how should they be defended?

On October 14, the Congress demonstrated that it could agree on something—a Declaration of Rights. They adopted a statement which declared that colonial rights were founded on the law of nature, the British constitution, and the colonial charters. The declaration left no doubt that the colonies would not give up the right to tax and legislate for themselves. They were not represented in the "British Parliament" and "from their local and other circumstances, cannot" be. While the delegates worked on the declaration, they also decided on the ways nonimportation, nonconsumption, and nonexportation could be made realities. They entered rough water almost immediately. The South Carolina delegation now revealed how tightly tied its tongue was to the pursestrings of planters at home. The South Carolinians told the Congress that unless rice and indigo were exempted from the ban on exports, they would not sign the "Association," as the agreement on trade restrictions was now called. This announcement drew protests, but after the Carolinians agreed that only rice had to be protected, Congress caved in.

The Association provided that the ban on imports from Britain would take effect on December 1; nonconsumption of East India Company tea would begin immediately; the prohibition of exports to Britain would, if it were still necessary, be observed after September 10, 1775. Everyone recognized that these instructions had little chance of success without force behind them. To give them force the Congress called for the election of a committee "in every county, city, and town" by those qualified to vote for representatives in the legislature. Under the Association, the committees were charged to operate as no government in America had ever operated. They were to inspect customshouse books, publish the names of offenders in local newspapers, and "break off all dealings" with violators, now baptized as "the enemies of American liberty." The delegates signed the Association on October 20. On October 26, Congress dissolved itself with the understanding that if need arose a second meeting would be held on May 10, 1775.

The delegates departed Philadelphia full of respect for one another. They had demonstrated that they and the people they represented shared common interests and values. For a while their interests, especially their economic interests, had threatened to pull them apart, but in the end they put together the Continental Association. The Association expressed values which tied Americans together and suggested that in their desire to protect their right to self-government there was a moral concern transcending the constitutional questions in conflict. Morality made its way into the Association through the resolve to "encourage frugality, economy, and industry." In declaring their intention to honor Puritan standards, Congress did not argue that it had found another weapon against tyrannical government. But of course it had. For it intended to remind Americans that their virtue—their commitment to the public interest—underlay their political freedom. Indeed the Congress intended that Americans should remember that without virtue all kinds of freedom would perish.

Parliament increased British authority over its colonies after 1763, and the colonies resisted it in protests and in the actions of the First Continental Congress. In *The American Revolution*, Gordon S. Wood considers the Americans' rejection of Parliament's sovereignty.

The colonists had been groping toward this denial of Parliament's power from the beginning of the controversy. For a decade they had engaged in a remarkable constitutional debate with the British over the nature of public power, representation, and the empire. This debate exposed for the first time just how divergent America's previous political experience had been from that of the mother country. During the eighteenth century the British electorate made up only a tiny proportion of the nation; probably only one in six British adult males had the right to vote, compared with two out of three in America.

In his famous *Letters from a Farmer in Pennsylvania*, John Dickinson rejected the idea that Parliament could rightly impose "external" or "internal" taxes and made clear that the colonists opposed all forms of parliamentary taxation. But Dickinson recognized that the empire required some sort of central regulatory authority, particularly for commerce, and conceded Parliament's supervisory legislative power so far as it preserved "the connection between the several parts of the British empire." The empire, it seemed to many colonists, was a unified body for some affairs but not for others.

To counter all these halting and fumbling efforts by the colonists to divide parliamentary authority, the British offered a simple but powerful argument. If Parliament even "in one instance" was as supreme over the colonists as it was over the people of England, wrote a subcabinet official, William Knox, in 1769, then the Americans were members "of the same community with the people of England." On the other hand, if Parliament's authority over the colonists was denied "in any particular," then it must be denied in "all instances," and the union between Great Britain and the colonies must be dissolved.

What made this British argument so powerful was its basis in the widely accepted doctrine of sovereignty—the belief that in every state there could be only one final, indivisible, and uncontestable supreme authority. This was the most important concept of eighteenth-century English political theory, and it became the issue over which the empire was finally broken. This idea that, in the end, every state had to have one single supreme undivided law-making authority had been the basis of the British position from the beginning.

The colonists could never share this traditional reverence toward Parliament, and on this issue they inevitably parted from their fellow Englishmen, not by rejecting the doctrine of sovereignty but by relocating it. By 1774 the leading colonists, including Thomas Jefferson and John Adams, were arguing that only the separate American legislatures were sovereign in America. It was now only a matter of time before these irreconcilable positions led to armed conflict.

The Continental Congress adopted a Declaration of Rights and imposed trade restrictions while colonies prepared for their defense. Attitudes toward war were ambiguous, as revealed in this letter from the American writer Mercy Otis Warren to Catharine Macaulay, the British historian (see page 42):

> But though America stands armed with resolution and virtue, she still recoils at the thought of drawing the sword against the state from whence she derived her origin.

In early 1775, Benjamin Franklin knew the officials in the British government to approach with the resolutions of the Continental Congress. He had lived in London from 1757 until 1762 and had returned in 1765. He had responsibilities as agent for the Assembly in Pennsylvania and later, also for New Jersey, Massachusetts, and Georgia. In *Benjamin Franklin: An America Life,* Walter Isaacson recounts Franklin's final efforts toward a compromise.

> In mid-December Franklin finally received the resolutions that had been approved by the First Continental Congress. At its meeting in Philadelphia, which lasted until late October, the rump assembly had reasserted America's loyalty to the Crown—but not to Parliament. In addition, it voted a boycott of British goods if Parliament did not repeal its coercive acts.
>
> Many of the colonial agents in London refused to have anything to do with the resolutions when they arrived. So Franklin and the other agents from Massachusetts took it upon themselves to deliver them to Lord Dartmouth, who "told us it was a decent and proper petition and cheerfully undertook to present it to his Majesty."
>
> In the meantime, Franklin was engaged in a variety of other back-channel talks and negotiations, most notably with Lord Chatham. The compromise that Chatham proposed would permit Parliament to regulate imperial trade and to send troops to America. But only the colonial legislatures would have the right to impose taxes, and the Continental Congress would be given official and permanent standing. Although Franklin did not approve of all its particulars, he readily agreed to lend his support by being present when Chatham presented the plan to the House of Lords on February 1.
>
> Chatham gave an eloquent explanation of his proposals, and Lord Dartmouth responded for the government by saying they were of "such weight and magnitude as to require much consideration." For a moment, Franklin felt that all of his back-channel talks and lobbying might be bearing fruit. Then Lord Sandwich, who as first lord of the admiralty had taken a hard line on colonial affairs, took the floor. In a "petulant, vehement speech," he attacked

Dear Madam   Plimouth N E   December 29, 1774

     Your kind Notice of my Last Emboldens me again to Interrupt your more important pursuits, by offering my Warmest acknowledgments, for the Expressions of personal Regard Contained in your agreeable favour of Sept 11th as well as for your Generous attention to the publick Calamities of my Country. though I never imagined that while you were Researching the Records of time, & by your Elegant pen Exhibiting to the World the most striking trait, of former tyrants, you was inattentive to the living agents of a Corrupt Court, who have been Long forming a system of Despotism that should Reach beyond the Atlantic, & involve this extensive Continent in the same thralldom that awaits the Miserable Asiatic. absurd will the plans of Modern policy appear when the faithful historian shall transmit to posterity the Late manœuvres of a British administration, when they shall Behold them plunging the nation still deeper in an immense debts, Equipping her fleet, to Harrass the Coasts, & her armies to Insult & subjugate these Loyal & populous Colonies, who from the first settlement of this once dreary Wilderness, to the mad project of shutting up the port of Boston, have been Voluntarily pouring their treasury into the Lap of Britain. Will not succeeding Generations, be astonished when told that this Maritime City was Blokaded at a period when her Commercial interests, were Closely interwoven with those of Britain. When the tracts of Cultivated Land, on this Continent, acknowledging the sceptre of Brunswick were almost inneaserable & when at the same time they Boasted their united Millions, Ready to pour out the Warm Blood as a Libation at the shrine of freedom ere they would submit to become the slaves of Arbitrary power.

     But tho America stands Armed with Resolution & Virtue, she still Recoils, at the thought of Drawing the sword against the state from whence she derived her Origen tho that state Like an unnatural parent has plunged her dagger into the Bosom of her affectionate offspring.

     But may I not hope to hear from you Madam who can Easily Deliniate their Character, that the New parliament principaly Consists, of men of more Conciliating tempers, of men who inherit the Glorious spirit which distinguished their noble Ancestors, & stimulated them to stand forth as the Barriers of English Liberty in the most perilous seasons, yet such is the prevailing Luxury & Dissipation of the times, such the undue influence of the Crown from the tribes of placemen. Pensioners, & Dependants Backed with a Large standing army, that Nursery of Slavery & Vice, that Bane of Every free state, that I fear there is Little Reason to Expect it.

Mercy Otis Warren to Catharine Macaulay, December 29, 1774. *(Courtesy of The Gilder Lehrman Institute of American History, GLC01800.01)*

Chatham's bill and then turned his aim on Franklin. He could not believe, he said, that the plan came from the pen of an English peer. Instead, it appeared to him the work of some American. As Franklin recounted the scene: "Turning his face to me, [he] said he fancied he had in his eye the person who drew it up, one of the bitterest and most mischievous enemies this country had ever known. This drew the eyes of many lords upon me; but…I kept my countenance as immovable as if my features had been made of wood."

Chatham replied that the plan was his own, but he was not ashamed to have consulted "a person so perfectly acquainted with the whole of American affairs as the gentleman alluded to so injuriously reflected on." He then proceeded to heap praise on Franklin as a person "whom all Europe held in high estimation for his knowledge and wisdom and ranked with our Boyles and Newtons; who was an honor not to the English nation only but to human nature." But Chatham was not only out of power, he was out of touch. Lord Dartmouth quickly abandoned his initial openness and agreed with Lord Sandwich that the bill should be rejected immediately, which it was.

For the next few weeks, Franklin engaged in a flurry of further meetings designed to salvage some compromise. He played a small role in one of the final and most eloquent pleas for peace. He spent the afternoon of March 19 with the great Whig orator and philosopher Edmund Burke. Three days later, Burke rose in Parliament to give his famous but futile "On Conciliation with America" speech. "A great empire and little minds go ill together," he proclaimed.

By then Franklin was already on the Philadelphia packet ship heading west from Portsmouth. He had spent his last day in London with his old friend and scientific partner Joseph Priestley. People who did not know Franklin, Priestley wrote, sometimes found him reserved, even cold. But that day, as they discussed the looming war and read from the newspapers, he grew very emotional. For a while, the tears in his eyes made it impossible for him to read.

The colonies had come together on a Declaration of Rights adopted by the First Continental Congress in 1774. The movement toward independence was hastened by British violations of those rights and its abuses of authority. In *Founders: The People Who Brought You a Nation*, Ray Raphael describes the abuse of authority in 1775 by Governor Dunmore against Washington, who was representing soldiers who had served the British.

Immediately after the Virginia Convention, upon his arrival home, George Washington received some unexpected bad news, seemingly off topic but in his mind very much to the point. Surveys for the two hundred thousand acres of bounty land, promised back in 1754 to soldiers who joined Washington's expedition into the Ohio country, had just been declared null and void. The problem, apparently, was that William Crawford, the surveyor, did not have the proper credentials. The previous year, Lord Hillsborough had tried to cheat Washington out of the lands he and other veteran officers had been promised in 1763—and now this! Initially, Washington treated the news as too "incredible" to believe; at worst, he thought, it was a trick of professional surveyors "to filch a little more money from us." But when the rumors continued, he wrote an impassioned letter to the governor, John Murray, Earl of Dunmore, begging him to intervene. Five years earlier, after going through all the proper channels, Crawford had been assigned to survey the two hundred thousand acres "with all possible expedition," Washington explained. Since that time, he continued, many of Crawford's patents had been officially granted "under your Lordships signature & the seal of the colony." How could all this be reversed at so late a date, and *why*? "It appears in so uncommon a light to me, that I hardly know yet how to persuade myself into a belief of the reality of it," Washington concluded.

To this letter, over one thousand words long, Lord Dunmore penned a perfunctory reply: the reason for declaring the surveys "null and void" was "a report that the surveyor who surveyed those lands did not qualify agreeable to the Act of Assembly directing the duty and qualification of surveyors." That's all he said. Dunmore's token response was penned on April 18, the day British soldiers set out from Boston toward Lexington and Concord.

Such a piece of bureaucratic chicanery pushed George Washington even further over the edge. William Crawford was his good friend, business associate, and indispensable agent in the West. With many years of experience and unsurpassed knowledge of the lands he surveyed, Crawford was certainly better qualified than any quill-pushing official three thousand miles away, and besides, he had been preapproved. In fact, Crawford knew the land so well that countless others had asked him to survey it, and Lord Dunmore himself had just relied on him to lead a dangerous expedition into Indian country. The move was so blatantly illogical that only one explanation remained: British authorities would stoop to any level to keep Americans from receiving legitimate title to lands across the mountains. There was no way for Americans to own the West without addressing the arrogant abuses of governmental authority coming from the East.

The acts of Parliament and the actions of British officials were backed by British military power. Jonathan R. Dull describes the sources of this power in *A Diplomatic History of the American Revolution*.

The enjoyment of "great power" status was not based directly on a large population or even on a given level of economic development. The direct basis of such status was some form of military strength. Great Britain universally was regarded as a great power even though her army was relatively small. (The British army comprised only some 27,000 men in April 1775, 7,000 of which were in North America.) Her power was based on several other factors. The first of these was her navy, the largest in the world. In time of war she could man nearly a hundred ships of the line, the gigantic battleships carrying fifty to a hundred cannon, upon whose number naval power was computed. (Even by the more demanding standard by which only ships with sixty-four or more guns were counted as ships of the line, Britain could command about eighty ships compared to sixty of France and fifty of Spain; lesser naval powers, in roughly descending order, were Russia, the Netherlands, Denmark, Turkey, Sweden, and Portugal.) The second factor was Britain's ability to expand her military forces in time of war by recruiting additional regiments, using militia, purchasing foreign troops, and subsidizing the armies of her allies. In 1747, for example, Britain, in conjunction with the Netherlands, hired an army of 36,000 Russians to fight the French; in the Seven Years' War she was able to tie down a large French army on the European continent by subsidizing the Prussian army and maintaining a mixed German-British army in western Germany.

Britain was able to attain such power in spite of a relatively small population—some eight million people in England, Wales, and Scotland. In large part this power was based on her huge colonial empire, which included Bombay and Bengal in India, Senegal and Gambia on the west coast of Africa, Ireland, Gibraltar, and Minorca in Europe, Jamaica and a dozen smaller islands in the Caribbean, the Bahamas, Bermuda, Quebec, Nova Scotia, Newfoundland, West and East Florida, and the thirteen North American colonies which later became the United States. Even though they were ultimately dependent on Parliament, many components of the empire had their own assemblies, although the British possessions in India were ruled through the East India Company and some other territories had only military governments. Her colonial trade helped make Britain the world's richest and most economically developed country, supporting on a population one-third that of France a comparable level of foreign trade and not greatly inferior government revenues. No other state could match in trade or government revenue France and Britain, leaving them unique in having the resources to subsidize other governments and armies. Britain, however, enjoyed a great advantage over France. Partly because her businessmen and bankers helped share in governing the country (through their direct or indirect representation in the House of Commons), Britain found it much easier and less expensive to borrow the money needed to wage a protracted war. Thus Britain generally could outlast her enemies, who eventually spent themselves into bankruptcy.

⚊≫✖✖✖≪⚊

6. Old North Church, Massachusetts

OLD NORTH CHURCH: CHRIST CHURCH IN THE CITY OF BOSTON IN
BOSTON NATIONAL HISTORICAL PARK
OPERATED BY THE OLD NORTH ASSOCIATION
SALEM STREET, BOSTON, MASSACHUSETTS

Christ Church in the City of Boston, known as Old North Church, was built in 1723. It was central to the plan that the Boston silversmith Paul Revere developed with patriot leaders in Charlestown and with the church sexton, Robert Newman. To warn patriots that British soldiers were advancing from Boston, toward Lexington and Concord, they planned to show two lanterns in the church steeple if the soldiers were coming by water and one if by land. On the night of April 18, 1775, Revere acted, described by David Hackett Fischer in *Paul Revere's Ride*.

Revere told his friends to go into the church and hang two lanterns in the steeple window on the north side facing Charlestown. Newman had found two square metal lanterns with clear glass lenses, so small that they could barely hold the stump of a small candle. Earlier that day he had carefully prepared the lanterns, and hidden them in a church closet. They went to a narrow ladder above the stairs and climbed higher, rung and rung, past the open beams and great silent bells. At last they reached the topmost window in the steeple. They threw open the sash, and held the two lanterns out of the northwest window in the direction of Charlestown.

While riders spread the general alarm in other areas of Middlesex County, Revere and William Dawes rode toward Lexington to warn residents of the approach of the British force. In *The Minutemen and Their World,* Robert A. Gross describes the actions of General Thomas Gage, the British commander.

The military blow Gage conceived was entirely predictable, given his political and strategic intelligence: a surprise pre-emptive strike to seize or destroy the ordnance and provisions at Concord. If the attempt succeeded, Gage would set back the provincial resistance for months, if not paralyze it for good. If it failed and the Americans took up arms against the British troops, they would bear the responsibility for starting the war. It is unclear whether the governor planned to arrest the top Whig leaders. In any case, all but Dr. Joseph Warren of the Committee of Safety were safely outside the capital. John Adams was at home with his wife, Abigail, in Braintree. Samuel Adams and John Hancock were lodging at Jonas Clarke's parsonage in Lexington, in close proximity to the political deliberations in Concord. Gage's plan was, as noted, what every well-informed colonist had been anticipating for weeks. The only question was *when* the governor would move, not *where*. But what neither side expected was the explosive combination of events that formed the so-called Battle of Lexington and Concord: an assault on unresisting militiamen at Lexington common, a military confrontation at Concord's North Bridge, and a classic guerrilla action by ill-disciplined provincials, drawing on Indian fighting experience to harry the British retreat to Charlestown on the bloody Battle Road.

In *Paul Revere's Ride,* David Hackett Fischer contrasts Gage's position with that of Revere and the American Whigs.

Had General Gage been the tyrant that many New England Whigs believed him to be, the outcome might have been very different. But Thomas Gage was an English gentleman who believed in decency, moderation, liberty, and the rule of law. Here again was the agony of an old English Whig: he could not crush American resistance to British government without betraying the values which he believed that government to represent. On the other side, Paul Revere and the Whigs of New England faced no such dilemma. Their values were consistent with their interests and their acts. That inner harmony became their outward strength.

On April 16 Revere and his friends in Boston, Cambridge, Charlestown, and Lexington considered a more pressing problem: how to send an early warning of movements by the Regulars from Boston on short notice, in the middle of the night, and when exits from the town were closed by General Gage. They worked out what a later generation would call a fail-safe solution that was typical of Revere's planning: "expresses" of the usual sort if possible, special messengers by clandestine routes, and if all else failed a back-up system of lantern signals from Boston to Charlestown.

To many Americans, the legend of the Lexington alarm conjures up the image of a solitary rider, galloping bravely in the darkness from one lonely farmstead to the next. This romantic idea is etched indelibly upon the national memory, but it is not what actually happened that night. Many other riders helped Paul Revere to carry the alarm. Their participation did not in any way diminish his role, but actually enlarged it. The more we learn about these messengers, the more interesting Paul Revere's part becomes—not merely as a solitary courier, but as an organizer and promoter of a common effort in the cause of freedom.

The more we learn about the range and variety of political associations in Boston, the more open, complex and pluralist the revolutionary movement appears, and the more important (and significant) Paul Revere's role becomes. He was not the dominant or controlling figure. Nobody was in that position. The openness and diversity of the movement were the source of his importance.

7. Buckman Tavern, Massachusetts

BUCKMAN TAVERN
1 BEDFORD STREET
LEXINGTON, MASSACHUSETTS

While the British regulars were marching toward Lexington in the early morning of April 19, 1775, men of the Lexington militia were gathering in John Buckman's tavern. Just before the regulars arrived, John Lowell, John Hancock's confidential clerk, reported to Paul Revere that Hancock and Samuel Adams had left a heavy trunk filled with important Whig papers in the tavern when they had fled Lexington. Lowell and Revere succeeded in hiding the trunk in the woods.

8. Colonel James Barrett Farm, Massachusetts

COLONEL JAMES BARRETT FARM IN
MINUTE MAN NATIONAL HISTORICAL PARK
448 BARRETT'S MILL ROAD
CONCORD, MASSACHUSETTS

Colonel James Barrett, a Massachusetts farmer in his sixties, was both a leader in Concord and a member of the Provincial Congress. He commanded a Middlesex County militia regiment and was in charge of military preparations for the Massachusetts Committee of Safety.

In October 1774, colonists began secretly to assemble military supplies in Concord, including on Colonel Barrett's farm, two miles from the town. All men between the ages of sixteen and sixty (with a few exceptions) were required to serve in the town militia, which included regular drills. The Provincial Assembly permitted some towns to have minute companies as well. The Minutemen were paid by their towns to train regularly so that they could be ready to march on short notice. Both the militia and the companies elected their own officers.

The British Regulars who marched to Concord on April 19, 1775, were intent on seizing weapons and other military supplies stored throughout the town. They did not find those hidden on Colonel Barrett's farm.

9. Lexington and Concord, Massachusetts

APRIL 19, 1775

MINUTE MAN NATIONAL HISTORICAL PARK
CONCORD, LINCOLN, AND LEXINGTON, MASSACHUSETTS

The 700 British regulars marching west from Boston were sent by General Thomas Gage, who was also the royal governor of Massachusetts. Commanded by Lieutenant Colonel Francis Smith and Major John Pitcairn, their orders were to march the eighteen miles to Concord and destroy the military supplies stored there and at Colonel James Barrett's farm. On April 19, 1775, Captain John Parker, in command of seventy militiamen lined up on the Lexington green, ordered the colonists to let the British troops pass by. Pitcairn, in the advance, ordered his 238 men onto the town common but told them not to fire. Suddenly someone did fire, and within minutes, eight colonials were dead and ten wounded. Colonel Smith arrived with his main force, brought the regulars under control, and ordered them to march on to Concord.

Middlesex County men continued to gather in Concord to carry military supplies away and hide them in nearby towns. At about 7:30 A.M. the British marched into the village and began their search. Colonel James Barrett led the militiamen across the North Bridge in Concord and then about a mile farther. The British destroyed all the supplies they could find and burned the town's liberty pole. When they saw smoke, the militia and Minutemen from Concord and Lincoln, who had been joined by those from Bedford and Acton, decided to return to Concord to protect their homes. Colonel Barrett ordered them to march to North Bridge but not to fire first. There were 400 colonials advancing against fewer than 100 British soldiers guarding the Bridge. The British at the east end of the bridge fired, killing two Acton Minutemen. Major John Buttrick, second in command of a regiment of Minutemen from Middlesex County, marching in front of the advancing Americans, gave the order for them to return the British fire.

Robert A. Gross describes the Concord fight and the British retreat in *The Minutemen and Their World*.

Major Buttrick leaped into the air, shouting, "Fire, fellow soldiers, for God's sake, fire." The resulting discharge wounded nearly a dozen of the enemy, three of them mortally. The provincials pressed on to cross the bridge; the British, jammed together at the end, panicked and ran, unpursued, toward town. The Concord fight—"the shot heard round the world"—had taken two to three minutes.

> You know the rest. In the books you have read,
> How the British Regulars fired and fled,—
> How the farmers gave them ball for ball,
> From behind each fence and farm-yard wall,
> Chasing the red-coats down the lane,
> Then crossing the fields to emerge again
> Under the tree at the turn of the road,
> And only pausing to fire and load.
>
> —FROM HENRY WADSWORTH LONGFELLOW, "PAUL REVERE'S RIDE"

Back in the village Colonel Smith once again made a fatal delay. With the countryside in arms, his worn and hungry men should have marched back to Boston as fast as they could. Instead, the slow-moving Smith vacillated on his course. Finally, about noon, the Redcoats began their retreat, leaving several of their wounded and a long legacy of bitterness behind them. They had been in Concord for four hours.

The British left the way they came, along the Bay Road, but this time without fife and drums. They were unaware they were walking into a trap. Above them, beyond the ridge which runs beside the road, the militiamen who had raced across the Great Fields poised to head off the Regulars' retreat. Ahead at Meriam's Corner, about a mile from town, where the ridge dies away and the road forks, the provincials lay in wait. Additional Minutemen from Reading and Billerica were approaching from the north and a force of East Sudbury men from the south. The provincials now numbered more than eleven hundred men. At the Corner, the road narrowed for a bridge over a small brook. As the British crossed, the shooting started.

The fighting grew fiercer and bloodier after the Redcoats left Concord. Outnumbered by an elusive, ever-increasing enemy and peppered by incessant fire, the beleaguered British used up their ammunition in often aimless shooting. They were exhausted after a virtually uninterrupted fifteen hours' march. The rout ended beyond Lexington village. By then, the nine-hundred-man armored First Brigade, dispatched that morning in response to Colonel Smith's message to Gates, had finally arrived in Lexington. "I had the happiness," Lord Percy, the brigade commander, remarked, "of saving them from inevitable destruction." It was Percy who inflicted the heaviest damage of the day upon the Americans, using cannon effectively to disperse approaching provincials and sending his men into houses from which sniper fire came, with orders to kill those within.

The British finally forced their way through to safety in Charlestown, encamping on Bunker Hill, in a position they foolishly abandoned several days later. Seventy-three Redcoats were dead, 174 wounded, and twenty-six missing—a casualty rate of close to 20 per cent. The comparable rate for the nearly four thousand American participants was only 2 or 3 per cent: forty-nine dead, thirty-nine wounded, four missing. No longer would Redcoats who knew Americans doubt their will to fight.

In *Paul Revere's Ride,* David Hackett Fischer points out how different the second battle of Lexington and Concord was from the first.

The second battle of Lexington and Concord was waged not with bayonets but broadsides, not with muskets but depositions, newspapers and sermons. In strictly military terms, the fighting on April 19 was a minor reverse for British arms, and a small success for the New England militia. But the ensuing contest for popular opinion was an epic disaster for the British government, and a triumph for American Whigs. In every region of British America, attitudes were truly transformed by the news of this event.

The colonists who began by leading the protests against acts of Parliament grew into the wise and far-sighted leaders known today as founders. In *Revolutionaries: A New History of the Invention of America,* Jack Rakove traces how they became revolutionary leaders.

The leaders of the colonial protests against Britain were all provincials before they became revolutionaries, revolutionaries before they became American nationalists and nationalists who were always mindful of their provincial roots. Understanding how these traits and experiences fit together and played upon one another is essential to explaining the puzzle that keeps drawing Americans back to the founding era. We find ourselves asking one recurring question: how do we explain the appearance of the remarkable group of leaders who carried the American colonies from resistance to revolution, held their own against the premier imperial power of the day, and then capped their visionary experiment by framing a Constitution whose origins and interpretation still preoccupy us over two centuries later?

Like many simple questions, it is not easily answered. The sense of historical destiny that surrounds the Revolution challenges our capacity to think our way back into the contingencies of the past and to appreciate how improbable an event it was. Part of that improbability lies in the record of misguided decisions that led the British government to fulfill its worst fears by driving the colonists down the road to independence. It took a peculiarly flawed process of framing bad policies and reacting to the resulting failures to convince the government of George III and Lord North that the best way to maintain the loyalty of their North American subjects was to make war on them. But that improbability immediately leads us to another. The men who took commanding roles in the American Revolution were as unlikely a group of revolutionaries as one can imagine. Indeed to call them revolutionaries at all is almost ironic. With the possible (and doubtful) exception of Samuel Adams, none of those who took leading roles in the struggle actively set out to foment rebellion or found a republic. They became revolutionaries despite themselves. Or rather, they became revolutionaries because a crisis in a single colony spiraled out of control in 1773–1774, and the empire's harsh response to the challenge to its authority persuaded colonists everywhere that the British government really was bent on abridging their basic rights and liberties. Until then, the men who soon occupied critical positions in the struggle for independence were preoccupied with private affairs and hopeful that the troubles that had roiled the empire in the 1760s would soon be forgotten. To catch them at those moments when they individually realized that would not be the case is to understand that the Revolution made them as much as they made the Revolution.

Yet if they were not revolutionaries by design, they became so in action. Their origins may have been provincial, and their involvement in the Revolution may have been forced upon them. But once engaged, they quickly grasped what an opportunity it was.

Ordinary men and women became extraordinary, as T. H. Breen points out in *American Insurgents, American Patriots*.

Along with rebels, mobs, and rabble, contemporaries used the word "insurgents" to describe American colonists who openly defied parliamentary acts. For our purposes, the word brings greater clarity to an understanding of the coming of national independence. The patriots who are generally credited with mounting the Revolution were in fact the beneficiaries of rebellious insurgents who initially sparked resistance. Without tens of thousands of ordinary people willing to set aside their work, homes, and families to take up arms in expectation of killing and possibly being killed, a handful of elite gentlemen arguing about political theory makes for a debating society, not a revolution. Such reflections raise arresting new questions. How did it happen that so many Americans reached a point of mutual commitment to a cause? When did they do so? The answers, it turns out, were hiding in plain sight. During the two years that preceded the Declaration of Independence, Americans launched an insurgency that drove events toward a successful revolution. In the process, American insurgents became American patriots. By restoring the insurgents to the story we tell ourselves about the nation's origins, we gain greater appreciation of the achievement of the patriots.

The process of rethinking the empire had begun during the summer of 1774. It drew upon the networks of communication, upon thousands of charitable donations for the poor, unemployed laborers of Boston, and upon newspapers that disseminated reports of local committees having punished ideological enemies. These marvelously creative links established effective political bonds of affinity between distant strangers, and so, when Americans learned that the insurgency had sparked a fatal military confrontation, they drew almost instinctively upon what had become a shared revolutionary identity.

The point is not that the death of innocent militiamen suddenly brought forth a binding sense of country. A common identity had already been established, the product of almost two years of popular resistance. News of the sacrifice at Lexington merely served to transform inchoate assumptions about an imagined solidarity—a country of the mind—into a force that we might call nationalism.

The irony is that Parliament's show of force—the occupation of Boston and a surge in troop strength—had been intended to give the "Friends of Government" greater confidence. The members of Lord North's cabinet reasoned that if the Crown's supporters in America felt safe, they would take the lead in restoring order. The debacle at Lexington and Concord put an end to such talk. Only two weeks after an insurgent army had driven British soldiers back to Boston, Gage sent

Dartmouth a candid assessment of the situation on the ground. The occupying forces had lost the contest for the hearts and minds of the Americans. "From what can be learned," the general explained, "it is not found that one province is in a better situation than another, the people called friends of government are few in all…[as are] those moderate men who abhor violent proceedings and wish for peace and quiet; the opposition party [is] numerous, active and violent." However much the report undermined his own credibility in London, Gage provided accurate intelligence.

It was perhaps too much to expect that the setback would provoke a serious review of colonial policy. According to George III, the lesson to be learned was that the occupying troops had been too small and too timid. "I cannot help being of opinion," he explained, "that with firmness and perseverance America will be brought to submission: if not, old England will perhaps not appear so formidable in the eye of Europe as at other periods." There could be no compromise. "America must be a colony of England or treated as an enemy. Distant possessions standing upon an equality with the superior state is more ruinous than being deprived of such connections."

～∞～

10. Fort Ticonderoga, New York

MAY 10, 1775

Fort Ticonderoga
Ticonderoga, New York

Between 1755 and 1759 the French built Fort Carillon at the narrows near the south end of Lake Champlain, where Lake George flows in over the rapids of the La Chute River. On July 8, 1758, during the Seven Years' War, the French successfully defended the fort against the British. When the British defeated the French the following year, the French blew up part of the fort.

In 1775, before Congress established the Continental Army, Benedict Arnold planned an offensive action against the British. He asked for and received a commission from the Massachusetts Committee of Safety to capture the fort—which had been renamed Fort Ticonderoga—and Crown Point. Ethan Allen, in command of the Green Mountain Boys had the same plan. After an agreement, Arnold and Allen led the assault together. On May 10, 1775, they crossed Lake Champlain, landed with eighty-three men, and marched to the south side of the fort. They surprised the forty-two-man garrison, demanded and received its surrender—and its artillery—in ten minutes.

On May 16, Arnold led his command down the Richelieu River into Canada, attacked the British military post at St. Johns, captured a sloop, and returned to Fort Ticonderoga.

The following winter, patriots led by Colonel Henry Knox delivered fifty-nine pieces of artillery from the fort to General Washington outside of Boston: two howitzers, forty-three cannon, and fourteen mortars.

11. Crown Point, New York

MAY 12, 1775

CROWN POINT STATE HISTORIC SITE
21 GRANDVIEW DRIVE
CROWN POINT, NEW YORK

In July 1759 during the Seven Years' War, the British took Fort Carillon at Ticonderoga. After this loss, the French destroyed the fort they had constructed at Crown Point, Fort St. Frédéric. The British took over the site and began constructing His Majesty's Fort of Crown Point. In 1773 a fire caused the destruction of the fort, and it was never rebuilt.

In May 1775 Seth Warner led the rest of the Green Mountain Boys north along the east side of Lake Champlain and crossed the lake to the dilapidated buildings where the British garrison was living near the old Grenadier Redoubt east of the remains of the fort. Encountering little resistance, they captured Crown Point and took prisoners: the nine-man garrison and ten women and children.

⸻∞⸻

12. Independence Hall and Yard, Pennsylvania

INDEPENDENCE HALL AND YARD IN
INDEPENDENCE NATIONAL HISTORICAL PARK
PHILADELPHIA, PENNSYLVANIA

The State House of the Province of Pennsylvania, now Independence Hall, was constructed between 1732 and 1756. From May 10, 1775, until March 1, 1781, it was the meeting place of the Second Continental Congress, except between December 20, 1776, and March 4, 1777, when it met in Baltimore, Maryland. During the British army's occupation of Philadelphia, Congress met in Lancaster, Pennsylvania, on September 27 and in York, Pennsylvania, between September 30, 1777, and June 27, 1778.

After the Articles of Confederation were ratified, the Confederation Congress met here from March 1, 1781, until June 21, 1783 (see #125).

The news of the battles at Lexington and Concord reached Philadelphia on April 24, 1775. On June 14 Congress voted to create the Continental Army and the following day appointed George Washington commander in chief. He took command of the Continental Army in Cambridge on July 3, 1775.

Georgia delegates had not attended the First Continental Congress in Philadelphia in September and October 1774. At its meeting in Savannah on July 4, 1775, Georgia's Second Provincial Council named delegates to the Second Continental Congress.

In *American Scripture: Making the Declaration of Independence,* Pauline Maier describes the Second Continental Congress.

As members of the Second Continental Congress assembled, the Virginian Richard Henry Lee observed that there had "never appeared more perfect unanimity among any sett of Men than among the Delegates," and that "all the old Provinces not one excepted are directed by the same firmness of union, and determination to resist by all ways and to every extremity." The Second Continental Congress would have to take charge of a country at war; it would become a government, the sole government of the emerging nation until 1781, when, in the final year of the war with Great Britain, the Articles of Confederation were finally ratified. Only in moments stolen from the daily work of wartime administration could it discuss broader issues, like the colonies' future, or consider documents of significance, such as the Declaration of Independence. Its decision to separate from Britain was one of the most important Congress made; and no other so seriously strained the sense of community with which the Congress began.

The delegates had hardly assembled when they received an address from the Massachusetts Provincial Congress reporting that it had taken steps during Congress's recess to raise 13,600 soldiers from its people and to secure additional men from New Hampshire, Connecticut, and Rhode Island. With the "greatest deference," the Bay Colony's Congress suggested that a powerful American army was the only way left to restrain "the rapid Progress of a tyrannical Ministry. Without a force, superior to our Enemies," it said, "we must reasonably expect to become the Victims of their relentless fury."

Ticonderoga and Bunker Hill made it abundantly clear that Congress faced a formidable task in controlling the popular military enthusiasm let loose with the outbreak of war. The creation of an American military command structure was a step in that direction. Congress, however, had no intention of founding a military establishment independent of its supervision: it continued not only to define the shape of the army and to appoint its officers, but also to determine as best it could where the troops would fight, and how.

It could not impose taxes, but it could borrow money, and found another independent if unstable source of financial support in the summer of 1775 when it decided to issue a continental currency. Moreover, even the most prominent colonies turned to it for directions on how they should proceed in political crises, which powerfully suggests that Congress had in its opening years an authority and even an eminence above and beyond that of any separate colony and, indeed, far beyond what the colonists conceded to Parliament.

The inefficiency of Congress's deliberations strained men's patience as effectively as its schedule drained their physical stamina. To accomplish anything of significance in Congress was extraordinarily cumbersome, Silas Deane explained, because "no motion or resolution can be started or proposed but what must be subject to much canvassing before it will pass with the unanimous approbation of Thirteen Colonies whose situation and circumstances are various. And Unanimity is the basis on which we mean to rise...." Under the circumstances, that strategy made sense: against the power of Britain, colonial strength lay in colonial unity. But it gave an obstructionist power to timid or recalcitrant minorities that continually irritated those who were—or were confident they ought to be—in the majority.

John Adams understood the nature of Congressional politics as well as any man, although the delays and compromises it demanded warred with his temperament. In time, that scrappy Massachusetts delegate, as ambitious for fame as Hancock but, as the child of an obscure family from the town of Braintree, with no inherited advantages in that pursuit except for his intelligence, would become one of the country's most vigorous and effective advocates for Independence. Adams's impulse from the earliest years of the Second Continental Congress was to rush forward, dissolve all governments under the Crown, set up democratically elected state governments "like that of Connecticut," form an "indissoluble" confederation for mutual defense, close the King's customs houses and open American ports to all nations—but he knew the colonies were "not yet ripe" for such measures. "America is a great, unwieldy body," he wrote on June 17, 1775. "Its progress must be slow. It is like a large fleet sailing under convoy. The fleetest sailors must wait for the dullest and slowest. Like a coach and six, the swiftest horses must be slackened, and the slowest quickened, that all may keep an even pace...."

Even the most radical members of Congress professed a strong preference for remaining in the empire. So late as August 25, 1775, Jefferson wrote in a private letter that he sincerely wished for reunion and "would rather be in dependence on Great Britain, properly limited, than on any nation on earth, or than on no nation."

In *Benedict Arnold, Revolutionary Hero: An American Warrior Reconsidered,* James Kirby Martin describes the effects of the capture of Fort Ticonderoga and Crown Point—which were offensive military actions—on the Second Continental Congress meeting in Philadelphia.

Much less sure of themselves, the patriots of 1775 had exhibited a robust determination to defend their families and property against wanton acts of political tyranny and military aggression, hoping in the meantime to realize the full restoration of their liberties. The forays in the Champlain region, however, stretched beyond credulity the bounds of any definition of defensive war. The attacks were clearly aggressive in intent and an invitation to expanded warfare, regardless of rationalizations about acquiring heavy artillery or preemptively securing a strong foothold in what could become a hotly contested theater of war.

Offensive operations so brash disturbed many delegates to the Second Continental Congress, which commenced deliberations in Philadelphia on the very same day that Allen, Arnold, and company seized Ticonderoga. Would this new Congress keep the Champlain forts, since their seizure made pronouncements about taking up arms only for defensive purposes look deceitful? Moderates in Congress worried lest this seeming incongruity undermine their attempts to resolve grievances with the parent nation, knowing full well that everescalating warfare would have the same effect.

Because Arnold had taken command in the Champlain theater, his name became ensnared in congressional wrangling over the forts and the larger issue of expanding the rebellion to include Canada. In the process his reputation suffered, mostly provoked by Allen and friends.

At the opening of the Second Continental Congress, many of the delegates were ready to establish a national army, while others wanted to appeal once again to King George III to end the crisis. In *The Ascent of George Washington*, John Ferling describes the petition to the king and Washington's surprising announcement after he was appointed commander in chief.

Congress had been in session only a few days when Virginia's Richard Henry Lee proposed the creation of a national army, but a month passed before the legislators took up the matter. The most conservative members, who at this point likely constituted a narrow majority, insisted on first petitioning George III to ask that he resolve the imperial crisis by rebuking Parliament. The more radical members thought such a petition ludicrous, but they could not afford to anger their colleagues. Unanimity was essential if war was to be waged. After protracted debate, an entreaty to the Crown was adopted during the second week of June. That cleared the way for Congress to create "the American Continental army" on June 14. As soon as the vote was taken, Massachusetts's John Adams took the floor and recommended Washington as commander of the new army. Washington had known this moment would come. Indeed, he had suggestively worn his new buff-and-blue uniform as he sat listening to the wearying days of debate. He immediately excused himself so his colleagues could talk freely. They talked for a day and a half. Some may have opposed Washington's appointment, but if so, it was from fear that New England's soldiers would not follow a non-New England commander or from anxiety that dumping General Artemus Ward might cause deep political divisions within Massachusetts. Considerable time was probably spent questioning Virginia's congressmen about Washington and discussing what authority was to be vested in the commander.

The issue was never in doubt, as Washington must have known. He was appointed commander of the Continental army on the second day of deliberations. Washington was chosen for numerous reasons, some military, some political. He had commanded Virginia's army for nearly five years. He exuded leadership qualities. Grave, formal, and, if not quite unapproachable, certainly exceedingly reserved, Washington conveyed a sense that he would brook no nonsense. He radiated vigor, was in good health, and at age forty-three was young enough in all likelihood to remain fit and to see a long war through to its conclusion. He was a Virginian, a son of the largest and wealthiest American province. He was also said to be a man of indomitable will. He was unassuming as well, "a compleat gentleman," said Thomas Cushing of Massachusetts, who added: "He is sinsible, amiable, virtuous, modest, & brave."

Washington started in spectacular fashion, winning adherents in separate statements made in the first days following his appointment. On the day after being named commander in chief, Washington returned to the Pennsylvania State House—known today as Independence Hall—to address Congress. It was one of the few speeches, if not the only one, that he made in the two congresses he attended. Washington rehearsed a litany that he had made familiar while commanding Virginia's army in the French and Indian War. He felt unequal to the task, but "as the Congress desire it I will enter upon the momentous duty, & give every power I possess in their service & for the Support of the glorious Cause." To that, he added a stunning and far more important announcement. Although Congress had already voted a salary of $500 per month for the army's commander, Washington said that "as no pecuniary consideration could have tempted me to have accepted this Arduous emploiment at the expence of my domestk ease & happiness," he would accept no pay. He asked only that he be reimbursed for his expenses. Few, if any, decisions that Washington made during the war were more important than his determination to eschew a salary.

In *General George Washington,* Edward G. Lengel considers explanations of Washington's view of command.

No one, of course, can know Washington's conscious or unconscious mental processes; but if we must speculate—and speculation is, after all, integral to the historians' art—keeping it simple is a good rule of thumb. With imagination, countless explanations are possible; and in this case several are plausible. Washington's ambition may have been so deep, even subconscious, that he did not realize its presence. Or perhaps it *was* conscious, in which case he chose to conceal his motivations from his wife, the Congress, and others. He might also have been of two minds, with his love of military achievement struggling against uncertainty and doubt. But what about the simplest explanation? Could it be that he meant what he said and really felt unfit for command?

Washington had already seen more than enough bloodletting to sate his youthful fancy. War no longer seemed the romantic adventure he had imagined it to be as a young man; rather it loomed now as a tragic necessity. As he explained in a letter to George William Fairfax after learning of the war's first skirmishes: "Unhappy it is…to reflect, that a Brother's Sword has been sheathed in a Brother's breast, and that, the once happy and peaceful plains of America are either to be drenched with Blood, or Inhabited by Slaves. Sad alternative! But can a virtuous Man hesitate in his choice?" The military aggressiveness that Washington would later show did not spring from any love of battle, but from his impatience and desire for quick, decisive resolutions to every problem.

In *George Washington: Man and Monument,* Marcus Cunliffe details the qualities that made Washington a great American commander.

Washington revealed himself as an aristocrat with radical leanings. At any rate, unlike some of the prominent citizens at Philadelphia, he was prepared to commit himself and his estates on the side of the colonies. His military apparel proclaimed the fact; his demeanor and his reputation preserved him from the charge of flamboyance. In Sam Adams and others Congress had patriots who could rouse a rabble; its imperative need was for someone who could discipline and lead a rabble, who could both look and behave like a commander on the European model and yet be a true American.

In *A Leap in the Dark: The Struggle to Create the American Republic,* John Ferling points to the importance of Congress's 1775 petition to the king in maintaining both unanimity in Congress and its control of America's relations with Britain.

With the army in existence, and General Washington off to the front, Congress on July 8 approved the "humble petition" to the king that in principle it had agreed to six weeks earlier. John Adams privately sneered at the naivete of such a step. Dickinson's faction, he said, held to the hope that Parliament would back down when it learned of the bloodshed at Lexington and Concord. Such expectations were chimerical, he believed, but those bent on reconciliation had to be accommodated lest "Discord and total Disunion" result. The petition, written chiefly by Dickinson, made no mention of American rights and blamed the imperial woes on the monarch's irresponsible ministers. It also cautioned the king that the war would only radicalize growing numbers of colonists, making reconciliation even more tenuous. It beseeched George III to act while time remained. Congress adopted the entreaty, in part to assuage those who held the hope of reconciliation, but also as historian Jerrilyn Marston has demonstrated, from a desire to centralize control of America's external affairs in its own hands. In 1774 New York and New Jersey had petitioned the Crown even while Congress was in session. Congress had not been happy. Such conduct demonstrated—or at least hinted at—divisions among the colonists. Congress wished London to believe that wartime America was undivided. From this point forward, America's relationship with the mother country was solely in the hands of the Continental Congress.

In *American Scripture,* Pauline Maier details Britain's rejection of reconciliation: the king's proclamation and the 1775 act of Parliament.

In fact, for all practical purposes George III had already answered the petition. On August 23, the King issued a proclamation that said the Americans had "proceeded to open and avowed rebellion," and that they were encouraged by persons within the Mother Country whose "traitorous conspiracies" would be suitably punished. Two months later, in a speech to Parliament on October 26, 1775, that would have an enormous impact on colonial opinion, the King asserted that the American rebellion was "manifestly carried on for the purpose of establishing an independent Empire." The time had come, the King said, "to put a speedy end to these disorders by the most decisive exertions." As a result, he had strengthened his naval and land forces and was also considering "friendly offers of foreign assistance."

Members of the pro-American minorities in the Lords and Commons protested that the colonists had not, as the King charged, openly avowed their revolt and rebellion. Congress explicitly denied any desire for Independence; in fact, its petition to the King offered a splendid opportunity for "extricating this country from the ruinous situation in which the folly of Administration has involved us." The majority in both houses nonetheless approved the King's speech, and later, after further debates, passed a "Prohibitory Act" that replaced previous restrictions on American trade. The new and more severe law prohibited all commerce with the thirteen North American colonies "during the continuance of the present Rebellion." It put the Americans outside the King's protection, declaring colonial vessels and their cargoes, whether in harbor or at sea, forfeit to the Crown "as if the same were the ships and effects of open enemies." The Act also allowed the impressment of those vessels' officers and crews into the Royal Navy, where, the Americans complained, they might be forced to fight against their countrymen. George III gave his approval on December 22, 1775, and American ships, ports, and seamen became the prey of the British Navy.

⤐⤐⤐

13. Bunker Hill, Massachusetts

JUNE 17, 1775

BUNKER HILL BATTLEFIELD AND MONUMENT IN
BOSTON NATIONAL HISTORICAL PARK
CHARLESTOWN, MASSACHUSETTS

Two months after Concord and Lexington and before Washington took command in Cambridge, General Gage launched an attack to protect the British control of Boston Harbor. The two heights that could control Boston harbor were Charlestown Heights and Dorchester Heights. When Artemus Ward, named major general by the Continental Congress, learned in June of 1775 that the British planned to occupy Charlestown Heights, he ordered Colonel William Prescott to command a force to construct fortifications on the Heights. Prescott gathered about 1,000 men on the Cambridge Common and led them toward Bunker Hill. Although the battle is called Bunker Hill, the redoubt and breastwork were built on Breed's Hill, closer to the harbor. When the British learned about the construction, they opened fire from their warships on June 17. When General William Howe attacked later in the afternoon, the patriot force included men from Massachusetts, Connecticut, and New Hampshire.

John Ferling details the battle of Bunker Hill in *Almost a Miracle: The American Victory in the War of Independence.*

The British infantrymen, wearing heavy wool uniforms and weighted down with equipment, were wedged into their amphibious craft. Each man carried a canvas knapsack crammed with a three-day supply of food and topped with a rolled grey blanket. Strapped to each man was a canteen, a haversack for personal items, including a cup, tools for cleaning his weapon, a scabbard filled with a two-pound bayonet, and a cartouche, or cartridge, box. Each man was additionally outfitted with a smoothbore, muzzle-loading musket popularly known as the Brown Bess, after its dark-hued walnut stock. The weapon was four feet, nine inches long, weighed twelve pounds, and fired a ball that was three-quarters of an inch in diameter. Muskets were notoriously inaccurate above fifty yards.

The redcoats landed unopposed near the southeast corner of the somewhat pear-shaped peninsula. Howe personally took charge of the British right that was to assault the rebels' left flank. He took about 1,100 men and gave the remainder, near 1,200, to General Robert Pigot, a veteran officer who was assigned responsibility for attacking the redoubt. Up the hill, Stark with five hundred men and two artillery pieces awaited Howe on the American left. To their right, between them and the breastworks, and ensconced in fleches—two-sided, V-shaped entrenchments—were fifty to seventy men, positioned so that Howe's force would be subjected to a fire from three sides—front, right, and left. Posted at the other end of the rebel lines, between Charlestown and the redoubt, were another seventy-five or so men from Connecticut, who were to pour small arms fire into the advancing red line of enemy soldiers. There may have been 1,500 men here, roughly 300 in the redoubt, the remainder behind the breastworks. Eight artillery pieces had been hauled to this sector.

Just after 3:00, on what had become an uncomfortably hot afternoon, the redcoats at last stepped off. When the regulars were at fifty yards, and near the point where they would deploy and charge, the Americans opened fire. The volley blew apart the redcoats' line. When the back rows stepped into the breach, they, too, were cut down by the salvos that followed. What the British were attempting, wrote historian Christopher Ward, was akin to "pushing a wax candle against a red-hot plane." Finally seeing the futility of it, the officers ordered a fallback.

Hard on the heels of this bloody rebuff, Howe readied the British lines further to the left for the attack on the redoubt. When the redcoats approached to within twenty-five yards, the order to fire was given at last. Howe was in the midst of it, but emerged unscathed, though all about him men fell, including two on his staff (in the course of day, every man on his staff would be killed or wounded). He halted the attempt to advance, pulling his men back several hundred yards below the redoubt.

A long, uneasy lull set in as the British awaited reinforcements. At last, Howe was ready. He now had four infantry regiments and a battalion of marines under his command. When the advancing regulars drew to within twenty-five yards, the beginning of the end commenced. This time the redcoats kept coming.

At last, it was over. More than three hours after it began, the shooting stopped. Fully 50 percent of the regulars who saw combat were killed or wounded—226 had died, 928 were casualties. Ninety British officers, nearly 40 percent of the officers in Boston, died or were wounded. In two engagements, on April 19 and now at Bunker Hill, Gage had lost nearly 1,500 men, almost a quarter of the force that occupied Boston. Colonial losses were heavy as well. Counting the dozen or so who died in captivity (of the roughly 40 who were taken prisoner), 160 Americans perished and at least 271 were wounded.

One of the cartographic special collections of the Library of Congress includes manuscript and printed plans of the eighteenth-century English publisher William Faden. These show different stages of the research and map production process which, in this case, depicts a series of maps related to the battle of Bunker Hill.

On July 7 after the battle of Bunker Hill, Benjamin Franklin wrote to his scientist friend, Joseph Priestley, in London. The letter is included in *Benjamin Franklin: Autobiography, Poor Richard, and Later Writings,* edited by J. A. Leo Lemay.

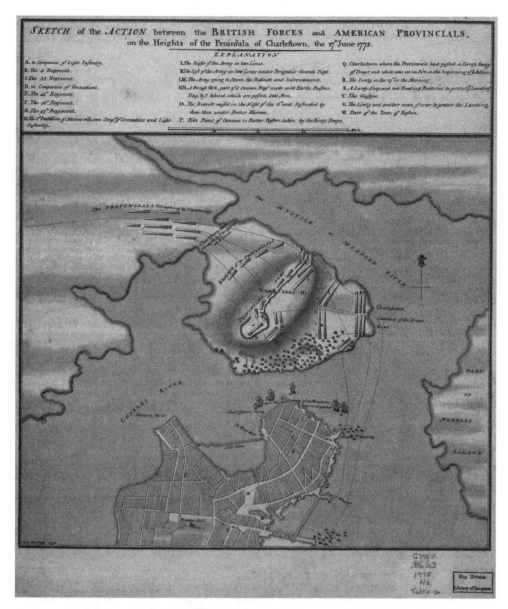

Action on the Heights of the Peninsula of Charlestown, 17 June 1775. John Humfrey. *Sketch of the action between the British forces and American provincials, on the heights of the peninsula of Charlestown, the 17th June 1775* [**London, 1775**]. *(Courtesy, Library of Congress, Geography and Map Division. http://hdl.loc.gov/loc.gmd/ g3764b.ct000251)*

The Congress met at a time when all minds were so exasperated by the perfidy of General Gates, and his attack on the country people, that propositions of attempting an accommodation were not much relished; and it has been with difficulty that we have carried another humble petition to the crown, to give Britain one more chance, one opportunity more of recovering the friendship of the colonies; which however I think she has not sense enough to embrace, and so I conclude she has lost them for ever.

She has begun to burn our seaport towns, secure, I suppose, that we shall never be able to return the outrage in kind. She may doubtless destroy them all; but if she wishes to recover our commerce, are these the probable means? She must certainly be distracted; for no trades-man out of Bedlam ever thought of encreasing the number of his customers by knocking them on the head; or of enabling them to pay their debts by burning their houses.

If she wishes to have us subjects and that we should submit to her as our compound sov-ereign, she is now giving us such miserable specimens of her government, that we shall ever detest and avoid it, as a complication of robbery, murder, famine, fire and pestilence.

In *Benjamin Franklin and the American Revolution,* Jonathan R. Dull details Frank-lin's civic involvement after he returned from London in 1775, including serving on many committees of Congress.

Franklin at first was more guarded with others about his political views; some, indeed, initially suspected him of being a British spy. Franklin eventually dispersed such suspicions by the range of his patriotic activities, not only in Congress but also as postmaster general, president of the Pennsylvania Committee of Safety, and president of the Pennsylvania Constitutional Conven-tion. He was also elected to the Pennsylvania Assembly and the Philadelphia Committee of In-spection and Observation, but lacked the time for them because of the demands of his service in the Continental Congress. Before Congress adjourned on August 1, 1775, for a six-week recess, it had appointed Franklin to committees dealing with the postal service, the drafting of a peti-tion to the king, the manufacture of saltpeter, the issuance of paper currency, the drafting of a declaration of the cause for taking up arms, the protection of American trade, the supervision of Indian affairs, the consideration of a resolution sent by Lord North, and the manufacture of lead.

The list of committees on which Franklin served indicates the dual nature of the task faced by Congress. On the one hand, it had to explore the possibility of negotiating a peaceful resolution to the dispute with Great Britain, a dispute that was becoming a full-scale war that few Americans wished. On the other, it had to create national institutions in order to coordi-nate the efforts of thirteen hitherto separate colonies to defend themselves.

With the British government unwilling to back down, the only hope for a negotiated settlement was through economic pressure, as had been successful in the past; should that fail, America would have to defend itself. Shortly after his return to America, Franklin wrote that he expected non-importation (already in effect) and non-exportation (due to come into effect in September) to end the controversy, but that he believed it absolutely necessary to be pre-pared to repel force by force.

There is a dramatic change in tone in Franklin's letters after the Battle of Bunker Hill on June 17. He was outraged by the British destruction of the nearby town of Charlestown before the battle, a seeming confirmation of British threats to burn American seaports. A common theme of these letters is Franklin's horror at the death of civilians, particularly women and children. This remained a concern of his; after the war he attempted to provide in various trea-ties for the future protection of noncombatants.

Before Congress adjourned, Franklin suggested that it offer an annual payment of £100,000 if Britain would make peace and give Americans the same privileges as Scotland. The proposal made little impact on his fellow delegates. He also circulated a suggestion that was more realistic—articles of confederation for "The United Colonies of North America." He would have to wait awhile before his colleagues were ready for such a complete break from Britain.

14. Old Cambridge, Massachusetts

LONGFELLOW HOUSE—WASHINGTON'S HEADQUARTERS
NATIONAL HISTORIC SITE
105 BRATTLE STREET
CAMBRIDGE, MASSACHUSETTS

General Washington arrived in Cambridge in July 1775, took command of about 14,000 soldiers, and made his headquarters in the house of John Vassall, a loyalist who had fled to England in 1774. It was his headquarters until the siege of Boston ended in March 1776.

Built in 1759, the house was a wedding present to the poet Henry Wadsworth Longfellow, and Fanny Appleton from her father when they were married in 1843. Longfellow lived in the house until his death in 1882.

15. Cambridge Common Encampment, Massachusetts

MASSACHUSETTS AVENUE AND GARDEN STREET
CAMBRIDGE, MASSACHUSETTS

Set aside in 1631, the sixteen-acre Cambridge Common was transferred to the City of Cambridge in 1769 to be a training ground for British soldiers. On April 19, 1775, Cambridge men gathered on the Common and marched to fight the British returning from the battles at Lexington and Concord.

Before the Battle of Bunker Hill, Massachusetts and Connecticut troops commanded by Colonel William Prescott marched in review on the Common. During the siege of Boston, the Common was the site of one of the Continental Army encampments. After the

British evacuated Boston on March 17, 1776, the Continental Army left Cambridge and began its march toward New York.

16. Gloucester, Massachusetts

AUGUST 8–9, 1775

Stage Fort Park, Gloucester Harbor
Gloucester, Massachusetts

During the siege of Boston, British naval vessels raided along the Massachusetts coast for food for the soldiers and fodder for their animals. On August 8 Captain John Linzee, commander of the HMS *Falcon*, captured an American schooner and chased another one into Gloucester Harbor. While he shelled the town, American artillery and musket fire hit the force that Linzee had sent toward shore to capture the schooner and burn the town. The Americans took British prisoners, freed the schooner and the sailors who had been impressed by Linzee, and drove off the *Falcon*.

The colonies needed naval vessels to supply their military needs and to protect towns along the coast. In *The First Salute,* Barbara W. Tuchman describes the early naval actions and the first vessels that became the United States Navy in 1775.

They were fortunate in a Commander-in-Chief who had formed in his own mind the fixed belief that the colonial forces could never achieve victory without sea power to use against the enemy. In August-September, 1775, to interrupt the British supply lines when he was besieging Boston, Washington had chartered and armed several small fishing schooners which had been commissioned by Massachusetts, Rhode Island and Connecticut to protect their coasts against British raids. By October 6, schooners commissioned by the Congress were watching the entrance of Boston harbor to fall upon British transports, which, not expecting naval action by the Colonies, carried no naval armament. "Washington's Navy," as the schooners came to be known, collected prizes of muskets, ball and powder and one fat 13-inch mortar, badly needed to bombard the British in Boston.

Rhode Island, with its great bays and long vulnerable seacoast, understandably shared the Commander-in-Chief's urgency about sea power. Going further than Washington, the colony, together with the associated Providence Plantations, passed a startling resolution in August, 1775, that no less than "an American fleet" should be built, and in the same month presented the resolve formally to the Continental Congress. Washington followed it in October with a request to Massachusetts for two armed ships to intercept two brigs loaded with military stores on their way from England to Quebec. Out of the need to organize this kind of enterprise on a larger scale and to interrupt British supply lines during the siege of Boston, the United States Navy was born. Privateers and fishing schooners manned by merchant seamen and fishermen were regularly commissioned and fitted out by the separate colonies. From this faint start Congress was being asked to authorize a national force responsible to the Continental government.

Congress decided to establish a national navy, and on October 13, 1775, appointed a Naval (later Marine) Committee to govern naval affairs, with authority to spend up to $500,000 to purchase and equip four armed ships and construct thirteen frigates, the class of warship carrying fewer than 44 guns, next below ship of the line. With some overconfidence, it was announced that they would be ready for sea in three months' time. The first four were purchased in November, marking the physical birth of the United States Navy, called at this time the Continental Navy. Because the United Colonies possessed no regular ships of war, merchant and fishing vessels had to be purchased, converted and armed. Hulls had to be reinforced, holes pierced to receive the guns for the broadside firing that was the basic and only tactic of naval warfare. Masts and rigging had to be strengthened for belligerent action and crews had to be recruited. Washington arranged for the small rough vessels newly transformed into warships to be chartered, armed and manned by soldiers recruited from New England regiments. Sailing crews had to be assembled by press-gang procedures because naval service in wet and squalid quarters and the smaller opportunity on national ships for prize money—of which the greater part went to the government, leaving much less to be divided among the owners and crews than on a privateer—offered few attractions to volunteer recruits. The greater danger on national ships than on privateers, which preyed largely on merchantmen, and the longer enlistments further discouraged volunteers. For the Continental Navy, press-gangs were a necessity.

Privateers were essentially ships with a license to rob issued to them by local or national governmental authority. The practice was a paradox in the development of law and order, which, as it progresses, is supposed to represent the advance of civilization. Privateers were fitted out for the express purpose of attack and seizure of commercial cargoes for the profit of owner and crews and of the authorizing power. In this business of maritime breaking and entering, the commission to a privateer authorized offensive action while letters of marque covered seizure of the cargo. Equivalent to a policeman giving his kind permission to a burglar, the theory was one of the happy hypocrisies that men fashion so ably when they want to combine law and greed.

Barbara W. Tuchman also details the navy's need for a flag.

A flag was as necessary as commodore or crew, for a national navy was nothing without it. If a flag for an army unit or a headquarters on land was a tradition to express a sense of pride and loyalty, for a ship on the trackless seas it was a necessity as a sign of identity so that it should not be taken for a pirate. Until now, ships commissioned by the separate colonies flew the colony's flag, like the pine tree of Massachusetts, or a personal standard, like the coiled serpent of George Washington with its device "Don't tread on me." For the Continental Navy, a flag was wanted to represent the hard-won confederation of colonies under one sovereignty, the great step that made feasible a war of revolution. This flag, made at the seat of Congress in Philadelphia, by a milliner, Margaret Manny, was to be the one to receive the first salute.

Everyone knows about Betsy Ross, why do we know nothing about Margaret Manny? Probably for no better reason than that she had fewer articulate friends and relatives to build a story around her.

Rather than venture into the tangled web of flag origins where a dispute attaches to every point, let us simply accept the fact that a red-and-white-striped flag made its appearance aboard a ship of the new navy at its dock in Philadelphia in December, 1775. What is on record here is that Margaret Manny, milliner, received from James Wharton of Philadelphia, 49 yards of broad bunting and 52 ½ yards of the narrow width with which to prepare an ensign. The goods were charged to the account of the ship *Alfred*, flagship of the squadron and, with 30 guns, largest of the first four. The finished product, leaving aside the question of who designed it, displayed thirteen red and white stripes, representing the union of the thirteen colonies, together with the combined crosses of St. Andrew and St. George in the canton or upper left quadrant retained from the Union Jack. The crosses had appeared on the British flag since 1707, when the two kingdoms of England and Scotland formed a union under the Crown of Great Britain. Their appearance on the American flag indicated that the Colonies were not yet ready to detach themselves from the British Crown or declare themselves a new sovereign state.

On a mid-winter day, December 3, 1775, the new flag was flown. "I hoisted with my own hands the flag of freedom," John Paul Jones recalled on the deck of his ship, the *Alfred*, at her dock in Philadelphia in the Delaware River, while the commodore and officers of the fleet and a cheering crowd of citizens hailed the event from shore. Washington, shortly afterward, on January I, 1776, raised what is believed to be the same flag on Prospect Hill in Cambridge, Massachusetts, during his siege of Boston. Testimony as to whether this flag, called the Grand Union, was carried at Trenton and Brandywine and other land battles is elusive, though it was soon to fly visibly in active combat at sea. The Grand Union gave way to the Stars and Stripes, officially adopted by Congress in June, 1777, with thirteen white stars on a blue field replacing the British crosses. In 1795, two stars were added, representing the adherence to the union of Kentucky and Vermont.

17. Edmund Fowle House, Massachusetts

Edmund Fowle House and Museum
The Historical Society of Watertown
28 Marshall Street
Watertown, Massachusetts

During the siege of Boston, the Massachusetts Provincial Congress met in Watertown, and committees of the Congress met in the Fowle House. It was the temporary home and headquarters of James Warren, husband of Mercy Otis Warren and paymaster general of the Continental Army. The house was moved from Mount Auburn Street to Marshall Street in 1872.

In *Founders,* Ray Raphael details the concerns of James and Mercy Warren about independence.

Throughout the second half of 1775, all events pointed in the direction of a separation from Great Britain. In August, King George III declared that not only the people of Massachusetts, but "divers wicked and desperate persons" throughout "our colonies and plantations in North America" were in a state of rebellion. To suppress the uprising, he dispatched thousands of additional troops and dozens of ships. The rebellious colonials could not successfully resist such an onslaught without material aid from Europe, yet European nations refused to interfere with Britain's internal affairs. Only if the rebels formed a separate union could they expect to receive the assistance they needed.

The logic was clear, and James Warren, among others, had little trouble figuring it out. On Wednesday, November 15, Warren wrote a letter to John Adams (still a delegate to the Continental Congress) from the master bedroom of the stately Fowle House on Mt. Auburn Street in Watertown, his temporary home and headquarters while he served as speaker of the Massachusetts Assembly and paymaster general of the Continental Army. Foreign powers were not willing to aid the patriots' cause, he noted, because Americans continued to acknowledge a "dependency" on the British Crown. To gain support, Congress needed to stop hesitating and take "capital and effectual strokes." What he meant, of course, was that Congress should declare independence from Britain, but he didn't say that. Even in the fall of 1775, over a year after the people of Worcester and other rebellious towns in Massachusetts had pushed for "independency," no recognized leader would dare step forth and embrace the *I* word.

As James wrote, Mercy sat beside him. (She had come to visit for a few days, since her husband was never free to travel home.) They must have been discussing the subject at hand, as they often did during letter-writing time, for Mercy suddenly barged in. James was being too soft in his choice of language, she thought, and she proceeded to dictate more forceful words of her own, insisting that her husband write them down:

> She [Mercy] sits at the table with me, will have a paragraph of her own; says you [Congress] "should no longer *piddle* at the threshold. It is time to *leap* into the theatre, to unlock the bars, and open every gate that impedes the rise and growth of the American republic, and then let the giddy potentate send forth his puerile proclamations to France, to Spain and all the commercial world who may be united in building up an Empire which he can't prevent.

Yes, Congress had indeed been piddling. The strategic logic of declaring independence, contrasted with the political need to disavow such a drastic measure, created a tension that colored every political move. Thomas Jefferson, who had taken George Washington's place in Congress, admitted on November 29 that only one thing stood in the way of taking the final plunge: "We want neither inducement nor power, to declare and assert a separation. It is will alone that is wanting."

John Dickinson (once revered as the Farmer, who wrote so lucidly in opposition to British taxation, but now known in the Adams-Warren circle as the chief "piddler" in Congress) took advantage of that lack of political will. At his urging, the Pennsylvania Assembly issued binding instructions to their representatives in the Continental Congress: "We strictly enjoin you that you, in behalf of this colony, dissent from and utterly reject any propositions, should such be made, that may cause or lead to a separation from our mother country or a change of the form of this government."

Delegates from New Jersey, Delaware, and Maryland also received instructions to oppose independence, while New York's contingent, conservative in bent, needed no prodding on that score. Early in January, James Wilson, a Pennsylvania delegate and political associate of both John Dickinson and Robert Morris, proposed that Congress itself take up the issue of independence, not to support it, but to come out once and for all against such a radical scheme. Wilson's motion was discussed and tabled, but his opponents, even as they argued against his measure, failed to declare their own support for independence. Precisely because their enemies called them traitors, patriots as rebellious as John and Samuel Adams had to demonstrate that they were not.

Robert Morris expressed the prevailing wisdom of the time: "For my part I abhor the name & idea of a rebel, I neither want nor wish a change of King or Constitution, & do not conceive myself to act against either when I join America in defence of constitutional liberty."

But Mercy Otis Warren had seen enough of all this piddling. She was ready to take the big leap, and so were others, if only they could find the nerve. For these people to come forth, however, someone would have to speak first, proudly and publicly, on behalf of independence.

---

18. Fort Western, Maine

OLD FORT WESTERN
16 CONY STREET
AUGUSTA, MAINE

In the summer of 1775, Congress ordered an attack on Canada. While one force launched an invasion from New York commanded by Brigadier General Richard Montgomery, General Washington ordered Colonel Benedict Arnold to command a force from Massachusetts through Maine to Canada. Arnold arrived at Fort Western in September 1775, assembled his force and supplies, including wooden boats built nearby, and headed north for the attack on Quebec. In the defeat in late December, Montgomery was killed, Arnold was wounded, and Captain Daniel Morgan and his men were captured. They were paroled eight months later.

In the summer of 1779 Fort Western helped the survivors of the failed Massachusetts attack on the British at Penobscot Bay and River in Maine (see #96).

The restored fort, a National Historic Landmark, is a little altered example of an eighteenth-century log fort/trading post. It was built in 1754 by the Proprietors of the Kennebec Purchase at the head of navigation on the Kennebec River to defend the area from attacks during the French and Indian War. It was a fortified storehouse for Fort Halifax, seventeen miles upriver. After it was decommissioned in 1766, James Howard, who had been its commander, purchased it and turned it into a trading post.

---

19. Williamsburg Powder Magazine, Virginia

COLONIAL WILLIAMSBURG
WILLIAMSBURG, VIRGINIA

Williamsburg was the capital of the Virginia colony from 1699 until 1776 and of the Commonwealth of Virginia until 1780, when the capital was moved to Richmond. The Powder Magazine, built in 1715, is the oldest building in Williamsburg.

John Murray, Earl of Dunmore, was appointed royal governor of New York in 1770 and royal governor of Virginia in 1771. The day after the royal governor of Massachusetts ordered a force to seize the colonists' military supplies in Lexington and Concord, Dunmore, fearing an uprising, acted on orders from London to protect the royal government. He sent Lieutenant Henry Collins and royal marines from the HMS *Magdalen* to remove the gunpowder from the powder magazine and take it to the HMS *Fowey*. When threatened by angry Virginians, Dunmore issued a declaration to free slaves, described by Cassandra Pybus in *Epic Journeys of Freedom: Runaway Slaves of the American Revolution and Their Global Quest for Liberty*.

> Anxiety about a slave insurrection was heightened when the embattled royal governor of Virginia removed all the gunpowder from the magazine in the colonial capital at Williamsburg on April 20, 1775. Confronted by an outraged citizenry, who believed Lord Dunmore had acted in order to expose them to the mercy of their slaves, the governor inflamed passions by announcing what he would do in the case of any retaliation: "I shall be forced to arm my own Negroes and receive all others that will come to me, who I shall declare free." Given that the planters of Virginia held some 180,000 people enslaved, to even hint at such a thing was truly shocking. Prominent Loyalists insisted that the governor would use such tactics if attacked, but their reassurance did nothing to diminish the terror of white Virginians for whom, it was said, "even the whispering of the wind was sufficient to rouze their fears."

At that time, a group of unidentified slaves had taken their lives in their hands to call on the governor and offer their service in support of the king, only to have him turn them away. In his besieged position in the governor's mansion, Dunmore was not prepared to risk more fury from the Williamsburg populace. His threats to free the slaves had "stirred up fears in them which cannot easily subside," he explained to the secretary of state in England, "as they know how vulnerable they are in that particular." By June, however, he had been forced to take refuge on a British warship in the James River (and to send his wife back to England) and he was only too happy to take advantage of the offer of service from fugitive slaves. From the relative safety of HMS *Fowey*, Dunmore began to assemble a squadron to strike back at the rebellious Virginians, welcoming any runaways that were able to make their way across to his fleet.

In November 1775 Lord Dunmore issued his proclamation, the impact of which Ray Raphael details in *Founders*.

> Patriots had suspected it might come to this, and finally it did. On November 14, 1775, from HMS *Fowey*, docked in the James River, the royal governor of Virginia, Lord Dunmore, issued his famous/infamous proclamation:
>> And I do hereby further declare all indented Servants, Negroes, or others, (appertaining to Rebels,) free, that are able and willing to bear Arms, they joining HIS MAJESTY'S Troops as soon as may be, for the more speedily reducing this Colony to a proper Sense of their Duty, to HIS MAJESTY'S Crown and Dignity.
> The impact was profound on both slaves and masters. Facing great risks and overwhelming odds, hundreds upon hundreds of African Americans, healthy men and women in their prime, left their plantations, crept through the woods to the water's edge, and swam or boated to British ships to cash in on Dunmore's offer of freedom. "Slaves flock to him in abundance," one bitter patriot wrote to another.

In *Slavery and the Making of America,* James Oliver Horton and Lois E. Horton provide estimates of the number of slaves seeking freedom by going to the British.

> Lord Dunmore recognized the slaves' desire for freedom and realized the strategic advantage to be gained by attracting slaves and indentured servants to the British cause. He well understood the psychological value of recruiting American slaves to fight against their former masters. A victory by black troops would be both humiliating and infuriating to the Americans. As Dunmore explained to his superiors in England, "by employing them you cannot desire a means more effectual to distress your Foes." In November 1775 he issued a proclamation offering freedom and a small payment to all slaves and servants who would fight for the British. Many slaves were attracted by the rhetoric of the American fight for freedom, but many others believed the English promised a more reliable route out of slavery. Hundreds of slaves joined Dunmore's Ethiopian Regiment. Although it is impossible to be certain how many sought

freedom by going to the British, estimates range as high as 100,000. Planters in South Carolina and Georgia were convinced that at least twenty thousand slaves would join Dunmore "in a fortnight." By 1778 Thomas Jefferson estimated that at least thirty thousand Virginia slaves had run away to the British, and at least thirty of these were from Jefferson's own Monticello plantation. Historians have placed the number of South Carolina's runaways at 25,000 or more between 1775 and 1783, while in Georgia more than 12,000 of the state's 15,000 slaves set out for freedom.

In *John Adams,* David McCullough documents the importance of slavery in the colonies.

In truth, black slavery had long since become an accepted part of life in all of the thirteen colonies. Of a total population in the colonies of 2,500,000 people in 1776, approximately one in five were slaves, some 500,000 men, women, and children. In Virginia alone, which had the most slaves by far, they numbered more than 200,000. There was no member of the Virginia delegation who did not own slaves, and of all the members of Congress at least a third owned or had owned slaves. The total of Thomas Jefferson's slaves in 1776, as near as can be determined from his personal records, was about 200, which was also the approximate number owned by George Washington.

20. Great Bridge, Virginia

DECEMBER 9, 1775

GREAT BRIDGE BATTLEFIELD AND WATERWAYS PARK AND
VISITOR/MUSEUM CENTER
1775 HISTORIC WAY
CHESAPEAKE, VIRGINIA

Slaves who responded to Governor Dunmore's proclamation and fled to freedom by joining the British army were organized into the Ethiopian Regiment and prepared for battle.

To protect the important port at Norfolk, Dunmore had to control the Great Road, the only land route between Norfolk and North Carolina. He ordered a fort built in Virginia along the road at the north end of the Great Bridge over the Southern Branch of the Elizabeth River.

In early December Colonel William Woodford's command of 900 patriots arrived to oppose Dunmore's 600-man force. Woodford led the 2nd Virginia Regiment, the Culpeper

Minutemen Battalion, and Virginia and North Carolina militia. Michael Kranish describes the Great Bridge battle in *Flight from Monticello: Thomas Jefferson at War*.

Woodford arrived on December 1, 1775, pitching camp in front of a small church at the southern end of the marshy area. The road from the church was lined with a dozen houses, which in turn led to a causeway with another seven houses. At the northern end of the causeway, the hastily constructed British fort was protected by two cannons. The Virginians set up their redoubts in the area between the two sets of houses but had no cannon, making a siege seemingly impossible. The only way to dislodge the British would be a head-on assault over the bridge, which risked making the Patriots easy targets for His Majesty's regiments.

The red-jacketed British grenadiers carried long muskets with fixed bayonets and were commanded by a tall, genteel captain named Charles Fordyce. The British wheeled their two cannons into place by dawn of December 9. The light forces prepared to charge. The grenadiers assumed position. Behind them were the Queen's Own Loyal Virginia Regiment and the freed slaves of the Ethiopian Regiment. The planks of the bridge, taken up earlier to prevent an assault by the Virginians, were put back in place.

Fordyce, acting on orders that presumably came from Dunmore, led the grenadiers across. In a strong, steady march, the first wave of British fired at the Virginians, reloading sharply in time, while the next row of men prepared to level their shot. The Virginians had been instructed to hold their fire until the last possible moment. Now, with British bullets and grapeshot whistling across the divide and the rising sun glistening off the water, the Virginians let loose. Fordyce was hit. He died as an officer was told to, leading his men. But he had also led them into disaster. The British, no longer protected by their fort, were exposed in a tight mass. The Virginians behind the breastworks fired at them and could hardly miss.

It was a stunning victory. A lone Virginian had injured a finger. Dunmore claimed only 17 dead, but he apparently tallied only the deaths of British regulars, not Virginia Loyalists or members of the Ethiopian Regiment. The Virginians captured many of the surviving members of the Ethiopian Regiment and decided to make examples of them, selling thirty-two into slavery in the Caribbean. The Virginia Convention passed a resolution that decreed death to "all Negro or other Slaves, conspiring to rebel or make insurrection."

The American victory opened the Great Road to North Carolina and the port of Norfolk, Virginia, to American ships. On January 1, 1776, Dunmore shelled Norfolk and set it on fire. The following May, he landed on Gwynn's Island in the Chesapeake Bay off the coast of Virginia with his loyalists, militia, and fleeing slaves, ending British rule in Virginia.

While independence was being debated, Britain encouraged it in Virginia by attacking patriots at Great Bridge and by Privy Council rulings against its commercial rights. Woody Holton details Virginia's address for commercial rights, which reveals the complexities within the American Revolution, in *Forced Founders: Indians, Debtors, Slaves, and the Making of the American Revolution in Virginia.*

From 1765, when the House of Burgesses took the most radical stance against the Stamp Act of any colonial legislature, to 1776, when Thomas Jefferson wrote the Declaration of Independence, Virginia was at the forefront of the American Revolution. Scholars studying the causes of the Revolution in Britain's most populous American colony have mostly focused on gentlemen—the likes of Jefferson, Washington, and Patrick Henry. Although no one can deny their importance, the Independence movement was also powerfully influenced by British merchants and by three groups that today would be called grassroots: Indians, farmers, and slaves. Some of the ways in which these groups helped—usually inadvertently—to sour crown-colony relations are evident in three documents produced by a unanimous House of Burgesses between 1769 and 1775. None of the three has received nearly as much attention as other Revolution texts.

The 1769 petition was for Kentucky. The second, adopted in 1772, was against the Atlantic slave trade. Three years later, assemblymen indicated in a formal address that free Virginians were willing to absorb some of the British Empire's American expenses—but only if Parliament granted them the same commercial rights that other British subjects enjoyed.

Today politicians as well as historians often portray the American Revolution as a tax revolt. This it certainly was, but it was also a conflict among social classes, for the British government did not act only on its own behalf. Like the modern American government, it responded to pressure from commercial interests and to a lesser extent from groups such as Native Americans. Indians and British merchants powerfully influenced the fate of the petitions that the Virginia House of Burgesses sent the Privy Council in 1769 and 1772 and of the address it adopted in 1775. Merchants organized to preserve their commercial privileges. Meanwhile, significant numbers of Ohio Valley and southern Indians united to try to keep their land. Pressured by the unified merchants and fearful of the united Indians, the Privy Council refused to comply with the burgesses' two petitions or with their 1775 address. The government's refusal angered all free Virginians that depended upon international trade, that considered African immigrants a threat to Virginia's economy and security, and that hoped to make (or recover) their fortunes selling Indian land.

The attacks by the military and the rejection of the colonies' addresses and petitions, such as those from Virginia, dimmed and then dashed any hope for reconciliation with Britain, as Pauline Maier points out in *From Resistance to Revolution.*

The most important single restraint on any decision for independence, however, was the hope that somehow, whether by action of the ministry, Parliament, King, or the British people, an accommodation within the framework of the empire might yet be made between the colonists and Britain, with the "terms and limits of our union" ascertained and fixed "upon clear and solid ground." This hope lingered on into late 1775; but with the failure of the English people to rise in support of the Americans it was extinguished, and independence became imperative.

In "James Ireland, John Leland, John 'Swearing Jack' Waller, and the Baptist Campaign for Religious Freedom in Revolutionary Virginia," in *Revolutionary Founders* edited by Alfred F. Young, Gary B. Nash, and Ray Raphael, Jon Butler points out that there were two revolutions in Virginia, one of which was for religious freedom.

James Ireland, John Leland, and John Waller, Baptists all, knew the dangers of pursuing freedom of religion and became major figures in the drive for the Revolutionary achievement of religious freedom in Virginia. They fought for two revolutions in Virginia, one for political freedom and one for religious freedom. They demonstrated how colonists of modest background led sophisticated discussions of fundamental political and religious principles; how the Revolution itself challenged all Virginia religious groups, including Baptists, in unexpected ways; and how a small, determined movement could profoundly change the long-vexed relationship between religion and government in Europe and America. They remind us how common men and women could shape society as profoundly as the well known and wealthy.

Virginia's Baptists worried about religious freedom because, as in most southern colonies, the Church of England—the Anglican Church—was Virginia's exclusive, legally established church, and non-Anglican "dissenters" worshipped only through government sufferance. Since the seventeenth century Virginia law had presumed all Virginians to be members of the Church of England. Residents were required to pay taxes to support it, and no one could preach in the colony without a license, a regulation reinforced in 1747 by the Virginia governor and council who demanded restraints on "all Itinerant Preachers." This meant that Virginia licensed only ministers it approved; could refuse to license dissenting preachers, such as Baptist and Presbyterian itinerant preachers who upset parish stability; and did not respect freedom of conscience, as did Pennsylvania.

Organized religion was scant in Virginia from 1607 until the 1680s, and questions of religious freedom were muted by early Anglican disorganization and spiritual indifference among early Virginia colonists. Church of England parish life lagged, ministers were few, and only Quakers offered competition, though in small numbers that attracted little negative attention. Between 1680 and the 1760s, however, Virginia developed a powerful Church of England establishment strongly inflected by wealth and social class. By the 1750s Anglican parishes in Virginia were renowned for large, beautiful church structures and generally well-paid ministers. Sunday worshippers drawn from the local planter aristocracy strengthened the authority of the Church of England and their own local and colony-wide prestige. After 1755 Baptists aggressively challenged this religious authority and personal prestige.

In an eighteenth-century society where hierarchy determined even how residents greeted each other, the Baptists' modesty, combined with their blunt assertiveness and claims of religious independence and spiritual vision, may be what most offended so many officials. Anglican authorities believed that the Baptists' modest social status simply gave them no right to ignore the established church, to preach without licenses. These very modest Baptists nonetheless shaped effective, dynamic communities outside the colony's established hierarchical religious and social order. And Baptists accomplished their goals by preaching in people's homes and the open air, beyond the church buildings Anglicans had worked so hard to construct in the previous half century.

Between 1770 and 1776 Virginia Baptists found ways to intensify their protests and demands while aligning themselves with political protests against British incursions against colonial rights and privileges. They accomplished this in three ways. First, they joined Presbyterians to support legislation applying the 1689 Act of Toleration to most Protestant dissenters in ways that stressed their common cause.

Second, the Baptists' (and Presbyterians') argument for broader freedoms took advantage of their own increasing numbers to make clear how restrictions against them were both unsuccessful yet increasingly problematic for the colony as a whole.

Third, by 1775 Baptist petitions linked their movement to the defense of the colony by its leading protesters against British actions. In August 1775 John Waller forwarded a letter as "clerk" of the Virginia Baptist Association to the Virginia Convention, which essentially governed the colony after Lord Dunmore dissolved the House of Burgesses in 1774, praising convention members as "Guardians of the Rights of Your Constituents[,] pointing out to them the Road to Freedom." The Baptist petition pointedly approved "a Military resistance against Great Britain, in regard to their unjust Invasion, and Tyrannical Oppression." Then the Baptists petitioned the convention to give four Baptist preachers "free Liberty to preach to the Troops at convenient Times without molestation or abuse." This deftly coupled vigorous support for colonial resistance to British tyranny with an approval of Baptist preaching that would overturn two decades of Virginia resistance to the Baptist cause.

Religious freedom was also deeply important to Thomas Jefferson, as John Ferling discusses in *Setting the World Ablaze: Washington, Adams, Jefferson and the American Revolution.*

The measure that was closest to Jefferson's heart concerned religious freedom. He subsequently referred to pre-Revolutionary Virginia, a province in which the Anglican Church was the established church, as a land of "religious slavery." However, change was in the air prior to the Anglo-American difficulties, and independence made change of some sort virtually inevitable. Virginia's large population of Methodists, Presbyterians, and Baptists, a citizenry being asked to soldier in defense of the Revolution, was ardent in the state. Thus, the state's Declaration of Rights, adopted in 1776 while Jefferson was yet in Philadelphia, asserted "the free exercise of religion" to all citizens.

Many Virginians, including Jefferson, had hoped for more. He believed the Declaration of Rights should have protected nonbelievers. He said it was proper for the state to concern itself with injuries that one person caused to another, but an affront to God was a matter between the offender and the deity. It "does me no injury for my neighbor to say there are twenty gods, or no God," he remarked. He thought each individual should have the right of "free inquiry" in matters of religion, as in matters of science and government. Although Jefferson was later attacked as an atheist, what he in fact sought was not so much freedom from religion, as the freedom for each person to pursue whatever beliefs his or her study and thought led them to, including the decision to believe in nothing. Therefore, in 1779 Bill No. 82, in the legal code that Jefferson introduced, provided that "no man shall be compelled to frequent or support any religious worship, place, or ministry," and that no person could be made to "suffer on account of his religious opinions or belief." His proposed legislation passed with slight modifications that did no damage to the sense of the original bill. Nothing that Jefferson accomplished in his public life gave him greater satisfaction, and little else that he touched has been of such lasting importance. He justly felt that he had acted to secure for each man the right to use his powers of reason in "the formation of his own [religious] opinions." He lived to see his statute serve as a model for legislation in other states and, ultimately, for the First Amendment to the U. S. Constitution.

<hr />

In January 1776, Thomas Paine's pamphlet was printed. Eric Foner describes *Common Sense* in *Tom Paine and Revolutionary America*.

On January 9, 1776, one of the most remarkable political pamphlets in the history of English writing appeared in Philadelphia. *Common Sense*, a forceful and brilliant argument for the independence of the American colonies from Great Britain and the superiority of republican government over hereditary monarchy, had an enormous impact on the subsequent decision for independence. By the end of the year, no fewer than twenty-five editions had been printed, reaching hundreds of thousands of Americans. The exact circulation of *Common Sense* is not known, but every scholar of the American Revolution agrees it was totally unprecedented in eighteenth-century America. In an age of pamphleteering, *Common Sense* was unique in the extent of its readership and its influence on events.

The author of *Common Sense* was Thomas Paine, "a gentleman," as John Adams described him, "about two years ago from England, a man who…has genius in his eyes." *Common Sense* marked the emergence of Paine as the greatest pamphleteer of the Age of Revolution, a career he would pursue in his *Crisis* papers in America, in *The Rights of Man, The Age of Reason* and *Agrarian Justice* in Europe, and in countless other pamphlets and newspaper articles. "I know not," Adams observed in 1806, "whether any man in the world has had more influence on its inhabitants or affairs for the last thirty years than Thomas Paine."

To understand Paine we must begin with his role as a pamphleteer of revolution. "The American and French Revolutions," Eric Hobsbawm has written, "are probably the first mass political movements in the history of the world which expressed their ideology and aspirations in terms of a secular rationalism and not of traditional religion." Paine was one of the creators of this secular language of revolution, a language in which timeless discontents, millennial aspirations and popular traditions were expressed in a strikingly new vocabulary. The very slogans and rallying cries we associate with the revolutions of the late eighteenth century come from Paine's writings: the "rights of man," the "age of reason," the "age of revolution," and "the times that try men's souls." Paine helped to transform the meaning of the key words of political discourse. In *Common Sense* he was among the first writers to use "republic" in a positive rather than derogatory sense; in *The Rights of Man* he abandoned the old classical definition of "democracy," as a state where each citizen participated directly in government, and created its far broader, far more favorable modern meaning. Even the word "revolution" was transformed in his writing, from a term derived from the motion of the planets and implying a cyclical view of history to one signifying vast and irreversible social and political change.

What made Paine unique was that he forged a new political language. He did not simply change the meanings of words, he created a literary style designed to bring his message to the widest possible audience. His rhetoric was clear, simple and straightforward; his arguments rooted in the common experiences of a mass readership. Paine helped to extend political discussion beyond the narrow confines of the eighteenth century's "political nation" (the classes actively involved in politics, to whom most previous political writing had been addressed). Through this new language, he communicated a new vision—a utopian image of an egalitarian republican society.

Toward the close of *Common Sense*, Paine moved beyond material considerations to outline in lyrical rhetoric a breathtaking vision of the meaning of American independence. "We have it in our power to begin the world over again...the birthday of a new world is at hand." Paine transformed the struggle over the rights of Englishmen into a contest with meaning for all mankind:

> O! ye that love mankind! Ye that dare oppose not only tyranny but the tyrant, stand forth! Every spot of the old world is overrun with oppression. Freedom hath been hunted round the globe. Asia and Africa have long expelled her. Europe regards her as a stranger, and England hath given her warning to depart. O! receive the fugitive, and prepare in time an asylum for mankind.

The immediate success and impact of *Common Sense* was nothing short of astonishing. At a time when the most widely circulated colonial newspapers were fortunate if they averaged two thousand sales per week, when the average pamphlet was printed in one or two editions of perhaps a few thousand copies, *Common Sense* went through twenty-five editions and reached literally hundreds of thousands of readers in the single year 1776. It also reached nonreaders; one report from Philadelphia in February said the pamphlet "is read to all ranks." Paine later claimed *Common Sense* had sold at least 150,000 copies, and most historians have accepted this figure as roughly accurate. As Paine exulted, it was "the greatest sale that any performance ever had since the use of letters."

Common Sense did express ideas which had long circulated in the colonies—the separateness of America from Europe, the corruption of the Old World and innocence of the New, the absurdity of hereditary privilege and the possibility of a future American empire. None of these ideas was original with Paine. What was brilliantly innovative was the way Paine combined them into a single comprehensive argument and related them to the common experiences of Americans.

21. Marblehead Town House, Massachusetts

OLD TOWN HOUSE
WASHINGTON STREET
MARBLEHEAD, MASSACHUSETTS

The Boston area was the focus of the war when General Washington took command in Cambridge in early July 1775. In Marblehead, just north of Boston, the Town House was the government center. Built in 1727, it was also the place where citizens gathered to protest the Stamp Act and the Boston Port Bill, organize Committees of Safety, Grievances, and Correspondence, and select the delegates for the Provincial Congress. The Sons of Liberty also met here.

In May 1775 John Glover was made colonel in the 21st Massachusetts. He organized 1,000 fishermen into a regiment and was commissioned head of it on June 16, 1775.

On January 1, 1776, the regiment became the 14th Massachusetts Continentals, described by David Hackett Fischer in *Washington's Crossing*.

George Washington had a special problem with a Yankee regiment that was by all accounts one of the best in the army. The Fourteenth Massachusetts Continentals were raised in Marblehead and recruited from fishing towns on the north shore of Massachusetts, especially Beverly, Salem, Lynn, and Marblehead. Their colonel was John Glover, prosperous owner of sloops and schooners in the Atlantic trade and member of the tight "codfish aristocracy" who dominated the north shore of New England. He was not a radical by nature, but he and his townsmen felt the sting of tyranny in writs of assistance, corrupt customs officers, and illegal impressments of Marblehead crews by the Royal Navy. These repeated acts turned a conservative ship captain into a revolutionary.

Many of his men were seamen and fishermen. The regiment also reflected the ethnic composition of New England maritime towns. Indians and Africans sailed in Yankee ships and settled in the seaport villages. They also enlisted in Glover's regiment. He knew these men as shipmates and welcomed them to his command. At first George Washington was not happy about the enlistments of African Americans, but after much discussion he worked out a sequence of compromises. The first was to allow African Americans to continue in the ranks but to prohibit new enlistments. The second was to tolerate new enlistments but not to approve them. By the end of the war, African Americans were actively recruited, and some rose to the rank of colonel in New England. Washington's attitudes were different from those of Colonel Glover, but here again he worked out a dynamic compromise that developed through time. It also kept the peace within the army, allowed men of different views to fight the war together, and encompassed another idea of freedom in the American Revolution. In that process the Continental army, beginning with the Marblehead regiment, became the first integrated national institution in the United States.

In *1776*, David McCullough describes the Boston area after General Washington took command of the army in July 1775.

By June a sprawling, spontaneous, high-spirited New England army such as had never been seen was gathered about Boston. Washington, arriving in the first week of July, was told he had 20,000 men, but no one knew for certain. No count had been taken until he made it a first order of business. In fact, there were 16,000, of which fewer than 14,000 were fit for duty. More than 1,500 were sick, another 1,500 absent. Nearly all his efforts and those of his senior officers were concentrated now on trying to hold the army together. The Connecticut troops, whose enlistments were to expire on December 9, were counting the days until they could start for home. Nothing, it seemed, could change their minds.

A stirring summons to renewed devotion to the cause of liberty, as strong and eloquent an appeal to the men in the ranks, "the guardians of America," as had yet been seen in print, appeared in the *New England Chronicle*, signed simply "A Freeman."

Notwithstanding the many difficulties we have to encounter, and the rage of our merciless enemies, we have a glorious prospect before us, big with everything good and great. The further we enter into the field of independence, our prospects will expand and brighten, and a complete Republic will soon complete our happiness.

At the Cambridge headquarters, Washington declared in his general orders for New Year's Day the commencement of a "new army, which in every point of view is entirely continental." And thus the army, though still 90 percent a New England army, had a name, the Continental Army.

Meanwhile, Washington put increasing trust in Nathanael Greene, as well as another impressive young New Englander, Henry Knox, to whom he assigned one of the most difficult and crucial missions of the war.

Colonel Henry Knox was hard not to notice. Six feet tall, he bulked large, weighing perhaps 250 pounds. He had a booming voice. He was gregarious, jovial, quick of mind, highly energetic—"very fat but very active"—and all of twenty-five.

It was Henry Knox who first suggested the idea of going after the cannon at far-off Fort Ticonderoga on Lake Champlain, an undertaking so enormous, so fraught with certain difficulties, that many thought it impossible.

The capture of Fort Ticonderoga from the British by Ethan Allen, Benedict Arnold, and a handful of Green Mountain Boys earlier in May had been sensational news, but the fort and its captured artillery were abandoned. When Knox told Washington he was confident the guns could be retrieved and hauled overland to Boston, Washington agreed at once, and put the young officer in charge of the expedition.

Henry Knox to George Washington, December 17, 1775. *(Courtesy of The Gilder Lehrman Institute of American History, GLC02437.00222)*

In a letter to General Washington (see opposite page), Colonel Knox details the difficulties in dragging the artillery from Fort Ticonderoga to Boston:

It is not easy to conceive the difficulties we have had in getting them over the lake owing to the advanced season of the year and contrary winds but the danger is now past.

Today monuments mark the trail over which Knox led the artillery train in the winter of 1775–1776.

22. Dorchester Heights, Massachusetts

MARCH 4–16, 1776

BOSTON NATIONAL HISTORICAL PARK
DORCHESTER HEIGHTS
SOUTH BOSTON, MASSACHUSETTS

Dorchester Heights, the hills south of Boston, was the critical height of land for General Washington's artillery in March 1776. David McCullough details the patriots' victory at Dorchester Heights in his book *1776*.

That Dorchester Heights could decide the whole outcome at Boston had been apparent to the British from the beginning. But while Gage had kept Bunker Hill heavily armed with cannon and manned by five hundred troops, he had done nothing about Dorchester. Nor had General Howe since taking charge after Gage's departure for home in October. Nor, indeed, had the Americans. Dorchester Heights remained a kind of high, windblown no-man's-land, neither side unmindful of its strategic importance, but neither side daring to seize and fortify it.

On January 14, two weeks into the new year, George Washington wrote one of the most forlorn, despairing letters of his life. He had been suffering sleepless nights in the big house by the Charles. "The reflection upon my situation and that of this army produces many an uneasy hour when all around me are wrapped in sleep," he told the absent Joseph Reed. "Few people know the predicament we are in." There was too little powder, still no money. So many of the troops who had given up and gone home, had, against orders, carried off muskets that were not their own that the supply of arms was depleted to the point where there were not enough for the new recruits. The single glimmer of hope was confirmation from Schuyler, on January 18, that the guns from Ticonderoga were on the way. As it happened, Colonel Knox, who had ridden on ahead, reached Cambridge later that same day.

Knox had been gone for two months and he had fulfilled all expectations, despite rough forest roads, freezing lakes, blizzards, thaws, mountain wilderness, and repeated mishaps that would have broken lesser spirits several times over. The guns Knox had come for were mostly French. After looking them over, Knox selected 58 mortars and cannon.

Knox's "noble train" had arrived intact. Hundreds of men had taken part and their labors and resilience had been exceptional. But it was the daring and determination of Knox himself that had counted above all. The twenty-five-year-old Boston bookseller had proven himself a leader of remarkable ability, a man not only of enterprising ideas, but with the staying power to carry them out. Immediately, Washington put him in command of the artillery.

The plan was to occupy the Heights on a single night, before the British knew what was happening, just as had been done at Bunker Hill. This time, however, there were the guns from Ticonderoga to haul in place. The move on Dorchester would begin after dark on March 4 and be completed by first light the morning of March 5, the anniversary of the Boston Massacre.

At daybreak, the British commanders looking up at the Heights could scarcely believe their eyes. The hope-for, all-important surprise was total. General Howe was said to have exclaimed, "My God, these fellows have done more work in one night than I could make my army do in three months." The shock of discovery threw the British into "utmost consternation." Their immediate response, a thunderous two-hour cannonade proved nothing, as their guns could not be elevated sufficiently to strike a target so high.

By nightfall a storm raged, with hail mixed with snow and sleet. The morning after, the winds continued to blow with a fury. Howe called off the attack and gave orders to prepare to evacuate Boston. Word had been passed—if allowed to depart peacefully, the British would spare the town.

Not until Sunday, March 17, St. Patrick's Day, did the wind turn fair and favorable.

It was a spectacle such as could only have been imagined until that morning. There were 120 ships departing with more than 11,000 people packed on board—8,906 King's troops, 667 women and 553 children, and in addition, waiting down the harbor, were 1,100 Loyalists.

The siege had been the stunning success it was proclaimed, and Washington's performance had been truly exceptional. He had indeed bested Howe and his regulars, and despite insufficient army and ammunition, insufficient shelter, sickness, inexperienced officers, lack of discipline, clothing and money. His patience with Congress had been exemplary, and while he had been saved repeatedly by his council of war from his headlong determination to attack, and thus from almost certain catastrophe, he had accepted the judgment of the council with no ill temper or self-serving histrionics.

He had kept his head, kept his health and his strength, bearing up under a weight of work and worry that only a few could have carried.

In *Washington's Crossing*, David Hackett Fischer describes General Washington after his first victory in the American Revolution.

It was March 17, 1776, the mud season in New England. A Continental officer of high rank was guiding his horse through the potholed streets of Cambridge, Massachusetts. Those who knew horses noticed that he rode with the easy grace of a natural rider, and a complete mastery of himself. He sat "quiet," as an equestrian would say, with his muscular legs extended on long leathers and toes pointed down in the stirrups, in the old-fashioned way. The animal and the man moved so fluently together that one observer was put in mind of a centaur. Another wrote that he was incomparably "the best horseman of his age, and the most graceful figure that could be seen on horseback."

He was a big man, immaculate in dress, and of such charismatic presence that he filled the street even when he rode alone. A crowd gathered to watch him go by, as if he were a one-man parade. Children bowed and bobbed to him. Soldiers called him "your Excellency," a title rare in America. Gentlemen doffed their hats and spoke his name with deep respect: General Washington.

～⚹～

23. Moores Creek, North Carolina

FEBRUARY 27, 1776

MOORES CREEK NATIONAL BATTLEFIELD
ROUTE 210
CURRIE, NORTH CAROLINA

While General Washington was preparing to end the siege of Boston, the royal governor of North Carolina, Josiah Martin, was organizing loyalists to battle other Americans. Martin had succeeded William Tryon as royal governor in August 1771 and was increasingly opposed by the colony's Assembly. In 1774 when Martin refused to call the Assembly into session, the Provincial Congress was established and elected delegates to the two Continental Congresses. By mid-1775 Martin was in exile on a British ship near the coast, urging London to send a force to join the thousands of loyalists he said were ready to fight.

In early January 1776 the Wilmington Committee of Safety began building earthworks to protect Wilmington from attack, and Martin learned that London had responded to his urging to send a force to link up with loyalists and regain royal control of North Carolina. A British fleet with regiments was sailing to meet the commander, General Henry Clinton, off Cape Fear. Martin launched his plan to organize loyalists for battle even though he did not know when the British troops would arrive.

The Cross Creek area of North Carolina, about 100 miles from the coast, had been settled by Scottish Highlanders who were loyalists. In mid-February Brigadier General

Donald MacDonald called for loyalists to gather at Cross Creek (today's Fayetteville). Only 1,400 responded, many fewer than the several thousand he had expected. Nevertheless, they marched toward the coast, planning to join the British forces when they arrived and take control of the colony.

The patriot militia under the overall command of Colonel James Moore marched to stop the loyalists. On February 25, 150 Wilmington militiamen led by Colonel Alexander Lillington arrived at the Moores Creek bridge and built earthworks on the east side of the creek. Colonel Richard Caswell with 800 North Carolina militiamen marched from New Bern to intercept the loyalists before they reached the coast. When they arrived at Moores Creek, Caswell's force camped west of the fifty-foot-wide creek. Warned of the pending loyalist attack, they moved to the earthworks on the east side on the night of February 26. They pulled up planks from the bridge and greased the log stringers with soap and tallow.

The persistent rain, muddy roads, and limited supplies caused more loyalists to desert so that the force was down to 800 when they attacked. MacDonald was ill, so Lieutenant Colonel Donald McLeod was in command. In the darkness before dawn on February 27 while drums rolled and bagpipes squealed, eighty broadsword men led by McLeod and Captain John Campbell charged across the bridge. The militia hit them with fire from muskets and their two cannon, nicknamed Mother Covington and her daughter. The Highlanders suffered thirty to seventy casualties, including McLeod and Campbell, in the less than five-minute battle. There were two American casualties.

Most of the rank-and-file loyalists taken prisoner were paroled and permitted to return to their homes after taking an oath not to fight as allies of the British. The officers, including MacDonald, were imprisoned in Halifax. In *Southern Campaigns of the American Revolution,* Dan L. Morrill describes the patriots' military advantages.

> Clearly, the enormous military advantages that the patriots possessed doomed Donald MacDonald and his men from the very outset of the campaign. The Tories had no artillery, and they demonstrated by their use of broadswords that they had no understanding of the tactics appropriate for the swamps and pine barrens of eastern North Carolina. Colonel Moore, on the other hand, was familiar with the terrain. Knowing that MacDonald was seeking to reach Brunswick on the lower Cape Fear, he was able to place his troops astride the only routes the Tories could take to the coast. In other words, Moore and his subordinate commanders were able to choose when and where to fight, able to occupy the battlefield first, and had ample time in which to erect formidable fortifications. The only hope the Tories had depended on the timely arrival of Henry Clinton and his sizeable body of regular British troops. Clinton's first ship, however, was delayed by bad weather, and did not reach the lower Cape Fear until April 18. The entire armada did not assemble until May 3, more than two months after the Loyalist troops had been overwhelmed.

In *Almost a Miracle*, John Ferling details the problems General Clinton and the Carolina loyalists encountered.

> The plan, put together in London, called for Clinton to rendezvous off Cape Fear with five Irish regiments that were crossing the Atlantic. His troop strength would be awesome: about 3,300 regulars in addition to the horde of eager Loyalists that Governor Martin had promised. Clinton arrived in March "big with expectation," according to his aide. He soon was disappointed. No Loyalists were waiting for him. Carolina rebels had crushed them two weeks earlier in a battle at Moore's Creek Bridge near Wilmington. Nor was he greeted by the invasion armada. Tossed by raging Atlantic storms, it did not arrive until six weeks later. While he waited, Clinton idled away much of the time on shipboard trying to decide what to do. Although he was given leeway to scrap the mission, the decisive events at Moore's Creek Bridge led him to believe that the southern Tories might be lost forever unless he took steps to rally them. Clinton shifted his thinking to Charleston, or more accurately to Sullivan's Island, which lies at the mouth of the city's harbor. Clinton doubted that Charleston could be taken without a protracted siege, and he also knew that even if it miraculously fell into his hands, it could not be held, as he and his men were to join Howe for the New York campaign. On the other hand, the naval squadron that he awaited was laden with 10,000 muskets for the Carolina Loyalists. From a toehold off South Carolina, it might be possible not only to distribute the weaponry, but to impede commerce into and out of Charleston. There was a dreamy quality to Clinton's thinking. It was never clear who would garrison Sullivan's Island or how it could possibly be supplied. Usually the most logical of British generals, Clinton appears to have succumbed to the pulsating passion to do something, anything, and to pray that it worked.
>
> With the Irish regiments and an armada of fifty sails, Clinton arrived off South Carolina early in June. Given his resources, including the formidable firepower of his fleet, he foresaw an easy go of it in taking Sullivan's Island.

The hundreds of thousands of Americans who were loyalists were varied and included wealthy Americans as well as artisans and farmers. Those who remained loyal to the king were willing to risk their lives by going into battle against other Americans. Among them were the men who fought at Moores Creek. Gary B. Nash presents an overview of the loyalists in *The Unknown American Revolution*.

> Called "Tories" by their patriot enemies, the Loyalists are known in the history books mainly as selfish ultraconservatives who preferred English rule to American self-governance. It is true that most Anglican clergymen, who owed their licenses to preach to the Church of England, remained loyal to England. So, too, large numbers of lawyers trained in England and wedded to English common law became Loyalists. Also, thousands of wealthy merchants and planters, with much to lose if an internal revolution succeeded alongside a victory over the British, swore fealty to the king. But these groups made up only a fraction of the Loyalists who numbered hundreds of thousands and made up about one fifth of the American population. Far more

numerous among the Loyalists were ordinary farmers, artisans, and others of modest means. Among these plebeian Loyalists were the tenants of the Hudson River valley; North Carolina Regulators still bitter over their treatment at the hands of those who were now leading the patriot movement; backcountry farmers in South Carolina who hated the patriot merchants and planters centered in Charleston; and ethnic German farmers and artisans in the middle states who feared control by an Anglo-American majority. In many cases, Loyalists "were the king's friends and others…were the patriot's enemies," as historian Ronald Hoffman has put it.

24. Halifax, North Carolina

HISTORIC HALIFAX
25 ST. DAVID STREET
HALIFAX, NORTH CAROLINA

Halifax, founded in 1760 on the south bank of the Roanoke River, was North Carolina's commercial and political center and a major supply depot during the American Revolution. North Carolina's Fourth Provincial Congress met here in April 1776 and voted unanimously to adopt a report later called the Halifax Resolves. The Resolves gave the North Carolina delegates the power to concur with those of the other colonies in the Continental Congress in declaring independence. The North Carolina state flag includes the date of the Halifax Resolves: April 12, 1776.

The following fall the Fifth Provincial Congress met in Halifax and approved North Carolina's first state constitution. On December 23 the Congress appointed Richard Caswell, who had led the militia to victory at Moores Creek, the first governor of the state of North Carolina.

25. Nikwasi, North Carolina

NIKWASI MOUND
EAST MAIN AND NIKWASI LANE
FRANKLIN, NORTH CAROLINA

In July 1776, Cherokee warriors attacked settlements on the North Carolina frontier. In September, Griffith Rutherford, a member of the North Carolina Assembly and a brigadier general, raised a 2,000-man militia. They burned Cherokee towns, including most of

Nikwasi on the banks of the Little Tennessee River. The Nikwasi Mound, the center of the village, was not destroyed. Barbara R. Duncan describes it in "Nikwasi Mound" in *American Indian Places: A Historical Guidebook,* edited by Frances H. Kennedy.

The Nikwasi Mound was the spiritual, political, and physical center of the town of Nikwasi, one of fifteen Cherokee Middle Towns along the Little Tennessee River from its headwaters to the Nantahala Mountains. The original Cherokee homeland extended over more than 140,000 square miles in eight present-day states. The mother town of Kituhwa was associated with the Middle Towns because it was on the Tuckaseegee River, a tributary of the Little Tennessee. For more than a thousand years the mound was the center of a Cherokee village, with houses, a dance ground, and fields for playing stickball and chunkey, surrounded by hundreds of acres of cornfields, gardens, and orchards. People gathered in a townhouse on top of the mound to make decisions, dance, and hold ceremonies.

26. Charleston, South Carolina

JUNE 28, 1776

FORT MOULTRIE IN FORT SUMTER NATIONAL MONUMENT
SULLIVAN'S ISLAND, SOUTH CAROLINA

In *Partisans and Redcoats: The Southern Conflict that Turned the Tide of the American Revolution,* Walter Edgar describes South Carolina before and during the early years of the Revolution.

On the eve of the American Revolution, South Carolina was the wealthiest colony in British North America. The aggregate wealth of inventoried estates in Charleston was more than six times that of Philadelphia. Charleston, one of the five great cities of colonial America, was the social, economic, and political capital of the colony. The elite who controlled South Carolina owed their wealth to rice, indigo, and the labor of thousands of black slaves. In 1775 there were 104,000 black Carolinians, but only 70,000 whites. Of these whites, nearly two-thirds (approximately 46,000) lived in what was called the backcountry.

The South Carolina backcountry began about fifty miles inland and stretched to the foothills of the Appalachians. Until the 1730s, this vast area was populated mainly by Catawba and Cherokee Indians. Then, in the 1740s and 1750s, hundreds of settlers poured into the Carolina backcountry. A majority of these new arrivals were Scots-Irish, but a fair number were English and German. They laid claim to lands that had for centuries belonged to Native Americans.

In 1760 the Cherokee, urged on by the French, launched an attack on the frontier settlements. In a panic, frontier families abandoned their homes for the safety of scattered forts. With the assistance of British troops, South Carolina eventually was able to defeat the Cherokee.

The Cherokee War had rent the fragile fabric of frontier society and attracted lawless individuals from other colonies. In 1766 and 1767, outlaws and bandits terrorized the law-abiding residents of the backcountry. Appeals to the colonial authorities in Charleston went unheeded. In desperation, those who had a stake in society formed a vigilante movement and called themselves Regulators—they were going to regulate society, create law and order. However, the Regulators went beyond ridding the backcountry of thieves and brigands. They also took it upon themselves to discipline those they termed "the lower sort," and they sowed the seeds for internal conflict that would later bear bitter fruit.

No sooner had the frontier begun to calm down than a heated constitutional dispute between the colonial assembly and imperial officials led to a government shutdown. After 1771, for all practical purposes, royal government ceased in South Carolina. Over the next four years, a number of extralegal organizations came into existence that eventually became the independent government of South Carolina.

The revolutionaries (or patriots, as they were beginning to call themselves) controlled Charleston and the lowcountry, but not much else. In the backcountry, there were individuals who had greater grievances with the South Carolina Commons House of Assembly than with the British Parliament. The patriots were in a quandary. With the large black majority in the lowcountry, they desperately needed the support of backcountry whites—a number of whom were loyalists—friends of the king (or as patriots derisively termed them, Tories). Initially the revolutionaries obtained a grudging pledge of neutrality from prominent backcountry leaders. Then, late in 1775, patriots imprisoned leading backcountry Tories, and in response, Tory militia units attacked patriot troops. In savage fighting that would presage the brutal nature of the American Revolution in South Carolina, the Tory uprising was suppressed.

After the North Carolina patriot militia defeated the British loyalists at Moores Creek, North Carolina, in February 1776, Commodore Sir Peter Parker and General Henry Clinton were forced to change their plans. They decided to raise loyalists in South Carolina. They sailed south on a squadron of warships and arrived off Charleston in June.

Clinton began his attack by trying to land men on Long Island (today's Isle of Palms). He had been given the false information that they could ford the inlet between Long Island and Sullivan's Island. On the morning of June 28, Parker's ships unsuccessfully bombarded the fort that was being constructed on Sullivan's Island. The fort had parallel walls of green palmetto logs sixteen feet apart, and the space between the walls was filled with sand. The sand and the green logs absorbed Parker's rounds while the commander of the fort, Colonel William Moultrie, directed his guns to damage the British ships.

When the British shot down the 2nd South Carolina regimental flag from its staff, Sergeant William Jasper retrieved the flag, tied it to a sponge rammer, and reset it while under fire, encouraging his fellow soldiers in the midst of the battle.

The patriots fought off nine warships and inflicted heavy casualties. In late July Clinton sailed north, ending his failed southern campaign.

Barbara W. Tuchman details the importance of seaborne commerce to the Americans in *The First Salute*.

Dutch merchants and mariners, alert to every opening for commerce, braved the physical and financial risks of seaborne commerce to make it pay richly. Wealth filled their warehouses. The American Colonies sent rich cargoes of their products—tobacco, indigo, timber, horses—to exchange for naval and military supplies and for molasses, sugar, slaves and furnishings from Europe. Their agents in Amsterdam arranged the purchases and the delivery to St. Eustatius for transshipment to the American coast. Vessels loaded with 1,000 to 4,000 pounds of gunpowder per ship, and in one case a total of 49,000 pounds, made their way to Philadelphia and Charleston (the nearest port). To the rebels with empty muskets, St. Eustatius made the difference.

As a free port, Eustatius had reaped the profits both as marketplace and as storehouse where goods waiting sale or transshipment could be safely housed against predatory foreign fleets in search of loot.

The measure of profit in the munitions traffic can be judged from the price of a pound of gunpowder, which cost 8.5 stivers of the local currency in Holland, and 46 stivers or almost five and a half times as much on Eustatius, because its proximity saved American customers time and the risks of a longer passage. Trade swelled to and from the Colonies. On a single day in March, 1777, four ships from the Colonies came via Statia into Amsterdam bringing 200 hogsheads of tobacco, 600 to 700 barrels of rice and a large shipment of indigo.

———

27. Independence Hall and Yard, Pennsylvania

INDEPENDENCE HALL AND YARD AND DECLARATION HOUSE IN
INDEPENDENCE NATIONAL HISTORICAL PARK
PHILADELPHIA, PENNSYLVANIA

The State House of the Province of Pennsylvania, now Independence Hall, was the meeting place of the Second Continental Congress when the colonies approved the Declaration of Independence. During the summer of 1776 Thomas Jefferson rented rooms in the house of Jacob Graff Jr., at 7th and Market Streets, where he drafted the Declaration. The house, now the Declaration House, was reconstructed on the site in 1975.

In the years since he defended the British soldiers in the trial after the Boston Massacre, John Adams had become a leader in Congress. While the delegates were considering independence, Adams was planning for government after independence. In *John Adams*, David McCullough details Adams's *Thoughts on Government*.

Adams's *Thoughts on Government*, as it would be known, was first set forth in a letter to a fellow congressman, William Hooper, who, before returning home to help write a new constitution for North Carolina, had asked Adams for a "sketch" of his views. When another of the North Carolinians, John Penn, requested a copy, this, too, Adams provided, in addition to three more copies, all written out by hand, for Jonathan Sergeant of New Jersey and Virginians George Wythe and Richard Henry Lee, who with Adams's consent, had the letter published as a pamphlet by the Philadelphia printer John Dunlap.

For Adams the structure of government was a subject of passionate interest that raised fundamental questions about the realities of human nature, political power, and the good society.

"It has been the will of Heaven," the essay began, "that we should be thrown into existence at a period when the greatest philosophers and law-givers of antiquity would have wished to live…

a period when a coincidence of circumstances without example has afforded to thirteen colonies at once an opportunity of beginning government anew from the foundation and building as they choose. How few of the human race have ever had an opportunity of choosing a system of government for themselves and their children? How few have ever had anything more of choice in government than in climate?"

He was looking beyond independence, beyond the outcome of the war, to what would be established once independence and victory were achieved. Much as he foresaw the hard truth about the war to be waged, Adams had the clearest idea of anyone in Congress of what independence would actually entail, the great difficulties and risks, no less than the opportunities.

The happiness of the people was the purpose of government, he wrote, and therefore that form of government was best which produced the greatest amount of happiness for the largest number. And since all "sober inquirers after truth" agreed that happiness derived from virtue, that form of government with virtue as its foundation was more likely than any other to promote the general happiness.

The greatest minds agreed, Adams continued, that all good government was republican, and the "true idea" of a republic was "an empire of laws and not of men." There should be a representative assembly, "an exact portrait in miniature of the people at large." Balance would come from the creation of a second, smaller legislative body, a "distinct assembly" of perhaps twenty or thirty, chosen by the larger legislature.

The executive, the governor, should, Adams thought, be chosen by the two houses of the legislature, and for not more than a year at a time. There must be an independent judiciary.

Finally and emphatically, he urged the widest possible support for education. "Laws for the liberal education of youth, especially for the lower classes of people, are so extremely wise and useful that to a humane and generous mind, no expense for this purpose would be thought extravagant."

Little that Adams ever wrote had such effect as his *Thoughts on Government*.

David McCullough describes Adams in his biography.

John Adams was a great-hearted, persevering man of uncommon ability and force. He had a brilliant mind. He was honest and everyone knew it. Emphatically independent by nature, hardworking, frugal—all traits in the New England tradition—he was anything but cold or laconic as supposedly New Englanders were. He could be high-spirited and affectionate, vain, cranky, impetuous, self-absorbed, and fiercely stubborn; passionate, quick to anger, and all-forgiving; generous and entertaining. He was blessed with great courage and good humor, yet subject to spells of despair, and especially when separated from his family or during periods of prolonged inactivity.

Ambitious to excel—to make himself known—he had nonetheless recognized at an early stage that happiness came not from fame and fortune, "and all such things," but from "an habitual contempt of them," as he wrote. He prized the Roman ideal of honor, and in this, as in much else, he and Abigail were in perfect accord. Fame without honor, in her view, would be "like a faint meteor gliding through the sky, shedding only transient light."

As his family and friends knew, Adams was both a devout Christian and an independent thinker, and he saw no conflict in that. He was hard-headed and a man of "sensibility," a close observer of human folly as displayed in everyday life and fired by an inexhaustible love of books and scholarly reflection. John Adams was not a man of the world. He enjoyed no social standing. There was no money in his background, no Adams fortune or elegant Adams home-stead like the Boston mansion of John Hancock.

It was in the courtrooms of Massachusetts and on the printed page, principally in the newspapers of Boston, that Adams had distinguished himself. Years of riding the court circuit and his brilliance before the bar had brought him wide recognition and respect. And of greater consequence in recent years had been his spirited determination and eloquence in the cause of American rights and liberties.

David McCullough points out in *John Adams* the importance of the resolution that John Adams and Richard Henry Lee, a Virginia delegate, presented to Congress in May 1776.

On Friday, May 10 came what many in Congress knew to be a critical juncture. John Adams had decided the time was ripe to make his move.

With Richard Henry Lee, he put forth a resolution recommending that the individual colonies assume all powers of government—to secure "the happiness and safety of their con-stituents in particular, and America in general." Not only was it passed, but with surprising unanimity. It awaited only a preamble which, as drafted by Adams, was a still more radical statement. This brought on three days of fierce debate, during which Adams repeatedly took the floor. In contrast to the resolution, Adams's preamble put aside any possibility of reconcil-iation and all but declared the colonies immediately independent.

What John Adams said was not recorded. But as the constant battler on the floor, with all that he had written, his work on committees, his relentless energy, industry, and unyielding determination, he had emerged a leader like no other, and when the breakthrough came at last on Wednesday, May 15, it was his victory more than anyone's in Congress.

The preamble was approved. He was elated. Congress, he wrote, had that day "passed the most important resolution that was ever taken in America."

At his lodgings two days later, Adams sat quietly writing to Abigail:

When I consider the great events which are passed, and those greater which are rapidly advancing, and that I may have been instrumental of touching some springs, and turning some wheels, which have had and will have such effects, I feel an awe upon my mind which is not easily described.

"I have reasons to believe," he added, "that no colony which shall assume a government under the people, will give it up."

The following is the transcript of the Lee Resolution on the National Archives website:

Richard Henry Lee, a delegate from Virginia, read a resolution before the Continental Congress "that these United Colonies are, and of right ought to be, free and independent States, that they are absolved from all allegiance to the British Crown, and that all political connection between them and the State of Great Britain is, and ought to be, totally dissolved."

On June 12, 1776, the fifth Virginia Convention adopted the Virginia Declaration of Rights. In *Founders,* Ray Raphael includes its importance to Thomas Jefferson as he drafted the Declaration of Independence.

In addition to the constitution itself, George Mason prepared the first draft of Virginia's Declaration of Rights, and his list of protections still resonates today: freedom of the press, the free exercise of religion ("unless, under colour of religion, any man disturb the peace, the happiness, or safety of society, or of individuals," Mason added), and a full list of protections for the rights of the accused.

The full Virginia Convention accepted the work of Mason and the drafting committee, but it added one more sweeping check on governmental power:

That a well-regulated militia, composed of the body of the people, trained to arms, is the proper, natural, and safe defence of a free state; that standing armies, in time of peace, should be avoided as dangerous to liberty; and that, in all cases, the military should be under strict subordination to, and governed by, the civil power.

Mason himself did not think to include this, for he implicitly trusted the current commander in chief of the Continental Army, who happened to be his friend, neighbor, and collaborator. But others thought it best to place some safeguards in writing.

Virginia's Declaration of Rights had great historical impact. In June of 1776, Thomas Jefferson consulted Mason's draft of the Virginia Declaration as he penned his own first draft of the Declaration of Independence. Mason's "all men are born equally free and independent" became for Jefferson "all men are created equal," while Mason's cumbersome "enjoyment of life the Com.^{ee} of the whole Congress to whom was referred the resolution and ~~of~~ the *Declaration* respecting independence. 17

Resolved   That these united colonies were and of right

ought to be free and independant States;

that they are absolved from all allegiance

to the british crown and that all political

connection between them and the state of

great Britain is and ought to be totally

Dissolved

Report of July 2. 1776.

N.5 the resolution for
independancy
agreed to July 2. 1776

383
90
87
96
26

64

Lee Resolution for Independence. June 7, 1776. *(Courtesy of the National Archives and Records Administration)* and liberty, with the means of acquiring and possessing property, and pursueing and obtaining happiness and safety" evolved into the more elegant "life, liberty, and the pursuit of happiness." (Both men, of course, were using the phrases of John Locke, repeated and refined by generations of European thinkers.) Shortly, four states placed passages from the preamble of the Virginia Declaration verbatim into their own constitutions, and finally, more than a decade later, Americans would use the Virginia Declaration of Rights as a model for their national Bill of Rights.

Gordon S. Wood describes the leaders of the Revolution in *The Radicalism of the American Revolution.*

We shall never understand the unique character of the revolutionary leaders until we appreciate the seriousness with which they took these new republican ideas of what it was to be a gentleman. No generation in American history has ever been so self-conscious about the moral and social values necessary for public leadership.

Pauline Maier summarizes the events that led to Independence and describes the Declaration of Independence in *American Scripture.*

Congress received news of George III's October speech to Parliament on January 8, 1776. It also learned that a British fleet had set sail with 5,000 troops. Norfolk was burned in the opening days of January, which, with the burning of Charlestown, Massachusetts, by the King's army during the Battle of Bunker Hill, and the destruction of Falmouth, Maine, in the fall of 1775, seemed to show how harshly George III was prepared to repress his American subjects. News of the Prohibitory Act arrived in February, further dimming the prospects for settlement. As John Hancock put it, "the making all our Vessells lawful Prize don't look like a Reconciliation."

　　Among those still hesitant on Independence, the idea of founding a republic gave another good reason for delay. In 1776, there were no regular, "republican" governments of the sort Paine advocated, in which all authority rested on popular choice and none on hereditary title.

　　Once again events in England undercut the arguments of those colonists most committed to preserving the empire. In late May, colonists learned that the King had rejected a petition from the City of London that asked him to define the terms of a just and honorable peace before turning the full force of British arms against the colonists. By June 5 even Robert Morris, who had done his best to hold off a decision for separation conceded that George III's response to London "totally destroyed all hopes of reconciliation" and made a "declaration of Independency" inevitable. For that event, he said, Great Britain could thank only herself.

　　On June 11 Congress appointed a committee to prepare a declaration of Independence. That committee had five members: Thomas Jefferson, John Adams, Benjamin Franklin, Roger Sherman of Connecticut, and Robert R. Livingston of New York. Seventeen days later, on

June 28, the committee presented its draft to Congress, which promptly tabled the report. By then only Maryland and New York had failed to allow their delegates to vote for Independence. That night Maryland fell into line.

On July 1, Congress again resolved itself into a Committee of the Whole "to take into consideration the resolution respecting independency." The debates went on through most of the day. When Congress reconvened on July 2, it received correspondence from Washington and others, mostly relating to the military situation. Congress then received from the Committee of the Whole the resolutions Richard Henry Lee had first proposed almost a month earlier. When the vote was put, the nine affirmative votes of the previous day had grown to twelve. A week later New York's Provincial Congress convention allowed its delegates to add the colony's approval to that of the other twelve colonies. In the end, there was no alternative; even the most hesitant agreed on that.

As the British began to bring the greatest fleet and the largest army ever assembled in North America into action against the Americans, Congress devoted the better part of two days to revising the draft Declaration of Independence. Wars, it understood, were not won by ships and sailors and arms alone. Words, too, had power to serve the cause of victory.

The final sentence was particularly wonderful in that it took a commonplace—one community after another in Massachusetts and elsewhere had movingly committed their "lives" and "fortunes" to the cause—and, by adding to it "our sacred honor," gave the passage more power, since honor remained a force of considerable significance, as well as a dignity and a mellifluousness as pleasing to the mind as it is to the ear.

What generations of Americans came to revere was not Jefferson's but Congress's Declaration, the work not of a single man, or even a committee, but of a larger body of men with the good sense to recognize a "pretty good" draft when they saw it, and who were able to identify and eliminate Jefferson's more outlandish assertions and unnecessary words. So successful an exercise of group editing probably demanded a text that required cutting, not extensive rewriting. Congress's achievement was remarkable nonetheless. By exercising their intelligence, political good sense, and a discerning sense of language, the delegates managed to make the Declaration at once more accurate and more consonant with the convictions of their constituents, and to enhance both its power and its eloquence.

Finally, on July 4, the Committee of the Whole reported that it had agreed upon a Declaration. Congress's journal says that the text was then read and that Congress accepted it, ordered it to be authenticated and printed under the supervision of the drafting committee, and provided for its distribution and proclamation.

The situation in 1776 also gives strong reason to think that the Declaration of Independence was designed first and foremost for domestic consumption. Independence itself was critical to securing support from the French government, but the purposes of Independence and of the Declaration of Independence must be distinguished. The willingness of the French court to back the Americans was founded on its rivalry with Britain, not on any commitment to the justice of their cause. No American had any doubt about that. Within the United States, however, the Declaration of Independence had many practical uses: it provided a vehicle for announcing Independence to the American people, and, if properly framed, might evoke a deeply felt and widespread commitment to the cause of nationhood and, above all, inspire the soldiers who would have to win the Independence that Congress proclaimed. The Declaration was, moreover, to be disseminated by print and also read aloud at public gatherings.

The historical significance of the Declaration did not lie in the principles it stated except insofar as it restated what virtually all Americans—patriot and Loyalist alike—thought and said in other words in other places. And that was exactly what the Declaration was meant to do: it was, according to Jefferson, "to be an expression of the American mind, and to give that expression the proper tone and spirit called for by the occasion."

In 1820, Secretary of State John Quincy Adams ordered William J. Stone to make an exact facsimile of the Declaration of Independence. Stone completed it in 1823.

The final paragraph of the Declaration of Independence ends with Americans' pledge to each other.

We, therefore, the Representatives of the united States of America, in General Congress, Assembled, appealing to the Supreme Judge of the world for the rectitude of our intentions, do, in the Name, and by Authority of the good People of these Colonies, solemnly publish and declare, That these united Colonies are, and of Right ought to be Free and Independent States; that they are Absolved from all Allegiance to the British Crown, and that all political connection between them and the State of Great Britain, is and ought to be totally dissolved; and that as Free and Independent States, they have full Power to levy War, conclude Peace, contract Alliances, establish Commerce, and to do all other Acts and Things which Independent States may of right do. And for the support of this Declaration, with a firm reliance on the protection of Divine Providence, we mutually pledge to each other our Lives, our Fortunes, and our sacred Honor.

Peter S. Onuf describes the Declaration of Independence in the "Introduction" of *Declaring Independence: The Origin and Influence of America's Founding Document*, edited by Christian Y. Dupont and Peter S. Onuf.

The Declaration of Independence is the touchstone of American nationhood, the document that marks the beginning of our history as a people. Eloquently articulating the principles and sentiments that drove patriotic subjects of King George III to resistance and revolution, the Declaration has served as a sacred text for subsequent generations of Americans. Other great state papers provided the blueprint for the national edifice, but none better defined the new nation's purpose. Americans have had—and certainly will have—a contentious and conflicted history, marked by ideological, sectional, economic, and religious strife. The federal Constitution itself inspired disagreement deep enough to unleash the "dogs of war" and threaten the survival of the union that the founders sought to perfect. Yet regardless of their disputes with each other, self-professed patriots have always proclaimed fealty to a common

William James Stone, Declaration of Independence [W.J. Stone facsimile on vellum], January 1, 1823. *(Courtesy of The Gilder Lehrman Institute of American History, GLC00154.02)*

set of beliefs, invoking the principles so memorably epitomized in the Declaration: "that all men are created equal, that they are endowed by their Creator with certain unalienable Rights, that among these are Life, Liberty and the pursuit of Happiness. That to secure these rights, Governments are instituted among Men, deriving their just powers from the consent of the governed . . ."

There are no final, definitive, authoritative interpretations because the Declaration must always be read through the ever-changing medium of the national history it initiated. We can make sense of the Declaration only if we grasp the larger contours of our nation's history. Likewise, a historically attuned understanding of the document's production and reception in its own time can help us gain a clearer idea of who "we, the people" once were, who we have come to be, and may still become.

David McCullough points out the importance of the first line of the Declaration of Independence in the "Preface" of *Declaring Independence,* edited by Christian Y. Dupont and Peter S. Onuf.

As has been amply documented down the years, but tends at times to be overlooked, those we call the founders of the nation were neither supermen nor gods. They were, without exception, perfectly capable of being mistaken, inconsistent, contradictory, vain, selfish, at times self-deceiving, at times dead-wrong—quite as much as the rest of us. History makes the point again and again. Thomas Jefferson made the point in the very first words of the first line of the Declaration of Independence. "When in the course of human events…" Read aloud, the accent should be on *human*.

But evidence of our humanity is not to be found in our failings alone, as history also makes abundantly clear, and as those same courageous notables who gave language and resolve to the American Revolution demonstrated with such far-reaching effect.

What is so magnificent, and ought always to command our respect as well as understanding, is that those same mere mortals, under the most trying circumstances and with no guarantee of success, could rise to achieve all that they did. And there are few more stirring examples of their noble attainments than the Declaration of Independence.

The Declaration of Independence is a statement of conviction and intent. When Jefferson wrote that "all men are created equal," he, a slave master, knew perfectly how much had still to be done by those who would follow to attain such a society in fact not theory. But that is part of our strength, that we Americans are called on, one generation after another, to achieve the promise. We have a star to steer by.

In *The American Revolution*, Gordon S. Wood points to the philosophy set forth in the Declaration of Independence.

Despite the failure of the Declaration of Independence to say anything about slavery, it nevertheless remained a brilliant expression of Enlightenment ideals—ideals that still reverberate powerfully in the lives of Americans and other peoples today. "That all men are created equal; that they are endowed by their Creator with certain inalienable rights; that among these are life, liberty, and the pursuit of happiness"—these "truths" seemed "self-evident," even to eighteenth-century Americans divided by great distinctions of status and confronted with the glaring contradiction of black slavery. The Declaration of Independence set forth a philosophy of human rights that could be applied not only to Americans, but also to peoples everywhere. It was essential in giving the American Revolution a universal appeal.

In *John Adams,* David McCullough quotes Adams on the creation of the Declaration of Independence.

It was John Adams, more than anyone, who had made it happen. Further, he seems to have understood more clearly than any what a momentous day it was and in the privacy of two long letters to Abigail, he poured out his feelings as did no one else:

> The second day of July 1776 will be the most memorable epocha in the history of America. I am apt to believe that it will be celebrated by succeeding generations as the great anniversary festival. It ought to be commemorated as the Day of Deliverance by solemn acts of devotion to God Almighty. It ought to be solemnized with pomp and parade, with shows, games, sports, guns, bells, bonfires, and illuminations from one end of the continent to the other from this time forward forever more.

Lest she judge him overly "transported," he said he was well aware of the "toil and blood and treasure that it will cost us to maintain this declaration." Still, the end was more than worth all the means. "You will see in a few days," he wrote in the second letter, "A Declaration setting forth the causes, which have impelled us to this mighty revolution, and the reasons that will justify it in the sight of God and man."

That the hand of God was involved in the birth of the new nation he had no doubt. "It is the will of heaven that the two countries should be sundered forever."

In *Revolutionary Characters: What Made the Founders Different*, Gordon S. Wood describes Thomas Jefferson.

It is true that much of Jefferson's thinking was conventional, though, as has been pointed out, he did have "an extraordinary gift of lending grace to conventionalities." He had to be conventional, or he could never have had the impact he had on his contemporaries. His writing of the Declaration of Independence, he later correctly recalled, was "not to find out new principles, or new arguments, never before thought of; but to place before mankind the common sense of the subject, in terms so plain and firm as to command their assent, and to justify ourselves in the independent stand we are compelled to take."

Jefferson's extraordinary impressionability, learning, and virtuosity were the sources of his conventionality. He was very well read, extremely sensitive to the avant-garde intellectual currents of his day, and eager to discover just what was the best, most politically correct, and most enlightened in the world of the eighteenth century. It was his insatiable hunger for knowledge and the remarkable receptivity of his antennae for all that was new and progressive that put him at the head of the American Enlightenment.

Robert M. S. McDonald considers Jefferson's role in writing the Declaration in "Thomas Jefferson's Strange Career as Author of Independence," in *Declaring Independence* edited by Christian Y. Dupont and Peter S. Onuf.

The most basic "fact" of United States history—that Thomas Jefferson authored the Declaration of Independence—was at first unknown to the public, became subsequently a matter of sometimes passionate dispute, and then only gradually a generally accepted premise. Several factors

Portable writing desk designed by Thomas Jefferson and used by him while writing the Declaration of Independence. *(Courtesy, Division of Political History, National Museum of American History, Smithsonian Institution)*

explain Jefferson's initial anonymity as author of the Declaration. First, it was common for eighteenth-century political tracts to be published without a signature or to be signed with a pseudonym. The trio of James Madison, Alexander Hamilton, and John Jay, for example, authored their Federalist as "Publius." Benjamin Franklin wrote as "Poor Richard," "Silence Dogood," and "Richard Saunders." When Philadelphia lawyer John Dickinson argued against the 1767 Townshend Acts, he assumed the identity of "a Farmer."

One of the hallmarks of eighteenth-century republican thought was the belief that men who took part in the government of others should be "disinterested"—a term that Jefferson used to praise George Washington for resisting "motives of interest or consanguinity, of friendship or hatred." Disinterested men did not openly seek political influence, for doing so would make them suspect of seeking office for private gain.

Authors who used pseudonyms or wrote anonymously not only wrote disinterestedly, they also showed their respect for the Enlightenment notion that an argument's authority came not from its author but rather from its logic. When Jefferson penned the Declaration, he invoked "self-evident truths." Similarly, Thomas Paine's *Common Sense*, which first appeared anonymously, contended that "who the Author of this Production is, is wholly unnecessary to the Public, as the Object for Attention is the *Doctrine itself*, not the *Man*." All that mattered, in other words, was the reasonableness of the argument, along with the reassurance that the author was "unconnected with any Party, and under no sort of Influence public or private, but the influence of reason and principle."

Around the country, Americans celebrated their newly declared independence. In *The Unknown American Revolution*, Gary B. Nash describes a July 1776 celebration in New York.

In one of the most telling celebrations of all, a milling crowd of New York City citizens roped the marble-mounted equestrian statue of George III, toppled it on Bowling Green, and fell upon the leaden monarch. Mutilating the face, cutting off the head, and displaying the royal visage atop a flagpole, they left the rest of the torso on the ground. It would end up in Litchfield, Connecticut, where women and children turned it into about 42,000 musket balls— hunks of "melted majesty," as one wit put it—to be fired at the king's redcoated troops.

In the "Introduction" Gordon S. Wood, editor of *The Rising Glory of America, 1760–1820*, details the moral quality of American society and the emphasis on the collective good in the American Revolution.

By the middle of the eighteenth century, and especially after the British attempt to reorganize the empire in the 1760's, American Whigs came to conclude that England was truly corrupt and bent on the subjugation and corruption of America as well. There were alarming signs appearing in the colonies of increasing individualism, widening social cleavages, and enhanced luxury, characteristics brought on by the colonists' emergence into more complicated and dynamic market societies, but interpreted by them as symptoms of regression and decay, a falling away of traditional moral and social values. All these changes bore a resemblance to what was happening in England and seemed to be connected in some way to English corruption. By the 1770's some of the Calvinist clergy began to shift the blame for these vices from America onto England, and on the eve of the Revolution the English Crown had become a scapegoat for a multitude of American sins. Even the "insignificance, insipidity, and ignorance" of America's provincial culture, one Virginian argued in 1776, were products not of the wilderness, but of the colonists' "connexion and dependence on Britain." England stood as "an insuperable barrier between us and the polished world, who, dazzled with the view of the primary planet, either knew not, or disregarded, the humble satellites which served to increase her splendor."

The Revolution thus became not only a rejection of the corrupted British empire, but as well an attempt to reform American society and to realize once and for all the moral values intellectuals had espoused for centuries—values that the Americans found summed up in the tradition of civic humanism or classical republicanism. For Americans in 1776, this republicanism represented an eighteenth-century secularized version of Puritanism, an updated, reactionary effort to bring under control the selfish and individualistic impulses of an emergent capitalistic society that could not be justified. It stressed a morality of social cohesion and promised the kind of organic state where men, as citizens, were indissolubly linked to one another in harmony and benevolence. It was a very beautiful but fragile ideal, for republics by definition and by their utter dependence on the people were the states most intimately related to the character of their people, both in their capacity for reformation and in their sensitivity to changes in that character. More than any other kind of polity, republics required an absence of selfishness and luxury; their existence in fact demanded an extraordinary moral quality in their people, a moral quality that the eighteenth century, like previous ages, designated as virtue—that is, the willingness of the people to sacrifice their private desires for the good of the whole. "A Citizen," declared Samuel Adams in a common exhortation of the Revolutionary years, "owes everything to the Commonwealth." He was, in fact, as Benjamin Rush said, "public property. His time and talents—his youth—his manhood—his old age—nay more, life, all belong to his country."

This virtue, or the unselfish devotion to the collective good, represented all that men of the eighteenth century, from Benjamin Franklin to Jonathan Edwards, sought in social behavior. It was generally assumed that those most willing to forego their selfish interest for the public good were those who privately practiced a mixture of classical and Puritan virtues—temperance, industry, frugality, simplicity, and charity. Hence, the sturdy independent yeomen, Jefferson's "chosen people of God," who were commonly regarded as the most free of private temptations and the most incorruptible, were considered to be the best citizens and the firmest foundation of a republic. The celebration of the farmer in the years following the Revolution was thus not a literary conceit, but a scientifically based imperative of republican government. It followed too that only a society marked by equality, where distinctions would be naturally rather than artificially based, could encourage men's willingness to obey authority and to subordinate their private desires to the general will. Hence, as American actions demonstrated in 1776, laws abolishing all legal distinctions and privileges were a necessary concomitant of republican government. The goal, however, was not to create a leveled society, but an organic hierarchy led by natural aristocrats who would resemble not the luxury-loving, money-mongering lackeys of British officialdom but the stoical and disinterested heroes of antiquity—men like Washington, who seemed to Americans to embody perfectly the classical ideal of a republican leader.

The republican obsession with virtue colored the entire Revolutionary movement and in time helped to shape America's cultural history in a way no part of the environment, the frontier included, ever could have. Indeed, much of what Americans came to believe and value grew out of their Revolutionary republicanism. It was a radical doctrine because, like Puritanism, it flew in the face of man's natural selfishness. Yet, in this new enlightened age, the most hopeful of the Revolutionaries believed that man was a malleable creature and that America especially was "in a plastic state" where "the benefactor of mankind may realize all his schemes for promoting human happiness." In fact, "it was possible," said Benjamin Rush, who personified the American Enlightenment, "to convert men into republican machines." As Samuel Stanhope Smith, soon to be president of Princeton, told James Madison shortly after Independence, new habitual principles, "the constant authoritive guardians of virtue," could be created and nurtured by republican laws, and these principles, together with the power of the mind, could give man's "ideas and motives a new direction." By the repeated exertion of reason—by "recalling the lost images of virtue: contemplating them, and using them as motives of action, till they overcome those of vice again and again . . . until after repeated struggles, and many foils, they at length acquire the habitual superiority"—by such exertions it seemed possible for the Americans to create a society of "habitual virtue." From these premises flowed the Revolutionaries' efforts at moral and social reformation; much of their republican iconography—the "Pomp and Parade," as John Adams called it, the speeches and orations, the bells and bonfires, the didactic history, even the "Painting, Sculpture, Statuary, Medalling, and Poetry"; and the republicans' devotion, in Smith's words, to "the great importance of an early virtuous education"—education that was designed not to release the talents of the individual, but to turn him into "public property." When the Americans of 1776 talked of their intention to "form a new era and give a new turn to human affairs" by becoming the "eminent examples of every divine and social virtue," they meant that they would become the special kind of simple, austere, egalitarian, and virtuous people that history and enlightened social science said was essential for the sustenance of a republic. The moral quality of their society thus became a measure of the success of their Revolution.

While American celebrated Independence, the 32,000-man British army commanded by General William Howe sailed into New York Harbor. On August 1, 1776, General Washington addressed his soldiers as he prepared for the British attack. His General Orders issued in New York are included in *This Glorious Struggle: George Washington's Revolutionary War Letters,* edited by Edward G. Lengel.

Washington's General Orders

AUGUST I

GENERAL ORDERS

Even with the enemy in sight, Washington struggled to create a sense of unity in his army.

Head Quarters, New York, August 1st 1776.

It is with great concern, the General understands, that Jealousies &c: are arisen among the troops from the different Provinces, of reflections frequently thrown out, which can only tend to irritate each other, and injure the noble cause in which we are engaged, and which we ought to support with one hand and one heart. The General most earnestly entreats the officers, and soldiers, to consider the consequences; that they can no way assist our cruel enemies more effectually, than making division among ourselves; That the Honor and Success of the army, and the safety of our bleeding Country, depends upon harmony and good agreement with each other; That the Provinces are all United to oppose the common enemy, and all distinctions sunk in the name of an American; to make this honorable, and preserve the Liberty of our Country, ought to be our only emulation, and he will be the best Soldier, and the best Patriot, who contributes most to this glorious work, whatever his Station, or from whatever part of the Continent, he may come: Let all distinctions of Nations, Countries, and Provinces, therefore be lost in the generous contest, who shall behave with the most Courage against the enemy, and the most kindness and good humour to each other—If there are any officers, or soldiers, so lost to virtue and a love of their Country as to continue in such practices after this order; The General assures them, and is directed by Congress to declare, to the whole Army, that such persons shall be severely punished and dismissed the service with disgrace.

On August 14, 1776, with the British in New York Harbor, the Provincial Congress concluded that Fishkill, New York, north of the Hudson Highlands and near the Hudson River, should be an armed encampment. The Fishkill Supply Depot became the major logistical center for the Continental Army in the north throughout the war. It included barracks for more than 2,000 soldiers, hospitals, magazines, workshops, stables, storehouses, and a prison.

There were many challenges confronting the Continental Army as it prepared to defend New York City in August 1776, described by Don Higginbotham in *The War of American Independence.*

The patriots were as aware as their adversaries of the strategic possibilities of the area. The city itself posed serious problems for its defenders, surrounded as it was by various bodies of water

Leather-covered writing case owned and used by George Washington while he was Commander in Chief during the Revolutionary War. *(Courtesy, Division of Political History, National Museum of American History, Smithsonian Institution)*

which would allow the British not only to dominate its approaches, but also to envelop the exposed American flanks by amphibious assault. When Washington sent Charles Lee to shore up New York's defenses, the latter estimated that while New York could not be held in a sustained campaign against overwhelming British military and naval power, it could be so fortified that the enemy would be severely bled in the process of taking it. A series of forts and the fortification of specific rugged locations were called for by Lee, whose works were far from completion when Congress ordered him south to save Charleston, leaving Washington's army, which had come down from Boston, to finish the job. Washington initiated additional projects such as the building of Forts Washington and Lee to guard the Hudson, the barricading of key streets, and the forging of a huge chain to be extended across the Hudson near West Point. To make any kind of an effective fight for the city itself meant a dangerous division of the American army. Large contingents of men and a quantity of artillery had to be ferried across the East River to Long Island, where the heights of Brooklyn commanded lower Manhattan, just as Dorchester Heights overlooked Boston. Nothing could keep the British from making a landing on the big, sprawling island. And with a superior enemy land force in their front and the likelihood of a British fleet in their rear in the East River, the Brooklyn regiments were in danger of catastrophe.

The catastrophe occurred in late August, the battle of Long Island. (There is no protected battlefield to visit.) Craig L. Symonds describes the battle in *A Battlefield Atlas of the American Revolution*.

In late June of 1776 while the Americans retreated from Canada, the first elements of a virtual British armada entered lower New York Harbor and began disgorging troops onto Staten Island. For weeks the British fleet grew in size until by mid-July ten ships of the line, twenty frigates, and nearly three hundred transports and supply vessels choked lower New York Harbor, their bare masts resembling a forest stripped of its leaves, according to one observer. General William Howe commanded the 32,000-man army, and his brother, Admiral Sir Richard Howe, commanded the escorting fleet. London had decided to take the war seriously.

To confront this impressive force, Washington had only about 19,000 soldiers, though reinforcements through the summer raised his total to 28,000 by August. This numerical imbalance was aggravated by the fact that the Americans had no naval forces at all, and Washington was painfully aware that he could be outflanked by sea almost anywhere in the New York

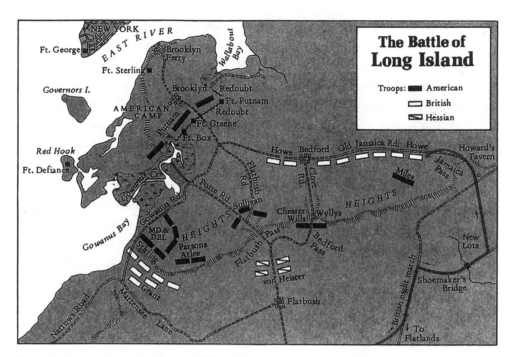

From: The Glorious Cause *by Robert Middlekauff (1982). Map from p. 345. By permission of Oxford University Press, USA.*

area. But New York City had tremendous political significance and Washington believed he could not abandon it without a fight. He therefore divided his army into five divisions, placing three of them in New York City at the southern tip of Manhattan Island, one at Fort Washington near the northern end of the island, and one under General Nathanael Greene on Long Island to protect Brooklyn Heights which, since it overlooked the city, was the key to New York. Alas for American fortunes, Greene fell ill and his second in command, John Sullivan, was junior to Israel Putnam, who assumed command. This was an unfortunate development for, though Putnam had plenty of courage, he was not an effective senior commander.

On August 22 Howe landed some 15,000 soldiers—about half his force—at Gravesend Bay on Long Island. The key geographical feature on Long Island was the long narrow ridge running roughly east-west known as the Heights of Guan. It was pierced by four passes: Gowanus Road, Flatbush Road, Bedford Pass, and Jamaica Pass. Howe feinted against both Flatbush and Bedford Passes and Putnam accordingly positioned most of his available troops there. Then on the night of August 26, Howe's main body of 10,000 men marched uncontested through Jamaica Pass. Sullivan's badly outnumbered forces at Bedford Pass and Flatbush Pass broke and fled for the fortified American camp around Brooklyn.

While Howe led the British main body through Jamaica Pass, the rest of Howe's force—some 5,000 men under Major General James Grant—assaulted Gowanus Pass. Grant's job was to hold the 1,600 Americans under Major General William Alexander, who claimed an Irish title as Lord Stirling, in their positions until Howe could attack them in the flank and rear. Accordingly, Grant was very tentative in his advance and he convinced Putnam to keep

Stirling's men in the closing trap. Putnam never really comprehended the developing situation. As a result, Stirling's men were pinned between two forces of nearly ten times their number, and forced to capitulate.

Recognizing potential disaster, Washington crossed the East River from New York and assumed direct command of the demoralized American force on Long Island. He knew that New York City could not be held without possession of Brooklyn Heights, and that Brooklyn Heights could be cut off by the Royal Navy. The only sensible recourse was to abandon the city, but he was unwilling to do that. He called for more reinforcements from Manhattan to boost American strength on Long Island to 9,500, still only about half the strength of the British.

Howe was now in a position to bag most of the Continental Army and its commander with it. But perhaps remembering the results of his hasty assault at Bunker Hill, he instead began constructing regular siege lines. Heavy rains slowed his progress, and in the interval provided by nature, Washington began to appreciate just how precarious his situation was. Finally on August 29 he ordered a retreat. That night, in six hours of heavy labor, all 9,500 men and all but six guns were successfully evacuated to Manhattan. Total American losses in the campaign for Long Island were 1,012 compared to British losses of only 392.

John Buchanan describes the difficult evacuation of Long Island in *The Road to Valley Forge: How Washington Built the Army That Won the Revolution.*

Washington was fortunate to have at hand that night two splendid regiments vitally important to the evacuation: 14th and 27th Massachusetts, most of their men hardy and experienced fishermen and sailors from the Essex county towns of Marblehead, Salem, Lynn, and Danvers. Israel Hutchinson (1728–1811) commanded the 27th. The 14th was led by one of the Continental Army's finest officers, Colonel John Glover, a forty-four-year-old master mariner become an officer of infantry. His regiment stood head and shoulders above the other Yankee regiments.

Beginning at ten o'clock on the night of 29 August, stealthily, by regiments, the cold and soaked and dispirited Rebel army moved off the heights and down the hill to the ferry landing where Glover and Hutchinson and their sturdy mariners waited to begin their long night on the swift, dark waters of the East River.

It was not until between roughly 7:00 and 8:00 a.m. that Hessian troops entered the empty Rebel lines and advanced through the fog across Brooklyn Heights and down to the ferry landing—just in time to fire at the last Rebel boat disappearing into the mist.

A British naval officer was flabbergasted by the event. Admiral Sir George Collier wrote, "To my inexpressible astonishment and concern the rebel army all escaped across the River to New York!…Now, I foresee they will give us trouble enough, and protract the war, Heaven knows how long."

After the tragic loss of more than 1,000 men in the battle, Washington made the difficult decision to fight a defensive war. In *Washington's Crossing,* David Hackett Fischer explains Washington's thinking.

The loss of Long Island caused much soul-searching in the American camp. On September 6, George Washington reported the result to Congress and called a "council of the general officers" to "take a full and comprehensive view of our situation." In Washington's thinking, the problem was to match a strategy to his soldiers. Washington observed that American troops were not willing to die for honor or duty. "The honor of making a brave defense does not seem to be a sufficient stimulus, when the success is very doubtful, and the falling into the enemy's hands probable."

From all this Washington concluded that "on our side the war should be defensive"; "we should on all occasions avoid a general action or put anything to the risque unless compelled by necessity." He resolved to keep his army in being, but it would be a "retreating army," defending what it could, yielding when it must, keeping the field and watching for an opportunity when "a brilliant stroke could be made with any probability of success."

28. Bentley/Conference House, New York

THE CONFERENCE HOUSE
298 SATTERLEE STREET
STATEN ISLAND, NEW YORK

General John Sullivan, who had been captured in the battle on Long Island, arrived in Congress on September 3, 1776, paroled by Admiral Richard Lord Howe, with Howe's request for a conference. On September 11, three representatives of the Continental Congress—John Adams, Benjamin Franklin, and Edward Rutledge—met with Howe on Staten Island at the home of a Tory, Colonel Christopher Billopp. The 1680 rubble stone masonry house is now The Conference House. Walter Isaacson describes the meeting in *Benjamin Franklin*.

Although Howe marched his guests past a double line of menacing Hessian mercenaries, the three-hour meeting on September 11 was cordial, and the Americans were treated to a feast of good claret, ham, tongue, and mutton.

Howe pledged that the colonies could have what they had requested in the Olive Branch Petition: control over their own legislation and taxes, and "a revisal of any of the plantation laws by which the colonists may be aggrieved." The British, he said, were still kindly disposed toward the Americans: "When an American falls, England feels it." He felt the same, even more strongly. If America fell, he said, "I should feel and lament it like the loss of a brother."

Adams recorded Franklin's retort: "Dr. Franklin, with an easy air and collected countenance, a bow, a smile and all that naïveté which sometimes appeared in his conversation and is often observed in his writings, replied, 'My Lord, we will do our utmost endeavors to save your Lordship that mortification.'"

The dispute that was causing this horrible war, Howe insisted, was merely about the method Britain should use in raising taxes from America. Franklin replied, "That we never refused, upon requisition."

Why then, Howe asked, was it not possible "to put a stop to these ruinous extremities?"

Because, Franklin replied, it was too late for any peace that required a return to allegiance to the king. "Forces have been sent out and towns have been burnt," he said. "We cannot now expect happiness under the domination of Great Britain. All former attachments have been obliterated." Adams, likewise, "mentioned warmly his own determination not to depart from the idea of independency."

The Americans suggested that Howe send home for authority to negotiate with them as an independent nation. That was a "vain" hope, replied Howe.

"Well, my Lord," said Franklin, "as America is to expect nothing but upon unconditional submission…"

Howe interrupted. He was not demanding submission. But it was clear, he acknowledged, that no accommodation was possible, at least for now, and he apologized that "the gentlemen had the trouble of coming so far to so little purpose."

In *The Glorious Cause,* Robert Middlekauff points to a particular characteristic of Franklin and other Revolutionary leaders.

"The use of travelling," Doctor Johnson wrote Mrs. Thrale, "is to regulate imagination by reality, and instead of thinking how things may be, to see them as they are." Johnson spoke for the age in this desire to see things as they are and to avoid the dangerous imaginings of how they may be. His England and much of pre-Revolutionary America shared a suspicion of what he called "airy notions"—the illusions of dreams and fancies. Johnson's great American contemporary, Benjamin Franklin, as a young man put aside speculations on the nature of reality in favor of living as a reasonable creature in contact with the world that presented itself through the evidence of his senses.

Franklin was a practical man. Practical men usually do not make revolutions; dreamers do. Yet Benjamin Franklin became a revolutionary with several million others in America. His action suggests one of the ironies of the American Revolution: its sources in a culture of men devoted to the hard realities of life—practical men, down-to-earth men like Franklin himself, men who in 1776 threw off their allegiance to the empire in the name of "common sense," a phrase Thomas Paine had chosen as the title of his great tract on behalf of American independence.

On September 12, 1776, after General Washington was assured that Congress did not require him to defend New York, the generals concurred and began the retreat off the island.

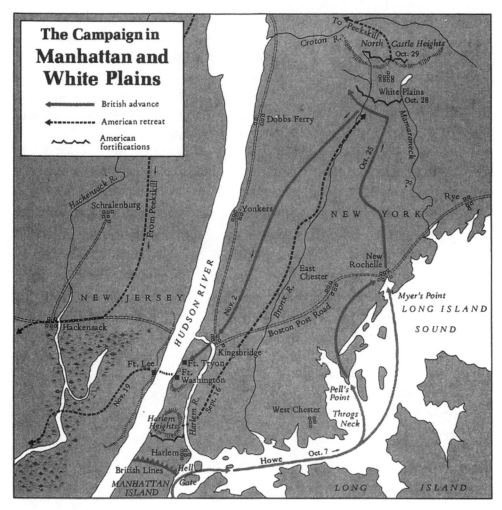

From: The Glorious Cause *by Robert Middlekauff (1982). Map from p. 345. By permission of Oxford University Press, USA.*

On September 15, five British frigates on the East River opened fire on the Connecticut militia, and when 4,000 British and German regulars landed at Kip's Bay (then an East River inlet between today's 32nd and 37th Streets in New York City), the militia fled. General Israel Putnam's command headed north toward Harlem Heights. The troop strength was diminishing because militiamen who were farmers were needed at home.

Piers Mackesy in *The War for America, 1775–1783* describes the battles at Kip's Bay, where General Washington endangered himself by riding into the fight, and at Harlem Heights.

> The defense had been deceived. Only a thin line of musketmen behind a breastwork guarded the beach at Kip's Bay, and their supports would not come up under the warships' fire. They broke and ran in disgraceful panic, with Washington raging vainly to check them. Clinton commanded the first wave; and if he could have thrust two miles across Manhattan to the Hudson, several thousand Americans in New York would have been cut off. But he had no

artillery, his orders were to hold a bridgehead for the second wave, and he stood fast on high ground to cover the landing place. Later he felt a chance had perhaps been missed, though Lord Rawdon thought otherwise. More curious, however, is a staff officer's journal which records that the escape route was still left open by the dispositions for the night, when Howe rejected his advice to post troops across the road by the Hudson. But Howe he wrote, was "slow, and not inclined to attend to whatever may be considered as advice, and seemed more intent upon looking out for comfortable quarters for himself..."

The landing had been a brilliant success. But before the assault Clinton had shown the misgivings which haunted the British command. He foretold strong resistance and a possible reverse, and later maintained that only the American blunder about the British plan had enabled him to succeed. "My advice has ever been to avoid even the possibility of a check," he had written that morning. "We live by victory." The British superiority was moral, not numerical. Hitherto the Americans had fled before them; raw men, whose military spirit, far from being broken, had not yet been created. In normal warfare risks are justified to exploit success. But the Americans had the resilience of innocence. Reverses quickly intimidated them; but the slightest run of success might transform them into an army. This was indicated the day after the landing. Washington had drawn away to the north and occupied a strong position on Harlem Heights. Two light infantry battalions supported by the Black Watch pressed impetuously forward into a disadvantageous action in front of the advanced posts, and were quickly withdrawn by Clinton on instruction from Howe. To the British it was an outpost skirmish; but the Americans had seen the redcoats' backs, and thought they had a major success.

Edward G. Lengel describes the effects on the soldiers of the victory at Harlem Heights in *General George Washington*.

Washington refused to risk his troops further and halted their advance, ordering them to break off the engagement and withdraw at about 2:00 P.M. Tilghman, who delivered the commander-in-chief's order, recalled that the troops "gave a Hurra and left the Field in good Order." This minor but victorious skirmish boosted morale even among the troops who had not been engaged. Among them, Colonel David Humphreys later wrote, "every visage was seen to brighten, and to assume, instead of the gloom of despair, the glow of animation." It was Washington's first battlefield victory of the war.

In the early fall of 1776 General Washington warned Congress that the Continental Army was on the verge of dissolution and that Congress should recruit soldiers for the duration of the war. Jack Rakove details the army's problems in *Revolutionaries*.

Congress in fact had just conceded Washington's basic point, resolving to recruit eighty-eight battalions to serve for the duration. Washington was not in the happiest mood when, from Harlem Heights on October 4, he answered President Hancock's letter enclosing this resolution. His orders for that day lambasted his troops yet again for their "shameful inatten-tion" to removing "the Offal and Filth of the Camp." Again warning that the army was near "political dissolution," Washington patiently explained why the new plan was both inade-quate in the terms it offered officers and soldiers alike and overly ambitious. "No time is to be lost in making fruitless experiments," he wrote. "If we have an army at all," he concluded, "it will be composed of materials not only entirely raw, but if uncommon pains is not taken, entirely unfit."

Washington wrote this letter in his own hand, in as firm a tone as he ever used with Congress. But however much he chafed at the restrictions under which he labored, he never scorned the authority of Congress. From the beginning of his command he accepted the prin-ciple of civilian supremacy over the military that has always been an axiom of American polit-ical thinking. His long experience in the Virginia assembly exerted greater influence over his political values than did the military service of his youth.

David Hackett Fischer's description in *Washington's Crossing* of the American army camps in New York in 1776 details the conditions that Washington criticized.

As the summer wore on, ill health began to plague the army. It had plenty of salt meat and hard bread but desperately lacked fresh food and green vegetables. The farmers around New York had a plentiful harvest in 1776 and began to bring their crops to the city. Undisciplined soldiers were so desperate that they seized the food on sight. Washington issued strict orders against this practice but could not enforce them, and the farmers stopped coming. In the midst of plenty, the army began to suffer from malnutrition, even from scurvy in the summertime.

The American camps were by all accounts much worse than those of the British and Hes-sians. American officers understood the importance of field sanitation but were unable to en-force it. The results were horrific. American troops lacked experience and camp discipline, and they paid a terrible price. They polluted their camps and fouled their water supply. The result was a polydemic of dysentery, "putrid fevers," typhoid fever, malaria, and enteric diseases.

At the same time that Congress struggled with army recruitment, it had to confront the nation's deepening economic crisis, detailed by John Ferling in *A Leap in the Dark*.

During the first winter of independence, signs of a swelling economic crisis became evident. The war devoured money almost with the speed that piranha on a feeding frenzy consume their prey. Congress adopted a Continental currency and issued $2,000,000 in June 1775. Within eighteen months it had put $25,000,000 into circulation and was printing new issues every fortnight. Not surprisingly, the value of the Continental currency began to collapse that autumn. Depreciation, resulting from overly generous emissions of paper money, as well as shortages occasioned both by the loss of British trade and the enemy's ever-tightening naval blockade, threatened economic collapse. To forestall that occurrence, the New England states convened in Providence in De-cember 1776 to seek agreement on price and wage regulations, and monetary policy.

Some in Congress, however, objected to any governmental tampering with the market-place, while others were put off by the intrusiveness of the states. These congressmen insisted that the economy, like diplomacy, was a national concern that should be left to Congress. Benjamin Rush of Pennsylvania argued that the "Salvation of this continent" hinged on re-peated demonstrations of the "sacred... Authority and character" of Congress to lead. To-gether with John Adams, he induced Congress to recommend that the states increase taxes. Furthermore, at Adams's behest, Congress raised from 4 to 6 percent the interest rate on loan certificates, which it had first issued only weeks earlier. Designed to be a source of investment, not a circulating medium, it was hoped that loan certificates would take money out of circula-tion and hence be a deflationary measure. But Congress went no further. The majority, which yet consisted of committed decentralists, preferred that the states find palliatives for their ec-onomic maladies. The alternative was for Congress to centralize its control of the economy, a move fraught with danger for a shaky union in the midst of a military crisis. Thus Congress not only approved the initiative of the New England states in seeking "to remedy the Evils occasioned by...exorbitant Prices" but also recommended that the middle and southern states convene in York, Pennsylvania, and Charleston, respectively, to consider solutions to their growing dilemma.

Following the victory at Harlem Heights on September 16, the American army con-tinued its retreat north on Manhattan, described by Craig L. Symonds in *A Battlefield Atlas of the American Revolution*.

The American victory at Harlem Heights was a tonic for Washington's soldiers, who had done little but retreat since the campaign opened. One American officer wrote home to his wife that "The men have recovered their spirits and feel a confidence which before they had quite lost."

The battle had the opposite effect on Howe. Reluctant as always to assault rebel en-trenchments, he decided once again to attempt to outmaneuver his enemy. On October 12, four thousand British soldiers embarked on transports at Kip's Bay, passed through Hell's Gate, and landed on Throgs Neck. Strategically the movement was a good idea, but Howe could hardly have chosen a worse place to land. The neck was nearly an island separated from the mainland by a single road that ran through marshes where a small group of Pennsylvania riflemen under the command of Colonel Edward Hand held the only bridge. Howe hesitated to force a crossing and Hand's men were reinforced. After six days, Howe decided to abandon Throgs Neck and moved his forces to Pell's Point.

At Eastchester a brigade of about 750 Americans under Colonel John Glover contested the road with Howe's 4,000 regulars. Though Glover was forced to withdraw, his men did so in good order after inflicting more casualties than they suffered. In another skirmish four days later, Colonel John Haslet's Delaware regiment attacked and mauled Colonel Robert Rogers's regiment of about 500 Loyalists at Mamaroneck.

Howe's move threatened to cut off the American army on Manhattan from the main-land, but Washington had already decided to abandon Manhattan and lower New York and fall back to White Plains. Sensitive to Congressional urgings, however, the American commander left some 2,800 men under Colonel Robert Magaw at Fort Washington in hopes of disrupting British transit of the Hudson River. Greene, with about 3,500 men, held Fort Lee across the river in New Jersey. Washington's main army of about 14,500 arrived in White Plains on October 22. Howe dallied at New Rochelle for two days, long enough to let Washington get safely to his new position. Then when 8,000 Hessians under Lieutenant General Wilhelm von Knyphausen arrived, Howe left half of them to garrison New Rochelle and started after Washington with about 14,000 men.

A week later on October 28 the two armies met in the Battle of White Plains. Putnam held the American right, Brigadier General William Heath the left, and Washington himself the center. But the key to the position was the high ground beyond the Bronx River known as Chatterton's Hill. About 4,000 British and Hessians attacked the 1,600 Americans under Colonel Joseph Reed on Chatterton's Hill. The American militia broke and fled, but the Continentals fought stubbornly. As at Harlem Heights and Eastchester, the Americans inflicted more casualties than they suffered, but they were forced to give up the hill, and its loss uncovered the American right. Washington had little choice but to withdraw northward to Castle Hill.

Howe, now reinforced to 20,000, did not follow. Instead he turned west to Dobb's Ferry, and then south to achieve the envelopment of Magaw's force in Fort Washington. Washington left Charles Lee in command of about 6,000 men at Castle Hill to block any northward move by Howe, and led the rest of his army northwest to Peekskill. From there he crossed the Hudson at Haverstraw (on November 10) and marched south to Hackensack, New Jersey.

Washington's decision to divide his already inferior forces and place the Hudson River between them was a serious error in military judgment. Equally questionable was his decision to leave Magaw's 2,800 men in Fort Washington where, on November 16, they were forced to capitulate. But in this, as in other things, Washington had acted in accordance with the wishes of Congress, and it could be argued that Washington's greatest service in the war was his definition of the role of commander in chief as subordinate to Congress. The loss of Magaw's 2,800 men was an unalloyed military disaster, but the solution urged by Charles Lee—a military dictatorship (with himself as dictator)—would have been a greater disaster.

29. Pell's Point, New York

OCTOBER 18, 1776

GLOVER'S ROCK ON ORCHARD BEACH ROAD IN
PELHAM BAY PARK, BRONX, NEW YORK

On October 18, 1776, General Howe landed 4,000 soldiers and six cannon near the mouth of the Hutchinson River on Pell's Point. Colonel John Glover in command of 750

Continentals slowed the British advance along a narrow road from the beach by firing from behind the protection of stone walls. John Ferling recounts the battle at Pell's Point in *Almost a Miracle*.

The British army had moved inland after the exchanges between the rival advance units on Split Rock Road, though considerable time had been required to bring up baggage wagons and field pieces, and to contrive a plan of action. Then the order to advance! Thousands of men, accompanied by horse-drawn artillery, moved in the direction that the enemy was last known to have been deployed.

Suddenly, without warning, a line of nearly 250 rebels rose up from behind stone walls only about thirty yards away. They fired in a staggered manner. The Americans to the right opened up, then as they ducked to reload, their brethren to the left, and then those in the center, laid down volleys. The British answered with small arms fire, although the artillery was rapidly brought forward. The cannon belched out a thunderous fire at the Continentals' stone barricade. The Americans got off seven volleys, taking a toll, before they—like the advance guard earlier in the morning—retreated.

The fighting at Pell's Point ended later in the afternoon. The Americans withdrew, yielding the area, but although outnumbered nearly six to one, they had held up the British long enough to permit the Continental army to escape Manhattan Island. The British had lost nearly two hundred men on that blood-soaked day. The Americans reported only twenty-one men lost, a figure that surely was far too low, though no doubt existed that their losses were considerably fewer than those suffered by their foe.

In the days that followed, Washington lavished praise on the men who had fought at Pell's Point. He spoke of their "merit and good behavior," and lauded Glover's "activity and industry," telling him: "you very well know the duty of a colonel" and "you know how to exact that duty from others." Glover continued to serve and fight long after this engagement.

30. Valcour Island, New York

OCTOBER 11–13, 1776

ADIRONDACK PARK
SOUTHEAST OF PLATTSBURGH, NEW YORK

While General Washington's Continentals were marching and fighting their way off Manhattan, Sir Guy Carleton, the royal governor of Canada, was planning to lay siege to Fort Ticonderoga and Mount Independence. He was delayed a month, while a flotilla was assembled in Canada at St. Johns about twenty miles south of Montreal.

General Horatio Gates, who had replaced Brigadier General John Sullivan, authorized Brigadier General Benedict Arnold to oversee the building of a small fleet at Skenesborough, New York, to counter Carleton. By October, Arnold had seventeen vessels on Lake Champlain.

On October 11 off Valcour Island, the Americans battled Carleton's force of nearly 2,000 men on twenty-five vessels. By sunset the British were winning. During the night in a heavy fog, the Americans sailed quietly away. Pursued by the British fleet, they fought again at Split Rock, suffered heavy losses, and destroyed their remaining vessels in today's Arnold Bay, near Panton, Vermont. Arnold's force escaped by heading south to Crown Point and on to Ticonderoga and Mount Independence.

Carleton continued sailing south but was delayed both by Arnold's attack and by strong headwinds. He concluded that winter was too near and his supply line from Canada too tenuous for him to attack Fort Ticonderoga. He withdrew to Quebec but left a crew at St. Johns to build ships and gunboats for a major invasion the following year.

The oldest surviving American fighting vessel, the *Philadelphia*, was one of Arnold's nine gundalows in the battle off Valcour Island. It weighed twenty-nine tons and was fifty-four feet long. Sunk in the battle, it was raised in 1935 and brought to the National Museum of American History in Washington, DC, in 1961.

In November 1776, the American generals decided to release the militia, furlough army soldiers, evacuate Crown Point—much of which had been destroyed in a 1773 fire—and concentrate the remaining 1,400 soldiers to garrison Fort Ticonderoga and Mount Independence under the command of Colonel Anthony Wayne.

---

31. Newport, Rhode Island

DECEMBER 8, 1776

FORT ADAMS STATE PARK
COLONY HOUSE
NEWPORT, RHODE ISLAND

In November 1776, while General Washington was crossing New Jersey, General Howe ordered General Clinton to capture Newport, Rhode Island, to assure an ice-free northern port for British ships. Clinton landed on Aquidneck Island and took Newport without a battle. The few defenders withdrew from the fortifications on the islands. By December 12 the occupying troops were in camps on Aquidneck and Conanicut Islands and quartered in Newport.

The British held Newport until October 1779. During their occupation, the British used the Touro Synagogue, designed by Peter Harrison and completed in 1763, as a hospital and an assembly hall.

In 1799 Fort Adams was built on the site of the Brenton Point Battery and named for President John Adams. The present Fort Adams, built on the same site, was begun in 1824.

Colony House was the primary meeting house for the General Assembly from its completion in 1739 until the current State House in Providence opened in 1901. On July 20, 1776, the Declaration of Independence was read from the front steps. The British used it as a barracks during their occupation of Newport. The Comte de Rochambeau honored General Washington at a banquet in the Great Hall in 1782.

While the British navy was moving to take control of Newport, a ship commissioned by the Continental Navy sailed into the St. Eustatius harbor. In *The First Salute* Barbara W. Tuchman describes the significance of the salute given the *Andrew Doria*.

White puffs of gun smoke over a turquoise sea followed by the boom of cannon rose from an unassuming fort on the diminutive Dutch island of St. Eustatius in the West Indies on November 16, 1776. The guns of Fort Orange on St. Eustatius were returning the ritual salute on entering a foreign port of an American vessel, the *Andrew Doria*, as she came up the roadstead, flying at her mast the red-and-white-striped flag of the Continental Congress. In its responding salute the small voice of St. Eustatius was the first officially to greet the largest event of the century—the entry into the society of nations of a new Atlantic state destined to change the direction of history.

The salute to the *Andrew Doria*, ordered on his own initiative by the Governor of St. Eustatius, Johannes de Graaff, was the first recognition following the rebel colonies' Declaration of Independence, of the American flag and American nationhood by an official of a foreign state. Dutch priority was not the most important aspect of the event, but as other claimants have disputed the case, let it be said that the guns of Fort Orange were confirmed as first by the President of the United States, in a plaque presented to St. Eustatius in 1939 over the engraved signature of the incumbent Franklin D. Roosevelt. The plaque reads, "In Commemoration of the salute of the flag of the United States fired in this fort November 16, 1776, by order of Johannes de Graaff, Governor of St. Eustatius, in reply to a national gun salute fired by the U.S. Brig-of-War *Andrew Doria*.... Here the sovereignty of the United States of America was first formally acknowledged to a national vessel by a foreign official."

The *Andrew Doria*, vehicle and protagonist of this drama, was not just any ship but already the possessor of a historic distinction. She was one of the first four ships, all converted merchantmen, to be commissioned into the Continental Navy created by act of the Continental Congress on October 13, 1775, and she was shortly to take part in its first active combat. She was a brigantine, a small two-masted vessel, refitted for belligerent action in the newly created American Navy. She had sailed from the New Jersey coast town of Gloucester near Philadelphia on October 23, under orders of the Continental Congress to proceed to St. Eustatius to take on military supplies and deliver a copy of the Declaration of Independence to Governor de Graaff. With only her limited sail area to catch the westerlies, her crossing in a little over three weeks to arrive by November 16 was a notable feat. Sailing times from North America to Europe and back varied widely depending on the type of ship, with the heavier warships taking longer than frigates and merchantmen, and depending on the wind, which might sometimes shift erratically from the prevailing westerlies blowing eastward to the reverse. At the time of the Revolution, the eastward passage to Europe, called "downhill," ordinarily took about three weeks to a month as opposed to the westward "uphill" voyage to America against the wind and the Gulf Stream, which took about three months.

~~~~

32. Fort Washington, New York

BENNETT PARK
FORT WASHINGTON AVENUE AND WEST 183RD STREET
NEW YORK CITY

The Americans had begun to build two forts on the Hudson River in July 1776, Fort Washington and Fort Lee. They were positioned to prevent the British fleet from moving up the river and separating the states. Fort Washington was on a 280-foot precipice above the east side of the river. Today, granite paving outlines its former contours. Fort Lee was built on the west side.

As the British approached Fort Washington on November 3, 1776, Major General Nathanael Greene, who was in overall command of both forts, argued for its defense. General Washington wanted to abandon the fort since it could not stop British ships on the Hudson River, but he concurred with Greene's plan.

On November 16, General Howe attacked with 13,000 British and Hessian troops, captured the fort, and took more than 2,800 prisoners, their supplies, and the artillery.

In *Washington's Crossing*, David Hackett Fischer describes General Washington after the loss of Fort Washington.

George Washington was shattered by the event. He was a witness to the final scenes, looking on helplessly from the Jersey Palisades across the Hudson River. Through his telescope he could see some of his troops fighting bravely, only to be driven back and defeated. The worst of it was to watch them surrender and see some of them put to the sword. This time there was no expression of anger by the American commander-in-chief. His feelings ran deeper than that. He blamed no one else for what had happened, took all the responsibility on his own shoulders, and judged himself more severely than anyone else could judge him.

It was the lowest point of Washington's long career. In the agony of that moment he felt that he had lost everything: lost the war, lost the Cause, lost his own way. But then this extraordinary man reached deep into his last reserves of inner strength. Not much was left, but enough to shake off a terrible despair. He looked away from Fort Washington and rallied his aides around him. Together, they would try again.

33. Fort Lee, New Jersey

NOVEMBER 20, 1776

FORT LEE HISTORIC PARK
HUDSON TERRACE
FORT LEE, NEW JERSEY

In November of 1776 General Howe began to implement his plan to occupy eastern New Jersey, where there were farms that could provide food for his soldiers during the winter. General Washington's intelligence sources informed him of Howe's plans, and on November 9 he began to move his army across the Hudson south of Peekskill to prepare for the British advance. On November 12 he set up his headquarters in Hackensack and ordered Greene to evacuate Fort Lee. Howe ordered General Charles Cornwallis with 5,000 soldiers to attack the fort. The British scaled an unguarded slope of the steep Palisades north of Fort Lee and took it in a surprise attack on November 20. Major General Nathanael Greene and most of the garrison escaped and crossed the Hackensack River at New Bridge on the night of November 20, ahead of the British.

In command of 10,000 men, Cornwallis pursued Washington, following Howe's orders to pressure Washington while avoiding a battle and to stop at New Brunswick. Washington retreated to Princeton, then to Trenton. To save his army, he took all of the boats along the Delaware River and ferried his army across it into Pennsylvania on December 8, just ahead of the British soldiers.

Howe stopped his pursuit and ordered his army into winter quarters in encampments between New York and Trenton. He offered pardon to residents in the New Jersey area who would pledge their loyalty to King George III and returned to New York to prepare for his winter leave in England.

Washington's army needed supplies as it marched across New Jersey in December. In *John Adams: A Life*, John Ferling relates the decisions in the year-long process that resulted in the aid that France delivered but kept secret from Britain.

> When war erupted, the French Foreign Minister, Charles Gravier, Comte de Vergennes, not only hinted to American businessmen in Europe that France might be willing to help the colonists, but in the fall of 1775 he sent a special agent, M. Achard Bonvouloir, to Philadelphia to encourage the American war effort and to intimate that French assistance was possible. At the same moment, Vergennes, through intermediaries, undertook a campaign to convince Louis XVI that France could benefit from Britain's woes and that it should secretly assist Washington's army. The French monarch demurred, at least until the sentiments of his ally, Spain, could be ascertained. But when Spain approved assistance to the American army—largely in the hope that Britain and the colonists would bleed one another to death, enabling Madrid to benefit from their exhaustion—Louis consented to Vergennes's wishes.

However, because the French navy was unprepared for war, neither Louis nor Vergennes gave any thought to open assistance, a belligerent act certain to result in a British declaration of war. Instead, it was decided that the goods would be sent clandestinely, through the dodge of a private and, of course, fictitious commercial enterprise, the so-called Roderigue Hortalez and Company. The first shipments of French goods, mostly arms and gunpowder, were speeding across the Atlantic as Washington's little army retreated across New Jersey in the fall of 1776.

Thomas Paine wrote *The American Crisis, NUMBER 1* while he marched with the Continental Army as it retreated across New Jersey and into Pennsylvania. The *Pennsylvania Journal* published it on December 19, 1776, and it was read to the Continental Army on December 23. This is the first paragraph of *NUMBER 1* in *Thomas Paine: Collected Writings,* edited by Eric Foner.

The American Crisis
NUMBER 1
December 19, 1776
THESE are the times that try men's souls: The summer soldier and the sunshine patriot will, in this crisis, shrink from the service of their country; but he that stands by it NOW, deserves the love and thanks of man and woman. Tyranny, like hell, is not easily conquered; yet we have this consolation with us, that the harder the conflict, the more glorious the triumph. What we obtain too cheap, we esteem too lightly:—'Tis dearness only that gives every thing its value. Heaven knows how to put a proper price upon its goods; and it would be strange indeed, if so celestial an article as FREEDOM should not be highly rated. Britain, with an army to enforce her tyranny, has declared that she has a right (*not only to* TAX) but "*to* BIND *us in* ALL CASES WHATSOEVER," and if being *bound in that manner* is not slavery, then is there not such a thing as slavery upon earth. Even the expression is impious, for so unlimited a power can belong only to GOD.

34. Mount Holly, New Jersey

DECEMBER 21–24, 1776
IRON WORKS PARK
MOUNT HOLLY, NEW JERSEY

On December 21, 1776, Colonel Samuel Griffin and 750 New Jersey militiamen skirmished with the Jäger Corps of the Hessian army commanded by Colonel Carl Emilius von Donop at the Petticoat Bridge north of Mount Holly. Reinforced on December 23, von Donop attacked the Americans in the Mount Holly area. They retreated in a running skirmish to their fortified positions along Pine Street and Iron Works Hill. When Donop

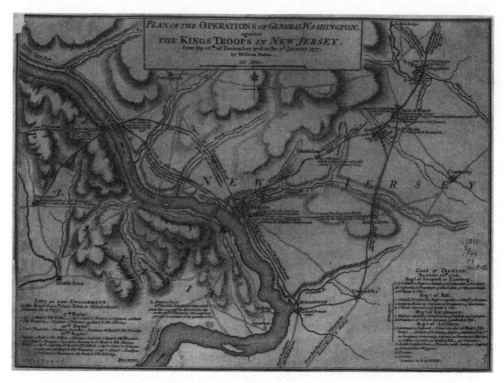

General Washington in New Jersey. William Faden. Plan *of the Operations of General Washington, Against the Kings Troops in New Jersey, from the 26th of December, 1776 to the 3d January, 1777.* London, 1777. *(Courtesy, Library of Congress, Geography and Map Division. http://hdl.loc.gov/loc.gmd/g3811s.ar127000)*

began shelling their positions from the Mount, Griffin withdrew during the night of December 24–25 to a nearby hill. Instead of marching his troops to Bordentown so that he could support Colonel Johann Rall at Trenton, von Donop kept them in Mount Holly where he stayed for three nights.

William Faden's map, published in April 1777, records General Washington's troop movements between December 26, 1776, and January 3, 1777. It is in the *American Map Collection* of the Library of Congress. Purchased in 1804, it was the first map collection acquired as a resource for Congress.

35. Thompson-Neely House, Pennsylvania

WASHINGTON CROSSING HISTORIC PARK
1112 RIVER ROAD
WASHINGTON CROSSING, PENNSYLVANIA

On December 25–26, 1776, General Washington led his army across the Delaware River at McConkey's Ferry, attacked Trenton, and returned to Pennsylvania on December 27.

The park includes the site of the crossing and historic buildings, including the Thompson-Neely House (on Lurgan Road) where sick and convalescing soldiers were treated.

36. Trenton, New Jersey

DECEMBER 25–26, 1776

WASHINGTON CROSSING STATE PARK
TITUSVILLE, NEW JERSEY
TRENTON BATTLE MONUMENT
PENNINGTON ROAD AND BROAD STREET
HISTORIC MARKERS IN MILL HILL PARK ON BROAD STREET
TRENTON, NEW JERSEY

Washington's army crossed the Delaware River into New Jersey and fought the battle of Trenton on December 26 against Hessians commanded by Colonel Johann Rall.

Washington Crossing State Park includes the site of the landing at Johnson's Ferry and the Johnson's Ferry House.

37. Trenton Barracks, New Jersey

OLD BARRACKS MUSEUM
101 BARRACK STREET
TRENTON, NEW JERSEY

Trenton Barracks, a fieldstone structure, was built in 1758 during the Seven Years' War. When General Washington attacked Trenton, there was skirmishing around the building against the Hessian troops stationed within. After defeating the Hessians, the Americans used the Barracks as a hospital. It was occupied at different times during the war by American, British, and Hessian troops as well as loyalist refugees and prisoners.

Washington Crossing the Delaware, the painting by Emanuel Leutze, is in The Metropolitan Museum of Art in New York. Its scale reflects the importance of the Crossing to General Washington and to America; it is more than twelve feet tall and twenty-one feet wide. In *Washington's Crossing*, David Hackett Fischer includes the painting in his description of the final days of December 1776 and Washington's great victory.

Emmanuel Leutze's painting shows only one side of this great struggle, but the artist clearly understood what it was about. He represented something of its nature in his image of George Washington and the men who soldiered with him. The more we learn about Washington, the greater his contribution becomes, in developing a new idea of leadership during the American Revolution. Emanuel Leutze brings it out in a tension between Washington and the other men in the boat. We see them in their diversity and their stubborn autonomy. These men lived the rights they were defending, often to the fury of their commander-in-chief. The painting gives us some sense of the complex relations that they had with one another, and also with their leader. To study them with their general is to understand what George Washington meant when he wrote, "A people unused to restraint must be led; they will not be drove." All of these things were beginning to happen on Christmas night in 1776, when George Washington crossed the Delaware.

In occupied New Jersey, General Howe had proclaimed a peace, but there was no peace. The pacifiers found themselves at war with an infuriated population. On Christmas Eve, Howe instructed his men in New Jersey not to travel alone on the roads, but to restrict their movements to large convoys, a few days each week. As law and order collapsed, the people of New Jersey were also at war with one another. During the dark days of December 1776, the Revolution was a civil war, which became an anarchy of cruelty and violence. This was life without liberty or law in occupied New Jersey.

The British commanders were coming up against a hard American reality, in the sheer size of the country that they were trying to control. Bands of New Jersey militia were roaming the countryside, and the Pennsylvania Navy controlled the river itself below Trenton Falls. Each of these movements in New Jersey had different drivers. The rising of the Hunterdon men in the north and west, the river raids of Ewing's Pennsylvania militia, the march and countermarch of Griffin's militia to the south, and the dalliance of Colonel von Donop with the beautiful young widow of Mount Holly all were spontaneous events. Washington was not the director of these events, but he and his staff were quick to recognize an opportunity.

Colonel Joseph Reed, Washington's adjutant, sent a message by express to Washington. "We are all of the opinion my dear general that something must be attempted to revive our expiring credit, give our Cause some degree of reputation & prevent total depreciation of the Continental money which is coming on very fast." He insisted that "even a Failure cannot be more fatal than to remain in our present situation. In short some enterprise must be undertaken in our present Circumstances or we must give up the cause."

That letter reached Washington by courier on December 22, 1776; Washington called a council of war. The general announced that the army had grown stronger; all of the reinforcements from New England had now arrived. The meeting debated Reed's plan for crossing the Delaware and attacking one of the enemy's posts in New Jersey. The council agreed very quickly, and a long discussion followed on how it might be done.

Even on Christmas day there was no respite, no celebration, and no heavy drinking by the Hessians in Trenton, as has often been alleged. In the night, a winter storm hit Trenton.

At last, in the midst of a howling northeaster, the Hessian garrison relaxed for the first time in eight days. Nobody thought that the enemy could attack in such weather.

Washington and his staff had planned the operation in great detail. He meant to cross the Delaware River on Christmas night and attack Trenton a little before dawn, with all the strength in his command. Field commanders were ordered to lead their men across the river in four separate movements, all at the same time. By midnight, the entire operation was on the verge of disaster. Of Washington's three forces, two were defeated by ice on the river. Only the northern force remained at McConkey's ferry. But there, at the water's edge, one important part of the plan went right. A large flotilla of small river craft was waiting when the men arrived. The Jersey militia of Hunterdon County had done their work well. Specially prized were the big Durham boats, sturdy freight boats built to carry heavy cargoes for the Durham Iron Works, after which they were named. Some were thirty or forty feet long, and others as large as sixty feet. A crew of four or five steered them downstream with oars and long eighteen-foot sweeps, and pushed them upstream with long "setting poles."

To manage the boats, the army recruited three groups of watermen. Most prominent were the men of Colonel John Glover's Marblehead regiment, salty seamen and fishermen from the North Shore of New England. These were the same men who helped to rescue the American army from Long Island and fought in the campaigns around New York. Once again they were doing double duty as boatmen and infantry.

The crossing was a challenge to all their skill that night. Ice had formed on the river and had broken apart into floating cakes and floes. The current had jammed large pieces along the banks in thick jagged rows. Washington had given command of the crossing to Henry Knox. He was a big, heavy man, taller than Washington and weighing in at nearly three hundred pounds. Many men remembered his "deep bass voice," which they could hear above the roar of the nor'easter. In the end it was nearly four o'clock in the morning when the American army began to march. The mission was now four hours behind schedule.

As they had planned, Washington ordered the army to divide at Birmingham crossroads. His generals knew their assignments. Nathanael Greene had the hardest task. He was to lead his division left at Birmingham crossroads to the Upper Ferry Road. It ran uphill away from the river to the Scotch Road and the Pennington Road, which would bring Greene's division into Trenton on its northern side. The other division of the army under Sullivan had orders to continue on the River Road and "enter the town by Water Street." On reaching the town, both divisions had the same instructions, which were to drive forward and attack with great speed and force. Sleet and snow were falling heavily again, with intervals of heavy rain. The men struggled to keep their flints and powder dry.

George Washington himself led the attack in the center. The time was a little past eight o'clock. Three minutes later, the heavy boom of American artillery was heard from the lower River Road. In the center of the town, German kettledrums suddenly began to beat the urgent call to arms. Both American wings attacked at nearly the same moment, through a heavy squall of snow that masked their approach. Against all expectation, they had taken the Hessians by surprise. The American brigades pressed forward. Washington ordered Fermoy's troops to move east across the country to block the Princeton Road.

On the River Road, the other wing of the American army advanced toward the lower end of the town at the same time. General Sullivan led from the front, with Captain John Flahaven's New Jersey troops in the van and Colonel John Stark's New Hampshire brigade close behind. John Stark had a reputation as a fighter. He was devoted to the Revolutionary cause and wrote to his wife that he was determined to "live free or die," a phrase that his state later made its motto. As the Hessian Jägers retreated toward Trenton, the Americans launched yet another part of their attack. Massed artillery on the Pennsylvania side of the Delaware began firing into the town. Trenton was now under heavy attack from three sides.

Colonel Rall decided to fight the Americans by attacking directly against their main strength inside the town of Trenton. It was a mistake of historic consequence. The American artillery overpowered the Hessian guns and laid down a concentration of fire at the vital center of the battle. Behind the German guns, the grenadiers of the Rall regiment in King Street were now exposed to the American artillery. They recoiled in disorder. Colonel Rall appeared, always in the thick of the fight.

Rall led both regiments of Hessian infantry east to a large apple orchard just behind the houses and turned them north. On the high ground above, George Washington saw the Hessian regiments rally in the apple orchard and watched them start up the hill toward his flank. Washington's quick reaction checked Rall's advance just as it was getting under way.

In the center of Trenton the battle became a bedlam of sound. The streets echoed with the thunder of artillery, the crash of iron on brick and stone, the noise of splintering wood and shattering glass, the roar of musketry, the clash of steel against steel, the mingled shouts and curses, and the cries of wounded men. Under heavy fire, the charge of Hessians failed. Reuber, the Hessian grenadier, believed that the turning point was the loss of Colonel Rall.

Colonel John Greenwood remembered that "General Washington, on horseback and alone, came up to our major and said, 'March on, my brave fellows, after me!' and rode off." Most American soldiers in this battle shared that memory of serving by the side of General Washington. They knew him not only as a leader but a comrade in arms.

The Americans had won a decisive victory. Altogether the Hessians lost 918 men. Of that number 22 were killed and 83 were seriously wounded. They seized enough material to equip several American brigades. Most prized by the victors were six excellent German cannon. Nobody counted the deaths from all causes during the campaign, but there are many indications that the number was not small.

On December 27, 1776, the Continental army struggled home to its camps in Pennsylvania. The men were worn out. They had marched and fought for sixty hours through snow, rain, sleet, and hail. Many were ill with fever, catarrh, consumption, and dysentery. Most were suffering from frozen faces, frostbitten hands, and lacerated feet.

Washington and his officers set a high standard in their treatment of Hessian captives at Trenton. He issued instructions that "the officers and men should be separated. I wish the former may be well treated, and that the latter may have such principles instilled in them during their Confinement, that when they return, they may open the Eyes of their Countrymen."

In Europe, the news from Trenton stimulated a controversy on the Hessian presence in America, the morality of the *Soldatenhandel*, or soldier trade, and the legitimacy of the government that engaged in it. Before 1776, this commerce had been widely accepted in Europe. After 1777 it came under strong attack. The affair at Trenton was a major factor, for it added the sting of defeat to the stain of moral disgrace. The events on the Delaware did not begin the debate on the soldier trade, but greatly expanded it. They also enlarged the international debate on the American Revolution and raised questions about the legitimacy of Europe's old regime. In all of these ways, the battle of Trenton transformed attitudes toward the War of Independence on both sides of the Atlantic.

The small battles near the Delaware were a collision between two discoveries about the human condition that were made in the early modern era. One of them was the discovery that people could organize a society on the basis of liberty and freedom, and could actually make it work. The ideas themselves were not new in the world, but for the first time, entire social and political systems were constructed primarily on that foundation.

Another new discovery was about the capacity of human beings for order and discipline. For many millennia, people had been made to serve others, but this was something more than that. It was an invention of new methods by which people could be trained to engage their will and creativity in the service of another: by drill and ritual, reward and punishment, persuasion and belief. Further, they could be trained to do so not as slaves or servants or robots, but in an active and willing way.

Washington and his generals decided to return to Trenton to force the British from West Jersey. After another difficult crossing of the Delaware River on December 30–31, following a six-inch snowfall and in bitter cold, Washington had to confront a greater problem: the enlistments of many experienced soldiers would expire on December 31. General Thomas Mifflin led Pennsylvania merchants in offering a bounty of ten dollars to each militiaman who would fight for six more weeks. Washington made a personal appeal with the same offer to the Continentals. They agreed, and Robert Morris, the Philadelphia merchant who was elected by Congress in 1781 to be Superintendent of Finance, found the money. Washington concentrated his 7,000 Continentals and militiamen in a fortified position on high ground south of the Assunpink Creek.

General Howe canceled General Cornwallis's leave and ordered him to return from New York to command the 8,000-man British force. In the second battle of Trenton on January 1–2, 1777, the British made unsuccessful attacks at the bridge across the creek and retreated. In *Washington's Crossing*, David Hackett Fischer describes the soldiers' courage.

This was the second battle of Trenton, an event largely missed until the accounts of many individual soldiers and junior officers on both sides emerged to document it in detail. It was not a general engagement, not an all-out assault by the British and Hessian forces, but a series of

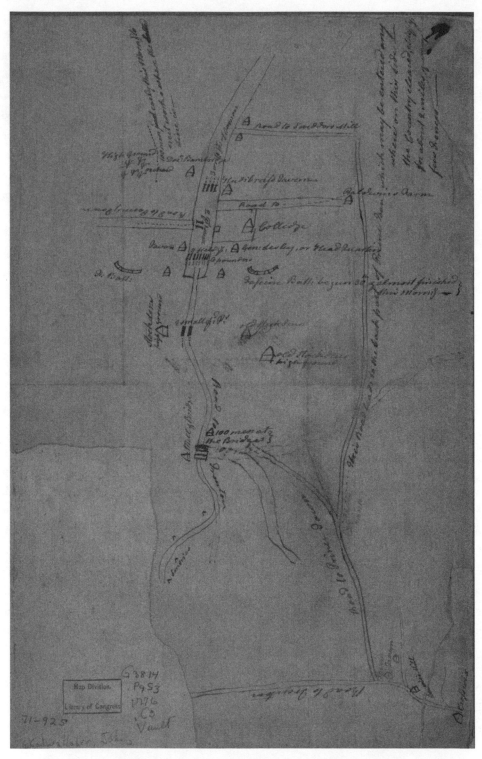

Revolutionary War Spy Map, 1777. John Cadwalader. *Plan of Princeton, Dec. 31, 1776* [1776]. *(Courtesy, Library of Congress, Geography and Map Division. http://hdl.loc.gov/loc.gmd/g3814p.ct000076)*

probing attacks, driven home with high courage by the Regulars. For the American troops it was a great victory. For their general it was a model of a brilliantly managed defensive battle in the same town where Colonel Rall had fought, but with very different results.

General Washington prepared for the attack on Princeton by sending a young spy into the town. This map (see opposite page) shows his information about British troop positions, defensive fortifications, and unprotected roads.

38. Princeton, New Jersey

JANUARY 3, 1777

PRINCETON BATTLEFIELD STATE PARK
500 MERCER ROAD
PRINCETON, NEW JERSEY

After the second battle of Trenton, Washington called a meeting of his general officers. They decided to attack Princeton. During the night of January 2–3, 1777, Washington ordered his soldiers to leave their campfires burning and march east of General Cornwallis's army toward Princeton. A drop in the temperature froze the formerly muddy roads.

Cornwallis had ordered Lieutenant Colonel Charles Mawhood to bring reinforcements from Princeton to Trenton. About daybreak on January 3 as Mawhood marched toward Trenton, the battle began between his force and General Hugh Mercer's 350-man brigade on the Quaker Road six miles from Princeton. In *A Battlefield Atlas of the American Revolution*, Craig L. Symonds describes this Washington victory.

> The two sides exchanged volleys, but the Americans were weary from so much marching and fighting in the past week and they could not stand up to a British bayonet charge. They broke and fled. Only when Washington himself appeared on the scene did the Americans rally. Washington assumed personal command and led them to the attack. "Parade with us, my brave fellows," he called out to those headed for the rear. "There is but a handful of the enemy, and we will have them directly!" Other American forces, marching to the sound of the guns, closed in on Mawhood's flanks. The British were nearly surrounded and they began to fall back. The jubilant Americans pursued them for several miles and rounded up fifty prisoners, but Washington called off the pursuit to turn his attention to the British regiment that Mawhood had left behind in Princeton. Most of that now-orphaned regiment escaped to New Brunswick, but nearly 200 barricaded themselves in Nassau Hall. Captain Alexander Hamilton brought up an artillery piece, fired two rounds into the building, and ordered a charge. The British capitulated.

Washington had achieved another improbable victory. The Americans had suffered 23 killed, among them the promising General Mercer, and 20 wounded. The British lost 28 killed, 58 wounded, and 323 captured. Washington was eager to continue up the chain of British outposts to New Brunswick, but the condition of his elated but exhausted men convinced him that he had pushed his luck about as far as it would go. He headed instead for his winter campsite in Morristown.

39. Nassau Hall, New Jersey

PRINCETON UNIVERSITY
PRINCETON, NEW JERSEY

Princeton University, then known as the College of New Jersey, opened Nassau Hall, a three-story sandstone building designed by Robert Smith, in November 1756. While the British occupied Princeton, they used Nassau Hall as a barracks, a storage facility, and a jail. During the January 1777 battle of Princeton, Captain Alexander Hamilton's artillery forced the British soldiers in the hall to surrender. It was heavily damaged during the war and only partially restored when the Continental Congress met in the Hall between June and November of 1783. The delegates had fled Philadelphia to avoid the soldiers demanding their back pay. After the Hall burned in 1802, the architect Benjamin H. Latrobe supervised the reconstruction.

General Washington reported to Congress on the battle in his letter to John Hancock, included in *This Glorious Struggle*, edited by Edward G. Lengel.

Washington won another victory at Princeton on January 3, but it was a close-run affair.

Pluckamin [N.J.] January 5th 1777

Sir

From the best Information I have received, Genl Howe has left no Men either at Trenton or Princeton. The truth of this I am endeavouring to ascertain that I may regulate my movements accordingly—The Militia are taking spirit and I am told, are coming in fast from this State, but I fear those from Philadelphia will scarce submit to the hardships of a winter Campaign much longer, especially as they very unluckily sent their Blankets with their Baggage to Burlington—I must do them the justice however to add, that they have undergone more fatigue and hardship than I expected Militia (especially Citizens) would have done at this inclement Season. I am just moving to Morris town where I shall endeavor to put them under the best cover I can. hitherto we have been without any, many of our poor Soldiers quite bear foot & ill clad in other respects. I have the Honor to be with great respect Sir Yr Most Obedt

Go: Washington.

In *Washington's Crossing,* David Hackett Fischer highlights the Americans' policy of humanity in the New Jersey campaign and in the war.

> Congress and the Continental army generally adopted Adams's "policy of humanity." Their moral choices in the War of Independence enlarged the meaning of the American Revolution.
>
> The most remarkable fact about American soldiers and civilians in the New Jersey campaign is that they did all of these things at the same time. In a desperate struggle they found a way to defeat a formidable enemy, not merely once at Trenton but many times in twelve weeks of continued combat. They reversed the momentum of the war. They improvised a new way of war that grew into an American tradition. And they chose a policy of humanity that aligned the conduct of the war with the values of the Revolution.
>
> They set a high example, and we have much to learn from them. Much recent historical writing has served us ill in that respect. In the late twentieth century, too many scholars tried to make the American past into a record of crime and folly. Too many writers have told us that we are captives of our darker selves and helpless victims of our history. It isn't so, and never was. The story of Washington's Crossing tells us that Americans in an earlier generation were capable of acting in a higher spirit—and so are we.

40. Morristown, New Jersey

Morristown National Historical Park
Morristown, New Jersey

Washington's army left Princeton on January 3, 1777, just before the British arrived, and marched toward Somerset and on to Morristown. Washington chose Morristown for the Continental Army's main winter encampment from January 6 until May 28. Its advantages included its distance from New York City—about a two-day march—which made it relatively secure from a surprise British attack. In the Morristown area there was also adequate wood for the men to cut for firewood and to build their huts.

In *His Excellency: George Washington,* Joseph J. Ellis points to the significance of Washington's decisions at Morristown.

> He made two important decisions at Morristown. First, he recognized that the smallpox problem required a more comprehensive solution. "If the Hospitals are in no better condition," he told Hancock, "our Regiments will be reduced to Companies by the end of the Campaign, and those poor Wretches who escape with life, will either be scattered up and down the Country and not to be found, or if found, totally enervated and unfit for further duty." Given

his manpower difficulty, he could ill afford to see a quarter of his troops incapacitated, as had occurred in New York; or else, he warned, "we must look for Reinforcements to some other places than our own States," presumably referring to the Kingdom of Heaven. In March 1777 he made inoculation mandatory and set up special hospitals in Philadelphia to implement the new policy.

Second, less out of conviction than a realistic recognition of his limited resources, Washington came to accept the fact that he must adopt a more defensive strategy and fight a "War of Posts." Also called a "Fabian strategy" after the Roman general Fabius Cunctator, who defeated the Carthaginians by withdrawing whenever his army's fate was at risk, it was a shift in thinking that did not come naturally to Washington. A Fabian strategy, like guerrilla and terrorist strategies of the twentieth century, was the preferred approach of the weak. Washington did not believe that he was weak, and he thought of the Continental army as a projection of himself. He regarded battle as a summons to display one's strength and courage; avoiding battle was akin to dishonorable behavior, like refusing to move forward in the face of musket and cannon fire. Nevertheless, he was now forced to face what he called "the melancholy Truths." New York had demonstrated that the Continental army could not compete on equal terms with British regulars on the conventional battlefield; and given the reduced size of his current force, "it is impossible, at least very unlikely, that any effectual opposition can be given to the British Army with the Troops we have." The most bitter and melancholy truth of all was that popular support for the war, the essential engine for producing new recruits, continued to sputter despite the Trenton and Princeton victories. (One French partisan of the cause claimed that "there is a hundred times more enthusiasm for the Revolution in any Paris cafe than in all the colonies together.") In effect, he had no choice but to become an American Fabius, or else simply surrender.

In late March 1777 he dispatched Nathanael Greene to brief the Continental Congress on his revised strategy. "I explained to the House your Excellency's Ideas of the next Campaign," Greene reported; "it appeared to be new to them." The Congress was apparently taken aback, because a Fabian strategy meant that Washington did not intend to defend Philadelphia at all costs if Howe chose to make it his target. His highest priority was not to occupy or protect ground, but rather to harass Howe while preserving his army. Adams, writing from Philadelphia, assured Abigail that he was safe: "We are under no more apprehensions here than if the British Army was in the Crimea. Our Fabius will be slow, but sure."

After an inactive winter and spring, General William Howe left New York and took command of the 16,000-man British army in New Jersey. On June 13, 1777, he marched to battle against Washington's army. The Americans' harassing actions were successful, and suffering from them and from the intense heat, the British withdrew to New York in late June. John Buchanan outlines the American strategy in 1777 in *The Road to Valley Forge*.

On 30 June 1777, the last units of the British army in New Jersey embarked on vessels for the short sail across the Kill van Kull to Staten Island, their efforts of the past eight months for naught. The opponents were right back where they had started the previous November, and the effects on the British army were ominous: the other ranks sullen, the officers in despair, Sir William Howe's reputation in tatters.

The New Jersey campaign of 1776–1777 was one of the most important of the war. It went from patriot despair at Washington's miserable retreat through the length of the state in 1776 to passionate joy over the victories at Trenton and Princeton. But the partisan campaign in the winter and spring of 1777 and Washington's refusal to be drawn into battle have received few accolades, although they combined to foil Sir William and drive his army to distraction.

Twenty-two-year-old Alexander Hamilton, then an aide-de-camp to Washington, penned one of the best contemporary descriptions of American strategy at the time and the principles behind it:

> I know the comments that some people will make on our Fabian conduct. It will be imputed either to cowardice or to weakness; But the more discerning, I trust, will not find it difficult to conceive that it proceeds from the truest policy, and is an argument neither of the one nor the other. The liberties of America are an infinite stake. We should not play a desperate game for it or put it upon the issue of a single cast of the die. The loss of one general engagement may effectually ruin us, and it would certainly be folly to hazard it, unless our resources for keeping up an army were at an end, and some decisive blow was absolutely necessary; or unless our strength was so great as to give certainty of success. Neither is the case.

He then summed up in one sentence the strategy of the campaign during the first half of 1777: "Our business then is to avoid a General engagement and waste the enemy away by constantly goading their sides, in a desultory, teasing way."

---

41. Ridgefield and Compo Hill, Connecticut

APRIL 26–28, 1777

RIDGEFIELD, CONNECTICUT
MINUTE MAN STATUE ON COMPO ROAD SOUTH
WESTPORT, CONNECTICUT

During the course of the Revolution, the British disrupted shipping along the coast and raided Connecticut towns in which supplies for the Continental Army were stored. William Tryon, the royal governor of New York who had taken refuge on a British ship in 1775, returned to a command in the army in 1777. On April 26, he sailed from New York, landed, and raided Danbury. Generals Wooster and Arnold attacked the British in Ridgefield.

On April 28 Arnold continued the running battle at Compo Hill as the British fought their way back to their ships.

In *Tories: Fighting for the King in America's First Civil War,* Thomas B. Allen recounts the raids led by Tryon at Danbury and Ridgefield.

A Loyalist spy identified only as "The Woman" reported "a very considerable Store of Provisions & cloathing and 80 pieces of Cannon" in Danbury, Connecticut, near the New York border, about twenty-five miles from the coast. General Howe authorized Tryon to lead a fleet of twenty-six ships to the mouth of the Saugatuck River, where he landed more than eighteen hundred men, including both Regulars and the Prince of Wales's American Volunteers Brigade. Tryon's style of pitiless warfare did not appeal to Howe, but this time he gave Tryon a sizable force because pilfering or destroying the Rebels' supplies made military sense.

Tryon met little opposition as his men marched to Danbury, where local Loyalists guided them to supply caches. The troops invaded and pillaged Patriots' homes, careful to spare the Anglican church and Loyalists' homes. Great piles of tents and provisions and thousands of shoes went up in flames. His mission accomplished, Tryon led his troops back toward the coast. But he discovered that his way was blocked by militiamen who had been hastily mobilized and led by Brig. Gens. David Wooster and Benedict Arnold.

Arnold was home in New Haven, brooding about the Congress's failure to promote him to major general, when at three o'clock one morning a messenger came with the report that a large force of Regulars and Tories had landed near Westport and were bivouacked in Weston, obviously on their way to Danbury. Arnold galloped off and was soon joined by sixty-six-year-old David Wooster, commander of the Connecticut militia. They quickly gathered one hundred mounted militiamen. Meanwhile Brig. Gen. Gold Selleck Silliman, commander of the Fairfield militia, had rounded up about five hundred more.

The next day Tryon left a burning Danbury behind him as he led his troops back to the shore and the waiting transports. He stopped at Ridgefield, where he supervised the torching of a Presbyterian church and seven Patriots' homes. Local Loyalists were said to have been spared because they had painted black and white stripes on their chimneys. Militiamen trailed Tryon's force, starting a short, fierce battle in which Wooster was fatally shot. A Continental soldier saw Arnold ride "to our front line in the full force of the Enemy's fire of Musquetry & Grape shot." His horse, riddled by nine shots, fell, trapping Arnold, who had been lamed in Quebec when a musket ball struck his left leg. As he struggled to free himself, a Redcoat demanded surrender at bayonet point. Arnold fatally shot him with a pistol and managed to escape.

Fighting continued on the third day, when Arnold, Silliman, and scores of additional militiamen arrived, firing at the invaders from houses, stone walls, and barricades. Arnold had another horse shot from under him as Royal Marines from the fleet landed and turned the battle, opening the way for the invaders to make it to boats that took them to the ships. In the three days of the invasion, about two hundred men in Tryon's forces were killed or wounded, as were about sixty militiamen.

42. Keeler Tavern, Connecticut

KEELER TAVERN MUSEUM, MAIN STREET
RIDGEFIELD, CONNECTICUT

The Keeler Tavern, built in 1713, became T. Keeler's Inn in 1772 and was a center of patriot resistance during the war. It was hit by artillery fire during the battle of Ridgefield on April 26–28, 1777, and a cannonball remains embedded in a corner post.

After the battle, Congress promoted Benedict Arnold to major general but did not restore his seniority over the five officers whom Congress had recently promoted over him to the same rank. In *Benedict Arnold, Revolutionary Hero,* James Kirby Martin points out the problems in the relationships of Congress with the Continental generals in 1777, especially General Philip Schuyler, the northern commander, and General Horatio Gates.

Among the politically favored officers, Gates came sprinting back to Philadelphia in mid-June after learning that Congress had sustained Schuyler in the northern command. He had no intention of again serving under the Yorker or as Washington's adjutant general. Nor did Gates seem to care that the main Continental army was on full military alert in New Jersey. Based on his actions, his singular concern was his own advancement over Schuyler.

Frothing with self-righteousness, Gates angrily presented himself to his New England friends as a man cruelly deceived by congressional allies. A chastened Roger Sherman cleared the way for Gates to be admitted to the floor of Congress on Wednesday, June 18, to present a report on military affairs in upper New York. To the delight of Schuyler's supporters, Gates soon lost his composure. He got into a shouting match with New York delegate James Duane, a close friend of Schuyler who took umbrage at the general's rambling commentary, which mostly had to do with Gates's sacrifices. The general eventually withdrew in a huff, even as pro-and anti-Schuyler delegates hurled insults at each other.

Attempting to regain their dignity, the delegates stated that any further communications from Gates should be in writing. That they did not vote to censure him as a general officer trying to influence their judgments, as they soon did with Knox, Greene, and Sullivan, was not lost on Benedict Arnold. What Congress had revealed was its own double standard. The delegates did not hold officers with significant political influence to the same punctilio of compliant behavior as those who lacked a strong base of congressional support. Arnold knew that if he had acted so indecorously, the delegates would have quickly called him to account. At no point, however, did Congress so much as hint that Gates should consider resigning, even though he had exhibited as much impertinence toward that body's decision-making prerogatives as had Knox, Greene, and Sullivan.

43. Fort St. Mark, Florida

CASTILLO DE SAN MARCOS NATIONAL MONUMENT
11 SOUTH CASTILLO DRIVE
ST. AUGUSTINE, FLORIDA

The contest for control of Florida during the Revolution was between the Americans and the British. In the early sixteenth century, it was between France and Spain. In September 1565, Admiral Pedro Menéndez de Avilés took possession of Florida for Spain and founded St. Augustine. The Spanish began building the masonry star fort, Castillo de San Marcos, in 1672. After the signing of the 1763 Treaty of Paris, the English took control of Florida and gave the fort an English name, Fort St. Mark. General Augustine Prevost became the commander of all forces in East and West Florida in 1776 and improved the defenses.

During the Revolution, East Florida was controlled by the British and was a haven for loyalists and their Seminole allies. Patrick Tonyn was the royal governor. The fort was the center of British military operations in East Florida, a supply base, and a prison. Americans tried repeatedly to capture it but always failed.

Britain ceded East and West Florida to Spain in 1783. The fort was once again Castillo de San Marcos. Florida became a US territory in 1821, and the fort was called Fort Marion. Florida became the twenty-seventh state in 1845, and in 1942 Congress restored the fort's original name.

44. Thomas Creek, Florida

MAY 17, 1777

HISTORICAL MARKER ON US 1 AT THOMAS CREEK
SOUTH OF CALLAHAN

The Americans in Georgia tried repeatedly to capture St. Augustine and stop the raids into Georgia by the East Florida Rangers and their Indian allies. On May 1, 1777, Colonel John Baker with 109 Georgia militiamen rode from Sunbury, Georgia, and arrived in East Florida on May 12. They waited at Sawpit Bluff for Colonel Samuel Elbert, whose flotilla was delayed by swollen rivers. The loyalists tracking Baker alerted their Seminole allies, who attacked Baker on May 4 and again on the night of May 14. On May 17 Lieutenant Colonel Thomas Brown leading forty loyalist Rangers, their Indian allies, and

100 British regulars led by Major Mark Prevost ambushed and defeated Baker's force at the battle of Thomas Creek. There were twelve American casualties. The Seminoles killed fifteen of the thirty-one militiamen taken prisoner; one of their warriors had been killed in the May 14 attack. On May 19, fifteen of Baker's troops met up with Elbert, who had arrived on Amelia Island the day before and reported on the defeat. Elbert returned to Satilla, Georgia.

45. Fort Tonyn and Alligator Creek Bridge, Florida

JUNE 30, 1778

HISTORICAL MARKER ON US 1 AT THE ALLIGATOR CREEK BRIDGE CALLAHAN, FLORIDA

The British built a fort on the St. Mary's River and named it for the East Florida royal governor, Patrick Tonyn. In June of 1778, the Continentals planned an attack on the fort: Georgia Continentals led by Major General Robert Howe, South Carolina Continentals led by Colonel Charles Cotesworth Pinckney, and South Carolina militia led by Colonel Andrew Williamson would join Georgia militia led by Governor Houstoun near the Altamaha River and attack with 3,600 troops. They arrived ten miles north of Fort Tonyn on June 25. When the Georgia militia arrived on June 28, Houstoun refused to permit his militia to be commanded by Howe. The compromise they reached was that Houstoun would march toward the forces blocking the King's Road at Alligator Creek Bridge while the army would take Fort Tonyn. The army's slow advance and the loyalists' reports on them gave the East Florida Rangers led by Colonel Thomas Brown time to burn the fort and retreat to Cabbage Swamp, south of the fort. Howe arrived at the remains of the fort on June 29 and fortified it.

After a short battle at Alligator Creek Bridge on June 30, an outnumbered detachment of Georgia militia led by Brigadier General Screven retreated to Houstoun's main force and north into Georgia. In the battle there were about fifteen casualties for each force. Howe occupied Fort Tonyn until July 11 when his soldiers burned it and retreated to Satilla, Georgia. More than 300 of his men had died and half of those who returned were sick. This was the third and final unsuccessful attempt by Americans to take control of East Florida.

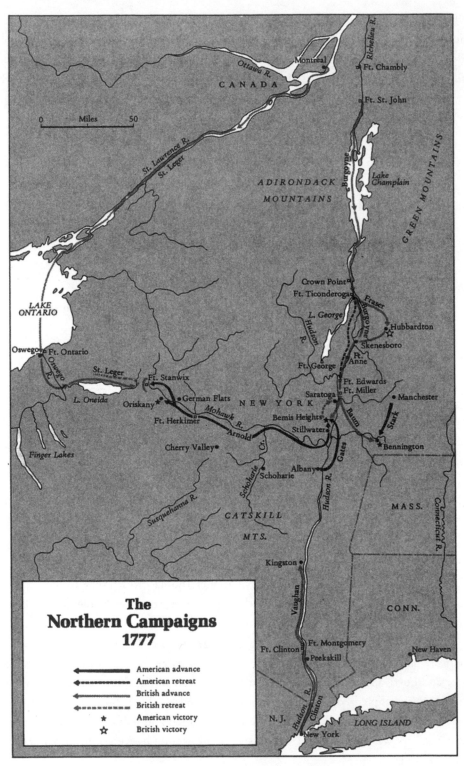

The
Northern Campaigns
1777

⟵ American advance
⟵ - - American retreat
⟵ British advance
⟵ - - British retreat
★ American victory
☆ British victory

From: The Glorious Cause by Robert Middlekauff (1982). Map from p. 375. By permission of Oxford University Press, USA.

46. Fort Ticonderoga, New York

July 5–6, 1777

Fort Ticonderoga
Ticonderoga, New York

Fort Ticonderoga was the first battle in General John Burgoyne's 1777 campaign from Canada south down the Hudson River. The battles are detailed in places #46–#57 and #60–#61. In *The American Revolution*, Gordon S. Wood presents an overview of the British strategy in 1777 and the consequences.

The British strategy for 1777 involved sending an army of 8,000, including 3,000 Germans and several hundred Indians, under General John Burgoyne southward from Canada by way of Lake Champlain to recapture Fort Ticonderoga. Near Albany, Burgoyne was to join a secondary force under Lieutenant Colonel Barry St. Leger, moving eastward through the Mohawk Valley, and General Howe, advancing northward from New York City through the Hudson Valley. The ultimate aim of the campaign was to isolate New England and break the back of the rebellion. It was assumed in Britain that General Howe would cooperate with Burgoyne. But Howe continued to believe that there was widespread loyalist support in the middle states and decided to capture Philadelphia, the seat of the congressional government. Howe moved on Philadelphia by sea and landed after much delay at the head of Chesapeake Bay in late August 1777. Believing he could not give up the Continental capital without a struggle, Washington confronted Howe at Brandywine, Pennsylvania, on September 11 and later on October 4 at Germantown and was defeated in both battles. But his defeats were not disastrous. They proved that the American army was capable of organized combat. And they prevented Howe from moving north to help Burgoyne. Howe's capture of Philadelphia demonstrated that loyalist sentiment reached only as far as British arms, and it scarcely justified what happened to Burgoyne's army in the North.

After St. Leger's force was turned back at Oriskany, New York, in the summer of 1777, Burgoyne and his huge, slow-moving entourage from Canada increasingly found their supply lines stretched thin and their flanks harassed by patriot militia from New England. Burgoyne's baggage train was over three miles long; his personal baggage alone took up over thirty carts. By felling trees, destroying bridges, and diverting streams, the patriots did all they could to make the wild terrain even more impassable than it was. Burgoyne had to build over forty new bridges as well as repair old ones. At one point he was covering less than one mile a day. This sluggish pace only worsened the problem of supply. One of his lieutenants declared that for every hour Burgoyne spent thinking how to fight his army he had to devote twenty hours figuring out how to feed it.

While Burgoyne's slow advance gave the American forces in the Hudson Valley needed time to collect themselves, the British army was diminishing. When 900 of Burgoyne's men attempted to seize provisions from a patriot arsenal in Bennington, Vermont, they were defeated by 2,000 New England militia under John Stark. Another 900 redcoats were detached to garrison Ticonderoga. Believing that his reputation rested on the success of his Canadian invasion, Burgoyne determined to press on. On September 13–14 he crossed the Hudson, cutting off his supply lines and communications with his rear. When he reached Saratoga, he confronted a growing American force of over 10,000 men under General Horatio Gates. Two bloody battles, in which General Benedict Arnold distinguished himself, convinced Burgoyne of the hopelessness of his situation, and in October 1777 he surrendered his entire army to the Americans.

Saratoga was the turning point. It suggested the reconquest of America might be beyond British strength. It brought France openly into the struggle. And it led to a change in the British command and a fundamental alteration in strategy.

In May 1775 an American force had captured Fort Ticonderoga (see #10). On July 2, 1777, General John Burgoyne ordered his army to advance against the fort. General Arthur St. Clair was in command of Fort Ticonderoga, Mount Independence, and the 2,800-man garrison. On July 5 General Simon Fraser's soldiers succeeded in hauling artillery up Mount Defiance (Sugar Loaf). In *1777: The Year of the Hangman,* John S. Pancake points to the fort's complex design as the problem for its defenders.

Ticonderoga was built on a high bluff overlooking the narrow neck of water at the upper end of Lake Champlain. Stretching to the south and east an arm of the lake continued for almost twenty miles to Skenesboro. Lake George formed a parallel arm to the west connected to Lake Champlain by an unnavigable creek. The fort was commanded by Major General Arthur St. Clair. Although the fort had undergone considerable repairs since its capture by the Americans in 1775, its defense still posed a number of problems.

In order to understand the geography of Ticonderoga it should be remembered that Lake Champlain makes a turn to the west so that a vessel sailing through the narrows to the upper arm of the lake is heading only one or two points south of due west. The headland on which the fort was located lay less than half a mile from the opposite shore which was dominated by a hill called Mount Independence. Since it was within cannon shot of Ticonderoga it had to be fortified. The American garrison had connected Mount Independence with the fort by a boat bridge and had constructed a log and chain boom across the narrows. They believed that this would effectively block the passage of vessels into the upper arm of Lake Champlain. They had also cleared a rough track through the forest from Mount Independence eastward to Hubbardton to link with the main road to the Hampshire Grants in Vermont. To the southwest of Fort Ticonderoga another hill called Sugar Loaf (Mount Defiance) rose 800 feet above the lake. Although it was only 1800 yards from the fort its slopes were considered too steep and rugged to allow guns to be mounted. The land approaches from the west were protected by a crescent-shaped series of trenches and redoubts called "the old French lines." Finally, to the northwest was Mount Hope which guarded the road and the stream from Lake George. Altogether Ticonderoga and its supporting positions constituted 2,000 yards of lines, fortifications and outworks.

The fort had been built originally by the French in 1755 and subsequent occupants had added to and refined it along lines dictated by European military engineers. Because it had figured so prominently in the military history of North America, Ticonderoga had acquired an impressive mystique as the "Gibraltar of North America." Its complex of lines and ramparts epitomized the kind of strong point which figured so prominently in the European doctrine of strategic posts guarding important geographic areas. The British were sure that Ticonderoga was the key to the conquest of New York, if not the entire continent, and Americans, including General Washington, thought so too. Their political ideology might be revolutionary but American military strategy was orthodox European.

The very complexity of the fortress was its greatest point of weakness. The French, the English, and now the Americans found that establishing and maintaining a garrison large enough to man the entire works presented formidable problems in logistics. This was why the fort had fallen so easily to the Americans in 1775, and it may well have been the consideration that led Carleton to abandon the upper end of Lake Champlain in 1776.

Burgoyne reached Crown Point in the last week in June and set up a temporary base. From there he moved his troops to a point about three miles from Ticonderoga and began to disembark. Fraser's advance corps and the British right wing were assigned to the western side of the lake with Riedesel and the Germans on the east. On July 2 Burgoyne ordered the advance. Riedesel's command was to move against Mount Independence and seal off the road to Hubbardton. Fraser was ordered to circle to the west and attack the old French lines. He also expected to cut off the garrison at Mount Hope, but St. Clair forestalled him. Early on the morning of the 2nd the garrison set fire to their works and hurried into the American lines.

The evacuation of Mount Hope gave the British access to the Sugar Loaf. One of Burgoyne's engineers, Lieutenant Twiss, reported to General Phillips that he thought a battery could be gotten to the summit. The old artilleryman was quick to seize the opportunity. "Where a goat can go a man can go and where a man can go he can drag a gun," he said and turned his furious energy to the task. By the morning of July 5 the British had a battery mounted which commanded both the interior of the fort and the narrows of the lake.

St. Clair did not hesitate. He paused only long enough for a hasty council of war to confirm his decision and then ordered a retreat. The baggage, the sick, and a guard of 600 soldiers were loaded into boats and evacuated up Lake Champlain towards Skenesboro. The rest of the army crossed the bridge under cover of darkness to Mount Independence. Scouts reported that the road to Hubbardton was still open so the army began its withdrawal. So silently did the Americans move that not until almost daylight did General Fraser realize they were gone.

47. Mount Independence, Vermont

JULY 5–6, 1777

MOUNT INDEPENDENCE STATE HISTORIC SITE
497 MOUNT INDEPENDENCE ROAD
ORWELL, VERMONT

In July 1776, soldiers had begun clearing the bluff on a high peninsula across Lake Champlain from Fort Ticonderoga. After the reading of the Declaration of Independence to the soldiers on July 28, 1776, it was named Mount Independence. Before most of the men left for the winter, they constructed a log boom across the lake and a floating bridge.

After withdrawing from Mount Independence, General St. Clair divided his force and took command of the larger one. He marched south to Hubbardton on a rough track cut through the woods. Colonel Pierce Long led the smaller force—his 600 New Hampshire soldiers and men from other regiments—and sailed south on Lake Champlain in five armed galleys and a convoy of bateaus. With them were women, children, invalids, and the heavy wagons and artillery.

General Burgoyne ordered 850 British regulars commanded by Brigadier General Simon Fraser and reinforced by 180 Germans led by Major General Baron Friedrich Adolph von Riedesel, to pursue St. Clair. Burgoyne broke through the log boom across the lake and sailed after Colonel Long with the rest of his forces.

After St. Clair evacuated Fort Ticonderoga and Mount Independence on July 6, 1777, the British and Germans occupied them and built more defenses. Following Burgoyne's surrender at Saratoga in October 1777, the British burned Mount Independence and left in November.

48. Hubbardton, Vermont

JULY 7, 1777

HUBBARDTON BATTLEFIELD STATE HISTORIC SITE
5696 MONUMENT HILL ROAD
HUBBARDTON, VERMONT

On the retreat from Fort Ticonderoga and Mount Independence, General Arthur St. Clair detached Colonel Ebenezer Francis and his 450-man command to serve as the rear guard. Before St. Clair headed south to Castle Town, he ordered Colonel Seth Warner to await Francis's force and take command of the rear guard. The 1,000–1,200 men included Francis's troops, Warner's 150 Green Mountain Boys from Vermont, and those from New Hampshire led by Colonel Nathan Hale. The rear guard arrived on July 6 after a demanding march of more than twenty miles in intense heat, leading the sick and disabled. Warner decided to make camp instead of following St. Clair's orders which were to march his command to join St. Clair by sunrise.

Early the next morning, Warner's pickets spotted British scouts. The battle against Brigadier General Simon Fraser's forces began along Sucker Brook and continued as the Americans moved to a defensive position on Monument Hill. General Riedesel's Germans arrived to reinforce Fraser. Their bayonet charge was successful, and Francis was killed. Warner ordered a retreat and told his men to flee as best they could toward Rutland. Both sides suffered heavy casualties in the three-hour battle, the Americans more than 300 and the British, 200.

The losses were tragic for the soldiers and for the people of Hubbardton, as Richard M. Ketchum points out in *Saratoga: Turning Point of America's Revolutionary War*.

> The community that was only beginning to take root after three years of incessant hardship and toil was decimated. Life was no different here from any other American frontier, after all—hard, infinitely demanding, a battle by men, women, and children against everything nature could throw at them, plus the constant threat of Indians, disease, and death. Yet they had persevered and survived, and though they knew the British were attacking Ticonderoga it probably did not occur to them that they would be in the path of the marauders who swept through their community and threatened to destroy in a few hours what they had struggled for years to build. The soldiers who fought at Hubbardton were by no means the only victims, in other words: civilians paid a heavy price.

49. Elijah West's Tavern, Vermont

OLD CONSTITUTION HOUSE STATE HISTORIC SITE
16 NORTH MAIN STREET
WINDSOR, VERMONT

On July 8, 1777, seventy-two delegates meeting in Windsor in Elijah West's Tavern— now the Old Constitution House—voted on and accepted the Constitution of Vermont, an independent state. Its constitution included a remarkable ban—on slavery. It was the first constitution in America to prohibit slavery, to establish universal manhood suffrage without requiring property ownership or specific income for voting rights, and to establish a system of public schools. Vermont was an independent state until 1791, when it was admitted to the United States as the fourteenth state.

In *Enjoy the Same Liberty: Black Americans and the Revolutionary Era,* Edward Countryman details the Vermont ban on slavery.

Vermont tore itself free of New York in 1777, after years of guerilla resistance to New York authority by Ethan Allen and his fellow Green Mountain Boys. Like everybody who opted for independence, the Vermonters had to create a new government, on terms that suited themselves. They adopted a very simple democracy, borrowing almost word for word from the democratic state constitution that Pennsylvania created in 1776. But the Vermonters went one step further, proclaiming as the very first item on their Declaration of Rights that "no male person, born in this country, or brought from over sea, ought to be holden by law, to serve any person, as a servant, slave or apprentice, after he arrives to the age of twenty-one Years, nor female, in like manner, after she arrives to the age of eighteen years, unless they are bound by their own consent."

What the Vermonters proclaimed was momentous in the growing assault on slavery. Lord Dunmore had offered freedom to slaves "appertaining to rebels" who would fight, but not to all slaves. Jefferson tried to blame both slavery and slaves' resistance on the king. The Vermonters showed no hesitancy and no confusion. Their ban was immediate and they intended it to be absolute. The United States census of 1790 did record sixteen slaves in the state, but that was a clerical error. The people to whom it referred were free. The Vermonters would not take part in the slave trade. They would not accept that enslavement under "positive law" elsewhere meant enslavement among them. No male in their state over twenty-one and no female over eighteen could be bound except "by their own consent."

The numbers involved were tiny. In 1790 the United States census recorded 255 free black people in Vermont. Nonetheless, for the very first time in the whole history of the colonized western hemisphere, there was a place where every adult man and woman was presumed free, no exceptions. Vermont remained a separate republic until 1791, when slaveholding New York finally abandoned its claim that Vermont was only a "pretended state" that the Vermonters were really New York's "revolted subjects." Congress admitted it as a state, bringing it under the Constitution. Until then, any fugitive slave who reached its borders could have claimed the same "Freedom Principle" that held in mainland France, or could have sought freedom in a Vermont court just as the Somerset ruling allowed in England.

50. Skenesborough, New York

JULY 7, 1777

HISTORICAL MARKERS
WHITEHALL, NEW YORK

After capturing Fort Ticonderoga and Mount Independence (see #46 and #47), General Burgoyne had the choice of two routes as he continued his campaign south. One was to retreat north on Lake Champlain with his main force, make the difficult three-mile portage to Lake George, sail south on the lake, and then march the ten miles overland to the Hudson River. The other, which he chose, was to sail after Colonel Pierce Long to Skenesborough (now Whitehall) and march south on the east side of the Hudson River through the dense forests.

Long moved too slowly and was forced to abandon his supplies at Skenesborough and head for Fort Ann. Before Burgoyne could advance, he had to wait for eighteen days at Skenesborough for supplies to reach him from Canada via Fort Ticonderoga.

The small fleet that Brigadier General Benedict Arnold had commanded in the Valcour Island battle in October 1776 (see #30) was built in the boat yard at Skenesborough.

51. Fort Ann, New York

JULY 8, 1777

HISTORICAL MARKERS ON US 4
FORT ANN, NEW YORK

General Burgoyne sent Lieutenant Colonel John Hill's British regiment toward Fort Ann to keep open his route south along the Hudson. Captain James Gray, leading a scouting party, skirmished with Hill's regiment for four hours on July 7. The next morning Colonel Pierce Long, reinforced by 400 New York militiamen commanded by Colonel Henry Van Rensselaer, attacked Hill's camp. They were running low on ammunition when Gray's men heard what they thought were Indian war calls. Fearing an attack by Indians arriving to reinforce Hill, the militia set the fort on fire and headed south to Fort Edward about fifteen miles away. The calls that protected the British had been made by Captain John Money of the 9th Regiment, who was Burgoyne's deputy quartermaster general.

In *Saratoga,* Richard M. Ketchum quotes General Philip Schuyler, the northern commander, on the problems he was confronting.

> To George Washington he confided on July 14: "Desertion prevails and disease gains ground...for we have neither tents, houses, barns, boards, or any shelter except a little brush. Every rain that falls, and we have it in great abundance almost every day, wets the men to the skin. We are...in great want of every kind of necessary, provision excepted. Camp kettles we have so few, that we cannot afford one to twenty men." A day later he begged Major General William Heath to send anything he could spare—adding the piteous note that "our whole train of artillery consists of two iron field pieces."

In mid-July, General Washington marched the Continental Army to the west side of the Hudson River to be partway between Generals Howe and Burgoyne. General Howe had a new plan, to take Philadelphia from the south via the Chesapeake Bay. He gathered his army on Staten Island and sailed past Sandy Hook on July 23 with 16,000 troops on 267 ships.

Burgoyne's challenges included his supply line, as Richard Ketchum points out.

> The linchpin of the army's supply line was Ticonderoga and its dependencies, and Burgoyne considered it so important that he detached two regiments to garrison the place. At the moment, Brigadier General James Hamilton was in charge. Possibly the sharpest thorns in Hamilton's side were the rebel prisoners, who had to be fed, housed, and continuously watched. He had them working through all the daylight hours, but they lost no opportunity to slip away into the woods. Eventually he had most of the garrison and all his able-bodied prisoners working to get the immense stockpiles of food and ammunition to the army, because Ticonderoga had become the bottleneck in the army's supply line. These exhausted men spent day after day manhandling boats, supplies, equipment, and thirty-three artillery pieces up the portage and across Lake George.
>
> Now was the time the realities of a wilderness campaign conducted far from a base hit home like a blow to the stomach, and what had seemed simple when Burgoyne studied his options on a map in London began to take on a daunting complexity. The business of furnishing food, ammunition, and other necessities for a force of some seven thousand men plus women, camp followers, and animals was beginning to assume awesome proportions if for no reason other than the length of the supply line and the time it took for any essential items to travel from Montreal or Quebec to Skenesborough or beyond.

In *1777: The Year of the Hangman,* John S. Pancake describes General Burgoyne's march south, slowed by Schuyler's axmen.

> The fall of Ticonderoga generated shock waves in England and America. Its exaggerated importance as the key to the continent produced unwonted despair in Philadelphia, and jubilation in Whitehall. In Philadelphia there was dismay on all sides and savage denunciations of Schuyler, especially from the New Englanders. They now felt vindicated in their support of Gates for command of the Northern Department.
>
> As the clamor over his behavior swelled Schuyler went to Fort Edward to do what he could to restore the situation. Twenty-three miles separated him from Burgoyne's base at Skenesboro. Finally St. Clair came in from Castleton and Colonel John Nixon arrived from Peekskill with 600 Continentals. This brought Schuyler's command to just under 4,500 men, a mixed body of 2,800 Continentals and about 1,600 militia. Schuyler did not intend to make a stand at Fort Edward, but he did want to make life as miserable as possible for the British. Emboldened by the fact that Burgoyne sent no advance parties to secure the route to the Hudson the American commander sent a thousand ax men back into the woods and swamps. They systematically destroyed every bridge and causeway. They dug ditches to divert streams and turned stretches of the road into muddy bogs. For days their axes rang through the virgin timber, felling huge trees so that the branches interlaced to create a nightmare tangle along the road.

Having created a veritable jungle to delay the enemy, Schuyler abandoned the ramshackle works at Fort Edward and withdrew his force down the Hudson to Saratoga. There he halted and sent out urgent pleas for reinforcements, but he was losing men by desertion almost as fast as he gained recruits. By August 3 Schuyler had retreated again, this time to Stillwater, twenty-five miles south of Fort Edward. The constant withdrawal in the face of the enemy was calculated to make Burgoyne's line of communication at Ticonderoga more tenuous, but it nevertheless fueled the criticism of Schuyler which had been mounting ever since the abandonment of Ticonderoga. His appeals to Washington for help placed the commander in chief in a dilemma. General Howe had embarked his army on transports on July 23 and disappeared over the Atlantic horizon; with his destination unknown Washington hesitated to send more reinforcements northward. In an effort to stimulate militia response in New England he dispatched Benedict Arnold and Benjamin Lincoln to report to Schuyler.

It took the British several days to collect their scattered forces and their baggage after their headlong pursuit of the Americans. By July 10 they had begun the laborious task of clearing away the ruin left by Schuyler's axmen. It was heavy work and the engineering parties were harassed by the sultry summer heat, and clouds of gnats and mosquitoes. Nearly a week was consumed in opening the road to Fort Anne and it was not until July 24 that the road to Fort Edward was finally clear. Burgoyne took four days to move fourteen miles to Fort Anne. On the 28th, Fraser's advance corps was sent forward and two days later the British right wing occupied Fort Edward. Bringing up the rear Riedesel's Germans came in and by August 9 Burgoyne's entire force was finally assembled on the Hudson.

52. Fort Edward, New York

JULY 30, 1777

HISTORICAL MARKER ON OLD FORT STREET
FORT EDWARD, NEW YORK

On July 23, 1777, General Schuyler led his forces to Moses Kill, four miles south of Fort Edward, and on July 30 issued orders to cross the Hudson River north of the village of Saratoga (today's Schuylerville). Some residents stayed, including Jane McCrea, the fiancée of Lieutenant David Jones who had joined Burgoyne's army. On July 27 she was found killed and scalped, resulting in outrage among the Americans in New York and a surge in their support for the war.

General Burgoyne's army arrived at Fort Edward but, because of the critical need for supplies, did not start crossing the Hudson River to Saratoga until September 13. Burgoyne's forces were slowed by having forty-two cannon and few horses to pull them.

53. Bennington, New York

AUGUST 16, 1777

BENNINGTON BATTLEFIELD STATE HISTORIC SITE
ROUTE 67
NORTHEAST OF HOOSICK FALLS, NEW YORK

General Burgoyne ordered Lieutenant Colonel Friedrich Baum, a German officer who spoke no English, to march toward Connecticut to recruit loyalists and get horses and supplies. When Burgoyne learned of the large supply depot at Bennington, Vermont, he redirected Baum to capture it. Baum advanced up the Walloomsac River and ordered his command to build breastworks on both sides of the river. John Stark was in command of the New Hampshire militia in the battle against the Germans.

W. J. Wood recounts the battle of Bennington in *Battles of the Revolutionary War*.

Because of the heavy rains, the American move did not begin until noon on 16 August. Two bodies of Stark's shirt-sleeved farmers were launched in an uncoordinated movement against deliberately prepared defensive positions which had no means of mutual support, to be followed by a central frontal attack by Stark's main body. With 200 New Hampshiremen, Colonel Moses Nichols was sent to make the four-mile northern circuit around the mountain to the northeast of the dragoon redoubt and attack from the north. Colonel Samuel Herrick with 100 Bennington militia and Vermont Rangers was dispatched to make a similar envelopment from the south. A small initial frontal attack was to be made by Colonels David Hobart and Thomas Stickney with 200 men against the enemy positions south of the crossing while a diversionary demonstration by 100 men was being made against Baum's main position. The central, main attack would be made by Stark with some 1,200 men, to jump off at the sounds of musketry from Nichols's and Herrick's attacks.

Incredibly, the whole American operation ticked away with clocklike precision. By 3:00 P.M. Nichols's men opened fire, with Herrick's attack getting off at about the same time. Hobart and Stickney then went forward with a neat little double envelopment of their own against the Tory redoubt, and John Stark mounted his horse to lead the main attack and—no account of the Battle of Bennington would be complete without it—made his famous cry, "We'll beat them before night, or Molly Stark will be a widow."

In no time the Tory redoubt was overrun. When its defenders had fled across the river, the Canadians and Indians swiftly departed. Only the dragoons and Fraser's men held out stubbornly in the dragoon redoubt. A fierce fire fight lasting for two hours ensued, which the battle-wise Stark later called "the hottest I ever saw in my life." Just as the ammunition in the defenders' pouches began to run out, the ammunition wagon caught fire and the last reserves blew up. Baum's dragoons drew their great swords and started to slash their way through their attackers. The Germans were actually hacking their way out to the road—the Americans had no bayonets to oppose them—when Baum fell mortally wounded. The fight went out of the dragoons, and they surrendered en masse. It was nearly 5:00 P.M., and what could be called the First Battle of Bennington was over.

Meanwhile, Heinrich Breymann's column, advancing from Sancoick's Mill at about 4:30 P.M., was about to bring on the second battle. Breymann advanced stolidly, beating off skirmishers who fired from the hillsides at his main column. What saved Stark was Warner's arrival with his 300 men. A new and equally hot fight began, lasting until daylight began to fail. By then Breymann's ammunition, like Baum's, had begun to run low, and the German ordered a retreat. The Americans continued to close in and retreat turned into rout.

The German and Tory losses for the day's fighting came to 207 killed and wounded and some 700 captured; of Baum's dragoons, only nine got back to base. The material losses were also severe: hundreds of muskets and jäger rifles, four ammunition wagons, 250 swords, and four cannon. The Americans claimed to have suffered only 30 killed and 40 wounded out of forces totaling about 2,000.

Even the loss of nearly 1,000 men, however, pales in comparison to Burgoyne's failure to capture the critical supplies he had so counted on, as well as the impact on British spirits and capabilities.

54. Fort Stanwix, New York

AUGUST 2–23, 1777

FORT STANWIX NATIONAL MONUMENT
ROME, NEW YORK

The British built Fort Stanwix in 1758 during the Seven Years' War to command the Mohawk River and the portage trail between the river and Wood Creek. The portage was on the major water route between New York and Lake Ontario. The British abandoned the fort after 1763, and in July 1776 the Americans began to garrison and restore it. During the revolution it was called Fort Schuyler to honor General Philip Schuyler. From April 1777 through the summer, Colonel Peter Gansevoort and his New York Continentals continued the restoration.

Lieutenant Colonel Barry St. Leger, in command of 750 troops, including regulars, Hessians, Canadians, and loyalists—Sir John Johnson's Royal Greens—and 800–1,000 Indians, headed from Canada into the Mohawk Valley in July 1777. They were to join forces with Burgoyne at Albany. They arrived before Fort Stanwix on August 2. Finding it too strong to capture, St. Leger began a siege.

During the battle at Oriskany on August 6 (see #55), Gansevoort sent Lieutenant Colonel Marinus Willett with 250 soldiers to raid the camps of St. Leger and the Indians. They were successful and made it back into the fort with the raided supplies and ammunition. Meanwhile, Schuyler ordered Major General Benedict Arnold to the fort. Arnold tricked St. Leger's Indian allies into thinking that he was approaching with a large force. That ruse and their losses caused the Indians to leave and, without them, St. Leger had to lift his twenty-one-day siege and head back toward Canada. He had failed in his objectives: to attract more loyalist and Iroquois allies and to join Burgoyne in Albany.

55. Oriskany, New York

AUGUST 6, 1777

ORISKANY BATTLEFIELD STATE HISTORIC SITE
ROUTE 69
ORISKANY, NEW YORK

In *Forgotten Allies: The Oneida Indians and the American Revolution,* Joseph T. Glatthaar and James Kirby Martin describe the August 1777 battle of Oriskany. General Nicholas Herkimer's patriot militia was reinforced by Oneida Indians—who were split between two leaders, Good Peter and Old Isaac—and Sir John Johnson's British force was reinforced by Senecas.

As Oneida adherence to neutrality slowly collapsed, Old Oneida residents were most likely to favor the British. By contrast, an overwhelming number of inhabitants at Kanonwalohale and Oriska ultimately aligned themselves with the rebels. Oquaga remained split, but a great many of the Oneidas there followed Good Peter's course and aided the revolutionaries rather than stand alongside Old Isaac and Joseph Brant. Their collective reasoning finally determined that with the breakdown of neutrality, aligning with the American rebels represented the safest and most sensible course for the People of the Standing Stone.

Chief Warrior Han Yerry had long since chosen the side he would favor should his fellow Oneidas enter the war. After the skirmishes at Lexington and Concord, he raised a band of Oneidas who were "friendly to the Americans in their struggle for liberty." Few surpassed Han Yerry in reputation among the Oneidas. Although he had flourished economically under British rule, Han Yerry disliked the Crown. Like other Oriska residents, he resented Sir William Johnson and his government for their actions in negotiating the Treaty of Fort Stanwix during 1768. By 1777 the Oneidas at Oriska, including the emissary Henry Cornelius, Han Yerry's brother Han Yost Thahoswagwat, Hendrick Smith, and Blatcop Tonyentagoyon, all prepared themselves to fight alongside Han Yerry against St. Leger's force.

Even before the British-Indian force reached Fort Schuyler, Brigadier General Nicholas Herkimer was back in German Flatts organizing assistance for Colonel Peter Gansevoort. At Fort Dayton, some eight hundred arms-bearing militiamen assembled. They began their journey on August 4, along a trail through flat terrain on the northern bank of the Mohawk River. Even as stragglers fell out, Herkimer picked up some fresh fighters along the way. Joining him near Oriska were a number of Oneidas, estimated at between sixty and one hundred. Just why Herkimer neglected to have Oneida scouts, who were much more familiar with the terrain, fan out well ahead and beyond the flanks of his troops on the morning of August 6, 1777, will forever remain a mystery.

About six miles from the fort, the road angled slightly to the northeast as it cut across a ravine. At about 10:00 a.m., the lead elements of Herkimer's force plunged into the crevasse, strode across the log bridge, and started scaling the opposite incline. Breathing heavily, they did not dawdle. Moments later, just behind the head of the column, an eruption of musketry fire shattered the calm. Herkimer had stumbled into a classic ambush.

The previous afternoon, Joseph Brant had received news from his sister Molly that Herkimer would be within ten or twelve miles of the fort that night with about eight hundred rebel militia. He recommended a surprise attack, and St. Leger concurred. Early the next morning, after much wrangling, Brant convinced the Senecas to participate, and they joined Sir John Johnson and a company of light infantry, which had moved out toward the ambush site the previous evening. All told, the Crown marshaled about five hundred men, four-fifths of them Indians, to attack Herkimer's force. Although Johnson was technically in command, the Iroquois designed and executed ambushes better than anyone, and Sir John wisely yielded battlefield leadership to the Seneca chief warriors Cornplanter and Old Smoke.

When Herkimer heard the thunder of musketry to his rear, he swung his large white horse around and reentered the ravine. A splendid target, the general did not last long. A musket ball shattered his leg about six inches below his knee.

About three hours into the struggle the skies opened up on the combatants, and passing thundershowers provided timely relief for the weary. When the rains subsided, the fighting began again and soon reached its earlier ferocity. Almost as quickly, the rage of battle began to fizzle out. Neither side could sustain the same level of intensity after the bloodstained morning engagement, and the heavy casualties on both sides were taking a psychological toll.

Herkimer's citizen soldiers had held the battlefield, but they had no victory. At least two hundred rebel partisans lay dead, with scores more wounded or captured. About 150 militiamen walked off the field at the end of the day, and they carried about 50 wounded friends and neighbors with them. Since few British and loyalist soldiers fought, their casualties probably amounted to about twenty-five or thirty. As many as three dozen Senecas perished in the fight, including six chiefs. Perhaps an equal number of fellow Iroquois never returned home. Although these numbers pale by comparison with the dead militiamen, they were devastating losses for so small a population group to endure.

Herkimer, his leg shattered, refused to leave the field until the fight had ended. Ten days after the battle, a surgeon unsuccessfully attempted to amputate the militia general's shattered leg. Herkimer bled to death, a Bible clutched in his hands and his family gathered around him.

Because most historians over the next century either ignored or did not know about Oneida participation in the battle, there were no tabulations of Oneida losses.

In August Congress relieved General Philip Schuyler of his command and named General Horatio Gates to replace him. Gates assumed command on August 19, and on September 9 he ordered the army to move north toward the British. On September 13 Burgoyne crossed the Hudson on a boat bridge north of the village of Saratoga (today's Schuylerville) and marched south. By September 15 the Continentals had completed the fortifications in Bemis Heights designed by Colonel Thaddeus Kosciuszko.

56. Fort Ticonderoga and Lake George, New York

SEPTEMBER 18, 1777

FORT TICONDEROGA
TICONDEROGA, NEW YORK

Patriots captured Fort Ticonderoga in May 1775 (see #10) but lost it to General Burgoyne in July 1777 (see #46). The contest for the fort continued in September. Under orders to disrupt Burgoyne's long communication and supply lines from Canada, Major General Benjamin Lincoln developed a plan to weaken Burgoyne by threatening British posts in his rear, forcing Burgoyne to detail soldiers to protect them. On September 18, 1777, Lincoln ordered Colonel John Brown and 500 militiamen on a surprise attack on Fort Ticonderoga while Colonel Johnson threatened Mount Independence across the lake, and Colonel Woodbridge headed south to Skenesborough—which the British had abandoned—to protect Brown's line of retreat. Brown attacked Brigadier General H. Watson Powell's soldiers at the Lake George landing at the outlet from Lake George into Lake Champlain and at Mount Defiance. Without heavy artillery, Brown could not take the fort, so his militia captured British boats and sailed south on Lake George. They survived a British attack but had to burn their boats and march toward Skenesborough.

In *Saratoga,* Richard M. Ketchum describes Colonel Brown's raid.

It was an amazing performance. At the cost of three or four killed and five wounded, Brown's raiders released 118 Americans who had been "confined, fatigued and dejected to such a degree that one could scarcely conjecture what they were. They come out of their Holes and Cells with Wonder and Amazement," Brown said, "indeed the Transition was almost too much for them." In addition, the colonel's men captured twelve British officers, 143 noncoms and privates, 119 Canadians, several hundred stands of arms, and a large quantity of baggage.

There was more to come: after some 150 bateaus in Lake Champlain and another fifty vessels in Lake George fell into his hands, Brown, in the flush of victory, sent a message under a flag of truce to the British commandant, demanding a surrender of Ticonderoga and Mount Independence in what he called "the strongest and most peremptory terms." The response was about what one might expect from a testy brigadier like Powell: "The garrison intrusted to my charge I shall defend to the last. I am, Sir, your humble servant. H. Watson Powell, Brig. Genl."

Despite the disappointing denouement, Brown's achievement (made possible in part by Brigadier H. Watson Powell's appalling negligence in allowing his men to be caught off guard) gave a boost to American morale, revealed the fragility of Burgoyne's line of retreat, and came as one more sober notice to his soldiers that the only way out of their dilemma was to break through Gates's lines.

57. Freeman's Farm at Saratoga, New York

SEPTEMBER 19, 1777

SARATOGA NATIONAL HISTORICAL PARK
STILLWATER, NEW YORK

The Saratoga National Historical Park Brochure includes the following description of the battle at Freeman's farm:

On September 19 the British advanced on the American camp in three columns. Two headed through the heavy forests covering the region; the third, made up of mostly German troops, marched down the river road. Seeing Burgoyne's army in motion, American scouts notified Gates, who ordered Col. Daniel Morgan's corps of Virginia and Pennsylvania riflemen to track the British march. About 12:30 p.m., some of Morgan's men brushed with the advance guard of Burgoyne's center column in a clearing—Freeman Farm—about a mile north of the American camp.

The ensuing battle raged back and forth over the farm for over three hours. Then, as outnumbered British lines wavered under deadly American fire, German reinforcements arrived from the river road. Hurling them at the American right, Burgoyne steadied his breaking line, gradually forcing the Americans to withdraw.

Burgoyne held the field but was stopped a mile north of the American lines, his army badly bloodied. Shaken by his victory, he ordered his troops to dig in near Freeman Farm and await support from Clinton, who promised to send troops north to aid Burgoyne. He waited nearly three weeks, but received no further word from Clinton.

In *Saratoga,* Richard M. Ketchum describes the British commander, General Clinton, in the Hudson Highlands.

Whatever else Henry Clinton might be planning, it did not include traveling to Saratoga to rescue his friend John Burgoyne. It was unthinkable that a man as cautious as Clinton would risk exposing Manhattan, Staten Island, and Long Island to attack by rebel raiders by removing too many of his troops for a protracted period of time. So, instead of heading north within ten days as Burgoyne had been led to believe, he dilly-dallied in Manhattan for yet another week, sent an attachment to New Jersey whose only accomplishment was to bring back some beef on the hoof, and finally, on October 3—four days after seventeen hundred reinforcements arrived at long last from Britain—set out with three thousand men aboard transports, bound not for Albany but for the rebel forts in the Highlands.

As his men were disembarking at Verplanck's Point, below Forts Clinton and Montgomery, a messenger from Burgoyne caught up with him. Captain Alexander Campbell of the 62nd Regiment had left Saratoga on September 20 and brought shocking news: Burgoyne's entire army did not exceed five thousand men and he had lost between five hundred and six hundred on September 19. The rebels—some twelve or thirteen thousand strong—were within a mile

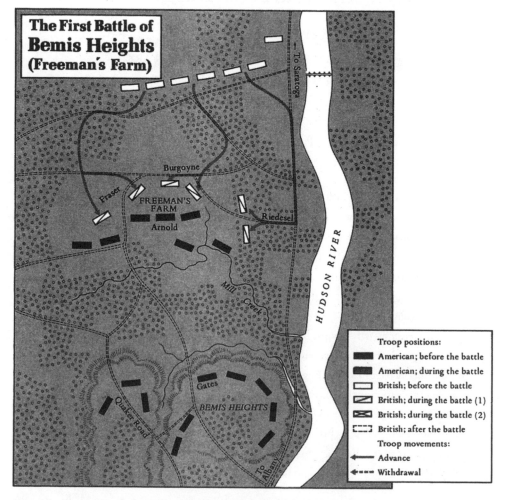

From: The Glorious Cause *by Robert Middlekauff (1982). Map from p. 379. By permission of Oxford University Press, USA.*

and a half of his lines, and another considerable force was threatening his rear. He estimated that his provisions might hold out until October 20 but said the only reason he had given up his supply line to Ticonderoga was his belief that an army from the south would join him at Albany.

58. Forts Clinton and Montgomery, New York

OCTOBER 6, 1777

THE SITE OF FORT CLINTON IS IN BEAR MOUNTAIN STATE PARK
ROUTE 9W
BEAR MOUNTAIN, NEW YORK
FORT MONTGOMERY STATE HISTORIC SITE
ROUTE 9W
FORT MONTGOMERY, NEW YORK

General Henry Clinton finally launched his 3,000-man diversionary force up the Hudson to take the forts protecting the vital river crossing and destroy their cannon. On October 5 he landed part of his force at Verplanck's Point, prompting Major General Israel Putnam—called "Old Put"—to prepare for an attack on his troops around Peekskill. The next morning, Clinton landed across the Hudson River at Stony Point and divided his command between Fort Clinton and, upriver, Fort Montgomery. He attacked the forts from the land side and was successful in taking both. George Clinton, the governor of New York and the commander of the forts, escaped. The British broke through the chain across the river, burned the American boats, and withdrew. General Clinton had no plans to continue upriver to Albany.

The British took Stony Point in June 1779 (see #93) but lost it to General Anthony Wayne in his daring raid in July (see #94).

59. Abraham Van Gaasbeek/Senate House, New York

SENATE HOUSE STATE HISTORIC SITE
296 FAIR STREET
KINGSTON, NEW YORK

This stone house, built in 1676 by Wessel Ten Broeck, became the home of Abraham Van Gaasbeek, a merchant. Protected from complete destruction by its stone walls when Kingston was burned, the house was rebuilt and has been restored.

After New York City fell to the British in 1776, the Provincial Congress met in White Plains, then in Fishkill, and next in Kingston (then named Esopus). On April 22, 1777, the Congress announced the approval of the state's first constitution. In June, George Clinton, a brigadier general in the militia, was elected the state's first governor.

On September 10, 1777, the New York State Senate met in the Van Gaasbeek house. In October, Major General John Vaughan in command of 1,700 troops moved up the Hudson River with Captain Sir James Wallace's naval squadron, forcing the legislature to adjourn. The small militia defending the town retreated, and on September 16, Vaughan ordered all buildings to be burned. After the British received news of Burgoyne's surrender, they sailed south.

In *A People in Revolution: The American Revolution and Political Society in New York, 1760–1790,* Edward Countryman describes the difficulties confronting the legislature.

On 10 September 1777 the legislature of the state of New York had a quorum for the first time. About half of the members of each house had made their ways to Kingston, where the governor had summoned them; of the rest, some were in Congress, some had died or been captured after Oriskany, some were marching to Saratoga, and some were tied up with local affairs. One was wearing George III's uniform. In British eyes all save that one were traitors, and all the more culpable for being leaders of the rebellion.

In the eyes of the people who had made up provincial New York their position was more complex. The new constitution was clear enough. It apportioned membership in the senate and the assembly. It declared who could vote in elections for each house and for the governorship. It stated that every year the voters would choose a whole new assembly and one-third of the senate, and it vested in the two houses together "the supreme legislative power within this state." It prescribed the procedure for making public policy, and it set up elaborate machinery for the final passage of bills and for naming officials. As a document, it was specific and matter-of-fact. It created a set of institutions that would endure for decades and that would be a model for those set up by the Federal Constitution a decade later.

But other things were less certain. Even while the first legislature was gathering, Burgoyne's army threatened the state's existence. Sixty miles below Kingston independent New York came to an abrupt end, and the occupied zone began. The British forces there showed their power less than a month after the legislature began business when a pillaging expedition sailed up the Hudson, captured and destroyed Kingston, and sailed back down—all virtually without opposition. As the redcoats advanced, the legislators scattered to their homes and militia units, leaving the state once more without regular government. For the time being, a few of them gathered in an utterly irregular Convention of the Members of the Senate and Assembly and took the little power there was to take.

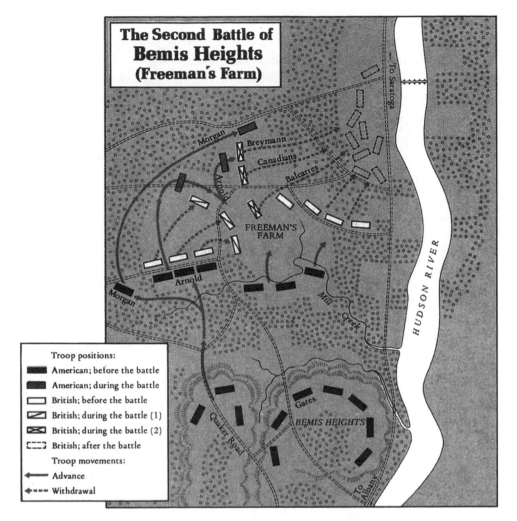

The Second Battle of
Bemis Heights
(Freeman's Farm)

From: The Glorious Cause *by Robert Middlekauff (1982). Map from p. 379. By permission of Oxford University Press, USA.*

60. Bemis Heights at Saratoga, New York

OCTOBER 7, 1777

SARATOGA NATIONAL HISTORICAL PARK
STILLWATER, NEW YORK

In *The Glorious Cause,* Robert Middlekauff recounts the second battle at Saratoga, Bemis Heights, in October of 1777.

By early October, Burgoyne recognized how bad his situation was. He was not yet cut off from Canada, but his soldiers were in no condition to make a rapid retreat: he had many wounded and sick; his transport was short; his supplies, shorter. He decided in the midst of weakness to try to smash through his enemy. On the morning of October 7 Burgoyne sent out from Freeman's Farm a heavy force in reconnaissance to test what he thought was the American left. If weakness was found there, he intended to attack with everything he had. His generals did not enter into this plan with much conviction: Riedesel proposed withdrawal to the Batten Kill, a small stream that fed into the Hudson, and Fraser agreed; Phillips refused to give any advice. Burgoyne detested the thought of withdrawal and persisted in his plan, sending the reconnaissance in three columns supported by ten fieldpieces ranging from six pounders to light howitzers. This party crept forward for three-fourths of a mile but discovered nothing. The three columns were then realigned to form a line of about a thousand yards. There the soldiers waited.

About two-thirty in the afternoon the Americans, whose knowledge of their enemy's dispositions was superior to the British, struck. Poor's brigade, New Hampshire regulars led by Enoch Poor, engaged the British left, and soon after Daniel Morgan swung wide and hit the left and found his way to the British rear. The British line began to give way, as the troops discovered Americans all around them. Burgoyne then sent his aide, Sir Francis Clarke, forward from Freeman's Farm with an order to pull the reconnoitering party back. Clarke received a bullet on the way and died before he could deliver the order.

61. The Siege of Saratoga, New York

OCTOBER 9–17, 1777

SARATOGA NATIONAL HISTORICAL PARK
STILLWATER, NEW YORK

By October 9 the British were blocked by 13,000 Americans and had suffered about 1,100 casualties. General Burgoyne ordered his 6,800 soldiers to retreat to the heights of Saratoga. By October 12 there was no possibility that the British could escape to the Hudson River, and surrender negotiations began the next day. On October 17, 1777, Burgoyne surrendered his army to General Gates.

In *Saratoga,* Richard M. Ketchum describes the British surrender.

Now the men in the ranks were to meet, in a manner of speaking. The prisoners were approaching with fifes and drums playing, and the waiting Americans lined both sides of the road, standing with muskets at their sides, eyes looking straight ahead or lowered in deference to the defeated men, though it was "a very agreeable sight," according to Ephraim Squier. What most impressed and gratified the tired, defeated soldiers in Burgoyne's ranks was that "not a single man gave any evidence or the slightest impression of feeling hatred, mockery, malicious pleasure or pride for our miserable fate." On the contrary, "it seemed rather as though they desired to do us honor."

The diplomatic maneuvering and the clash of armies and navies often obscured what the Americans were fighting for. It was, to be sure, independence from England, but it went deeper than that, and an example of what it was all about occurred on the shore of Lake Champlain. On November 20, Horatio Gates wrote New York's Governor Clinton to say that Ticonderoga and Mount Independence had been evacuated by Brigadier Powell on the 8th of the month. Ebenezer Allen, a captain of Herrick's Vermont rangers, had his scouts follow the British to make certain they were really withdrawing, and on November 12 those men got into a skirmish with Powell's men near Gilliland's farm on the Bouquet River and took a few prisoners, including a black woman named Dinah Mattis. The scouts brought her back to headquarters at Pawlet, and on November 28, 1777, Captain Allen gave the woman a highly unusual letter that suggested what some of these young men had in mind when they turned out to fight Burgoyne's army of invasion:

> To whom it may concern. Know ye that whereas Dinah Mattis a negro woman with nancey her Child of two months old was taken Prissnor on Lake Champlain...by a scout under my command, and according to a Revolve passed by the Honorable Continental Congress that all [prisoners] belong to the Captivators thereof I being conscientious that it is not right in the sight of god to keep Slaves...I do therefore give this said Dinah mattis and Nancey her child [their] freedom to pass and repass any where through the United States of America...as though she was born free, without being Mollested by any Person or Persons....
>
> (SIGNED) EBENEZER ALLEN *Capt.*

Burgoyne returned to England on parole. The soldiers, known as the Convention Army, were marched to a camp in Cambridge, then in 1779 to Charlottesville, and later to Fort Frederick, Maryland, and to Camp Security in York, Pennsylvania.

Piers Mackesy details the resignations of the British commanders in America in *The War for America, 1775–1783.*

The defeat at Saratoga is the clearest turning point of the war. It marked the beginning of a general war waged throughout the world; and it was the beginning of North's real parliamentary troubles. In the House of Commons and the Lords a hurricane broke over the heads of the Ministers. For a time the country gentlemen held firm, and Lord North maintained his large majority. But as the session dragged on and war with France drew near, these supporters began to fall away, and at the beginning of March an Opposition motion on the Budget was defeated by only six votes in a House of 288. Much of the political trouble turned on the treatment of the generals.

Saratoga was marked by the resignation of all the Commanders-in-Chief in America, and was the beginning of what was soon to become a characteristic misfortune of the war: bitter feuding between the Ministers and their naval and military commanders. By the end of

1777 both Carleton and Sir William Howe had resigned; and their example was to be followed by Lord Howe in the course of the coming year.

After Washington learned that General Howe had sailed south from New York, he ordered his 11,000-man army to march south. Washington rode at the head of the army on the march through Philadelphia on August 24 and on to Wilmington, Delaware, the next day. The Marquis de Lafayette, the young French nobleman who had arrived in Philadelphia to volunteer for the Americans, rode beside him.

The British finally landed at the head of the Chesapeake Bay near today's Elkton, Maryland, on August 25, 1777. In *1777: Year of the Hangman,* John S. Pancake describes General Howe's slow journey and his reply to Lord George Germain, the American secretary.

It took the British fleet two weeks to reach Cape Henry, for the ponderous armada could only proceed as fast as the slowest ship. Ten days were consumed sailing up the great bay to the Head of the Elk. Twenty-five days from Delaware Bay Howe landed his army—ten miles farther from Philadelphia than if he had landed at Reedy Island. Altogether it had taken the British commander thirty-three days to bring his army some twenty miles closer to Philadelphia than it had been at Perth Amboy in June. Moreover, it was an army whose men were exhausted from more than a month at sea in the summer's heat. The army's horses—those that survived—were physical wrecks. But the most severe blow was the fact that there were virtually no Loyalists to welcome Howe. Many farms and villages were deserted and in some cases the people of the neighborhood had burned their crops to prevent the enemy from using them. No more than a handful of people came forward to greet Sir William and pledge their allegiance to the English cause. So the hope of a Loyalist rising in Pennsylvania and a campaign that would end with the conquest of the middle states secured by an occupation force of provincial troops disappeared in the smoke of the burning fields. Howe abandoned his intention of seizing the supply depots (if indeed he ever had such intention) and ordered his victualing ships back to the Delaware—presumably to brave the fire ships and floating batteries which he had earlier avoided. He would, he told Admiral Howe, allow ten days for them to reach New Castle, by which time he expected to be in position to destroy the rebel army.

On August 30 Howe finally replied to Germain's May 18 dispatch which had approved the movement to Pennsylvania by sea on condition that Burgoyne was properly supported. Howe had received this on August 12 while he was still at sea. Now his belated reply revealed between its lines the ruin of Sir William's strategy. He would, he said, be unable to cooperate with Burgoyne; and "the prevailing disposition of the inhabitants [of Pennsylvania]...I am sorry to observe, seem to be, excepting a few individuals, strongly in enmity against us...." He reminded Germain that his previous request for reinforcements had not been met, and that "in the present extended situation of the King's southern army" the American Secretary should not expect the war to be ended by the present campaign. Read out of context Howe's dispatch makes it appear almost as if Germain were responsible for the deplorable state of affairs. Sir William had by now become quite accomplished at laying his faults on others.

62. Hale-Byrnes House, Delaware

606 STANTON-CHRISTIANA ROAD
NEWARK, DELAWARE

The Georgian brick house was enlarged by Daniel Byrnes, a Quaker preacher and miller, after he bought it in 1773. The property, southwest of Wilmington and at the intersection of two major roads, was the site of Continental Army artillery that protected supplies stored in the area. Washington's General Orders September 5, 1777, scheduled a general officers' meeting at the house.

63. Brandywine, Pennsylvania

SEPTEMBER 11, 1777
BRANDYWINE BATTLEFIELD PARK
1491 BALTIMORE PIKE
CHADDS FORD, PENNSYLVANIA

On September 3, the British began their march from Maryland toward Philadelphia. General Washington positioned his army west of Newport, Delaware, on September 8. When General Howe ordered his main force around Washington's right, Washington redeployed to Chadds Ford on the Brandywine, the route between Kennett Square and Philadelphia. Howe reached Kennett Square on September 10.

In *The War of American Independence,* Don Higginbotham describes the Brandywine battle.

> As the Americans made repeated harassing strokes, Howe became fearful that the Virginian would retire toward the mountains to the west and dog his advance as he had done in New Jersey earlier that season. But Washington's countrymen expected him to interpose his army between Howe and the capital, and Washington himself showed not the slightest inclination to shy away. When Howe entered Kennett Square, Pennsylvania, he found Washington with

8,000 Continentals and 3,000 militia in position on the northern banks of Brandywine Creek. Washington anticipated a frontal assault across the stream, but he should have remembered Howe's flanking measure at Long Island. The American right wing under the ill-starred John Sullivan, victim of the earlier thrust in 1776, failed to reconnoiter or patrol adequately beyond its sector. While General Knyphausen with 5,000 men demonstrated before Chad's Ford on the main Philadelphia road, Cornwallis led the bulk westward, traversed the Brandywine at an unprotected ford above the American right, and crashed down upon Sullivan's flank and rear. As rumor of Howe's maneuver got to Washington before the assault itself, the American briefly considered a sudden plunge across Chad's Ford to destroy Knyphausen, and indeed he might have succeeded but at the risk of the total loss of Sullivan's force. Restraining his impulse, he hastened Nathanael Greene's division from his center to support the hard-pressed New Hampshire officer. Greene's men, some of them covering four miles in only forty-five minutes, fought splendidly as they held firm against repeated volleys and then bayonet charges, allowing Sullivan's disorganized regiments to escape. With darkness approaching, Greene retired in good order and joined Washington, who, denuded by Greene's departure from the center, had been thrown back by Knyphausen's Germans and redcoats.

At Brandywine as at Long Island, American intelligence proved defective, and for the second time Howe had outgeneraled Washington, but the Virginian had quickly recovered his presence at Brandywine by speeding Greene to the scene of potential disaster. Owing to fatigue among his own troops and the lateness of the hour, Howe did not pursue Washington, whose regiments finally were halted and reformed at Chester. Washington's casualties in all categories numbered about 1,000 men, Howe's approximately half that many.

64. Paoli, Pennsylvania

SEPTEMBER 21, 1777

PAOLI BATTLEFIELD HISTORICAL PARK AND PAOLI MEMORIAL GROUNDS
MONUMENT AVENUE
MALVERN, PENNSYLVANIA

Craig L. Symonds describes General Charles Grey's attack on American troops under General Anthony Wayne at Paoli in *A Battlefield Atlas of the American Revolution*.

After his defeat at Brandywine, Washington withdrew to Chester to reorganize, then marched via Philadelphia to a position some twenty miles west of the city near White Horse Tavern in order to guard the fords of the Schuylkill River. Much more than the Brandywine, the Schuylkill was a significant barrier to any army and Howe would have to cross it to attain his goal.

Leisurely as usual, Howe waited a day before sending Cornwallis in pursuit, then four days later he set his army in motion northward through Turk's Head (now West Chester) to clash with Washington's army on September 16 two miles south of the American camp. The British had much the better of the battle, and were threatening both American flanks when a torrential downpour halted the battle and perhaps saved Washington's army from a catastrophic defeat. Following this "Battle of the Clouds" as it came to be called, Washington retreated west to Yellow Springs, then even further west to Warwick Furnace to obtain dry powder and other supplies.

Howe, meanwhile, dispatched a column to seize the small American supply depot at Valley Forge where the British set up camp. With Washington's main army so far from the Schuylkill fords, Howe was in a position to make a dash for Philadelphia. But Washington had left Brigadier General Anthony Wayne and 1,500 men behind near Paoli Tavern to fall upon Howe's baggage train. Learning of Wayne's whereabouts from captured messages and Tory spies, Howe determined to launch a surprise night attack on Wayne's camp.

Howe assigned the mission to 5,000 men under the command of Major General Charles Grey, and ordered Grey to make the attack with bayonets only. In order to ensure surprise, Grey ordered his men to take the flints out of their muskets so that no accidental firings would alert the American sentries. Grey's column set out on September 19. Also on that day Wayne wrote to Washington that the British were very quiet in their camp. "I believe he knows nothing of my situation," Wayne wrote. He was about to find out how wrong he was.

The British column approached the American camp at one o'clock in the morning of September 20. Wayne had pickets out, but the British drove them in and charged into the American camp before Wayne could organize an effective resistance. Though Wayne had his men up and on the move in a matter of moments, in the confusion orders were misunderstood. Lieutenant Colonel Richard Humpton, who commanded the American rear guard, twice faced his men in the wrong direction and had to be set straight. In the meantime, the British could see the Americans clearly, silhouetted by the light of their own campfires. Grey's men smashed into the American camp and employed their bayonets with grim effect. Many of the Americans did not have bayonets and they had little opportunity to reload in the wild melee that ensued.

Fifty three Americans were killed and another 100 wounded before the rest fled westward. The British suffered relatively minor losses of 4 killed and 7 wounded. For that reason alone, the battle has gone down in history as a "massacre." But the name is misleading; the British forces were guilty of no offense beyond one-sided success in battle.

Grey's force rejoined Howe's main body the next day. But Howe's chance to cross the Schuylkill uncontested had fled with his decision to smash Wayne's command. Washington had crossed the Schuylkill at Parker's Ford and was now at Evansburg in position to dispute a river crossing by the British. Howe therefore employed a simple ruse to divert Washington away from the river. He marched westward toward the upper fords, causing Washington to parallel his movements north of the river and then he counter-marched at night and crossed the Schuylkill at Flatland's Ford near Valley Forge on September 23, a move which put him between Washington and Philadelphia. The British army entered Germantown on September 25 and marched into Philadelphia the next day amid the cheers of the Tory residents.

In *The Road to Valley Forge,* John Buchanan considers the surprise attack at Paoli.

> The action that night of 20 September 1777 is called the Paoli Massacre. We should observe, however, that the escape of most of Wayne's command means that it was not a massacre. Nor was it a full-scale battle. Action at Paoli would be a better description. In 1783 a British historian delivered this verdict:
>
>> General Grey conducted this enterprise with equal ability and success though perhaps not without that humanity which is so conspicuous in his character.... A severe and horrible execution ensued.... The British troops as well as the officer that commanded them gained but little honour by this midnight slaughter. It shewed rather desperate cruelty than real valour.
>
>> Perhaps. According to American participants, British soldiers were heard to call out "No quarter," but no evidence has been found that General Grey or other officers gave such an order, and the prisoners taken argue against it. But we can argue that the mere order to either unload weapons or remove flints and rely solely on swords and bayonets invited unnecessary killing, because when soldiers come to close quarters the instinct for survival magnifies and creates an uncontrollable frenzy to kill before you are killed. Yet the British army was in a delicate situation, with enemies in front and behind. Grey's mission was critical to remove the danger behind, secrecy and silence were absolutely necessary, and the possibility that careless soldiers could compromise the mission was real. The argument could go on and on. "War is hell," Sherman said. It always will be.

65. The Occupation and Evacuation of Philadelphia, Pennsylvania

SEPTEMBER 26, 1777– JUNE 18, 1778

INDEPENDENCE NATIONAL HISTORICAL PARK
PHILADELPHIA, PENNSYLVANIA

On September 19, 1777, the Continental Congress fled from Philadelphia, and the British marched into the city on September 26. Congress met in Lancaster, Pennsylvania, on September 27, and in York, Pennsylvania, between September 30, 1777, and June 27, 1778. On November 15, 1777, Congress, while meeting in York, agreed to the Articles of Confederation. The final state ratified the Articles four years later, in 1781.

The British occupation ended when General Clinton evacuated Philadelphia on June 18, 1778. In *Almost a Miracle,* John Ferling describes General Howe during the occupation.

Anticipating that the ministry would accept the resignation he had submitted in October, Howe occupied his time preparing his defense for the almost certain parliamentary inquiry into his failure to suppress the American rebellion. He knew, too, that many blamed him for Burgoyne's fate, and for some that would have served as a catalyst for action that might bring redemption. Not so for Howe. He had nearly 17,000 regulars with him in Philadelphia, at least twice the number that Washington could put under arms to defend Valley Forge. Howe might also have conducted a winter campaign in the South, which he had once promised. He had access to a fleet and London's authorization to take the war further south. But Howe had come to the end of his tether. He offered up the now customary excuses: he had too few men and the Loyalists were untrustworthy. In reality, Howe's problem with attacking Valley Forge lay in Bunker Hill's ineradicable hold on him. With the one exception of Brandywine, since June 1775 he simply had been unable to conceive of an attack on a well-entrenched American force of any size.

Thus, the British army languished in Philadelphia throughout the winter and spring. It was the regulars' most comfortable winter yet. Once the Delaware River was opened, provisions flowed in from New York and across the sea, and from nearby farmers who succeeded in getting their goods through the rebels' cordon. Not only were the soldiers well fed, many residents of Philadelphia—about 20,000 of the city's 30,000 inhabitants remained throughout the occupation—welcomed them with open arms. Parties for the officers were common. There were young women to date, and the citizenry formed clubs for the soldiers' entertainment, gave concerts, and welcomed them to their churches and theaters. It was the polar opposite of gloomy Valley Forge, and more than 1,100 of Washington's soldiers defected to the British in Philadelphia.

General Howe submitted his resignation in October 1777. When it was accepted in May 1778, he sailed from Philadelphia to Britain. In *The Howe Brothers and the Revolution,* Ira D. Gruber describes the failures in America of Admiral Howe, who resigned his command in September 1778, and General Howe.

Admiral Lord Howe carried his forty-eight years well. Seamen called him "Black Dick," celebrating both his complexion and his solemn courage. Howe's education, which was more social and moral than intellectual, was well suited for the son of a nobleman destined for a career at sea.

Major General William Howe, a professional soldier of forty-five, possessed many of the personal qualities and social advantages of his older brother. He had risen in society, the army, and politics with the help of his powerful family and the favor of royal relations. But if his family had provided for his education (through tutors and four years at Eton) and if it had helped him purchase his way to a lieutenancy at eighteen, a captaincy at twenty-one, and a lieutenant colonelcy at twenty-eight, he had won for himself a sound reputation as a soldier. Serving in America and along the coast of France during the Seven Years' War, he became known as a strict disciplinarian whose battalion was once described as "the best trained... in all America." No one doubted his bravery, energy, or integrity." But William lacked the confidence, the sense of responsibility, and the professional dedication that distinguished Lord Howe. Under the pressures of command, he betrayed a fundamental lack of confidence: he was reluctant to surround himself with able subordinates, rarely asked advice, and avidly sought approbation. He was, all considered, a man better suited to the command of a regiment than of an army.

The Howes failed primarily because they and a majority of the ministry were working in separate and mutually destructive ways toward the restoration of British government in America. Indeed so different were their intentions that the Howes succeeded in becoming commanders in chief and peace commissioners only by exploiting a combination of misconceptions and fortuitous circumstances.

Although the Howes got the appointments they sought, they did not get the authority to negotiate an end to the rebellion; in fact, their failures in 1776 were largely a result of their efforts to make peace without the authority to do so. The ministry expected them to crush the rebellion.

In pursuing unsuccessfully their own dreams of conciliation, the Howes sacrificed the ministry's best prospect for regaining the colonies. It does, of course, seem paradoxical that their efforts to restore royal authority and American goodwill should have blasted the ministry's hopes and contributed to the loss of the colonies. But they did, because the ministry had to rely on coercion, because it was not free to negotiate a settlement with the colonies. Even had North and a majority of his colleagues been willing to make concessions on those issues that the colonists considered fundamental—to grant them the right to tax themselves and regulate their domestic affairs—they could not have done so. The king and nearly all members of Parliament were too passionately attached to the principle of parliamentary supremacy and too confident in their ability to sustain that supremacy to tolerate concessions. Under these circumstances the ministry's best prospect of recovering America lay in coercion, in destroying all armed resistance, dispersing the rebels, and restoring loyalists to power.

By the time Germain and Sandwich succeeded in provoking the Howes to resign, Burgoyne had surrendered in the wilderness and Britain was on the brink of a world war. The North ministry had lost its best prospect for ending the rebellion. Never again would its commanders have the opportunities that the Howes had spurned in the cause of peace.

66. Peter Wentz Homestead, Pennsylvania

PETER WENTZ FARMSTEAD
SHEARER ROAD
WORCESTER, PENNSYLVANIA

Peter and Rosanna Wentz completed their stone house in 1758. It was General Washington's headquarters before the battle of Germantown on October 4, 1777, and again in October 16–20.

In *The Glorious Cause,* Robert Middlekauff details Washington's preamble to his general order to the army before the battle of Germantown.

With Howe ensconced in Philadelphia, Washington made camp along Skippack Creek twenty-five miles to the west. He had no intention of sitting quietly, however. The old desire for action worked within him, drawing strength from his conviction that his troops, young and inexperienced as they generally were, would fight well given half a chance. By early October that chance had appeared. Howe had not found life in Philadelphia full of comfort and ease. He held the city but not the Delaware River, which provided an important line of access to it. The American forts on the river blocked all traffic and denied British ships the opportunity to bring in supplies and reinforcements. In his isolated circumstances Howe feared to spread all his troops throughout Philadelphia in inns and houses and had bivouacked around nine thousand at Germantown on the east side of the Schuylkill River five miles to the north. Another three thousand had been sent to protect the transport of supplies from Elktown, which of course involved a slow move over land. Four battalions remained in Philadelphia and two more had marched off to attack Billingsport twelve miles below the city on the Delaware. Howe was now spread all over the map.

When Washington learned of the scattered condition of the enemy, he decided to attack the largest concentration at Germantown. His troops probably needed no persuasion to fight, but Washington felt compelled once more to review the reasons why they should. The preamble to his general order to the army conveyed something of his own eagerness and, what is probably more important, just how far his understanding of the Revolution and of his army had proceeded. He now recognized that a professional pride existed at least in several of his regiments, and he appealed to it by reminding them that far to the north their comrades had delivered a heavy blow to Burgoyne at Freeman's Farm. He coupled this reminder of the northern success to invocation of the cause of America. "This army, the main American Army, will certainly not suffer itself to be outdone by their northern Brethren; they will never endure such disgrace; but with an ambition becoming freemen, contending in the most righteous cause rival the heroic spirit which swelled their bosoms, and which, so nobly exerted has procured them deathless renown. Covet! my Countrymen, and fellow soldiers! Covet! a share of the glory due to heroic deeds! Let it never be said, that in a day of action, you turned your backs on the foe; let the enemy no longer triumph."

These appeals of pride, to heroism, to honor had been made before, but their linkage to a cause which was "righteous" as well as glorious and which was shared by the "Country" marked a subtle departure, a broadening understanding. Washington ended by bringing these grand concepts into conjunction with the immediate and personal interests of his troops. The enemy, he reminded them, "brand you with ignominious epithets. Will you patiently endure that reproach? Will you suffer the wounds given to your Country to go unavenged?" These questions concerned his soldiers' families, especially since a revolution that failed would undoubtedly be regarded as treason: "Will you resign your parents, wives, children and friends to be the wretched vassals of a proud, insulting foe? And your own necks to the halter?"

Perhaps only in a revolutionary war do soldiers go into battle with a conception of a "righteous cause" competing with an image of their necks in a halter. These men could have no doubts about what they were fighting for, though they may have blurred some of the fine distinctions in republican ideology. What they had to understand was that their fight was for themselves, not for an overmighty lord and master.

Don Higginbotham recounts the October 4 battle at Germantown in *The War of American Independence.*

For the first time in the war, Washington moved forward to attack the major part of a British army: 9,000 troops Howe had placed in quarters at Germantown, seven miles from Philadelphia. It was to be another of Washington's characteristic night movements. Since Howe had divided his army and had not required the Germantown contingent to erect defenses, the idea of an assault was militarily sound, but the plan may have been "too intricate for inexperienced officers and imperfectly disciplined troops." Four columns—two of regulars, two of militia— started for Germantown on the evening of October 3 from their encampment near Skippack Creek, sixteen miles away. The two militia columns, moving on the outside, were to pass beyond the British front lines and assail the flanks and rear, while the Continental divisions under Sullivan and Greene were to hit the enemy's left and right fronts respectively. Although the militia, hardly trustworthy in such an operation, failed to execute their assignments, Sullivan's division at daybreak hurled the British advance parties back in wild confusion. Greene's division, having lost valuable time on the wrong road, finally arrived and drove all before it as far as the village market place. But the tide was already turning. Part of Sullivan's command had halted to flush several companies of the British 40th Regiment from the large stone house of Justice Benjamin Chew. Despite a heavy cannonading from Knox's artillery, the thick stone masonry served as an excellent fortress (though it took three carpenters all the next winter to restore the interior). Sullivan's delay and Greene's late appearance gave Cornwallis vital time to speed reinforcements from Philadelphia. Then, too, a heavy fog fell over the ravined, four-mile long battle front making it even more difficult for the American units to coordinate their actions. In the confusion General Adam Stephen, in disobedience to orders (he was drinking heavily), swung his Continentals out of line and coming upon Anthony Wayne's rear, mistakenly opened fire upon fellow Americans.

Washington, who according to Sullivan exposed himself "to the hottest fire," turned to steady his officers and men, but the turmoil was too much for most of them. Panic overcame several of the American regiments, especially as ammunition in Sullivan's division began to run out. Since the Americans' luck was unbelievably wretched, Washington could take heart from the results, imperfect as they were. Actually defeated, for they had given up the field and suffered total losses of roughly 1,000 compared to Howe's 534 casualties in all categories, the patriots had nevertheless scared the daylights out of their opponents in several hours of vigorous action. It was a superior American army to the one that had fought the campaign of 1776. If the Continentals still had not worsted the enemy in formal combat, they made his victories highly expensive.

～～～

67. Fort Mercer, New Jersey

OCTOBER 22, 1777

RED BANK BATTLEFIELD PARK
100 HESSIAN AVENUE
NATIONAL PARK, NEW JERSEY

The British needed to control the Delaware River in order to bring supplies to Philadelphia for their troops and for the loyalists. In early October 1777 the British fortified the crossing of the Schuylkill River to Province Island (now the site of the airport) and began to build batteries on the island and floating batteries to fire on Fort Mifflin on Mud Island (see #68). On October 11, American galleys shelled the British north battery, and a 100-man force captured sixty British defenders.

Fort Mercer, across the Delaware River from Fort Mifflin, was named to honor General Hugh Mercer, who was killed in the battle of Princeton on January 3, 1777 (see #38). The fort had been strengthened under the direction of the French artilleryman Chevalier de Mauduit du Plessis. The two forts and a triple row of chevaux de frise in the river between them prevented British ships from sailing upriver to supply Philadelphia.

On October 22, General Howe ordered Colonel Carl von Donop and 2,000 Hessians to cross the Delaware River at Cooper's Ferry, approach the fort from the landward side, and capture it. The commander of the garrison, Colonel Christopher Greene, ordered his men to hold their fire until the Hessians gained access to the outer walls and were ascending the new inner earthworks and then hit them with musket fire. Rowing galleys on the river also fired on the Hessians. The Americans won the battle, suffering 37 casualties and inflicting 400, including von Donop. The survivors retreated to Cooper's Ferry that night.

The loss of Fort Mifflin on November 16 and the approach of General Cornwallis, in command of 5,000 soldiers, forced the evacuation of Fort Mercer the night of November 20–21. The Delaware River was open to the British.

68. Fort Mifflin, Pennsylvania

NOVEMBER 10–16, 1777

FORT MIFFLIN ON THE DELAWARE
FORT MIFFLIN AND HOG ISLAND ROADS
PHILADELPHIA, PENNSYLVANIA

The British built Fort Mifflin on the Delaware River in 1771. General Howe put Fort Mifflin and its 400-man garrison under siege in October 1777 and on November 10 began a heavy naval bombardment. More than half of the Americans were injured or killed. The survivors evacuated the fort on the night of November 15–16.

In 1795 the fort was rebuilt to a design by Pierre L'Enfant. When it was closed in 1954, it had been in continuous use longer than any fort in the nation. The white stone walls are the only remains of the original fort.

In *Founders,* Ray Raphael describes life for Private Joseph Plumb Martin at Fort Mifflin.

For Private Joseph Plumb Martin, war was more about survival than honor. But Martin and other privates sent into harm's way did not possess much control over whether they survived or not. Witness Martin's experience at Fort Mifflin, which, along with Fort Mercer, guarded the Delaware River a few miles downstream from Philadelphia. Once the British had taken the city, these two forts assumed great strategic significance, for as long as they remained under American control, British ships could not sail up the river to supply the occupying army. Hoping to dislodge the Americans from their last bastions in the region, British artillerymen unleashed a continuous barrage of projectiles from the best warships in the world upon a sixteen-year-old lad from Connecticut and others who shared his assignment. Martin described the bombardment in graphic detail:

> During the whole night, at intervals of a quarter or half an hour, the enemy would let off all their pieces....I was in this place a fortnight and can say in sincerity that I never lay down to sleep a minute in all that time....The cannonade was severe, as well it might be, six sixty-four-gun ships, a thirty-six-gun frigate, a twenty-four-gun ship, a galley and a sloop of six guns, together with six batteries of six guns each and a bomb battery of three mortars, all playing at once upon our poor little fort, if fort it might be called.
>
> The enemy's shot cut us up. I saw five artillerists belonging to one gun cut down by a single shot, and I saw men who were stooping to be protected by the works, but not stooping low enough, split like fish to be broiled....When the firing had in some measure subsided and I could look about me, I found the fort exhibited a picture of desolation. The whole area of the fort was as completely ploughed as a field. The buildings of every kind hanging in broken fragments, and the guns all dismounted, and how many of the garrison sent to the world of spirits, I knew not. If ever destruction was complete, it was here.

After weathering two weeks of intermittent fire, followed by six days of round-the-clock bombardment, Private Martin and his commanding officers had had enough. On the night of November 15, they abandoned Fort Mifflin, but even that was fraught with peril. Martin and some others were left behind to set the remaining structures ablaze, and by the light of their flames British artillerymen were able to take some final deadly shots.

Joseph Plumb Martin survived, but he was shaken to the core.

⟩⟩⟩⟩⟩

69. Fort Randolph, West Virginia

OCTOBER–NOVEMBER 1777

THE SITE OF THE FORT IS NEXT TO TU-ENDIE-WEI STATE PARK
A REPLICA OF THE FORT IS IN KRODEL PARK
POINT PLEASANT, WEST VIRGINIA

Fort Randolph, built in 1776, was one of Virginia's two principal military forts on the Ohio River. It was named to honor Peyton Randolph who was twice president of the Continental Congress. In *The Shawnees and the War for America,* Colin G. Calloway recounts the murder of the Shawnee chief Cornstalk at Fort Randolph in October 1777.

In early October, Cornstalk visited the American garrison at Fort Randolph on the Kanawha River, at the site where he had fought the Virginians exactly three years earlier. A Shawnee chief called Red Hawk and another Shawnee called Petalla accompanied him. Colonel Charles Stuart, who was at the fort, recalled what happened. Cornstalk apparently made no secret of the Indians' disposition. He said he was opposed to joining the war, but the current was so strong against the Americans that the Shawnees would have to run with the stream, in spite of all his efforts. Hearing this, the post commander, Captain Matthew Arbuckle, decided to take the three Shawnees hostage, to try to prevent the nation from joining the British. A month later, Cornstalk's son Elinipsico came to see what had happened. Father and son "embraced each other in the most affectionate manner." Meanwhile, however, soldiers brought in the body of a young man who had been killed and scalped. Some of the militia immediately yelled, "Let us kill the Indians in the fort." Despite Stuart and Arbuckle's efforts to stop them, they burst into the building where the Shawnee hostages were held. As Cornstalk rose to meet them they shot him dead in a hail of bullets. His son was shot as he sat on a stool, and Red Hawk was gunned down as he tried to escape up the chimney. The governors of Virginia and Pennsylvania sent urgent messages to the Shawnees; George Morgan conveyed Congress's regret; and Patrick Henry denounced the murders, but it was too little and too late. General Edward Hand recognized, "If we had anything to expect from the Nation it is now Vanished."

Thomas Jefferson, governor of Virginia during the war, wanted to see the Ohio Shawnees exterminated or driven from their lands, and he advocated turning other tribes against them. Almost every year now American troops from Kentucky invaded Shawnee country and burned crops and villages. In 1779, John Bowman led a campaign against Chillicothe. A handful of warriors repelled and harassed the attackers, but Black Fish was wounded and died a week later. A severe winter followed but Shawnees hit the frontiers again in the spring. They raided settlements in the Ohio Valley, forced the Americans to abandon Fort Randolph, and effectively closed the Ohio River to American traffic.

Colin Calloway also provides an overview of the Shawnees' defense of their homelands.

In the struggle over land and culture that lies at the heart of America's story, the Shawnees earned a reputation for stiff resistance against encroachment on their territory and for staunch defense of their way of life. For more than sixty years, they stood in the front lines, waging a war of territorial and cultural resistance that ranged across the present-day states of Pennsylvania, West Virginia, Kentucky, Ohio, Indiana, and Missouri. As one Shawnee leader told the British, "We have always been the frontier."

The war primarily concerned land. The one-thousand-mile-long Ohio River drains a huge area of northeastern North America before emptying into the Mississippi. Pioneers like Daniel Boone flooded into Kentucky, and Shawnee warriors fought them back as trespassers on their hunting lands. Kentucky became a bitterly contested "dark and bloody ground." The Ohio River became the major highway for settlers traveling west. The conquest of Kentucky and the Ohio Valley "was the first and greatest hurdle" for American national expansion. For almost twenty-five years, throughout the American Revolution and the years that followed, Shawnees fought to stop white settlement at the Ohio. Never again would Indians face Americans on such nearly equal terms as they did here; never again would Indians win victories of the magnitude they did here. As the United States moved west, so did Shawnee resistance.

The Shawnees' defense of their own homeland merged into a broader defense of Indian country. Shawnees regularly allied with other Indian nations and time and again they took the lead in marshaling multitribal confederations. The Ohio Valley that was key to European empire-building and American nation-building was also home to Indian nations whose cultural, economic, and societal values were often directly at odds with those of the invaders. The contest was not only about who should occupy the land, but about what kind of societies should exist there and what meanings the land would hold for them. From the moment they set foot on the continent, Europeans and then Americans depicted their conflicts with the Native peoples as an elemental battle between two ways of life, between, as they described it, civilization and savagery. The Shawnees no doubt saw it that way, too, although, had they used the terms, they would have had their own ideas about who was civilized and who was savage.

In histories and memories of the Old West, the Shawnees often featured as frontier terrorists. They burned cabins, killed and scalped settlers, routed American militia, and like the whites they fought, sometimes committed unspeakable atrocities. They were infamous for capturing Daniel Boone's daughter, and for capturing Daniel Boone himself on more than one occasion. In their own minds, of course, Shawnees were freedom fighters, not terrorists. At a time when American patriots were urging colonists to unite against British imperialism, Shawnees urged Indians to unite against American expansion.

Shawnee communities were based on clan and kinship; deference was paid to age, not to wealth or station; custom and public opinion, not laws and government, checked individual conduct. Women farmed, men hunted. Shawnees measured wealth in gifts given and in social capital rather than in money and material goods. They valued sharing and reciprocity as both an ideal and a practical way of living. Tribal homelands were hallowed ground held in common. As it was for other Native peoples, land was vital to their identity. Land was not just acreage, it was the total physical environment they inhabited: earth and sky, rivers and lakes, mountains and meadows.

The gulf separating the Shawnees from the people who invaded their land was not an impassable chasm. There was much that brought Indians and Europeans together, and there were many who attempted to reach across the cultural gulf to fashion new relationships. Travelers from the East often said they saw little difference between backcountry settlers and Indians. Indians and Europeans entered into trade, alliances, and other arrangements of mutual interest based on shared understandings. But the escalating competition for land submerged common humanity in a sea of antagonisms. The line dividing Indians and whites drew increasingly tight, and became increasingly contested and racial, leaving little room for men like Blue Jacket and Daniel Boone and little opportunity for new kinds of societies to grow from the confluence of cultures.

While American troops battled the Shawnees in the Ohio Valley, states in the South were successful in their treaties with the Cherokees. In *The American Revolution in Indian Country: Crisis and Diversity in Native American Communities*, Colin G. Calloway details the treaties with the Cherokees. Two of the Cherokee chiefs were Old Tassel and the Raven; Dragging Canoe was a younger chief.

In May 1777, the Lower Cherokees came to terms with Georgia and South Carolina at DeWitt's Corner, surrendering all remaining land in South Carolina except a narrow strip on the western border. Two months later, the Overhill Cherokees met to make peace with Virginia and North Carolina at Long Island. Chains of friendship were established between Chota and Williamsburg, as well as Chota and New Bern; Virginia and North Carolina each appointed agents to live at Chota. Old Tassel delivered a spirited speech questioning the Americans' assumptions of conquest, but the Overhills ceded all lands east of Blue Ridge as well as a corridor through the Cumberland Gap. The Raven hoped the new boundary would act as "a wall that reached up to the skies." Together, the two treaties stripped the Cherokees of more than five million acres.

The British and Americans both recognized that shortage of provisions drove the Cherokees to make peace. That spring, the homeless inhabitants of Big Island, Tellico, Toqua, and Chilhowee followed Dragging Canoe south and west and built new towns, with the same names, along the Chickamauga.

The Chickamauga "secession," as it is often called, was not an unmitigated disaster. It relieved Chota of the need to hand over Dragging Canoe to the Americans as the price of peace, and it allowed the peace party to disavow the actions of dissidents over whom they had no control.

━━━≫≪━━━

70. Valley Forge, Pennsylvania

WINTER 1777–1778

VALLEY FORGE NATIONAL HISTORICAL PARK
1400 NORTH OUTER LINE DRIVE
KING OF PRUSSIA, PENNSYLVANIA

As the Continental Army was marching toward Valley Forge for the winter, General Washington was worrying about how to get adequate supplies for the men. *The Boisterous Sea of Liberty* by David Brion Davis and Steven Mintz includes Washington's letter to the president of Congress about the use of military power to provide for his soldiers.

George Washington, December 14–15, 1777, to the President of Congress (GLC 5572)

I confess I have felt myself greatly embarrassed with respect to a vigorous exercise of military power. An ill-placed humanity, perhaps, and a reluctance to give distress, may have restrained me too far; but these were not all. I have been well aware of the prevalent jealousy of military power, and that this has been considered as an evil, much to be apprehended, even by the best and most sensible among us. Under this idea, I have been cautious and wished to avoid as much as possible any act that might increase it. However, Congress may be assured, that no exertions of mine, as far as circumstances will admit, shall be wanting to provide our own troops with supplies on the one hand, and to prevent the enemy from getting them on the other.... I should be happy, if the civil authority in the several states, through the recommendations of Congress, or their own mere will, seeing the necessity of supporting the army, would always adopt the most spirited measures, suited to the end. The people at large are governed much by custom. To acts of legislation or civil authority they have ever been taught to yield a willing obedience, without reasoning about their propriety; on those of military power, whether immediate or derived originally from another source, they have ever looked with a jealous and suspicious eye.

The encampment of the Continental Army at Valley Forge began on December 19, 1777, and ended on June 19, 1778. The first disaster, a lack of food, hit soon after the patriots arrived and another, floods and more shortages, came in February. The location, twenty miles northwest of Philadelphia, was far enough from the main British army in winter quarters in Philadelphia to provide protection from a surprise attack.

In *Revolutionaries,* Jack Rakove quotes the letter Washington wrote on December 23 to Henry Laurens, the president of the Continental Congress, on the conditions at Valley Forge.

Whether out of political calculation or self-righteous anger, Washington justified his blunt account of the dire conditions of his men with a direct appeal to "my own reputation." He had sounded the same theme a year earlier in private letters citing frustration over soldiers' pay, enlistments, and discipline as a threat to the "character" he wanted to establish. Hitherto he had been "tender" about "lodging complaints" against the various administrative reforms that Congress had imposed against "my Judgement." But "finding that the inactivity of the Army" had now been "charged to my own account, not only by the common vulgar, but those in power, it is time to speak plain in exculpation of myself." There followed not only a detailed review of the needs of the army, from the basics of food and clothing down to soap and vinegar, but also pointed digs at the local officials who had dissuaded him from using the confiscatory powers Congress had vested in him, with assurances that Pennsylvania would do its duty. "I can assure those Gentlemen, that it is a much easier and less distressing thing, to draw Remonstrances in a comfortable room by a good fire side, than to occupy a cold, bleak hill, and sleep under frost & snow without Cloaths and Blankets." Yet even at this moment of urgency, his concern lay as much with the future campaign as the immediate crisis. "We have not more than three months to prepare a great deal of business in," he estimated; "if we let these slip or waste, we shall be labouring under the same difficulties all next Campaign, as we have done this."

Thus began the Valley Forge winter, that episode in privation that summons images of gaunt, half-clad, barefoot soldiers huddled in the snow around flickering fires, staring vacantly into gruel-filled cups, bitterly aware that the enemy was sleeping warm and well fed in nearby Philadelphia. The first crisis followed hard upon the army's arrival at Valley Forge, when spontaneous chants of "No meat! No meat!" rang across the encampment. A second graver one occurred in mid-February 1778, when drenching rains washed out roads, swelled rivers, and badly disrupted the flow of supplies to camp. Over two thousand soldiers died that winter. Outright starvation was not the immediate killer, but rather the lowered resistance to disease that repeated food shortages and inadequate clothing fostered in the overcrowded huts the army had hastily erected.

In *American Creation: Triumphs and Tragedies at the Founding of the Republic*, Joseph J. Ellis details the famine at Valley Forge.

At least on the face of it, two unquestioned facts about the conditions at Valley Forge appear irreconcilable. On the one hand, the chronic food shortages of December and January became a full-fledged famine in February. Several officers commented on the deplorable situation, describing troops on the verge of both starvation and desertion, horses dying for lack of forage, their decaying bodies filling the air with a sickening stench. On the other hand, the arc of the army's deployment ran directly across the most fertile and productive farming region in the country. Gouverneur Morris, one of the delegates on the Camp Committee, put it most succinctly: "An American Army in the Bosom of America is about to disband for the want of something to eat." In effect, the Continental Army was starving to death while located squarely in the middle of America's most bountiful breadbasket. How could that possibly be?

The short answer is that the bulk of the local farmers preferred to sell their crops to the British army in Philadelphia. "I can assure Your Excellency," explained one officer on patrol duty, "not less Flour than is sufficient to maintain Eight or Ten Thousand men goes daily to Philadelphia…and scarcely a day passes but a Number gets into that Place by the different roads on this side of the Schuylkill." A veritable caravan of grain and livestock flowed from the countryside into the city to feed British troops, the wagons often driven by women and children in order to minimize the likelihood of arrest if stopped by American patrols. "I am the more chagrined at the want of provisions to which I am informed your Army is reduced," wrote William Livingston, the governor of New Jersey, "as I believe it is partly owing to the boundless Avarice of some of our Farmers, who would rather see us ingulphed in eternal Bondage, than sell their produce at a reasonable price."

Actually, at least from the point of view of the farmers, price was the problem, because the Continental Army purchased supplies with certificates whose value was tied to the vastly inflated Continental currency, making the certificates nearly worthless. The British paid in pounds sterling, a much more reliable medium of exchange. And so their decision to sell to the British army was not so much a political statement as it was a wholly rational economic calculation based on self-interest.

But even that explanation oversimplifies a more complicated question of allegiance throughout the countryside surrounding Valley Forge. For it implies that the bulk of the populace identified with the patriot cause, but were forced to put their patriotism aside in order to feed their own families. The social and political reality, in truth, was much messier. If we could draw a map of the adjoining counties and color the pro-British areas red and the pro-American areas blue, the result would resemble a random pattern of red and blue patches, but the largest area would need to be colored purple, reflecting a population that remained equivocal: Quakers who were conscience-bound to a posture of neutrality; lukewarm patriots or loyalists whose allegiance shifted in accord with the military balance of power in their neighborhoods; and a substantial segment of indifferent citizens who just wanted the war to go somewhere else and allow them to get on with their lives.

Such a map exposes the utter inadequacy of two political assumptions prevalent at the time and resonant in the history books ever since. The first assumption claimed that the vast majority of the American citizenry supported the war. That was probably true in 1775–76, but it was no longer true by 1777–78. The second assumption claimed that the two political camps, labeled Whig and Tory or patriot and loyalist, were clearly delineated and permanent categories. That was never true, and the longer the war went on, the more fluid and dynamic these categories became, and the larger the population became that did not fit neatly into either political camp. In effect, the countryside around Valley Forge constituted a microcosm of the increasingly muddled allegiances that a protracted war had created in those middle states where the conflict had generated its greatest havoc.

And the worse the famine within the Valley Forge encampment became, the worse the muddle and the havoc became for the local residents. With the army facing starvation, Washington felt obliged to order a "Grand Forage," sending Greene with a detachment of nearly a thousand troops to forcibly purchase, which meant to confiscate, all the cattle, horses, and grain that remained in the region. The ever-resourceful Greene vowed to do his duty, despite the distasteful business of watching whole families collapse in sorrow and desperation as his soldiers carried away everything they owned. Greene reported that the scenes could break your heart, but also that the pickings were surprisingly slim because British foraging expeditions out of Philadelphia had already picked the country clean. "We take all the Horses and Cattle, Hogs and Sheep fit for our use," he explained, "but the Country has been so gleaned that there is but little left in it." Most of the local farmers tried to hide whatever crops and livestock not already sold to the British in nearby swamps in order to feed themselves during the remainder of the winter. And it was almost impossible to get reliable intelligence on these hidden caches, because, as Greene explained, "Whigs here are afraid to give any information respecting the Tories for fear that when we are gone they will be carried prisoners into Philadelphia."

Indeed, the war in the countryside had become a series of foraging fights between the two armies, with the local residents trapped in between. One farmer, who claimed allegiance to the cause of American independence, described the vicious cycle that resulted from the evershifting situation on the ground: "That we can neither stay at our Houses, go out nor come in with Safety. That we can neither plough, plant, sow, reap nor gather. That we are fast falling into Poverty, Distress, and into the Hands of our Enemy." And farmers of a loyalist persuasion suffered the same fate whenever the Continental Army was in the area. Those attempting to avoid recriminations by claiming neutrality quickly discovered that no such thing existed.

If the local residents were trapped between the unpredictable arrivals of two marauding armies, Washington was caught between two equivalently incompatible courses: confiscating the food that prevented the starvation of his soldiers, which understandably alienated the very people the American Revolution was intending to defend, or maintaining his revolutionary principles while watching his army dissolve. This was never a difficult choice, though Washington preserved his conscience by insisting that all confiscated crops must be paid for in certificates. While worthless, they provided a moral balm. As for the women and children driving supplies into Philadelphia, they should not be physically harmed, but their horses and wagons should be confiscated. And those men identified as ringleaders in this illicit traffic should be arrested and hanged in public executions designed to make a statement. He did not reverse a request from the commander of one patrol outside Philadelphia to fire on all men carrying food into the city, then leave their bodies on the road as warnings to those similarly disposed. He drew the line, however, short of what we now call "pacification." When presented with a proposal to deny Howe's army access to the farms within a ten-mile radius of

Philadelphia by forcibly removing all the inhabitants to more distant locations, he rejected the suggestion as a solution that was worse than the problem it solved, concluding that "the horror of depopulating a whole district...would forbid the measure."

These sorrowful scenes and difficult choices exposed a major new development in the strategic chemistry of the war. In the countryside around Valley Forge it became clear for the first time that the American Revolution, while still and always a struggle for independence, was also now a civil war for the hearts and minds of the American people. And the two contests were closely connected.

Until now, Washington had viewed the war as a conventional contest between two armies. His whole effort had focused on sustaining a fighting force in the field that could match and eventually defeat the British army. While he never entirely abandoned that conventional conviction, the foraging fights around Valley Forge forced him to confront the unconventional dimensions of the emerging conflict. Greene had warned him that "the longest purse" usually won a protracted war, a viewpoint that made an eventual British victory, like the added sums of an accountant's ledger, almost a mathematical certainty. Now, however, the volatile political chemistry of the countryside changed the terms of the equation, for the new variable was not money but allegiance. Even the longest purse could not defeat the deepest resistance.

A new term entered Washington's military vocabulary, "cover the country," signaling the recognition that deployment of the Continental Army and local militia units as a kind of roving police force that controlled the countryside was a crucial new mission, in many ways more important than set-piece battles with the British army. This was a new way of thinking for Washington, not easy for him to embrace given his honor-driven sense of battle as much like a summons to duel. Nor did it arrive in his mind as lightning flash or epiphany. (Temperamentally, Washington was incapable of epiphanies, and indisposed to trust them in others.) But as the snows at Valley Forge began to melt, he was gradually coming to grasp the wisdom of a defensive strategy designed to make control of the countryside as crucial as winning battles.

In *The Road to Valley Forge,* John Buchanan notes the importance of Quartermaster General Greene at Valley Forge.

At Valley Forge the problem was the all-important logistical system. It broke down. Its fixing did not begin until Nathanael Greene was appointed quartermaster general in March 1778 and with ruthless efficiency undertook a job he wanted no part of. For as he wrote, "No body ever heard of a quarter Master in History." He served in that position for 2 ½ years, before going on to win immortality in his brilliant Carolina campaign.

For make no mistake about it. The army almost perished at Valley Forge. A mild winter, yes, but winter is still winter, and no time to be poorly clothed and poorly fed. As the winter progressed and the situation grew worse, Washington was driven to put into effect the power Congress had given him to seize supplies from civilians. He knew this might alienate the people, which was why he took so long to do it, but the army's precarious condition drove him to it.

This was no mission for the tenderhearted. Greene wrote to one of his officers,

You must forage the Country naked, and to prevent their complaints of the want of Forage we must take all their Cattle, Sheep, and Horses fit for the use of the Army.

If the food supply was erratic and at times desperate, it was surpassed as a problem by the lack of proper clothing. Letter after letter raises the specter of half-clothed soldiers in a wintry environment.

In his letter written at Valley Forge on April 21, 1778, to John Banister, a Virginia delegate to the Continental Congress, General Washington expressed his concern about the number of officers who had resigned from the army. The letter is in *George Washington: Writings*, edited by John Rhodehamel.

Men may speculate as they will; they may talk of patriotism; they may draw a few examples from ancient story, of great atchievements performed by its influence; but, whoever builds upon it, as a sufficient Basis for conducting a long and bloody War, will find themselves deceived in the end. We must take the passions of Men, as Nature has given them, and those principles as a guide, which are generally the rule of Action. I do not mean to exclude altogether the Idea of Patriotism. I know it exists, and I know it has done much in the present Contest. But I will venture to assert, that a great and lasting War can never be supported on this principle alone. It must be aided by a prospect of Interest or some reward. For a time it may, of itself, push Men to Action; to bear much, to encounter difficulties; but it will not endure unassisted by Interest.

Benjamin Franklin commended to General Washington a former Prussian officer, Baron Friedrich Wilhelm von Steuben, who arrived at Valley Forge on February 23 and instituted a standardized training regimen for the Continental Army. He was so effective that Washington recommended that Congress appoint him inspector general with the rank of major general. Thomas Fleming presents the challenges von Steuben confronted at Valley Forge in *Washington's Secret War: The Hidden History of Valley Forge*.

Baron von Steuben's reforms were not only a struggle against mounting chaos; they were a race against time. By the first weeks of March, when the Baron was getting to work on reforming the army, the starving time of mid-February had subsided into a precarious balance between supply and demand. It soon became clear that there was no hope of one man doing the job. To back up the Baron, Washington selected fourteen inspectors—one for each infantry brigade—from among the most talented and intelligent majors in the army. They would be Steuben's assistants. But the big question remained: where to begin?

Steuben decided the key to reviving the army was a manual that would enable the troops, with sufficient practice and instruction, to march and maneuver with precision and confidence on a drill field and on a battlefield. No such manual existed, and Steuben decided he would write one specifically for the American army in its present situation. So began a drama of large historical importance that now and then degenerated into comedy. The Baron's English remained rudimentary. None of his pupils spoke a word of his two principal languages, French and German. Nor did any of the brigade inspectors. His only interpreter was Duponceau, who still had zero grasp of military terminology.

Even in the first lessons, Steuben was teaching something far more important than the mechanics of drilling and marching and handling a gun. He was showing these men and the spectators that doing these things right made a soldier proud of himself. Marching in exact formations gave him a sense of confidence in himself and his brothers in arms. Here and in future lessons in his manual the Baron was inculcating the idea that being a soldier required far more hard work and attention to detail than civilians imagined.

The Baron was not satisfied with transforming the drill and marching procedures of the Continental Army. He wanted to see a psychological, even a spiritual change in the relationships between the officers and men. He wrote succinct summaries of the duties of each officer in a regiment, from the colonel to the lieutenants. Perhaps the most important were the instructions to the captain. The opening lines are worth reading because they remain the cornerstone of the U.S. Army's philosophy of leadership today.

> A captain cannot be too careful of the company the state has committed to his care.... His first object should be, to gain the love of his men, by treating them with all possible kindness and humanity.... He should know every man of his company by name and character. He should often visit those who are sick, speak tenderly to them, see that the public provision, whether of medicine or diet, is duly administered and procure them besides such comforts and conveniences as are in his power. The attachment that arises from this kind of attention to the sick and wounded, is almost inconceivable.

In *The Unknown American Revolution,* Gary B. Nash emphasizes the importance of the foot soldiers in the Continental Army.

For six long years of war, climaxing at Yorktown in October 1781, but not culminating for another year, the men who fought under Washington were a far cry from the celebrated minutemen. Especially those who fought in the Continental army had shallow roots in *any* community. They were overwhelmingly from the lower layers of society and were mainly enlisted to bear arms so that the mythic citizen-soldier could avoid military service and stay at home. This led to tension, dissension, and disillusionment with the Continental Congress among the common enlisted men. Finally, it led to mutiny.

One of the main problems of the war was how to fill the thirty-eight regular regiments, which at full strength consisted of some eight thousand men (not even half the soldiers the British fielded throughout the war). Upon inspection, most of these soldiers turn out to be those with pinched lives, often fresh from Ireland or Germany, recently released from jail, or downright desperate. In fact, only a small sliver of white American males of fighting age served in the Continental army under Washington and his generals.

In the mid-Atlantic states, as in New England, the yeoman farmer of revolutionary lore, shouldering his weapon and bidding his family goodbye, was mostly a myth. Mostly landless, drawn from unskilled laborers or lower artisans (such as shoemakers), and overwhelmingly drawn into service by bounties provided by those wanting to avoid Continental service, they differed from the dispossessed New Englanders only in one respect: The majority were foreign-born, and most of them had only recently arrived in North America.

In the southern states the recruiting process was much the same. Maryland's Continental soldiers, who froze at Valley Forge in the winter of 1777–78, were mostly young, poor, landless, voteless, and, in about half the cases, immigrants. Maryland was unusual only in trying to take choice out of the hands of the dispossessed. By legislative decree, any local court could require a person considered a vagrant to serve at least nine months in the Continental army. Prime candidates for this kind of conscription were the thousands of convicts transported by the British to Maryland and Virginia—some 24,000 from 1746 to 1775—in order to sweep clean the jails of England. In Virginia, substantial bounties lured lower-class youths, some as young as fourteen, into the regular army. By the end of 1776, looking for more men, the Virginia government followed Maryland by authorizing the impressment of "rogues and vagabonds"—a vagabond being described as any man neglecting to pay his county and parish taxes or any man with no visible estate.

Washington's officers had no illusions about the human material they had to shape into fighting units. "Food for Worms…, miserable sharp looking caitiffs, hungry lean faced Villains," Anthony Wayne labeled them. Notwithstanding all these unpleasant comments, Continental army officers could not do without such men. Absent such human material, the war would have quickly ended with a British victory. What is more, it was these down-and-outers who were most likely to endure the awful conditions of camp life and battlefield gore.

For all his obscurity, the foot soldier was, in fact, one of the main reasons that the Americans were able to sustain a series of disheartening defeats in the first two years of the war and still continue the fight. Washington and his generals relied on the poor unsung youth—the guerrilla fighter whose capacity to survive in horrendous conditions proved crucial. Washington understood what would later become a famous dictum of war, one that also applied in Vietnam two centuries after the American Revolution. The standing army that does not win, loses; the guerrilla army that does not lose, wins. Private Joseph Plumb Martin, an out-of-work farm laborer who joined the Eighth Connecticut Regiment, was the kind of young, penniless soldier who made all the difference. In plainspoken but penetrating prose, inscribed in a diary kept through several enlistments, the seventeen-year-old Martin, born in the tiny farming village of Becket in western Massachusetts, showed what the common soldier faced, endured, and—sometimes—survived.

~~~~∞~~~~

While the Continental Army was enduring the winter at Valley Forge, the American representatives in Paris were moving toward an alliance with France. In *Benjamin Franklin,* Walter Isaacson describes Franklin and the two treaties.

After a full year of deflecting requests for an alliance, the French were suddenly impatient as 1777 drew to a close. They were prodded not only by America's success at Saratoga and the completion of their own naval rearmament program, but also by a new gambit by Franklin. He began to play the French and British off against one another and to let each side discover—and here is where he relied on the spies he knew were in his midst—how eager the other side was for a deal. In the meantime, the British sent to Paris the most trusted envoy they could muster, Paul Wentworth, their able spymaster.

Not quite sure who was spying on whom, Franklin pursued the cleverly naïve approach he had described a year earlier. It was in his interest that the British discover (as they did through their spy Bancroft) how close the Americans were to a deal with France. And it was in his interest that the French discover (as they did through their own constant surveillance of Wentworth) that the Americans were having discussions with a British emissary. Everything he said to Wentworth he was happy to have the French overhear. As Yale historian Jonathan Dull has noted, "The ineptitude of the British government presented Franklin with a chance to play one of his best diplomatic roles: the innocent who may not be so innocent as he pretends."

Thanks to Franklin's maneuvers as well as the victory of Saratoga, the French now wanted an alliance as eagerly as America did. Franklin was told that the king would assent to the treaties—one on friendship and trade, the other creating a military alliance—even without the participation of Spain. France made one stipulation: America could not make peace with Britain in the future without France's consent. And so the treaties of friendship and alliance were won.

The two treaties were signed in Paris on February 6, 1778, by France's minister to the United States, Conrad Alexandre Gerard, and by the three American representatives: Silas Deane, Benjamin Franklin, and Arthur Lee. Congress ratified the treaties on May 4, 1778.

Congress elected John Adams to replace Silas Deane, and Adams arrived in Paris in April 1778.

———❦———

71. Fort Roberdeau, Pennsylvania

APRIL 1778–1780

FORT ROBERDEAU
383 FORT ROBERDEAU ROAD
ALTOONA, PENNSYLVANIA

Daniel Roberdeau combined his rugged individualism—he was a successful Philadelphia merchant—with important civic involvement. He was an opponent of the Stamp Act, a delegate to the Second Continental Congress, a strong advocate for independence, and a signer of the Articles of Confederation for Pennsylvania; he also served as a brigadier general in the Pennsylvania military.

During the war, the Continental Army had a critical need for lead for bullets. When Roberdeau learned in April of 1778 about lead deposits in western Pennsylvania, he led an expedition into the wilderness, to today's Altoona. He confirmed the report and oversaw the construction of a fort to protect the lead mining and smelting operations and the local people. In his June 4, 1778, letter to General Washington, he described the fort as being fifty yards square with a bastion at each corner, guarded by seventy men who were mostly militia and a few Continental soldiers.

The mine closed in 1780. The present fort, a reproduction of Fort Roberdeau, was completed in 1976 in commemoration of the Bicentennial.

---

72. Monmouth, New Jersey

JUNE 28, 1778

MONMOUTH BATTLEFIELD STATE PARK, ROUTE 33B
MANALAPAN, NEW JERSEY

Several changes in the war emerged in the summer of 1778. General Howe, who had submitted his resignation in October of 1777 (see #65), sailed from Philadelphia to Britain in late May and was succeeded by General Clinton as the commander in America. The next change was the result of America's alliance with France: Clinton was ordered to evacuate Philadelphia and move his army to New York. On June 19, Washington's new army marched out of Valley Forge and prepared for the attack on Clinton as he headed north, the battle of Monmouth. Piers Mackesy, in *The War for America, 1775–1783*, details the orders to Clinton.

> Clinton had only been in Philadelphia for a day when the *Porcupine* sloop arrived from England with the Cabinet orders of 21 March. They changed the whole character of his task. France was now an enemy in fact if not yet in name. Clinton learnt that he was to expect no reinforcements and no recruits, and would lose 8,000 men to Florida and the West Indies. His first act as Commander-in-Chief would be to abandon Philadelphia and remove the gutted remnant of his field army to New York. There was no glory in this.
>
> The army in the rebel colonies had a strength at that moment of nearly 27,000 rank and file fit for duty: 8,400 at New York, 3,500 at Rhode Island, and 14,700 with the main force in Philadelphia. The detachments for the West Indies and Florida would leave about 8,000 rank and file fit for duty to withdraw from Philadelphia. But Clinton resolved to postpone departure of the expeditions to the southwards till his own movement to New York was complete. His reason was the impossibility of providing simultaneous naval protection for both movements.

In *Washington's Secret War,* Thomas Fleming describes the army and its commander as they headed toward Monmouth after the winter at Valley Forge.

On June 19, exactly six months to the day after they arrived, the rest of the Continental Army marched out of Valley Forge, regimental flags flying, fifers shrilling, and drummers beating the step for the slow march. They were a new army, with new pride and new confidence, thanks to Baron von Steuben and the tall man who rode at the head of the column.

George Washington had demonstrated his mastery of a new kind of leadership in those six grim months, a blend of the military and the political, which necessity had forced upon him. He had taken command of the entire army and its support services and placed men of his choice in charge of them. He had testified to his solidarity with his officer corps, the "band of brothers" as he sometimes called them, by winning them higher salaries and half pay for seven years after the war.

He had also established a core of support in Congress, which the extremists around Samuel Adams could not overcome with their true whig rants. In the name of the men who had stayed the bitter course at Valley Forge, General Washington would no longer suffer slanders and insults silently. He was the army's commander in chief, with a new depth and dimension to the title—which he would soon make clear on the field of battle—and in the politics of high command.

To help the loyalists escape from Pennsylvania, General Clinton provided ships for 3,000 loyalists and several thousand Hessians. On June 18 he marched his army out of Philadelphia in a column twelve miles long, across New Jersey toward New York.

General Washington prepared to attack.

Thomas Fleming describes the battle at Monmouth in *Washington's Secret War.*

General Charles Lee led his division of the army across the Delaware River at Coryell's Ferry (present-day Lambertville) north of Trenton on June 20. General Washington followed him with the rest of the army on the twenty-first and twenty-second. Washington's detailed orders to Lee reveal his distrust of his second in command. Meanwhile, Washington did everything in his power to impede Clinton's progress toward New York. Bridges on the royal army's route were burned, roads were blocked by chopped down trees, buckets and ropes were removed from wells to retard the enemy's march.

Sir Henry Clinton, meanwhile, had advanced to Monmouth Court House (now Freehold) where on June 27 he paused to give his troops a badly needed rest. The weather remained insufferably hot. General Washington sent Lee orders to attack the British rear guard. He made it clear that Lee was expected to assault and hold the rear guard in place until Washington arrived with the rest of the army. The ever-more reluctant Lee did nothing all day Saturday, the twenty-seventh. When he summoned Lafayette, Anthony Wayne, and two other generals who would lead the assault for a council of war at 5 p.m., Lee neither gave them a plan nor asked them what they had seen from their forward positions. They were simply told to be

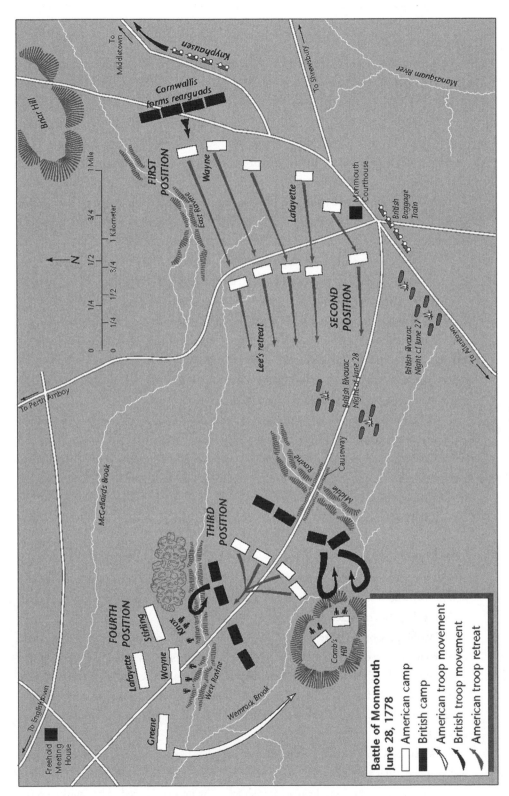

**Battle of Monmouth
June 28, 1778**

- ▭ American camp
- ■ British camp
- ⬈ American troop movement
- ⬈ British troop movement
- ⬈ American troop retreat

FIRST POSITION

Cornwallis forms rearguads

Knyphausen

To Middletown

Briar Hill

To Englishtown

To Perth Amboy

McCellard's Brook

FOURTH POSITION

Lafayette Wayne Knox Stirling

THIRD POSITION

West Ravine

Greene

Wemrock Brook

Comb's Hill

Middle Ravine

Causeway

British Bivouac
Night of June 28

British Bivouac
Night of June 27

To Allentown

To Shrewsbury

Manasquan River

Monmouth Courthouse

British Baggage Train

Lee's retreat

SECOND POSITION

Lafayette

Wayne

East Ravine

Freehold Meeting House

N

0   1/4   1/2   3/4   1 Kilometer
0   1/4   1/2   3/4   1 Mile

From: Almost a Miracle *by John Ferling (2007). Map from p. 302. By permission of Oxford University Press, U.S.A.*

ready to advance in the morning. Lee's actions (or better, inactions) underscore an ironic, seldom considered fact about this self-proclaimed military genius: he had never commanded an army in battle before.

On June 28 at 5 a.m., Washington received a message from the commander of the New Jersey militia, General Philemon Dickinson, that the British army had begun its march toward Middletown and its ultimate destination, Sandy Hook. Washington immediately ordered the main army to begin its march and sent one of his aides, Richard Kidder Meade, to Lee telling him to begin his pursuit and "bring on an attack as soon as possible." The temperature soared into the nineties as Washington's 7,800 men trudged down a sandy road toward Monmouth Court House. The general rode to the crest of a ridge that overlooked a large swamp and saw coming down the road two regiments in some disorder, all but staggering with heat exhaustion. Their colonels told the stunned Washington that the whole advanced corps was retreating.

Finally there appeared the one man who could answer General Washington's questions: General Charles Lee, followed by several aides, his dogs, and hundreds more retreating men. An infuriated Washington rode up to him and shouted: "What is the meaning of this?" What Washington heard—and saw—was Lee's ineptitude as a general. With two-fifths of the Continental Army (Lee's men) groggy with fatigue and falling back with no orders to take a position, and Washington's main army coming up the road behind him, also without a plan, the stage was set for a rout that might destroy the Continental Army and would certainly ruin the commander in chief's reputation forever.

A moment later General Washington experienced what might be called a military epiphany. In a letter to his brother John Augustine "Jack" Washington, he told how he suddenly sensed "that bountiful Providence which has never failed us in the hour of distress" had arranged for him to encounter Lee at this place. It was all but perfect for defense. Washington began giving orders. Then came a sight that stirred relief and joy: General Anthony Wayne and the rest of his men, marching in perfect formation as if they were on Valley Forge's Grand Parade.

British cavalry opened the attack on Anthony Wayne's thin line with a thunderous charge. American cannon raked them at long range and blasts of musketry from the hedgerow and nearby woods sent men and horses plunging to the sandy earth, writhing in agony. The surviving dragoons retreated in disorder.

Washington ordered Steuben to bring up the regiments he had reorganized. Steuben's reinforcements moved out to make the attack with "great spirit," Washington later said. But the combination of the suffocating heat and the oncoming darkness aborted the assault. Washington ordered the army to rest for the night in their forward positions and prepare to resume the offensive in the morning. The general spread his cloak on the ground and slept among his troops.

When the Continentals awoke in the morning, they found General Clinton and his army had vanished. After giving his men several hours to recover from the heat of the day, the British commander had put them on the road at midnight. The heat continued to be murderous and water was in short supply. Washington saw no point in wearing down his men. They had done their job. They had proven they could meet the best of the British army and fight them to a standstill.

In *A Battlefield Atlas of the American Revolution,* Craig L. Symonds summarizes the actions at Monmouth.

Monmouth was really two battles: the disgrace of Lee's skirmish in the morning, and the steadfastness of the

Camp mess chest including field accoutrements used by General George Washington during the Revolutionary War. *(Courtesy, Division of Armed Forces History, National Museum of American History, Smithsonian Institution)*

Americans under Washington in the afternoon. The troops had proven their ability to stand and fight even against British regulars, if properly led. The one dark spot was Lee's shameful conduct. But he was not at all shamefaced. He asserted his innocence in a sharp letter to Washington and demanded a court martial. Washington obliged him, submitted formal charges, and placed him under arrest. Six weeks later a military court found him guilty as charged and suspended him from the service.

This Glorious Struggle, edited by Edward G. Lengel, includes the letter General Washington wrote to Henry Laurens, the president of the Continental Congress, after the battle of Monmouth.

Washington describes the ensuing campaign, which culminated on June 28 in the Battle of Monmouth, in this letter to the president of Congress.

English Town [N.J.]
1st July 1778

Sir

I embrace the first moment of leisure, to give Congress a more full and particular account of the movements of the Army under my command, since its passing the Delaware, than the situation of our Affairs would heretofore permit.

Were I to conclude my account of this days transactions without expressing my obligations to the Officers of the Army in general, I should do injustice to their merit, and violence to my own feelings. They seemed to vie with each other in manifesting their Zeal and Bravery. The Catalougue of those who distinguished themselves is too long to admit of particularizing individuals: I cannot however forbear mentioning Brigadier General Wayne whose good conduct and bravery thro' the whole action deserves particular commendation.

The Behaviour of the troops in general, after they recovered from the first surprize occasioned by the Retreat of the advanced Corps, was such as could not be surpassed.

The peculiar Situation of General Lee at this time, requires that I should say nothing of his Conduct. He is now in arrest. The Charges against him, with such Sentence as the Court Martial may decree in his Case, shall be transmitted for the approbation or disapprobation of Congress as soon as it shall have passed…

Go: Washington

In *The American Revolution,* Gordon S. Wood points to the most important characteristics of General Washington.

Washington's ultimate success as the American commander in chief, however, never stemmed from his military abilities. He was never a traditional military hero. He had no smashing, stunning victories, and his tactical and strategic maneuvers were never the sort that awed men. Instead, it was his character and political talent and judgment that mattered most. His stoicism, dignity, and perseverance in the face of seemingly impossible odds came to symbolize the entire Revolutionary cause. As the war went on year after year, his stature only grew, and by 1779 Americans were celebrating his birthday as well as the Fourth of July. Washington always deferred to civilian leadership and never lost the support of the Congress, even when exaggerated rumors of a cabal involving Thomas Conway, an Irish-born French officer, and General Horatio Gates, the victor at Saratoga, seemed to threaten his position in the fall and winter of 1777–78. He was always loyal to his fellow officers in the Continental Army and they to him; they trusted him, and with good reason. What he lacked in military skill he made up with prudence and wisdom. When in the wake of the French alliance the French nobleman the Marquis de Lafayette, who had been in the struggle since 1777, proposed a Franco-American scheme for conquering Canada, the excited Congress readily agreed. Washington, however, pointed out that France had her own interests and was scarcely to be trusted in the retaking of Canada, and the scheme quietly died.

━━◈━━

73. Newport, Rhode Island

AUGUST 5–31, 1778

CONANICUT BATTERY
BUTTS HILL FORT
NEWPORT, RHODE ISLAND

The British had occupied Newport and the islands in Narragansett Bay since their capture by General Clinton in December 1776 (see #31). By the end of July 1778, General Robert Pigot held the islands with a garrison of 6,000 troops. After conferring with General Washington, Admiral Comte d'Estaing agreed to sail his fleet of twelve ships-of-the-line and three frigates north to Rhode Island where he would join an American force and attack Pigot. Washington ordered 2,500 Continentals led by Major General the Marquis de Lafayette and Brigadier General James Varnum from White Plains, New York, to join Major General John Sullivan in Providence. Thousands of New England militiamen and state troops were gathering to march to Tiverton, Rhode Island.

The French fleet arrived in Narragansett Bay on July 29. The plan agreed upon by d'Estaing and Sullivan called for the Americans to move from Tiverton down the east side of the island while the French attacked from the west with their 4,000 regulars and marines. The two forces would trap the British in Newport and cut off British forces posted to the north.

On August 9 Admiral Howe's fleet arrived off the Rhode Island coast. Admiral d'Estaing ordered the marines he had just landed on Conanicut Island back on his ships and sailed out to meet the British. While the two fleets maneuvered for position, a violent storm blew in, damaging both fleets. They sailed away to make repairs, the British to New York and the French to Boston. Lafayette rode to Boston to urge d'Estaing to return but was unsuccessful.

Sullivan moved from Tiverton in the early morning of August 9. The Americans marched south toward Newport and dug siege lines within a mile of Pigot's fortifications. After the loss of the French forces, the departure of militia, and illnesses among his command, Sullivan had too few effective soldiers. He began to withdraw from Aquidneck Island on the night of August 28–29 and head north to Butts Hill. Major General Nathanael Greene's division and Brigadier General John Glover's division defended the Americans' move off the island. Sullivan's force had about 210 casualties and Pigot's, 260.

74. Beavertail Light and Conanicut Battery, Rhode Island

BEAVERTAIL STATE PARK, BEAVERTAIL LIGHTHOUSE MUSEUM
CONANICUT BATTERY, BATTERY LANE
JAMESTOWN ON CONANICUT ISLAND, RHODE ISLAND

The first Beavertail Lighthouse was a wooden tower built in 1749 under the direction of the Newport architect Peter Harrison on the southern tip of Conanicut Island in Narragansett Bay to guide mariners. After it burned four years later, it was replaced by a fieldstone tower. The British damaged the lighthouse in 1779 when they retreated from Rhode Island. It was later demolished; some of the foundation remains.

In 1776 the Rhode Island Assembly ordered the construction of a battery on Beavertail. After the British took Newport, they reinforced the battery and fired its cannon at the

French fleet in July 1778 (see #73). The British spiked the battery's guns and destroyed its powder magazines when they left in October 1779.

75. Fort Barton, Rhode Island

FORT BARTON WOODS
HIGHLAND ROAD AT LAWTON AVENUE
TIVERTON, RHODE ISLAND

Fort Barton, an earthen redoubt, was built to defend Tiverton against the British on Aquidneck Island. It overlooks the site of Howland's Ferry where General John Sullivan's troops embarked on August 9, 1778, for their advance onto the island.

The fort was named in honor of William Barton, a lieutenant colonel of a Rhode Island state regiment. On a dark night in July 1777 Barton had led about forty-five men who rowed past British warships, captured British Major General Richard Prescott without firing a shot, and returned to the mainland.

76. Butts Hill Fort, Rhode Island

OFF SPRAGUE STREET
PATRIOTS PARK AT ROUTES 24 AND 114
PORTSMOUTH, RHODE ISLAND

In 1776 Americans built an earthwork on Butts Hill, the highest ground in the northern area of Aquidneck Island. The British took the fort in December 1776 and expanded it, including building barracks for 200 soldiers. General John Sullivan's forces captured the fort when they moved onto the island in the 1778 Newport campaign (see #73), and it was Sullivan's headquarters during the August 29 battle. After the Americans completed their withdrawal from Aquidneck Island, the British occupied the fort until they abandoned the island in October 1779.

Patriots Park, a National Historic Landmark, is the site of the battle. The granite monument is a memorial to the 1st Rhode Island Regiment and the battle.

Christian M. McBurney describes the battle of Rhode Island in *The Rhode Island Campaign: The First French and American Operation in the Revolutionary War.*

The military significance of the Battle of Rhode Island has been underestimated. Aside from the battles at Bunker Hill, Lexington and Concord, and Bennington, Vermont, it caused more casualties than any New England engagement of the war. And while the August 29, 1778, clash ended allied attempts to recapture Newport, it revealed numerous positive signs. Continental troops on the American army's left wing had fought with vigor against seasoned British regular troops. And on its right (which featured the 1st Rhode Island Regiment, an outfit filled with freed slaves and other persons of color) Continentals repelled three charges by Hessian regulars, forcing them to flee the field—a rare accomplishment. Along with the June 1778 Battle of Monmouth, the Battle of Rhode Island proved that solid instruction and battlefield experience were shaping the Continental army into an effective fighting force. The battle also highlighted the improving accuracy of American artillery, and even the fighting potential of New England militia units.

For the Americans, who as Greene wrote "had so often been necessitated to turn our backs" to the enemy, the sight of stalwart Hessian professionals withdrawing before them was a rare and glorious one. "To behold our fellows, chasing the [Hessians] off the field of battle, afforded a pleasure which you can better conceive than I describe," Greene added. Greene happily boasted to George Washington that "I had the pleasure to see them run in worse disorder than they did at the Battle of Monmouth." Lieutenant Colonel Livingston wrote exuberantly that not "since the commencement of the war" had the enemy "receive[d] so unexpected a check." In his official report to Congress, Sullivan noted simply that "The enemy were at length routed and fled in great confusion to [Turkey] Hill, leaving their dead and wounded in considerable numbers behind them."

In fact, neither Sullivan nor Pigot wanted a full-scale battle. Sullivan sought merely to get his American army off Aquidneck Island intact before the arrival of Clinton's reinforcements. Even if he inflicted a major defeat on the British, he could not, without naval support, have held the island against both Pigot and Clinton. Pigot in turn had no desire to risk his entire force— and possession of Newport—just for a chance to bloody Sullivan. Now he just wanted the American army to leave the island. However, inflated estimates of that army's size—which he and his subordinates believed to be from 15,000 to 20,000 troops—may have influenced him. Pigot had visited the summit of Quaker Hill to observe the action at 2:00 p.m. Two hours later he ordered the Hessian Landgrave and Ditfurth Regiments to march to von Lossberg's support, and they dutifully arrived at 7:00 p.m. Like Sullivan, he would commit to no more. Aside from sporadic artillery fire and light skirmishing that continued until nightfall, the Battle of Rhode Island was over. The rattle of musketry and booming of cannon had lasted for seven hours.

During the night of August 30–31 New England boatmen, many from General John Glover's former regiment, ferried Sullivan's troops off the island just ahead of General Henry Clinton's arrival at Newport on September 1 with a small fleet carrying more than 4,000 reinforcements.

In October 1779, the British evacuated Newport. On July 10, 1780, Commodore the Chevalier de Ternay's French fleet carrying the Comte de Rochambeau in command of more than 5,000 troops arrived off the coast. They remained in Rhode Island until June 1781, when they marched south to join General Washington's Continental Army near White Plains, New York, on July 6.

After the British evacuated Newport, they made no attempt to take it from the French. In *Victory at Yorktown: The Campaign that Won the Revolution,* Richard M. Ketchum points out that the failure to attack the French was one of the consequences of British headquarters infighting.

The failure of the British to attack, and possibly fatally wound, the French at Newport was calamitous in the long run. Because of the feud between General Clinton and Admiral Arbuthnot the French troops, who were, after all, some of the finest units of a veteran, first-class army, remained unharmed and within easy sailing distance of New York. Their presence in Rhode Island was a constant threat to the British, and, as George Washington discovered, even the pretense of an attack was likely to alter whatever plans Sir Henry might have made.

Nor was the French army the only beneficiary of the British headquarters infighting. Ternay's capital ships—seven of them—remained in Newport, a menace Arbuthnot had to deal with by maintaining a blockade, tying up vessels that could be more profitably employed elsewhere. And the blockade, as the French were to discover, was no guarantee that those seven ships of the line could not escape.

During that summer of 1780 Sir Henry Clinton lost the initiative and never regained it. For eight more months he and Admiral Marriot Arbuthnot would remain locked in a harness of mutual hatred that precluded any possibility of cooperation between the services they led.

—≫≪—

77. Bedford-Fairhaven, Massachusetts

SEPTEMBER 5–6, 1778

FORT PHOENIX STATE RESERVATION
GREEN STREET
FAIRHAVEN, MASSACHUSETTS

The people of Fairhaven, a town on Buzzard's Bay, completed a fort in 1777 to protect it from British naval attacks. After the Battle of Rhode Island, General Clinton sailed south from Newport to New York. He detached General Charles Grey, who had led the attack on General Anthony Wayne's force at Paoli (see #64), with a 4,000-man force and ordered him to raid along the Massachusetts coast and destroy the privateers and their storage buildings.

Sir James Murray led the soldiers who raided the New Bedford harbor, drove the thirty-four-man militia from the fort, burned the barracks, and destroyed the fort and ten of its eleven cannon. They burned buildings, wharves, and warehouses in New Bedford and Fairhaven and vessels in the Acushnet River. Their successful raid destroyed the privateer fleet and the local economies, which did not recover until after the war when the area became a major whaling port.

The fort was later rebuilt and named Fort Phoenix. It was attacked by the British landing from the HMS *Nimrod* in June 1814 and taken out of service in 1876.

78. Martha's Vineyard, Massachusetts

SEPTEMBER 8–15, 1778

MARTHA'S VINEYARD, MASSACHUSETTS

General Grey continued raiding along the coast of Massachusetts. His forces entered Vineyard Haven Harbor on September 10, 1778, and demanded animals, food, and weapons. After the residents responded by driving in livestock, giving up public funds, and surrendering arms, Grey ordered his men to raid the island, including today's West Tisbury, Chilmark, Edgartown, and Vineyard Haven. They seized townsmen and took more than 10,000 sheep as well as cattle, hay, and weapons, all without firing a shot. After destroying their saltworks and boats, including their whaling boats, Grey sailed away on September 15, leaving the islanders destitute, without adequate food or the means to produce it before winter began.

79. Old Tappan, New Jersey

SEPTEMBER 28, 1778

BAYLOR MASSACRE BURIAL SITE
RIVERVALE ROAD AND RED OAK DRIVE
RIVER VALE, NEW JERSEY

General Grey's next attack was a night surprise, like Paoli in September of 1777 (see #64). Washington sent small forces to harass General Henry Clinton's large foraging parties in the Hudson River Valley. In late September 1778 he ordered Brigadier General Anthony Wayne to operate against General Cornwallis on the west side of the river. Wayne posted the 3rd Continental Light Dragoons, commanded by Colonel George Baylor, near the bridge over the Hackensack River. The twenty-six-year-old Baylor led a 100-man force that was inexperienced and poorly armed. On September 28, Grey led his light infantry in a night surprise attack on the Dragoons with bayonets—as he had at Paoli—inflicting more than fifty American casualties. Those taken prisoner included Baylor, who was wounded in the attack.

80. Lake Champlain, Vermont

NOVEMBER 6–9, 1778

ADDISON COUNTY ALONG OTTER CREEK FROM
MIDDLEBURY NORTH THROUGH VERGENNES, VERMONT

The British launched raids in 1778 against patriot forces, including those at Fairhaven and Old Tappan, and others that devastated civilians, including at Martha's Vineyard in September, and two in Vermont and New York in November.

Major Christopher Carleton, in command of 454 men, including 100 American Indians, sailed south from Canada on Lake Champlain with orders to destroy Americans' vessels, sawmills, and gristmills; to raid communities of supplies, provisions, and animals; to take the men prisoner and to send their families away. On November 6 Carleton landed 107 men south of Chimney Point. They raided east to Middlebury, where they burned all but one of the buildings, a barn built of logs too green to burn. The next day they continued their raid north along Otter Creek to Vergennes. A second party came ashore near today's West Bridport and marched on the Crown Point Road east to destroy Moore's sawmill, but were stopped by Americans near the mill and withdrew.

81. Cherry Valley, New York

NOVEMBER 11, 1778

HISTORICAL MARKERS
CHERRY VALLEY MUSEUM
49 MAIN STREET
CHERRY VALLEY, NEW YORK

Joseph T. Glatthaar and James Kirby Martin describe the Cherry Valley raid in *Forgotten Allies.*

In early November 1778, an Oneida warrior named Nicholas Sharp, also called Saucy Nick and Loghtaudye (He Continues Speaking), conveyed important intelligence to Peter Gansevoort, commanding at Fort Schuyler. An Onondaga Indian had just returned from the Susquehanna Valley and described a "great Meeting" in which Indians and Tory rangers decided to attack Cherry Valley. Gansevoort rushed the information to the rebel commander at Cherry Valley, Colonel Ichabod Alden. With gross incompetence, Alden refused to shelter local settlers in the recently built fort. He and other officers kept their billets in a private residence some distance away.

The British had assembled more than five hundred Indians, Tories, and regular soldiers for the attack. Captain Walter Butler, who had escaped from the patriots back in April, assumed command of the expedition, more in name than anything else. Haughty and arbitrary, he was in charge only because his father, John, was suffering from a severe bout of rheumatism. Young Butler quickly alienated the Indians and many of the loyalists. Ninety of Brant's Tory followers refused to fight under Butler and went home, despite the latter's threats to treat them like traitors to the king. Friends implored Brant to remain. He did so grudgingly.

Shortly after dawn on November 11, the British force swooped down on the settlers of Cherry Valley. Those in the fort were able to repel the assault. Outside the fort, the affair turned ugly. Indians and Tories began slaughtering men, women, and children. Efforts by Butler and Brant failed to restrain the attackers. When the smoke cleared, the Crown raiders had butchered thirty-one residents and grabbed seventy-one prisoners, thirty-eight of whom they later released. In addition, twenty-six rebel officers and soldiers, including Alden, lost their lives, and fourteen more became prisoners. The Indians and Tories stripped the area of livestock and left almost no structures standing.

⟞⟋⟍⟝

In May 1777 Georgians had attacked Thomas Creek, Florida, to stop the raids into Georgia by the East Florida Rangers and their Indian allies and to capture St. Augustine (see #43). In the spring of 1778 while General Washington's army was at Valley Forge, Georgians fought back a British naval attack on April 19. (see #82) In June they tried again in Florida at Fort Tonyn and Alligator Creek Bridge but failed (see #45).

82. The Capture of the HMS *Hinchinbrooke* and the Sloop *Rebecca*, Georgia

APRIL 19, 1778
HISTORICAL MARKER ON
FREDERICA ROAD NEAR FORT FREDERICA NATIONAL MONUMENT
ST. SIMONS ISLAND, GEORGIA

Georgia had a small navy to protect the inner passages along its coastline. The galleys, highly maneuverable, flat-bottomed, oared vessels that could carry heavy ordnance, had

The Southern Campaigns 1778-1781

From: The Glorious Cause by Robert Middlekauff (1982). Map from p. 439. By permission of Oxford University Press, USA.

been built by shipwrights sent from Philadelphia to Savannah. The British issued orders to the HMS *Hinchinbrooke,* the *Hatter,* and the *Rebecca* (captured from South Carolina) to capture Georgia's galleys for the British to use in the rivers and channels where their larger vessels could not maneuver. When Colonel Samuel Elbert, the commander of the Continental line forces in Georgia, learned that British vessels were near Frederica, he boarded his 350-man command on three galleys, the *Washington* under Captain John Hardy, the *Lee* under Captain John Braddock, and the *Bulloch* under Captain Archibald Hutcher. Captain George Young was in command of a flatboat loaded with artillery. They headed into the Frederica River from the north.

On April 19, they met the British and opened fire. The British attempted to escape downriver but grounded the *Hinchinbrooke* and the *Rebecca* and were forced to abandon them. The *Hatter* rescued the British crews and sailed to Jekyll Island. The Americans won the battle, captured the ships, and suffered no casualties.

83. Fort Morris, Georgia

NOVEMBER 25, 1778, AND JANUARY 6–9, 1779

FORT MORRIS HISTORIC SITE
2559 FORT MORRIS ROAD
MIDWAY, GEORGIA

In 1776 the Continental Congress ordered Fort Morris to be built on a low bluff on the Medway River to protect Sunbury, an important seaport south of Savannah. On November 25, 1778, a British force demanded the surrender of the fort and its 200-man garrison. Colonel John McIntosh refused, responding: "Come and take it." Instead, the British withdrew to Florida, taking cattle, sheep, horses, and slaves with them.

After Lieutenant Colonel Archibald Campbell took Savannah in December 1778, the fort was the last American stronghold in Georgia. Campbell joined forces with Major General Augustine Prevost, who had marched north from St. Augustine in command of 2,000 British regulars, loyalists, and American Indians. On January 9, 1779, General Prevost's younger brother, Lieutenant Colonel James Marc Prevost, fired his artillery on Fort Morris, forcing the commander, Major Joseph Lane, and his 200 Continentals and militia to surrender.

The British renamed it Fort George in honor of King George III. Captured American officers were paroled and held in house arrest in Sunbury. When the siege of Savannah began the following September, the British garrison was ordered to Savannah.

84. Savannah, Georgia

DECEMBER 27–DECEMBER 29, 1778
SEPTEMBER 12–OCTOBER 9, 1779
BATTLEFIELD MEMORIAL PARK
LOUISVILLE ROAD AND MARTIN LUTHER KING, JR. BOULEVARD
SAVANNAH, GEORGIA

On September 25, 1778, Congress appointed Major General Benjamin Lincoln to replace Major General Robert Howe as commander of the Southern Department. Lincoln arrived in Charleston in December. Howe was still in command in Savannah when the British captured it on December 29.

Robert Middlekauff describes the capture of Savannah in *The Glorious Cause.*

Germain now had an idea of how the war might be won—tap the loyalist support in the South and further its spread northward. From the beginning of Clinton's assumption of command, Germain had tried to push him into a new expedition. The entrance of France into the war diverted even Germain, but the order to dispatch troops from Philadelphia to Florida in March 1778 helped keep alive the possibility of a campaign in the southern colonies. By November, Clinton was prepared for a first effort. On the 27th he dispatched Lt. Colonel Archibald Campbell with the 71st Regiment, two regiments of Hessians, four Tory battalions, and a small contingent of artillery—altogether about 3500 rank-and-file on an invasion of Georgia. Two days before Christmas, Campbell arrived off Tybee Island at the mouth of the Savannah River, some fifteen miles below the town of Savannah.

The American commander in Georgia, Robert Howe, rushed to the town's defense from Sunbury, a distance of thirty miles. He was badly outnumbered, however, and his force—700 Continentals, 150 militia—was soon outflanked when Campbell was guided by a slave through a swamp to a vulnerable point in the not very formidable American defenses. The battle that ensued on December 29 resembled many in the war: the Americans collapsed and fled, leaving almost 100 dead and 453 prisoners. The British lost three dead and ten wounded. In the next month, Campbell with the support of Prevost, who came up from Florida, took control of Georgia.

Nine months after the capture of Savannah, in September 1779, the French fleet arrived off the Georgia coast to retake it. Edward J. Cashin describes the siege of Savannah in "Revolutionary War in Georgia" on the *New Georgia Encyclopedia* website, www.georgiaencyclopedia.org.

Governor Sir James Wright returned to Georgia on July 14, 1779, and announced the restoration of Georgia to the crown, with the privilege of exemption from taxation. Thus Georgia became the first, and ultimately the only one, of the thirteen states in rebellion to be restored to royal allegiance. Governor Wright had hardly settled to his duties when on September 3, 1779, a French fleet of twenty-five ships appeared unexpectedly off the Georgia coast. Count Charles Henri d'Estaing intended to oblige George Washington by stopping off on his way back to France to recapture Savannah. He disembarked his army of 4,000–5,000 men at Beaulieu on the Vernon River and proceeded to besiege Savannah. Major General Benjamin Lincoln hurried over from South Carolina with his army to join in the siege.

D'Estaing demanded the surrender of Savannah on September 16, but General Augustine Prevost asked for twenty-four hours to give an answer. During that day, Lieutenant Colonel John Maitland brought his 800 redcoats in from Beaufort, South Carolina, to bolster the British defenses. Then Prevost declined to surrender.

On October 9, 1779, the allies launched a grand assault upon the British lines and suffered 752 casualties, while the British defenders lost only 18 killed and 39 wounded. Count Casimir Pulaski, a Polish nobleman who had volunteered to fight for the cause of liberty, died at the head of the men he led. Sergeant William Jasper, the hero of the 1776 battle in Charleston harbor, also died. The battered French army withdrew to its ships, and Benjamin Lincoln's troops returned to Charleston.

85. Kettle Creek, Georgia

FEBRUARY 14, 1779

KETTLE CREEK BATTLEFIELD
WAR HILL ROAD
SOUTHWEST OF WASHINGTON, GEORGIA

After Lieutenant Colonel Archibald Campbell captured Savannah in December 1778, he marched on to Augusta, occupied it on January 29, 1779, and waited for Colonel James Boyd. Boyd was trying to build a force from among the loyalists in the Carolinas, but he had recruited only 350 men. Boyd headed toward Augusta and was joined by 250 North Carolinians commanded by John Moore. Patriots fought Boyd at the crossing at Vann's Creek and followed him into Georgia. Meanwhile, Campbell was threatened by gathering forces that could cut him off from Savannah, so he moved out of Augusta toward Savannah on February 14.

Boyd, unaware of Campbell's withdrawal or of the militia monitoring his march, camped in a bend of Kettle Creek. The 340-man militia led by Colonel Andrew Pickens of South Carolina and Colonel John Dooly and Lieutenant Colonel Elijah Clarke of Georgia attacked, defeated the loyalists, and mortally wounded Boyd. Each force suffered about twenty killed and wounded. The militia took prisoners after the battle and gathered up more as they headed toward Augusta. They marched 150 prisoners into South Carolina, held trials, and sentenced five to hang—those who had coerced men to join the loyalists by threatening their families and property. Recruitment of loyalists continued to decline.

By December 1778 the British had captured four American cities—New York, Philadelphia, Newport, and Savannah—and would take Charleston in 1780. Benjamin L. Carp describes the effects of the revolution on the cities in *Rebels Rising: Cities and the American Revolution*.

Political activity in the cities helped lead the colonists to independence, but in the process, the cities rendered themselves obsolete. As the Revolutionary War began, urban taverns and narrow streets ceased to be the focus of revolutionary politics. The committees and militia units of the countryside had become politically mobilized, and city dwellers now became minority populations within the larger movement. The war's cataclysmic events deprived the cities of their role in the nation's political development, as the seaport towns were abandoned, occupied, and immobilized. When the British armed forces descended on the shores of America, they seized the cities as essential posts for prosecuting the war against the rebellious colonists. In time the British withdrew from each of the cities, but Americans would no longer think of their seaports as centers for political mobilization; indeed, they would forget or suppress the part that the cities had played in the years of resistance.

The British, faced with the task of salvaging their crumbling empire, now sought to take advantage of the cities' deep harbors, public buildings, and importance as centers of commerce and communication to shelter and supply the armed forces. As they occupied New York City, Newport, Philadelphia, Savannah, and Charleston, the British hoped to mobilize the local Loyalists and reestablish colonial rule using the cities as strong points. Patriots, on the other hand, found they could no longer depend upon the cities. This situation left them with three choices: defend the cities, abandon them, or destroy them. Local leaders, understandably, begged the Continental Congress to defend American cities. This strategy unfailingly placed the Continental Army at great risk, and generally ended in disaster. The British Navy was powerful enough that it could successfully support an assault on almost any coastal position. As a result, Americans surrendered more men during the battles around New York City in 1776 and during the unsuccessful defense of Charleston in 1780 than they did during the entirety of any given year of the war.

In other cases, the Patriots decided to abandon the cities. These retreats rankled many Patriots because they handed the British all the advantages of the ports. Still, the alternative was often the destruction of the Continental Army—hence, the British took Newport without firing a shot in 1776 and faced minimal opposition at Philadelphia in 1777 (though the Continental defense of the Delaware River proved more tenacious). Many Patriots would never return to these cities, which helped to diffuse the memory of the cities' political mobilization.

Since the Continental Army could not defend the cities, since the British could reap great civilian and military benefit from the cities, and since Loyalists owned much of the cities' property, many radical Patriots did not hesitate to suggest burning coastal cities or allowing the British to destroy them. When the British began shelling Norfolk, Virginia, on New Year's Day, 1776, Patriot forces took the opportunity to burn the rest of the city themselves. Six days after the British occupation of New York City on September 15, 1776, a sixth of the city burned. Patriots were the likely culprits in this instance as well, though after both fires, Patriot newspapers deflected blame toward the British.

---

86. Camp Reading Cantonment, Connecticut

PUTNAM MEMORIAL STATE PARK
ROUTES 107 AND 58
REDDING, CONNECTICUT

After the August 1778 battle at Newport (see #73), General Clinton's forces stayed in and near New York. Those he had ordered south took Savannah in late December. As winter approached, Washington's army went into encampments in Connecticut, New Jersey, and near West Point.

Putnam Memorial State Park is the site of the New Hampshire brigade's camp, one of Major General Israel Putnam's three winter encampments from December 1778 until May 1779. Putnam's division included a New Hampshire brigade under Brigadier General Enoch Poor, a Canadian Regiment led by Colonel Moses Hazen, and two brigades of Connecticut troops: 2nd Brigade Connecticut Line regiments commanded by Brigadier General Jedediah Huntington and the 1st Brigade Connecticut Line regiments commanded by Brigadier General Samuel H. Parsons.

The encampment was positioned so that the soldiers could cover Long Island Sound and West Point, if needed, and could protect the supply depot at Danbury.

Private Joseph Plumb Martin wrote about the hunger and cold that he and the other men in their Connecticut brigade suffered. Ray Raphael quotes Martin in *A People's History of the American Revolution: How Common People Shaped the Fight for Independence.*

Starting in 1779 and continuing through 1783, two years after the surrender at Yorktown, dozens of minor mutinies plagued the Continental Army. Most followed a similar pattern: hungry and frustrated men who had received no pay made a show of force, gained the attention of officers or politicians who offered them promises, and then backed off. On July 29, 1779, when "the biger part of the Regement had turn'd out in Muterny" and "marcht off for Greenwich," Jeremiah Greenman, by now a sergeant, went off with his men in hot pursuit; two days later the mutineers "all return'd to camp all pardined."

Whereas Sergeant Greenman remained faithful to the established military order, Joseph Plumb Martin, still a private, defiantly joined with the protesters. In January of 1779, growing weary of "our old Continental line of starving and freezing," Martin and his colleagues "concluded that we *could* not or *would* not bear it any longer." They decided to parade in front of their huts with no officers, a clear violation of military rule. The officers "endeavored to soothe the Yankee temper…with an abundance of fair promises," but "hunger was not to be so easily pacified." Although the protesters disbanded, they harassed the officers through the night by the firing of arms, "making void the law." Rations improved slightly over the next few days, "but it soon became an old story and the old system commenced again as regular as fair weather to foul." The men paraded once more on their own, this time with arms, threatening to march to the state capital at Hartford and then to "disperse to our homes" if still unsatisfied. But they never made good on their threats: "[T]he old mode of flattery and promising was resorted to and produced the usual effect. We all once more returned to our huts and fires, and there spent the remainder of the night, muttering over our forlorn condition."

<hr />

87. Hopewell Village and Furnace, Pennsylvania

HOPEWELL FURNACE NATIONAL HISTORIC SITE
ROUTE 345
ELVERSON, PENNSYLVANIA

The iron furnaces that produced shot and cannon were vital to sustaining the Revolution. Ironworks were built in remote, forested areas because the furnaces used charcoal, made from wood, for fuel. Iron ore, charcoal, and limestone were put into the furnace. The limestone removed impurities in the ore and, when the furnace was tapped, pure liquid iron emerged. The furnace at Hopewell produced pig iron and products created by pouring the iron into molds. Hopewell's most famous product was the Hopewell stove, which significantly improved women's lives by enabling them to put food on the stove to cook and then turn to their other work instead of having to remain before the hearth fire, tending it.

Mark Bird inherited his father's iron business and expanded it. He built the Hopewell Furnace on French Creek (1771–1883), where there were iron ore and limestone deposits as well as sources of water and wood. The Hopewell Furnace produced shot and cannon for the Continental Army and Navy.

Bird was a colonel in the Berks County militia and outfitted the men at his own expense. He also served as Deputy Quartermaster General of Pennsylvania and provided flour to the soldiers at Valley Forge. After the war the Continental Congress's payments to

Bird were insufficient, and he never recovered from the economic downturn of the 1780s. He died in North Carolina in 1816.

Hopewell passed through several owners until 1800, when the Buckley-Brooke partnership bought it and operated it for eighty-three years. They expanded the operations and built the now restored iron plantation buildings. Clement Brooke was the ironmaster from 1816 until 1848. In "The Iron Plantations" in *Hopewell Furnace,* W. David Lewis describes the importance of the iron industry in America.

> Rapid expansion of the colonial iron industry in the early 18th century was one of the early causes of conflict with England. That country's mercantilist philosophy of keeping its colonies in a state of economic dependence led to passage by Parliament in 1750 of a law prohibiting the building of any further colonial ironworks for the making of plates, nail rods, or steel. Colonial ironmasters scoffed at these restrictive efforts, however, and by the outbreak of the Revolution, the American iron industry accounted for about one-seventh of the world's output of pig iron, wrought iron, and castings.
>
> Pennsylvania was by far the most important iron manufacturing colony. By 1770 when Mark Bird chose Berks County as the site for Hopewell Furnace, the area was already becoming a center of American industry. The iron plantations were built on very different social and economic foundations from those of the southern agricultural counterparts, but there were parallels in their size, rural setting, and concentration on one product. There was usually a spacious, richly furnished "Big House," surrounded by thousands of acres of woodland. The ironmaster who resided there often emulated the style of the English gentry, complete with elegant carriages and a pack of hunting hounds. He was at the pinnacle of an essentially self-contained, rural society that often numbered over 100 people, all of whose work was directly or indirectly related to the production of iron.

88. Cornwall Furnace, Pennsylvania

CORNWALL IRON FURNACE
94 REXMONT ROAD
CORNWALL, PENNSYLVANIA

In 1742 Peter Grubb built the iron furnace in Cornwall because all of the raw materials required by the smelting process—iron ore, limestone, and wood for charcoal—were available nearby. It closed in 1883 and is the only charcoal-fueled blast furnace in America that has survived intact. The furnace, blast equipment, and buildings are as they were in the mid-nineteenth century.

89. Jerusalem Mill, Maryland

GUNPOWDER FALLS STATE PARK
2813 JERUSALEM ROAD
KINGSVILLE, MARYLAND

Americans were sustained by the grains they grew and the gristmills that milled the flour. One of the largest mills in Maryland was on the Little Gunpowder River. In 1772 David Lee, a Quaker, began milling flour in the new gristmill, in partnership with Isaiah Linton. Linton built eight water-powered mills along the Little Gunpowder River. The Quaker village also included a sawmill and a building known as the Gunshop. The mill operated until 1961.

In *Revolutionary Mothers: Women in the Struggle for America's Independence,* Carol Berkin details the work of women to help the troops during the war.

For most women, the struggle to survive and to protect their children and their homes was challenge enough. Yet, they were pressed, and they pressed themselves, to do more—and there was much more to be done. General Washington's Continental troops were woefully short of everything from ammunition to clothing. State regiments lacked necessary supplies as well. If the production of homespun had been a political gesture in the years before the Revolution, now it was a critical necessity. Only a few months after the battles of Lexington and Concord, a call went out in Philadelphia to "the SPINNERS of this city, the suburbs, and country" to return to cloth production. Wool and cotton would be distributed to every spinner who came to Market and Ninth streets with a letter of reference from a "respectable person in their neighborhood." The broadside, posted across the city, declared that this was a call to public service that could be answered by the humblest of women. "The most feeble effort to help to save the state from ruin, when it is all you can do, is...entitled to the same reward as they who, of their abundant abilities, have cast in much." Local leaders in Hartford, Connecticut, pre-ferred to order rather than urge the women of their town to produce clothing for the troops. Their production quota for 1776 was 1,000 coats and vests and 1,600 shirts. In the South, patriot leaders appealed to women to plant crops that could feed the local armies.

Most of the women who contributed to the "public defense" did not need to be coerced. In the midst of their private struggles they found the time to aid their country's cause. If the army needed saltpeter, women made saltpeter, boiling together wood ash and earth scraped from beneath the floors of their houses, adding charcoal and sulfur to produce the powder. If the army needed clothing, women like Mary Fraier of Chester County, Pennsylvania, went door-to-door, soliciting clothes from their neighbors, then cleaned and mended them before delivering them to nearby troops. When the word spread that the military needed metal to produce bullets and cannon shot, women melted down their own pewter tableware, clock weights, and window weights, and solicited their neighbors to do the same. One New Englander even donated the name plaques from her family's tombstones.

And wherever the battlefield yielded its wounded, women volunteered to provide beds and care for the soldiers.

90. Fort Frederick, Maryland

FORT FREDERICK STATE PARK
11100 FORT FREDERICK ROAD
BIG POOL, MARYLAND

The construction of the large stone fort began in 1756 during the Seven Years' War. Under the command of Colonel Moses Rawlings, it was turned into a prison during the American Revolution. British and German soldiers taken at Saratoga in 1777, known as the Convention Army, were imprisoned in the fort as were soldiers surrendered with General Cornwallis at Yorktown in 1781. Prison life for American and British soldiers was difficult and often tragic (see #100).

⇢⟫⟨⇠

91. Fort Laurens, Ohio

FEBRUARY–MARCH 1779

FORT LAURENS STATE MEMORIAL
11067 FORT LAURENS ROAD NORTHWEST
BOLIVAR, OHIO

Ohio, like other frontiers, was the site of violent interactions between settlers and the British regulars with their American Indian allies. Fort Laurens, the only fort in Ohio, reveals the hardships of war west of the Allegheny Mountains. In late 1778 General Lachlan McIntosh, a Georgian in command of 1,200 men, headed into the Ohio Territory to attack Indian villages along the Sandusky River. In mid-November, winter forced him to abandon his campaign. He built a fort named to honor Henry Laurens, the president of the Continental Congress. McIntosh garrisoned the fort with 200 men commanded by Colonel John B. Gibson and returned to Fort Pitt.

In February 1779, Captain Henry Bird, leading fifty British regulars, and Simon Girty, with 180 Indians—including Wyandot, Mingo, Munsee, and Delaware—attacked and killed or captured a detail from the fort and held it under siege for a month until both sides were suffering from starvation. After the British lifted the siege, McIntosh sent a relief force with supplies. Most of the garrison returned to Fort Pitt. The fort was abandoned in August 1779.

92. Vincennes, Indiana

FEBRUARY 23–25, 1779

GEORGE ROGERS CLARK NATIONAL HISTORICAL PARK
401 SOUTH 2ND STREET
VINCENNES, INDIANA

In the summer of 1778, twenty-six-year-old Colonel George Rogers Clark, supported by Governor Patrick Henry of Virginia, led a force of frontiersmen against the British in the West. They took control of Kaskaskia and Cahokia along the Mississippi River near St. Louis, which were populated by French settlers, and then took Vincennes without firing a shot. The British Lieutenant Governor Henry Hamilton left Detroit in command of a force and retook Fort Sackville in Vincennes on December 17, 1778.

The following is from the George Rogers Clark National Historical Park website.

Determined to capture Hamilton, Clark and his force of approximately 170 Americans and Frenchmen made an epic 18-day trek from Kaskaskia through the freezing floodwaters of the Illinois country. At times in icy water up to their shoulders, it was Clark's determined leadership that brought them through this incredible midwinter journey. They arrived in Vincennes after nightfall on Feb. 23, 1779. The French citizens, eager to again renounce the British, warmly greeted Clark's men, providing food and dry gunpowder. Hamilton's garrison now consisted of approximately 40 British soldiers and a similar number of French volunteers and militia from Detroit and Vincennes. These French troops were not enthusiastic to fire upon the enemy when they realized that the French inhabitants of the town again had embraced the Americans.

Clark's men surrounded the fort and gave the impression of having a much larger army. Flags sufficient for an army of 500 had been brought from Kaskaskia and now were unfurled and carried within view of the fort. The American soldiers, who were experienced woodsmen, could maintain a rate of fire that convinced the British that the army indeed was large in number. These woodsmen were armed with the famed long rifle. And their aim was accurate.

At this time, an event occurred which caused the British to realize what might be their fate if the Americans were forced to storm the fort. An Indian raiding party, sent out by Hamilton to attack American settlers along the Ohio River, returned to Vincennes. Their entrance came during a lull in the battle and they saw the British flag flying, as usual, from the fort. The unsuspecting warriors, gleefully yelling and firing their weapons in the air, realized their mistake too late. Several Indians were killed or wounded by the frontiersmen while others were captured.

In retaliation for Indian raids in which numerous men, women and children had been slaughtered, Clark ordered five of the captured warriors to be tomahawked in full view of the fort. The executions were intended to heighten the psychological pressure upon the British, while also illustrating to Indian observers that the redcoats no longer could protect those tribes who made war on the Americans.

Following this grim scene, the lieutenant governor reluctantly agreed to Clark's final terms which were just short of unconditional surrender. Hamilton described his thoughts at having to surrender. "The mortification, disappointment and indignation I felt, may possibly be conceived…" The defeated British army marched out of Fort Sackville and laid down their muskets before their victors. The surrender occurred 10 a.m., Thurs., Feb. 25, 1779.

<hr>

93. Verplanck's Point, New York

MAY 30–JUNE 1, 1779

HISTORICAL MARKERS ON RIVERVIEW AVENUE
VERPLANCK, NEW YORK
STONY POINT BATTLEFIELD STATE HISTORIC SITE
BATTLEFIELD ROAD
STONY POINT, NEW YORK

General Washington had ordered two blockhouses built on the Hudson River to secure King's Ferry, the Americans' southernmost ferry crossing of the Hudson River. The small fort on Verplanck's Point on the east bank, Fort Lafayette, was held by a seventy-man brigade commanded by Captain Armstrong.

General Henry Clinton had returned to New York after the June 1778 battle of Monmouth. With the objective of taking control of this crossing, he ordered seventy sailing vessels and 150 flatboats upriver. On May 30 a force commanded by Major General John Vaughan landed on the east bank of the Hudson at Teller's Point several miles below the fort and marched north. When Clinton landed a smaller force the next day, south of the Stony Point fort on the west bank of the river, the forty-man garrison under Major William Kears burned the blockhouse and fled. Clinton had artillery emplaced on Stony Point and shelled Fort Lafayette. Vaughan cut off Armstrong's retreat, forcing him to surrender the entire garrison, which was accepted by Major John André. The British had one casualty.

94. Stony Point, New York

JULY 15–16, 1779

Stony Point Battlefield State Historic Site
Battlefield Road
Stony Point, New York

After the loss to the British of both forts at King's Ferry on the Hudson River in early June 1779, General Washington and Brigadier General Anthony Wayne developed a carefully planned surprise attack to retake the fort on Stony Point, 150 feet above the river on the west bank. Wayne, in command of light infantry, marched more than twelve miles under tight security and arrived near the fort after dark on July 15. In the midnight attack, they overwhelmed the garrison with bayonets and swords and took more than 500 prisoners. Wayne's disciplined soldiers honored the cries for quarter. There were fifteen Americans killed and twenty British.

After the victory, Washington concluded that an effective garrison would require too many soldiers and ordered Wayne to remove the supplies and the fifteen cannon and destroy the fortifications. The Americans withdrew on July 18. The victory was an important morale builder for the Americans. The British reoccupied the remains the next day and rebuilt it, only to abandon it the following October.

95. New Town, New York

AUGUST 29, 1779

Newtown Battlefield State Park
451 Oneida Road
Elmira, New York

In response to the raids on the frontier in 1778, Washington ordered Continentals to attack Iroquoia, the lands of the Iroquois confederacy which was known as the Six Nations. In late August 1779 the combined forces of Major General John Sullivan and Brigadier General James Clinton came up the Chemung River. A force led by Major John Butler, Joseph Brant, and the Seneca war chief, Sayenqueraghta, had built breastworks of brush and logs one-half mile long near New Town, an Indian village. One of Sullivan's advance riflemen climbed a tree and saw the loyalists and Indians behind their breastworks. Sullivan turned his artillery on them, and the Indians and loyalists retreated after a short battle.

In *The Divided Ground: Indians, Settlers, and the Northern Borderland of the American Revolution*, Alan Taylor describes the invasion.

During the summer the main Patriot invasion advanced in three prongs. From Pittsburgh, Colonel Daniel Broadhead marched north against Seneca villages in the Allegheny Valley. From the Mohawk Valley, General James Clinton led his brigade down the Susquehanna River to Tioga to meet the main thrust, commanded by General John Sullivan, who marched up that river, past the ruins of Wyoming. Samuel Kirkland joined the Sullivan expedition as a chaplain, mixing Christianity with patriotism to inspire the troops. In mid-August at Tioga, Clinton rendezvoused with Sullivan, creating an army of 3,000 men, more than three times the number of Loyalists and western Iroquois mustered to resist.

At Newtown Point on August 29, Sullivan's soldiers brushed aside resistance led by Brant, Butler, and Sayenqueraghta. The Patriot troops then methodically located, looted, and burned the Iroquois villages around the Finger Lakes and in the Genesee Valley, while Broadhead did the same in the Allegheny Valley. Everywhere, the soldiers marveled at the substantial villages of log cabins, the broad fields of Indian corn, and the extensive orchards of apple, peach, and cherry trees, all of which they systematically destroyed. Patriot torches claimed Kanadasega, Sayenqueraghta's home village that had hosted Kirkland's original mission in 1765. On September 15, Sullivan turned back, returning via the Chemung and Susquehanna rivers to Pennsylvania. In retrospect, he boasted of destroying 40 Iroquois villages and at least 160,000 bushels of corn. Impressed by Iroquoia's fertile soil, many officers and soldiers eagerly anticipated a postwar return as conquering settlers.

The Iroquois plight seemed dire by war's end. Whether allied to the British or to the Patriots, all the Iroquois had suffered devastating raids that destroyed almost all their villages by 1781. The violent dislocations promoted malnutrition and disease, reducing Iroquois numbers by a third, from a prewar 9,000 to a postwar 6,000. Becoming refugees either at Schenectady, on the American frontier, or at Montreal or Niagara, within the British orbit, the Iroquois left behind a broad and bloody no-man's-land. After the war, American settlers and speculators meant to fill that vacuum, inspired by favorable reports from the soldiers in Sullivan's invasion.

---

96. Penobscot Bay and River, Maine

JULY 21–AUGUST 13, 1779

FORT GEORGE

BATTLE AVENUE

EXHIBIT AT THE CASTINE HISTORICAL SOCIETY

17 SCHOOL STREET

CASTINE, MAINE

The British determination to occupy the Penobscot Bay area was driven by the need for a trading post on the coast, a safe area for loyalists, a source of pine masts for ships, and a naval base. In the summer of 1779 Brigadier General Francis McLean arrived in present-day Castine in command of 700 troops. The British began to build a fort, later named Fort George.

Since Maine was a province of Massachusetts, the Provincial Assembly took action to oppose the British. In the largest amphibious operation of the Revolutionary War, Massachusetts sent Commodore Dudley Saltonstall in command of naval craft that included troop transports, supply vessels, and a thirty-two gun frigate from the Continental Navy. Brigadier General Solomon Lovell commanded the 1,000 inexperienced militiamen, and Lieutenant Colonel Paul Revere was in charge of the artillery. In the last week of July, Lovell made a daring landing with 400 troops near the fort. To Lovell's surprise, Saltonstall refused to engage the three British sloops. When Vice Admiral Sir George Collier in command of seven armed British warships sailed in, Saltonstall retreated up the bay. With no outlet, his crews had to burn and abandon their vessels. The Americans escaped into the Maine woods and made their way toward Boston.

After the navy's court-martial, Saltonstall was dismissed from the service. The British retained control of the coastal trade in northern New England.

Naval action was not limited to the American coast. In June 1777 Congress had made Captain John Paul Jones commander of the sloop *Ranger*. The following April he took the Revolutionary War across the Atlantic Ocean by raiding along the British coast. In 1779 he sailed toward England in command of four ships, one of which he had named the *Bonhomme Richard* to honor Benjamin Franklin. Along the coast of Yorkshire on September 23, he battled the HMS *Serapis*. Paul Aron describes the battle in *We Hold These Truths*.

The *Serapis* fired a series of devastating broadsides at the *Bonhomme Richard*. The battle certainly appeared lost to gunner's mate Henry Gardner. Not seeing Jones, assuming he was dead, and realizing the *Bonhomme Richard* was soon likely to sink or blow up, Gardner called "Quarters!"—a signal to the British that he was ready to surrender. Jones, furious, flung his gun at Gardner's head, knocking him out.

On the *Serapis*, Captain Richard Pearson had heard Gardner's calls and responded, "Have you struck? Do you call for Quarters?"

It was then, according to the *Bonhomme Richard*'s first lieutenant, Richard Dale, that Jones uttered his memorable line: "I have not yet begun to fight!"

The tide of battle turned when the *Serapis*'s bowsprit became entangled in the *Bonhomme Richard*'s starboard quarter. About three hours after the battle began, with more than 150 of the Americans and more than 130 of the British dead or injured—about half of the crew members on both sides—Pearson surrendered. The *Bonhomme Richard* sank the next day, and Jones sailed on to Holland in the damaged but still seaworthy *Serapis*.

Jones's famous words have been the subject of much debate, with historians differing over at what point in the battle he spoke them and whether he spoke them at all. Whatever the exact words, there is no denying Jones loudly refused to surrender, then went on to win the battle. There is also no denying the effect of his victory. By taking the war to the shores of

Great Britain, by defeating a British warship, Jones shattered the aura of invincibility surrounding the Royal Navy.

Franklin rightly praised Jones for spreading "terror and bustle" along the British coasts.

---

97. Morristown, New Jersey

MORRISTOWN NATIONAL HISTORICAL PARK
MORRISTOWN, NEW JERSEY

Morristown was the winter encampment for the Continental Army from January 6 until May 28, 1777 (see #40) and again from December 1, 1779, until June 23, 1780. The Historical Park includes most of the 1779–1780 encampment areas, which are southwest of the village, and the Ford Mansion, Washington's headquarters. In *Almost a Miracle,* John Ferling quotes General Washington on the source of the army's problems at Morristown.

Snow began falling in December, and just after Christmas a blizzard struck that raged for nearly thirty-six hours. Fresh snow fell every few days throughout January and February, piling atop the old snow. With but a single blanket apiece, the men often slept huddled together in search of warmth. Early in January, General Greene anguished for the "Poor Fellows," half of whom were "naked, and above two thirds starved." A month later he reported that the army was on "the point of disbanding for want of provisions."

The supply service was emasculated when numerous staff employees left in 1779 for better paying jobs in the private sector. Congress's decision to relinquish to the states the job of supplying the army also haunted the cold, hungry soldiers at Jockey Hollow. Most states were not up to the challenge. More than at any other moment in the war it was this winter of deprivation and despondency that the seeds sprouted for what later would be called the "nationalist" or "consolidation" movement, the drive to create a strong and sovereign national government, a quest that culminated in the Constitutional Convention in 1787. It was while the miseries of Morristown were fresh on his mind that Washington first despaired that "our measures are not under the influence and direction of one council, but thirteen." He added that unless Congress possessed "absolute powers in all matters relative to the great purposes of War, and of general concern," and that the states were restricted to "matters of local and internal polity," the United States was "attempting an impossibility and shall very soon become (if it is not already the case) a many headed Monster…that never will or can, steer to the same point."

98. The Siege of Charleston, South Carolina

FEBRUARY 11–MAY 12, 1780

A REMNANT OF THE HORN WORK, THE TABBY FORTIFICATION AT THE
CENTER OF THE AMERICAN LINES, IS IN MARION SQUARE
CHARLESTON, SOUTH CAROLINA
FORT MOULTRIE IN FORT SUMTER NATIONAL MONUMENT
SULLIVAN'S ISLAND, SOUTH CAROLINA

In *Partisans and Redcoats,* Walter Edgar describes the siege of Charleston, which began on February 11, 1780.

As 1779 drew to a close, the British were planning a major southern campaign. Encouraged by their successes in Georgia and the reports of loyalists in the Carolinas, they envisioned a quick victory that would roll up the southern states one by one. South Carolina was the key to their strategy. "I had long determined," wrote Sir Henry Clinton, "on an expedition against Charleston, the capital of South Carolina." On the day after Christmas 1779, a British fleet sailed from New York with an army of eighty-five hundred. On 11 February 1780, British forces landed on John's Island, south of Charleston. General Lincoln and his army withdrew into Charleston and prepared to defend the city. On 1 April, the British began to construct their siege works. On 9 April, a British fleet of fourteen warships slipped past the forts defending Charleston and sailed into the inner harbor. Now the city was vulnerable to cannon fire from both land and sea.

The noose was tightening around the American garrison, but rather than save his army, General Benjamin Lincoln let local politicians browbeat him into remaining in the city. On 13 April, Governor John Rutledge and several members of his council escaped the beleaguered city. Those state officials who remained were determined to resist to the last man, and when Lincoln made plans for evacuating his troops, they threatened to open the city's gates to the enemy.

On 12 May 1780, after a forty-two-day siege, Lincoln surrendered his army of approximately five thousand men. It was one of the greatest disasters in the annals of the U. S. Army. By refusing to stand up to civilian authorities, he placed the entire future of the United States in jeopardy. There was now no American army in the South to oppose Clinton. South Carolina, the key state in Clinton's grand southern strategy, lay open to the victorious British army.

Carl P. Borick details the fall of Charleston in *A Gallant Defense: The Siege of Charleston, 1780.*

Whereas Clinton could include as captured all men in the garrison, during the siege Lincoln could only count on those who were capable of performing duty. Of the Continentals and militia in the garrison, a large proportion were either sick or wounded or lacked proper clothing and arms, and as such were unfit for duty. For instance, Lincoln's effective strength at the end of April was probably at most only 4,000 men under arms.

In addition to the men captured, the soldiers of the garrison suffered 89 killed, most of whom were Continental troops; 138 men had been wounded. These figures to be sure do not include American casualties suffered at Biggin's Bridge and Lenud's Ferry. The civilian populace shared in the horrors of war throughout British operations in the lowcountry, and they certainly did so during the siege of the city, where British fire killed approximately twenty civilians. Altogether, the campaign against Charleston took the lives of some 150 Americans. Official returns for the British army showed 76 men killed and 189 wounded, while losses among the navy were 23 killed and 28 wounded, for a total of 99 killed and 217 wounded among British forces. It was a relatively small price to pay for their victory. Not only had they captured the largest and most important city in the southern states, but they had taken an entire army as well. They also took possession of 400 pieces of cannon, over 5,000 muskets, and large quantities of ammunition. Meanwhile, the Royal Navy commandeered three Continental warships, *Providence, Boston,* and *Ranger*, and the South Carolina navy's *L'Aventure*, plus assorted smaller vessels. The Continental navy could ill afford the loss of three frigates while the South Carolina state navy came near to going completely out of existence.

By all accounts, losses sustained in the fall of Charleston were disastrous for the American cause, not only in the south but throughout all the states. Most costly was the loss of 3,465 officers and enlisted men of the Continental regiments, which all but eliminated the Continental lines of three states, Virginia, North Carolina, and South Carolina.

99. Powder Magazine, South Carolina

POWDER MAGAZINE
79 CUMBERLAND STREET
CHARLESTON, SOUTH CAROLINA

By 1704 Charles Town, now Charleston, was surrounded by a wall to protect it from French, Spanish, and American Indian attacks. The Powder Magazine, a National Historic Landmark, is the city's oldest public building. It was completed in the northwest corner of the town in 1713 to store Charles Town's supply of gunpowder.

100. The Exchange, South Carolina

THE OLD EXCHANGE
122 EAST BAY STREET
CHARLESTON, SOUTH CAROLINA

The brick custom house was completed in 1771 with a cellar for storage and an exchange floor for merchants. The third floor housed customs offices and the Great Hall, where in 1774 delegates were elected to the First Continental Congress. In 1776 the Declaration of Independence was read from the front of the Exchange. The British used the cellar as a prison after they captured Charleston in May 1780.

Almost a Miracle by John Ferling includes an overview of prisoners of war in America, in England, and on ships.

Charleston yielded the largest collection of prisoners taken by Britain in a single engagement, a number that exceeded the combined total captured at Quebec and Fort Washington, the two other battles in which record numbers of Americans surrendered. Each man who was led away into captivity entered a world that was perhaps more dangerous than anything he had previously experienced as a soldier. Scholars believe that at least 8,500 of the 18,154 Continental soldiers and sailors who were captured in this war died while in captivity. In contrast, the best estimate is that about 6,800 Continentals died in battle and 10,000 perished in camp of disease. Put another way, whereas one Continental soldier in eighteen was killed in action and one in ten died of a camp disease, an astonishing 47 percent of those who became prisoners of war perished in captivity.

The largest numbers were confined in four places—England, New York, on prison ships, or at Haddrell's Point, about six miles from Charleston. Though some installations were spacious, overcrowding was a common problem. The British resolved the matter by converting obsolete naval and merchant vessels into prison ships, the most loathsome, and dangerous, facility that any prisoner could face. Provided with rations that were two-thirds those allotted British soldiers, a prisoner's diet was inadequate in quantity and nutrition, and sometimes the food was spoiled or chock-a-block with maggots or worms. Those held captive on ships were confined below deck in lethally squalid surroundings.

The acute class-consciousness of that day was evident in the treatment of prisoners. Virtually all officers were paroled and lived in what was tantamount to an indulgent house arrest. Captive officers in New York were allowed to reside in private homes, paying room and board to the owner, to move about freely within the city, though they could not leave Manhattan.

The United States also took prisoners. Some men were housed in jails, but the most fortunate wound up in newly constructed barracks. Captive British and German officers were paroled and rented rooms in private residences. The enlisted men held captive by the Americans, like their rebel equivalents, faced a difficult life. Often unable to adequately provision their armies, it was usually beyond the capability of the Americans to provide for their prisoners. Although many prisoners faced deprivation, and many died in captivity, the Americans—with one glaring exception—did not set out to deliberately mistreat their prisoners. The black stain on America's record was its treatment of captive Loyalist soldiers, who often were consciously subjected to inhuman treatment.

Escape aside, there were three principal ways in which a prisoner might gain his freedom. Both sides offered captives freedom in return for defecting and joining their armed forces. Far greater numbers were released from confinement through paroles. Set free, a parolee pledged not to soldier again before he had been formally exchanged. Prisoner exchanges were the third method of liberating captives. Washington favored exchanges, fearing that if the American captives were left in British hands for years, the public would be persuaded that military "service [was] odious." The commissioners in Paris secured three exchanges of naval captives and in 1779 and 1780 Franklin arranged for the release of nearly 275 American prisoners by swapping some of the captives taken by John Paul Jones.

101. Waxhaws, South Carolina

MAY 29, 1780

BUFORD BATTLEGROUND MARKERS AND MONUMENTS
SC 9 AND SC 522
EAST OF LANCASTER, SOUTH CAROLINA

John S. Pancake recounts the Waxhaws battle in *This Destructive War: The British Campaign in the Carolinas, 1780–1782.*

At the time of the surrender of Charleston, a force of 350 Virginia Continentals under Colonel Abraham Buford was on its way to reinforce the besieged city. They had gotten as far as Lenud's Ferry on the Santee when news of the fall of Charleston reached them, so Buford started back to North Carolina. Determined not to let this force escape, Cornwallis detached Tarleton's Legion and sent it in pursuit. The young dragoon drove his command 105 miles in fifty-four hours and caught up with Buford at the Waxhaws near the North Carolina border. Tarleton called on Buford to surrender, and when the American refused Tarleton launched a driving attack spearheaded by his mounted men. The Virginians gave way before the charge, "the battalion was totally broken and slaughter was commenced...." Buford and his officers now tried to surrender, but the dragoons continued to cut down the Americans. Tarleton reported that his horse was shot from under him at just the time when the Americans were raising a white flag, but he was accused of refusing to give quarter and so earned for himself a notoriety that he may not have altogether deserved. One hundred and thirteen Americans were killed and

150 wounded. Reports that Tarleton's men bayoneted the wounded are hardly consistent with the fact that the British paroled the wounded and "surgeons were sent for from Camden and Charlotte town to assist them." Buford escaped with the remnant of his command. The Legion lost five killed and fourteen wounded. The Patriots were naturally anxious to overlook the fact that the British, bone-weary from their forced march, had defeated a force that outnumbered them three to two. Whatever the facts, "Tarleton's quarter" became symbolic of British barbarity, and the tough Legion commander was soon spoken of as "Bloody Ban."

How much this grim little engagement and its aftermath contributed to the renewal of resistance is difficult to say. Perhaps it was too much to expect that partisans on both sides who had been clawing at each other for more than a year could now live in peace. At least two dozen clashes between Whigs and Tories had taken place since the fall of Savannah in 1778. Nor did the behavior of the British troops help matters. The regulars were the same redcoats who had plundered in New Jersey, New York, and Pennsylvania and who, from first to last, had never had much regard for Americans whether Whig or Tory. Major Patrick Ferguson's militia inevitably contained many who were eager to avenge the abuses they had suffered from their Whig neighbors.

It was certainly unfortunate for the British that within a few weeks raiding parties had burned out Thomas Sumter. With predictable dispatch this partisan leader took the field, but he was not the first. On the same day as the battle at the Waxhaws, Colonel William Bratton scattered Loyalist militia at Mobley's Meeting House near Winnsboro. Then in a four-day period in mid-July Whig and Tory partisans clashed at Union Court House, Williamson's Plantation, Cedar Springs, Gowen's Old Fort, and McDowell's Camp on the Pacolet River.

In *The Southern Strategy: Britain's Conquest of South Carolina and Georgia, 1775–1780,* David K. Wilson considers Lieutenant Colonel Banastre Tarleton's responsibility for the casualties in the battle at Waxhaws.

Buford's defeat was ultimately the result of the inexperience of his troops, and of his own mistake in holding his fire a few seconds too long. However, what is most controversial about the battle at Waxhaws is whether a massacre took place after the surrender and, if so, whether Tarleton ordered or condoned it. Dr. Brownfield's dramatic account of the battle's aftermath is now one of the most famous and most often referenced pieces of prose regarding the Revolutionary War in the South: "The demand for quarters, seldom refused to a vanquished foe, was at once found to be in vain;—not a man was spared—and it was the concurrent testimony of all the survivors, that for fifteen minutes after every man was prostrate. They went over the ground plunging their bayonets into every one that exhibited any signs of life."

So what really happened? The casualty figures given by Tarleton in his official report to Cornwallis tell the real, unbiased story. Tarleton reported that the Americans suffered 113 killed "on the spot"; 150 wounded were "unable to travel, and left on parole"; and a mere 53 Americans were taken prisoner. Henry Lee says that "Lieutenant-Colonel Buford, with the horse, escaped, as did about eighty or ninety of our infantry, who fortunately being advanced, saved themselves by flight." Contrast Buford's losses with those of Tarleton, who reported only 5 killed and 12 wounded—a total of 17 casualties.

Even though Tarleton may be innocent of ordering an atrocity, he is certainly guilty of failing to restrain his men once the engagement ceased to be a battle and became a simple slaughter. Charles Stedman, who was serving as chief of Cornwallis's commissary on this expedition, said of the battle: "The king's troops were entitled to great commendation for their activity and ardour on this occasion, *but the virtue of humanity was totally forgot*" [emphasis added]. This condemnation, coming from a British officer who served alongside Tarleton and his legion, serves as authoritative confirmation of the American accusations of brutality leveled against Tarleton and his troops after this battle.

In *A Battlefield Atlas of the American Revolution,* Craig L. Symonds points to the problems General Henry Clinton's proclamations caused in South Carolina.

The fall of Charleston and the capture of the entire American southern army did a great deal to encourage loyalism in the South. Clinton established a string of British outposts across South Carolina, and all over the state Americans declared their loyalty to the crown. Clinton's first proclamations were designed to reinforce this mood. He declared that all those who had rebelled against King George would receive a pardon so long as they now went home and behaved themselves. Most Whig leaders did just that. But on June 3 Clinton reversed himself. His new proclamation declared that passive neutrality was not enough. Only those who took "an active part in settling and securing His Majesty's government" would be forgiven. Many men who might have remained out of the war altogether were thereby forced to choose between active support and opposition. Having issued this declaration, Clinton left Charleston two days later and returned to New York, leaving Cornwallis in command. Almost from the moment of Clinton's departure the Carolinas erupted into virtual civil war.

On June 5, 1780, General Cornwallis assumed command of the British army in the South.

In May 1780 General Washington had to confront the loss of Charleston and the surrender of almost 3,500 Continentals. He also knew that the Revolution was threatened by the British success in the war and by Congress's lack of fiscal responsibility and authority. In *His Excellency: George Washington,* Joseph J. Ellis describes Washington's views on the problems confronting the Continental Congress.

Up until now, when Washington thought about the importance of virtue as a source for patriotic commitment, he thought in personal terms: the courage of soldiers advancing against a British artillery position; the silent sacrifices of half-naked troops trudging through the snow at Valley Forge; his own decision to risk everything to serve a cause he believed in. Another more impersonal version of virtue now began to circulate in his thinking, a version not dependent on sheer willpower but rather on institutions capable of delivering resources. If the essence of personal virtue was bravery, the essence of institutional virtue was fiscal responsibility. And if the latter version of virtue determined the current contest, Washington acknowledged that "my feelings upon the subject are painful," for he was saddled with a fiscal system that seemed designed to produce, as he put it, only "false hopes and temporary expedients."

His initial understanding of the political liabilities afflicting the Continental Congress, like his initial understanding of virtue, emphasized personal failures of will. The best men, he told Benjamin Harrison of Virginia, preferred to serve in the state governments, where they could "slumber or sleep at home…while the common interests of America are mouldering and sinking into irretrievable…ruin." While the second-tier delegates in the Continental Congress dithered over trifling issues, where were the first-tier leaders from Virginia? "Where is Mason, Wythe, Jefferson, Nicholas, Pendleton, Nelson and another [i.e., Harrison] I could name?" Why was the Congress failing to prosecute profiteers and "forestallers" (hoarders who jacked up the prices of supplies needed by the army), who were obviously "pests of society," all of whom ought to be "hung in Gibbets upon a gallows five times as high as the one prepared by Haman?" How could a responsible group of legislators allow the currency to become a standing joke—not worth a Continental—and the inflation to spiral to such heights that "a rat, in the shape of a Horse, is not to be bought at this time for less than £200?" Given any semblance of equivalent resources, he was prepared to take on the British army and promise victory. But the failure of political leadership at the national level, which had permitted inflation, corruption, and broken promises to become "an epidemical disease," meant that sheer indifference had become a more formidable enemy "infinitely more to be dreaded than the whole force of G. Britain." It was beyond belief, he confided to an old Virginia friend, to watch America's best prospects become "over cast and clouded by a host of infamous harpies, who to acquire a little pelf, would involve this great Continent in inextricable ruin."

The real problem, which Washington came to recognize only gradually, was less personal than structural, not so much a lack of will as a deep-rooted suspicion of government power that severely limited the authority of the Continental Congress. Parliament and the British ministry could impose taxes and raise armies because they possessed the sovereign power to speak for the British nation. During the early months of the war the Continental Congress had assumed emergency powers of equivalent authority, which rendered possible the creation of the Continental army and Washington's appointment to head it. But by behaving as a national legislature, an American version of Parliament, the Congress made itself vulnerable to the same criticism that the colonies had directed at Parliament itself. The central impulse of the American Revolution had been a deep aversion to legislation, especially taxes, emanating from any consolidated government in a faraway place beyond the direct control and supervision of the citizens affected. From the perspective of Virginia and Massachusetts, the delegates gathered in Philadelphia were distant creatures who could not tax them any more than could the House of Commons in London. And since voting in the Continental Congress had always been by state—one state, one vote—it could not plausibly claim to represent fairly or fully accurately the American population as a whole. The Articles of Confederation, officially adopted in 1781, accurately embodied the same one-vote principle and did not create, or intend to create, a unified American nation but rather a confederation of sovereign states.

Washington had given little thought to these political questions before the war. His revolutionary convictions, to be sure, included a staunch rejection of Parliament's power over the colonies. But the core of his hostility to British power had been rooted in questions of control rather than an aversion to political power per se, in the fact that it was *British* more than it was power. Personally, he despised the British presumptions of superiority that rendered him a mere subject. Politically, he believed that only an independent America could wrest control of the untapped riches west of the Alleghenies from London nabobs. He had left more finely tuned arguments about the proper configuration and character of an indigenous American government to others.

In 1780 he decided that he could no longer afford to remain silent.

General Washington corresponded regularly with Congress and, occasionally, with the members he knew. On May 31, 1780, he wrote a letter that included a warning to Joseph Jones, a member of Congress from Virginia. His letter is in *George Washington: Writings,* edited by John Rhodehamel.

Certain I am that unless Congress speaks in a more decisive tone; unless they are vested with powers by the several States competent to the great purposes of War, or assume them as matter of right; and they, and the states respectively, act with more energy than they hitherto have done, that our Cause is lost.

This my dear Sir is plain language to a member of Congress; but it is the language of truth and friendship. It is the result of long thinking, close application, and strict observation. I see one head gradually changing into thirteen. I see one Army branching into thirteen; and instead of looking up to Congress as the supreme controuling power of the united States, are considering themselves as dependent on their respective States. In a word, I see the powers of Congress declining too fast for the consequence and respect which is due to them as the grand representative body of America, and am fearful of the consequences of it.

———— ⟫⟫⟫⟫ ————

102. Logan's Fort, Kentucky

MAY 30–JUNE 1, 1777
Martin Luther King Street
Historical Markers on the Courthouse grounds and at
MLK Street and Danville Avenue
Stanford, Kentucky

In the 1770s settlers and land speculators moved into Kentucky and Ohio. The settlements violated treaties and invaded Indian homelands. The raids were tragic for both settlers and

Indians. By 1777 the three remaining settlements in Kentucky were Logan's Fort (today's Stanford), built by Benjamin Logan a few months before the attack, Boonesborough and Fort Harrod.

American Indians attacked Boonesborough on May 23 and Logan's Fort on May 30. Logan led the militia in their successful defense of the fort, which encouraged future settlements in Kentucky.

103. Fort Boonesborough, Kentucky

SEPTEMBER 7–18, 1778

FORT BOONESBOROUGH STATE PARK
KENTUCKY RIVER MUSEUM
4375 BOONESBORO ROAD
RICHMOND, KENTUCKY

Daniel Boone came to Shawnee lands in 1769 to hunt. He founded Boonesborough in April 1775 and by September 1778 there were twenty-six log cabins and four blockhouses. In January 1778 Boone was one of the men captured by Shawnees who escaped and returned to Boonesborough. The men of the settlement successfully defended it during the September 1778 siege by several tribes led by Black Fish. Boone moved away the following year, and by 1815 the village was deserted.

Colin G. Calloway recounts the capture of Daniel Boone by the Shawnees in *The Shawnees and the War for America*.

Black Fish, who had been a rival of Cornstalk for the position of principal chief, led a large war party into Kentucky and headed for the settlement at Boonesborough. En route they surprised Boone and a party of men at the salt springs on the Licking River. Caught off guard in a snowstorm, Boone persuaded his twenty-six companions to surrender rather than throw their lives away and indicated that he would be willing to talk Boonesborough into surrendering in return for guarantees of good treatment. The Shawnees headed north with their captives. They made Boone run the gauntlet, between two lines of people striking him with clubs and sticks, but after they reached Chillicothe most of the captives were adopted into Shawnee families. Black Fish adopted Boone to take the place of a dead son. Boone recalled that Black Fish and his wife were kind to him and that he grew attached to his adoptive family. But he also dissembled to buy time for Boonesborough. When the chance came he made good his escape, returned to Boonesborough, and helped organize its defenses. Most of the other captives also eventually managed to escape. Shawnee warriors raided Fort Randolph and the Kanawha Valley in the spring, and lay siege to Boonesborough in September but the settlement held out. Despite Boone's dissembling, Black Fish maintained warm relations with his adopted son.

104. Ruddell's Station, Kentucky

JUNE 24, 1780

HISTORICAL MARKER FOR RUDDELL'S MILLS ON ROUTE 1940
NEAR ROUTE 1893
SOUTHEAST OF CYNTHIANA, KENTUCKY

Among the settlements in Kentucky was Ruddell's Station, a group of cabins fortified in 1779 by Isaac Ruddell, where Pennsylvania German families lived.

In 1780 the British increased their raids on the western frontier. The first occurred in June, when British Captain Henry Bird led 150 troops of the Detroit Militia, the British 8th Regiment, and 700 American Indians from several tribes up the Ohio River into the Licking River, and overland to Ruddell's Station. Their cannon fire resulted in the surrender of Ruddell's Station on June 24, and the Ruddells were among the settlers taken prisoner. After their release, they returned to the area and later built the mills.

105. Martin's Station, Kentucky

JUNE 26, 1780

HISTORICAL MARKER ON ROUTE 27 NEAR BRENTSVILLE ROAD
NORTHWEST OF PARIS, KENTUCKY

Two days after the attack on Ruddell's Station, the nearby Martin's Station also surrendered to Captain Bird. He was forced to end the campaign because of a shortage of food and the threat of Colonel George Rogers Clark's attacks on Indian villages (see #106). The British headed back to the Licking River with more than 300 prisoners who were forced to march and row boats—without adequate food—to Detroit.

106. Piqua, Ohio

AUGUST 8, 1780

GEORGE ROGERS CLARK PARK
936 SOUTH TECUMSEH ROAD
SPRINGFIELD, OHIO

Governor Thomas Jefferson ordered Colonel George Rogers Clark to leave the Vincennes area and head to the Ohio country to protect the Kentucky settlements. In August of 1780, he led 1,000 Kentucky militiamen against Piqua, a Shawnee village. In the six-hour battle, the militia shelled the council house, burned the village and crops, and suffered twenty-seven casualties.

In *The Shawnees and the War for America,* Colin G. Calloway describes the violence in the Shawnee homelands.

Shawnee warriors routinely ambushed settlers traveling downriver on flatboats, sometimes assisted by white Shawnees who lured the emigrants closer to shore. The British reported that the Shawnees and their allies brought scalps to Detroit every day. Shawnee warriors also joined a multitribal assault into Kentucky led by British officer Henry Bird, along with McKee, Elliott, and the Girty brothers. They captured two settlements, Ruddell's and Martin's Stations, and took more than three hundred prisoners. Among the captives were a twelve-year-old boy named Stephen Ruddell, and his six-year-old brother Abraham. Their parents and siblings were soon released, but the two boys remained with the Shawnees for years. They gave Stephen a Shawnee name, Sinnamatha or Big Fish, and he became a close friend of Tecumseh, who was about his age.

In retaliation, George Rogers Clark invaded Shawnee country with one thousand men. The Shawnees burned Chillicothe rather than see it fall to the Big Knives; they made a stand at Piqua on the Mad River and did not withdraw until Clark turned his six-pound cannon on the village council house where many of the people had taken refuge. The Americans killed some old people they found hiding in the cornfields and spent three days burning the crops. Some men plundered Shawnee graves for burial goods and scalps. Shawnee losses were slight but the destruction of their corn hit them hard that winter. Refugees filtered into Detroit asking for food and shelter. "We see ourselves weak and our arms feeble to the force of the enemy," said one Shawnee chief in a council held there in spring 1781.

107. Oneida Castle, New York

JULY 25–26, 1780

SKENANDOAH BOULDER HISTORICAL MARKER
ONEIDA CASTLE, NEW YORK
SHAKO:WI CULTURAL CENTER, 5 TERRITORY ROAD, ONEIDA, NEW YORK

British forces continued their raids in New York. In late June 1780, loyalists and Iroquois arrived at Old Oneida to urge the Oneidas, who were allies of the Americans, to go with them to Niagara. Eleven warriors joined them when they left. Those who remained decided to abandon Old Oneida and Kanonwalohale (today's Oneida Castle) and go to Fort Schuyler (called Fort Stanwix before and after the Revolution; see #54) where they could be protected, taking as much as they could with them.

When Joseph Brant arrived in late July at Kanonwalohale with 300 warriors, it was deserted. In *Forgotten Allies,* Joseph T. Glatthaar and James Kirby Martin recount the next tragedy for the Oneidas.

> Brant soon learned that the residents had fled to Fort Schuyler. Leaving Kanonwalohale behind in a heap of glowing embers, the Mohawk chief and his raiders pressed on to the outskirts of the post. At the Indian field, with unenthusiastic support from Skenandoah, Brant attempted to persuade the Oneidas to switch their allegiance. One hundred thirty-two agreed to join the Crown; the others resisted. As tension mounted and the Oneidas felt more threatened, some at the Indian field started taking flight for the fort. Brant and his party pursued. Most of the Oneidas were able to get inside the gates, but two were not so fortunate. They were shot down before they reached the fort.
>
> For the next day or so, Brant's followers fired sporadically inside the post, and the garrison responded with musket shot and cannon blasts. After wasting much ammunition, the raiders then gathered up the Oneida cattle grazing outside Fort Schuyler and vanished. Skenandoah, Good Peter, and a few guides led those Oneidas who had agreed to switch allegiance, and the animals, to Niagara, while Brant directed his warriors eastward, toward rebel settlements. Under pressure from Guy Johnson to prove their loyalty and contribute to the British war effort, these 132 Oneidas produced only 20 warriors for military campaigning.
>
> Despite their rage against the Oneidas and the destruction of Kanonwalohale, the British and their Iroquois allies left Old Oneida standing. Throughout the Revolutionary War, its residents maintained a reputation for neutrality. Most of the military-age men, eager to earn esteem in combat, had already linked in some way to one side or the other. Old Oneida became a kind of haven for older people, women, children, and those who wanted nothing whatsoever to do with the war.

108. Canajoharie District, New York

AUGUST 1–2, 1780

VAN ALSTYNE HOMESTEAD, MOYER STREET
CANAJOHARIE, NEW YORK
FORT PLAIN MUSEUM AND HISTORICAL PARK
FORT PLAIN, NEW YORK
INDIAN CASTLE CHURCH, LITTLE FALLS, NEW YORK

Joseph Brant's response to General Sullivan's invasion of Iroquois lands in August of 1779 was to continue raiding in the Mohawk Valley. The following summer, he circulated a rumor that he was going to attack a supply vessel on the river, prompting the commander of Fort Plain to leave the Canajoharie District unprotected while his force protected the vessel. On August 1, 1780, Brant, leading 450 Indians and loyalists, took 300 cattle and horses, destroyed crops, burned more than fifty houses and other buildings in about twenty-four square miles, and killed sixteen people.

109. Johnson Hall, New York

JOHNSON HALL STATE HISTORIC SITE
HALL AVENUE
JOHNSTOWN, NEW YORK

Sir William Johnson was appointed superintendent for Indian affairs in 1756 and lived in Old Fort Johnson, west of Amsterdam, New York. He was successful in his effort to ally the Iroquois Confederacy with the British toward the end of the Seven Years' War. In 1763 he built Johnson Hall, where he lived with Molly Brant, sister of the Mohawk leader, Joseph Brant. His estate included a mill, a blacksmith shop, an Indian store, and barns.

Sir William negotiated the 1768 Boundary Line treaty at Fort Stanwix, which moved the 1763 boundary line farther south and west. The controversial treaty opened lands that are now parts of six states to settlers and land speculators, including Johnson. Colin G. Calloway details the importance of Johnson Hall in *The Scratch of a Pen: 1763 and the Transformation of North America.*

> Johnson Hall became a pivotal place in the conduct of British-Indian relations. It was a meeting ground of cultures. Johnson employed Dutch, German, and Irish workers on his estate and owned some African American slaves. He also attracted emigrant Highland Scots to settle as tenants on his lands. Delegations from dozens of tribes made their way to Johnson

Hall, as did soldiers and travelers. Even before the house was finished, Johnson held meetings there with Iroquois and other delegates, to divide the Indian confederacy and isolate Pontiac. In the next eleven years, the Irish baronet presided over countless councils at Johnson Hall, while servants worked to feed the assembled delegates and interpreters worked to communicate the conversations across multiple languages. Johnson's efforts matched those of the French in cultivating good relations with Indian people and entailed great expense and tireless politicking. The relationship seems to have been mutually beneficial: the Mohawks elevated their status as much important confederacy business was now conducted in Mohawk country rather than at Onondaga; Johnson diverted much of the management of Indian affairs and Indian trade from Albany to Johnson Hall. He complained regularly that every room and corner of his house was "Continually full of Indians of all Nations," "each individual of whom has a thousand things to say, & ask and any person who chuses to engage their affections or obtain ascendancy over them must be the greatest Slave living & listen to them all at any hour."

But he didn't have much to complain about. He was both friend and exploiter of the Iroquois, an agent of empire and an independent entrepreneur pursuing his own goals. He built himself a personal empire as marcher lord on Indian lands. By the time of his death in 1774, he was the largest landowner in the Mohawk valley.

John Johnson inherited his father's title and Johnson Hall. He fled to Canada in May 1776, joined St. Leger's failed expedition in the Mohawk Valley in 1777 (see #54), and led destructive raids in the Valley in 1780, including the raid on Stone Arabia on October 19. After the war, he and his family remained in Canada.

110. Stone Arabia, New York

OCTOBER 19, 1780

HISTORICAL MARKERS AT ROUTE 10 AND STONE ARABIA ROAD
PALATINE BRIDGE, NEW YORK

The agricultural settlements in the Mohawk Valley were a major source of food for the states until British and Indian raiders began destroying them. By 1776 settlers were fortifying their buildings and surrounding them with log stockades. In October 1780 Sir John Johnson and Joseph Brant led between 800 and 1,500 raiders—regulars, Tories, and Iroquois warriors—up the Mohawk River on the north bank, burning buildings and crops.

Colonel John Brown led his men from Fort Paris in the village of Stone Arabia and met the raiders in the early morning of October 19. Brown was killed, and Major Oliver

Root took command. The survivors reached Fort Paris and protected it with its cannon. Johnson destroyed Stone Arabia, including the two churches.

111. Klock's Field, New York

OCTOBER 19, 1780

FORT KLOCK HISTORIC RESTORATION
ON ROUTE 5 NEAR ROUTE 67
ST. JOHNSVILLE, NEW YORK

In 1750 Johannes Klock built a stone house on the north bank of the Mohawk River with walls two feet thick pierced with holes through which muskets could be fired. In 1776 he built a log stockade around the house, which also served as a fur trading post, to protect it during raids by the British loyalists and their American Indian allies.

After the battle at Stone Arabia, Sir John Johnson and Joseph Brant continued up the Mohawk River Valley. Later on the morning of October 19, Brigadier General Robert Van Rensselaer and the Albany County militia, led by sixty Oneidas, attacked Johnson's force in Klock's fields. They took forty prisoners and their plunder.

Governor George Clinton estimated that Johnson and Brant had burned 200 dwellings and 150,000 bushels of wheat. General Schuyler was concerned about the Oneidas who were also suffering from the raids.

Joseph T. Glatthaar and James Kirby Martin quote Schuyler in *Forgotten Allies*.

In October 1780 he had reminded Congress of the many contributions of the Oneidas and then urged that body "to attend to their situation and afford them some relief." In early December Schuyler advised Congressional leaders that "their case is at present much more critical." With the local cupboard all but bare, the situation was truly grim. "Their affection for us," he cautioned, "hath hitherto induced them to turn a deaf ear, to the repeated offers of the Enemy, and enabled them to support the misfortunes they experienced, with fortitude, and temper." Concern for the Oneidas reached down into the Schuyler household. Measuring up to his own words, the general dipped into his private larder, until he had doled out much of his personal stock of food. In mid-January, he informed Congress that he would tap his own credit to purchase food and clothing, and he also drafted a personal note for a thousand dollars to acquire 200 blankets for his Oneida allies.

112. Fort St. George, New York

NOVEMBER 23, 1780

MANOR OF ST. GEORGE

NEIGHBORHOOD ROAD AND SMITH ROAD

SHIRLEY, NEW YORK

In the late seventeenth century, Colonel William "Tangier" Smith received manorial grants that included thousands of acres in the area of today's Brookhaven. He built a house near Mastic Beach which he named the Manor of St. George. During the Revolution, British soldiers and loyalist refugees from Rhode Island seized the manor, fortified it, and renamed it Fort St. George.

In November 1780, Major Benjamin Tallmadge led eighty soldiers from Fairfield, Connecticut, across Long Island Sound. They landed at Mt. Sinai, left a detail to guard their boats, and marched across Long Island. On November 23 they surprised the British and the loyalists at the Manor, defeated them in the short battle, and took 200 prisoners, including 150 loyalist noncombatants. The killed and wounded included one patriot and seven British. Tallmadge marched the patriots and their prisoners back across the Island and burned 300 tons of hay that had been collected at Coram for the British army.

The property was later restored to the Smith family. In 1718 the Floyd family purchased more than 4,400 acres of the Smith estate. William Floyd, a signer of the Declaration of Independence, inherited the property, including Old Mastic House, which is now in the Fire Island National Seashore.

━━━◦◦◦━━━

113. Ramsour's Mill, North Carolina

JUNE 20, 1780

RAMSOUR'S MILL BATTLEGROUND

JEB SEAGLE DRIVE

HISTORICAL MARKER AT NORTH ASPEN STREET AND PAUL LAWING ROAD

LINCOLNTON, NORTH CAROLINA

In May 1780, the British had taken Charleston, and Lieutenant Colonel Banastre Tarleton had won at Waxhaws. In June the North Carolina militia were the victors at Ramsour's Mill.

Lieutenant Colonel John Moore of the North Carolina Loyalist Volunteers, who had returned home after serving with General Cornwallis in South Carolina, began to gather a force of loyalists in June of 1780. When the North Carolina militia leader in the Charlotte area, Brigadier General Griffith Rutherford, heard about the force, he directed Colonel Francis Locke to raise a militia force to battle them. Colonel Locke's 400 men on horseback and on foot surprised 1,000 loyalists in a daybreak attack near Ramsour's Mill on June 20.

In *The Road to Guilford Courthouse: The American Revolution in the Carolinas,* John Buchanan describes the fighting at Ramsour's Mill.

There was apparently no officer coordinating Rebel movements. Captain Graham wrote that "after the actions commenced, scarcely any orders were given by the officers. They fought like common soldiers, and animated their men by their example, and they suffered severely. Captains Falls, Dobson, Smith, Borman and Armstrong were killed; and Captains Houston and McKissick wounded."

Small parties of Rebels, anxious to continue the fight but seeking better cover from the galling fire, worked their way to opposite ends of the slope and began turning both Tory flanks. This is an age-old tactic, and they probably acted instinctively. That they turned the Tory flanks simultaneously was certainly fortuitous. The Rebel center at the same time held firm. The Tories began retreating up the ridge to their left and ran into advancing Rebels. Now the fighting came to close quarters and became ugly. It was hand to hand. Rebels and Tories, Americans all, began bashing in skulls with clubbed muskets. Screams, shouts, and curses rent the air. The Rebels began to get the better of it. Some Tories discarded their green twigs and mingled with the Rebels to escape death or capture. Others started to flee across the ridge and down its back toward Ramsour's Mill. The Rebels pursued until they possessed the entire ridge. Incredibly, Lock's small band, minus the faint of heart whose number we do not know, had driven almost 1,000 armed Tories off the high ground.

There were no official returns after militia clashes. We are dependent on participants whose reports often conflict with each other. The best estimate for Ramsour's Mill is that the Tory losses equaled the Rebels', which gives us a total of 140 killed and 200 wounded. Three hundred and forty men scattered about. That was serious fighting, and the scene on the ridge and its surrounding slopes must have made a deep impression on the survivors.

It was a humiliating defeat for the Tories. Twice the King's men in North Carolina had risen prematurely, and twice they had been crushed by Rebel militia. The first clash, in 1776 at Moore's Creek Bridge near the coast was when Highland Scots trying to rendezvous with the British at Cape Fear had been knocked out of the war. Now Ramsour's Mill, and "in a few days," wrote William Richardson Davie, "that district of country lying between the [Catawba] River, the mountains" and the South Carolina line "was entirely cleared of the enemy."

On July 12, the patriots defeated Captain Christian Huck's loyalists and a detachment of the British Legion in the New Acquisition District of the Catawba River Valley in South Carolina. It resulted in the increase in Brigadier General Thomas Sumter's command to 600 and a decrease in the number of loyalists willing to take up arms. The site of the battle is in Historic Brattonsville.

On July 13 Congress appointed Major General Horatio Gates as commander of the Southern Department to replace Major General Benjamin Lincoln, who had been captured at Charleston. Gates assumed command in North Carolina on July 25.

114. Hanging Rock, South Carolina

AUGUST 6, 1780

HANGING ROCK STATE HISTORIC SITE
SATELLITE SITE OF ANDREW JACKSON STATE PARK
FLAT ROCK ROAD AND HANGING ROCK ROAD
SOUTH OF HEATH SPRINGS, SOUTH CAROLINA

After the British captured Charleston in May (see #98), they established loyalist outposts in South Carolina. Hanging Rock was one of the two in the Catawba River Valley. On August 6, 1780, Brigadier General Thomas Sumter and Major William Richardson Davie in command of 800 riders from North and South Carolina attacked 500 loyalist regulars and militia commanded by Major John Carden camped at Hanging Rock, protected only by earthworks.

Thirteen-year-old Andrew Jackson was in Sumter's command. Forty-eight years later, he was elected president of the United States.

John Buchanan recounts the battle at Hanging Rock in *The Road to Guilford Courthouse.*

With a coolness under fire usually attributed only to regulars and with tactics that twentieth-century infantry could not improve upon, "these brave men took instinctively to the trees and bush heaps and returned the fire with deadly effect. In a few minutes there was not a British officer standing, one half of the regiment had fallen, and the others on being offered quarters threw down their arms." The remaining British prepared for a last stand. They "drew up in the center of the cleared grounds in the form of a Hollow Square" and fixed bayonets. The Rebels were on the verge of a crushing victory and the destruction of a British strongpoint.

Then the men who had attacked with elan and displayed intrepid behavior under fire fell apart. The lure of loot overwhelmed them. Hundreds of partisans began plundering the British camp, found the liquor supplies, and started getting roaring drunk. Sumter and his officers implored them in vain to return to their duty. Only Major William Richardson Davie's dragoons and about 200 infantry could be formed at the edge of the woods, and the fire they directed at the British proved ineffectual. Then the Legion infantry, Hamilton's volunteers, and Tory militia were observed rallying at the edge of the woods on the other side of the British camp. Fearing a flank attack, Davie led his little band of horsemen around the camp under cover of trees and charged the British. Although Davie was outnumbered, the British, still reeling from their previous reverses, "were routed and dispersed."

The affair now took on a comic-opera appearance. An hour was spent plundering the camp and drinking its liquid supplies, "taking the paroles of British officers, and preparing litters for the wounded. All this was transacted in full view of the British troops, who in the mean time consoled themselves with some military music & an interlude of 3 cheers for King George, which was immediately answered by cheers" from the Rebels. Finally, loaded with plunder, reeling from strong drink, the Rebels marched off, if march is the proper word. Major Davie had a good view of their progression from his post as commander of the rear guard. "It is easy to conceive that this retreat could not be performed according to the rules of the most approved Tacticks. However under all these disadvantages they filed off unmolested along the front of the Enemy about 1 O'clock."

They left behind 200 Tory casualties while suffering only twelve killed and forty-one wounded. They had not fulfilled their main purpose of destroying the strongpoint, but it was a clear-cut victory nonetheless over the kind of trained, disciplined Tory regulars the British expected to be a key factor in retaking the Carolinas. Sumter's tactics would remain primitive, but his ability to rally men and lead them on grand enterprises was vital to the cause. And young William Richardson Davie had again shown himself a leader of uncommon ability and judgment.

115. Camden, South Carolina

AUGUST 16, 1780

HISTORIC CAMDEN REVOLUTIONARY WAR SITE
222 BROAD STREET
CAMDEN, SOUTH CAROLINA

After their victory at Charleston in May (see #98), the British marched inland to control the area from Georgetown, South Carolina, to Augusta, Georgia. They made the courthouse town of Camden their supply base, garrisoned it with 2,500 soldiers, and occupied it from June 1, 1780 to May 10, 1781. In *Partisans and Redcoats,* Walter Edgar describes the battle of Camden and the failures of General Horatio Gates.

Gates, anxious to win more laurels for himself, had pushed his army to the point of exhaustion. On 15 August, Cornwallis moved out from Camden with Gates's army as his objective. Almost simultaneously, Gates ordered his army forward to seek out the British. The Americans were ill prepared for battle. Besides being physically worn out from forced marches, their evening rations on 14 August had caused them nothing but misery. Because of Gates's haste to engage the enemy, the meat was only partially cooked and a dessert of molasses and corn mush caused diarrhea.

Early on the morning of the sixteenth, the advance parties met. Although the Americans outnumbered the British three thousand to two thousand, only nine hundred of Gates's command were Continentals; the remainder were Virginia and North Carolina militia. Nearly 70 percent of the British army were either British or Tory regulars; the rest were North Carolina militia.

As the two armies maneuvered for battle, Gates made one military gaffe after another. He assigned unseasoned militia troops to cover the American left and a portion of the regulars to the right. He kept the remainder of his Continentals in reserve. It was no contest. At the first sight of the British advancing with fixed bayonets, the militia broke and ran. Some accounts said they threw down their loaded weapons and never fired a shot. The Continentals under DeKalb stood their ground. Twice they turned back the British, but eventually they were overwhelmed. The brave DeKalb suffered eight bayonet and three bullet wounds. Three days later he died.

General Gates did not stick around to see the final outcome of the battle. He mounted his horse and did not stop until he reached Charlotte, North Carolina, about 70 miles away. He then procured a fresh horse and galloped off another 120 miles to Hillsboro—to put as much distance as he could between himself and Cornwallis's victorious army.

If ever there was a military disaster, the Battle of Camden was one. Of the 3,000-plus members of Gates's southern army who entered the battle, only about 700 regrouped at Hillsboro. Estimates of the number of killed range from 250–800; between 900 and 1,000 men were wounded and taken prisoner. The rest of the army simply vanished. All of the American artillery and almost all of its ammunition and supply wagons were captured.

116. Musgrove's Mill, South Carolina

AUGUST 19, 1780

MUSGROVE MILL STATE HISTORIC SITE
398 STATE PARK ROAD OFF SC 56
NORTH OF CLINTON, SOUTH CAROLINA

On August 18, 1780, Colonel Elijah Clarke led Georgians, Colonel James Williams led South Carolinians, and Colonel Isaac Shelby led Overmountain Men as they rode toward the area defended by Major Patrick Ferguson's loyalists. They planned a surprise attack with their 200-man force on the 200 loyalists guarding the ford at Musgrove's Mill on the south side of the Enoree River about thirty miles north of Ninety Six. Just before their attack on August 19, 1780, the Americans learned from a local man that Lieutenant Colonel Alexander

Innes had arrived from Ninety Six with 300 men, including 200 Tory regulars. Unable to retreat because their horses were exhausted from carrying them forty miles during the night of August 18, the Americans lured the enemy toward them into an ambush. They hit the loyalists with rifle fire at about seventy yards and wounded Innes.

John Buchanan describes the defeat of the loyalists in *The Road to Guilford Courthouse.*

Through smoke "so thick as to hide a man at twenty yards," recalled Isaac Shelby, the Tories "broke in great confusion…dead men lay thick on the Ground over which our men pursued the enemy." It was during this pursuit that the man who had played such a key role in planning and executing the fight was killed in action. Captain Shadrach Inman was shot seven times, once in the forehead, and fell dead under an oak tree.

The entire action probably lasted about one hour, with the fierce struggle on Shelby's flank taking some fifteen minutes. The British defeat was complete, and this did not bode well for the Tory cause. In the middle of strong Tory country a small band of daring Rebel guerrillas had badly hurt and sent flying in disarray regulars and militia more than double their number. The British loss was sixty-three killed, ninety wounded, seventy taken prisoner, a total of 223 out of Innes's combined force of 500. The Rebels lost four killed and seven wounded. They were elated. Different emotions swept through the inhabitants of the countryside as anxious relatives of Tory militiamen arrived to peer at dead faces, hoping they would not find those they were looking for.

John Buchanan also notes the importance of horses in the war.

Writing after the war, Banastre Tarleton's deputy, Major George Hanger, put his finger on the tactical problem faced by the British: "The crackers and militia in those parts of America are all mounted on horseback, which renders it totally impossible to force them to an engagement with infantry *only*. When they chuse to fight, they dismount and fasten their horses to fences and rails; but if not very confident in the superiority of their numbers, they remain on horseback, give their fire, and retreat, which renders it useless to attack them without cavalry: for though you repulse them and drive them from the field, you can never improve the advantage, or do them material detriment." Sir Henry Clinton had left Cornwallis with only about 240 regular cavalry: Tarleton's British Legion, and the forty troopers of the 17th Light Dragoons. They were quite simply not enough to fight the type of war chosen by the partisans, especially as the Tory mounted militia were inferior to the Rebel horsemen.

General Washington left his headquarters in New Jersey and rode with his staff and body-guards to West Point. On September 18, 1780, he had dinner with Benedict Arnold, who had sought and received the command of West Point. Washington continued on to Hartford, Connecticut, to his first meeting with the Comte de Rochambeau on September 20. On September 25, Washington learned that Arnold had defected.

117. DeWint House, New York

LIVINGSTON STREET AND OAK TREE ROAD
TAPPAN, NEW YORK

General Washington stayed in the DeWint House four times while he was in Tappan. The first was August 8–24, 1780. The third was May 4–8, 1783, when he met with Lieutenant General Sir Guy Carleton about the British evacuation of New York and the exchange of prisoners. The last was November 11–14, 1783, when a snowstorm stopped him en route to West Point.

His second stay, September 28–October 7, 1780, followed the arrest on September 23 of Major John André as a British spy. General Henry Clinton had put André in charge of the negotiations with Benedict Arnold about turning over West Point to the British in exchange for money. André had met with Arnold near West Point and was trying to return to New York when he was captured. The board of officers headed by Major General Nathanael Greene found André guilty of spying. Arnold escaped to the British, and André was hanged on October 2.

In October 1777, Arnold had been seriously wounded in the battle at Bemis Heights and returned to the army as commander in Philadelphia the following May. In August of 1780, at his urging, Washington named him commander of West Point. In *Benedict Arnold, Revolutionary Hero,* James Kirby Martin describes Arnold as he became a traitor.

> Since Arnold was still too physically incapacitated to take an active field assignment after returning to the army in May 1778, Washington named him the military commander of Philadelphia in anticipating the British evacuation of June 1778. In trying to be supportive of Arnold, the commander in chief made a poor choice for his disillusioned, resentful, embittered subordinate by stationing him where he would have regular contact and likely conflict with self-possessed civilian leaders in Congress—and even the Pennsylvania state government.
>
> Arnold assumed his new command post with a withering sense of service to the cause of liberty. Had he been reasoning with his usual clarity of purpose and strategic insight, he would have realized how the Franco-American alliance had seriously undercut British prospects of ever regaining the colonies—despite widespread popular apathy and instances of flawed civilian leadership. He would have appreciated how his own audacious generalship and the success of more than two years of campaigning in the northern theater, with the capstone triumph at Saratoga, had established the conditions that would make winning the War for Independence a distinct possibility. Instead, Arnold, as he dwelled on being used and abused, began to lose his broader vision. Having served the cause of liberty so well, he would increasingly put the emphasis on serving himself first—with the long-term consequence of everlasting infamy.
>
> Seasons of mounting bitterness lay behind Arnold's transformation from an intensely enthusiastic patriot to a dangerous enemy of the Revolution. Deeply bruised by so many personal confrontations and disappointments, he had come to regard the cause of liberty in the same battered terms. "The mass of the people are heartily tired of the war," he had written secretly to

I mean, I can with the greatest truth assure you, that he never mentioned a syllable to me in his life injurious to you in the least possible degree, nor have I any reason to believe that _he_ ever did to any Gen.r of my Family.

The bare report of a coolness which is said to subsist between you & the Gen.r I have in view, has given me great concern, because I have a warm friendship for both & consider harmony essential to our interest. — There is nothing if he is the person, which would give me more pleasure than to hear that you were in perfect amity again.

Let it be the case — Let all differences subside — the situation of our affairs never required it more — and in the emphatical terms of your and General Irwine's letter of which you inclosed a copy — Let all be as a band of Brothers, & rise superior to every injury whether real or imaginary and persevere in the arduous but glorious struggle in which we are engaged till peace & Independence are secured to our Country. — I am certain you wish do it — and I will only add that

I am with the most perfect
y.r friend & obed.t serv.t
G.o Washington

George Washington to Anthony Wayne, September 6, 1780. *(Courtesy of The Gilder Lehrman Institute of American History, GLC02872)*

John André in July 1780, and he compared the "present struggles" convulsing the patriot war effort to "the pangs of a dying man, violent but of a short duration."

Because of his feelings of ingratitude and his perception of rejection by the Revolutionary community, an embittered Arnold thus forsook the cause to which he had given so much of himself. Just as he had done so many times before, he stood in defiance of those persons whom he felt had falsely wronged him and rejected the movement they represented in favor of returning his allegiance to the British empire, an entity that he had deemed completely tyrannical only a few years before. In doing so, Arnold provided handsomely for his family, more than amply recovering what he had sacrificed financially. Still, he failed miserably in his other objective of becoming the pied piper of reconciliation with the parent nation.

The British commissioned Arnold a brigadier general in the regular British army, but they were hesitant about cashing in on their investment. Even if he was America's fighting general, he was still a mere provincial—and one who irritated many British officers because he was not bashful about telling them how they had mishandled the war effort.

In December 1780, on orders from Commander in Chief Henry Clinton, Arnold led a force of sixteen hundred troops by sea to Virginia. The resulting raids and capture of Richmond reduced the flow of patriot supplies southward into the Carolinas for use by Nathanael Greene's Southern Department troops as they dueled with British units under Lord Cornwallis. When the earl himself moved into Virginia in May 1781, ultimately to become entrapped by combined Franco-American forces at Yorktown, Clinton recalled Arnold to New York City.

In December 1781, Arnold sailed for England, hoping to convince imperial leaders not to give up, despite the loss of Cornwallis's army at Yorktown. Once in London, he had meetings with ranking cabinet officials as well as George III, and they spoke highly of his vigor of martial purpose. Arnold even presented a plan designed to bring about a reunited empire, predicated on Britain's "willingness to carry on the war." As at Quebec, however, he had arrived too late. Because of so many enemies and setbacks on so many fronts, peace sentiment was ascendant. Negotiations were already getting underway to end the war and concede American independence.

This Glorious Struggle, edited by Edward G. Lengel, includes a letter from Washington written soon after Arnold defected.

OCTOBER 13
TO LIEUTENANT COLONEL JOHN LAURENS
On and off for the remainder of his life, Washington would ponder Arnold's treason, without ever really understanding why it had happened.

Hd Qrs Passaic Falls [N.J.]
13th Oct. 1780.

My dear Laurens...

In no instance since the commencement of the War has the interposition of Providence appeared more conspicuous than in the rescue of the Post & Garrison of West point from

Arnolds villainous perfidy. How far he meant to involve me in the catastrophe of this place does not appear by any indubitable evidence—and I am rather inclined to think he did not wish to hazard the more important object of his treachery by attempting to combine two events the lesser of which might have marred the greater.

A combination of extraordinary circumstances—an unaccountable deprivation of presence of Mind in a Man of the first abilities—and the virtuous conduct of three Militia Men—threw the Adjutant General of the British forces in America (with full proofs of Arnolds treachery) in to our hands—and but for the egregious folly—or the bewildered conception of Lieutt Colo. Jameson who seemed lost in astonishment and not to have known what he was doing I should as certainly have got Arnold.

André has met his fate—and with that fortitude which was to be expected from an accomplished Man—and gallant Officer—But I am mistaken if at *this time*, Arnold is undergoing the torments of a mental Hell. He wants feeling! From some traits of his character which have lately come to my knowledge he seems to have been so hackneyed in villainy—& so lost to all sense of honor and shame that while his faculties will enable him to continue his sordid pursuits there will be no time for remorse. . . . your Sincere friend and obliged Servant

Go: Washington

General Anthony Wayne had served in Washington's army since the campaign in Canada in 1775. Washington's letter (see page 232), written in September 1780 just before Arnold defected, reveals his relationship with his generals. Washington thanked him for his letter and for his friendship and continued:

Let us be as a band of brothers and rise superior to every injury whether real or imaginary and persevere in the arduous but glorious struggle in which we are engaged till peace and Independence are secured to our country.

118. Overmountain Victory
National Historic Trail, South Carolina

THE TRAIL INCLUDES EIGHTY-TWO MILES OF PUBLIC PATHWAYS,
A COMMEMORATIVE MOTOR ROUTE, AND HISTORIC SITES.
HEADQUARTERS 2635 PARK ROAD BLACKSBURG, SOUTH CAROLINA

General Cornwallis expected the British victory in the battle of Camden to deter American attacks, but by the first week of October, patriot militia from North Carolina and Virginia were riding to battle the loyalists.

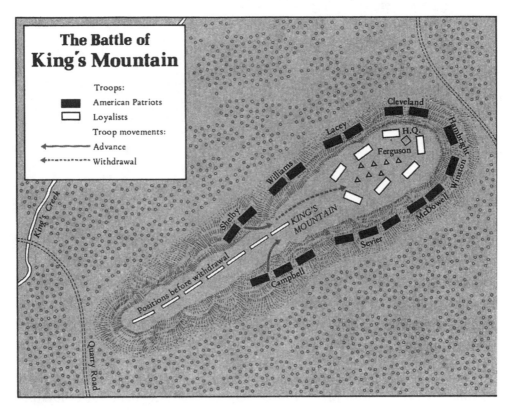

From: The Glorious Cause *by Robert Middlekauff (1982). Map from p. 473. By permission of Oxford University Press, USA.*

The Overmountain Victory National Historic Trail commemorates the primary routes taken by the patriot militia who tracked the loyalists led by British Major Patrick Ferguson to Kings Mountain on October 7, 1780.

In *Victory at Yorktown*, Richard M. Ketchum describes the over-mountain men.

In late September the over-mountain men began to gather, and a curious lot they were. Most were North Carolinians: Colonel Isaac Shelby with 240 men from Sullivan County; Colonel John "Nolichucky Jack" Sevier with 240 from Washington County; and Colonel Charles McDowell with 160 from Burke and Rutherford counties; plus Colonel William Campbell, leading 400 men from Washington County, Virginia. They made their way through snow in the gap and on the bank of the Catawba picked up Colonel Benjamin Cleveland and his 350 men from Wilkes and Surry counties. Shelby was there for a good reason: Ferguson had sent a patriot he took prisoner to tell Shelby if he did not surrender, Ferguson planned to cross the mountains and burn his whole county.

These frontiersmen from the Watauga settlements in what is now Tennessee did not take that sort of threat lightly. They were acutely aware of what the enemy had done at the Battle of the Waxhaws.

Most of the over-mountain irregulars were Scotch-Irish hunters and Indian fighters—big, tough men who had learned combat in the no-quarter warfare of the southern frontier—and they were out to get Ferguson and his Tories after he sent a warning that he planned to hang their leaders and lay waste their homes and settlements. They were deadly shots with their long-barreled rifles, and they traveled light, on horseback, with not much more than a blanket, hunting knife, and a pouch full of ground parched corn sweetened with maple syrup. They were in North Carolina because they preferred to have the fighting here, rather than back home on their farms, near their wives and children.

119. Kings Mountain, South Carolina

OCTOBER 7, 1780
KINGS MOUNTAIN NATIONAL MILITARY PARK
2625 PARK ROAD
BLACKSBURG, SOUTH CAROLINA

The over-mountain men rode from their farms in Virginia, Tennessee, and North Carolina, tracking British Major Patrick Ferguson and his command of loyalists. They met up at Kings Mountain in South Carolina, just south of the state border. John W. Gordon describes the loyalist defeat at Kings Mountain in *South Carolina and the American Revolution*.

An ace up Cornwallis's sleeve and one of his most trusted officers was Major Patrick Ferguson. Most importantly, Ferguson was a highly capable officer who had proven his ability to lead Americans—loyalist ones—in combat. Ferguson was in charge of organizing all loyalist militia in South Carolina. Ferguson's message to the Over-Mountain settlements on the other side of the Appalachians—that they would have to declare for the king or else face attack from the king's forces—was singularly ill-chosen. It roused the independent-minded Watauga pioneers to fury. They now resolved to strike at Ferguson before he could strike at them. Mounted on horses for faster movement, they swarmed after Ferguson and his loyalists. This turn of events surprised Ferguson; he initially retreated. He soon, however, made the decision—although the safety of Cornwallis's base was within two days' march—to hold atop a sixty-foot-high, footprint-shaped piece of partially wooded ground called King's Mountain. The riders pushed all through a drizzly night, eventually reaching, by early afternoon on October 7, a position from which they could dismount for an attack.

The Americans who tied or handed off their horses to holders and advanced up the hill in weather now clearing of rain were a coalition much the same as that which had fought at

Musgrove's Mill a month and a half before. Their leaders were Isaac Shelby and John Sevier, who commanded the Tennessee Over-Mountain men (and both of whom Ferguson had threatened to hang); William Campbell, who commanded nearly two hundred Virginia riflemen; and Charles McDowell, Benjamin Cleveland, and Joseph Winston, who between them had some three hundred or so North Carolinians.

The Americans had camped the night before at a place called Hannah's Cowpens some thirty-five miles west of King's Mountain. At the Cowpens the American groups already described were joined by four hundred or so South Carolina riflemen under James Williams. The total force arrayed against Ferguson was nearly two thousand, although the number actually riding in advance to commence the attack—again the best-mounted riflemen—was a little less than a thousand men (probably around 930–960).

What appears to have happened is that the Americans, under their coalition of commanders, divided the hill and its defenders into sectors before the attack and fanned out to commence their approach. In this way Shelby and Campbell, taking the southwestern portion of the ridge, attacked at opposite sides of the mountain. Williams, Sevier, and McDowell hit the next portion, which contained Ferguson's camp; and Cleveland and Winston hit from the northeast.

Slipping through the trees, the riflemen managed to reach Ferguson's camp almost before his sentries could give the alarm. They opened up a deadly fire on Ferguson's ranks. Ferguson had not chosen to improve his position with breastworks or an abatis. In woods fighting of this bushwhacking sort, the long rifle was supreme, enabling the rebels to pick off their enemies with well-aimed, deliberate fire. The loyalist ranks, receiving fire from all sides, began to flag. Ferguson, the rifle and irregular warfare theorist and expert, had lured himself into a situation where he could be destroyed by his own kind of warfare. He tried to lead a breakout charge. He was struck down.

The battle had been one between Americans. Ferguson had been the only actual British soldier present. The killed and wounded on the rebel side amounted to ninety men or just under 10 percent of the attacking force, and included two of the main commanders. Williams of South Carolina and William Chronicle of North Carolina both died in (or soon after) the battle. The British side lost roughly a third of the force, or 311 in killed and wounded. Approximately 660 of Ferguson's men were captured. The fight at King's Mountain, only an hour long, was a bitter fight, with the Americans continuing to pour in fire well after the point where the Americans on the other side had tried to surrender. Wounded loyalists were left where they had fallen, given neither food nor water. Dead loyalists were thrown into a long, shallow grave. Those captured were marched off toward Hillsborough, North Carolina. As quickly as they could, the victorious rebels held a court-martial of their newly gained prisoners of war. Thirty-six were soon tried, a dozen sentenced to be executed, and nine immediately hanged.

But King's Mountain was much more even than the loss of a thousand-man force and a valued officer. It was a smashing defeat that showed in starkest terms the inability of British arms to acquire and employ a substantial force of loyalists.

120. Blackstock's Plantation, South Carolina

NOVEMBER 20, 1780

MONUMENT ON MONUMENT ROAD
HISTORICAL MARKER AT ROUTE 49 AND BLACKSTOCK ROAD
NORTHEAST OF CROSS ANCHOR, SOUTH CAROLINA

General Cornwallis ordered Lieutenant Colonel Banastre Tarleton to pursue and defeat Brigadier General Thomas Sumter. Sumter halted his force at Blackstock's plantation on the Tyger River. John W. Gordon recounts the battle in *South Carolina and the American Revolution.*

In the afternoon Mary Dillard—at obvious personal risk—rode in to tell Sumter that Tarleton's column, which had earlier passed by her house, contained cavalry and mounted infantry, but that the artillery and the rest of the British infantry, moving on foot, was some miles behind the mounted group. Consulting with his commanders, Sumter planned a defense around the buildings comprising Blackstock's plantation. The Gamecock positioned Henry Hampton and his South Carolina riflemen to hold the main buildings at Blackstock's, supported by riflemen from Georgia. He himself occupied the ridge across the road.

Tarleton's mounted force arrived, coming up the road and deploying for attack. Despite odds of less than three hundred British or loyalist provincials against nearly a thousand Americans, the British attack began boldly and well. The redcoats of the 63rd Foot, now dismounted and fighting as the infantry they were, by their volleys and bayonet attacks drove back the American riflemen covering Sumter's left flank. But the momentum of their advance carried them into the zone of Hampton's riflemen, and these began picking off redcoats. Tarleton decided to lead the dragoons in a charge. The dragoons spurred forward up the hill—and were stopped by Hampton's riflemen firing from their covered positions. Sumter was badly hit by buckshot in the shoulder, chest, and back. Covered by Lacey's riflemen, he was led from the field.

Indeed, his whole force departed Blackstock's that night. The Americans had given up the position after dark and had lost three men killed and five men wounded. Tarleton was in possession of the field but had lost fifty-one killed and wounded (some accounts double this figure), and Sumter was still loose. Tarleton, heavily outnumbered, claimed victory. Yet the Americans saw things differently. For the first time Tarleton had been stopped in a battle.

In *This Destructive War,* John S. Pancake points to the failures of the North administration to support General Clinton in 1780.

For a brief time in the summer of 1780 Sir Henry Clinton was England's hero. The news of the fall of Charleston and the conquest of South Carolina reached London at a most fortuitous moment for the American Secretary and the ministry. Earlier in the summer, twenty-five English counties had passed resolutions denouncing the corruption of Parliament and the dictatorial power of the King. In June the Gordon riots broke out in London, and for three days the city was in chaos. Clinton used the opportunity to press his demands: that Arbuthnot be replaced; that reinforcements be sent; and that transports and supply ships be placed under the control of the army. He accompanied these with his oft-repeated assertion that if the ministry could not demonstrate its confidence in him by meeting his requests he stood ready to resign.

All during the late summer and fall, the cabinet considered the situation in America. It finally came up with answers that were becoming increasingly characteristic of the North administration. By mid-October it had decided to relieve Arbuthnot, but no replacement was designated, although Clinton had suggested six admirals with whom he would be pleased to work. The cabinet also decided that Clinton should receive "such reinforcements as can be spared." His other requests were ignored, and he was plainly told that if he wished to resign the King would not refuse him.

Thus instead of boldness there was timidity. Instead of grasping at opportunities for victory the cabinet sought to avoid failure, lest the Opposition seize upon it and drive the members from office. Even Germain, who had once been the driving force behind the war in America, seemed to have lost his nerve. He was full of strategic suggestions for Clinton, but he would not arbitrarily order them. Ever since Burgoyne had claimed (without justification) that he had been committed by his orders to march to Albany in 1777, Lord George had avoided binding a commander in the field.

On October 14, 1780, Washington named Major General Nathanael Greene to succeed Major General Horatio Gates as commander of the Southern Department. John Buchanan summarizes Greene's first month in command in *The Road to Guilford Courthouse*.

Gates was in Charlotte with what passed for an army. Greene arrived on 2 December 1780. To describe the two men as not close would be a gross understatement. It could have been an awkward moment, but both carried it off with aplomb. Greene behaved toward the beaten general with respect and kindness. Gates retained his dignity. Otho Holland Williams was there, and described their conduct as "an elegant lesson of propriety exhibited on a most delicate and interesting occasion." The new commander of the Southern Department was cut of different cloth than the old. Nathanael Greene was superior to Horatio Gates in all respects. His planning for the southern campaign was masterly. He also excelled as an organizer and administrator, making men forget Gates. And he was a genuine not an ersatz fighter, exhibiting a judicious mixture of caution and daring.

The command to which Greene succeeded was in a pitiful state. On his arrival it numbered 2,307 men, of whom 1,482 were present and fit for duty. Absent were 547; of those 128 were on detached duty. Continentals for the crack Maryland and Delaware Lines numbered 949. They were the backbone of the army. But of the overall total, only 800 men were properly clothed and equipped. As small as his army was, there were not adequate provisions and forage for them in the immediate countryside.

On 3 December 1780 a living legend rode into Nathanael Greene's camp at Charlotte to report to his new commander. Rarely have two men of such uncommon martial gifts had the opportunity to complement one another. Renowned from Quebec to the Carolinas, celebrated in one army and feared by another, his life a succession of dramas one of which would be enough for most men, Brigadier General Daniel Morgan of the Virginia Line was by far the Continental Army's finest battle captain. He was at the beginning of a long and remarkable journey. A commanding presence combined with valor, a high natural intelligence, and a stirring capacity to lead men would take him from the bottom of the heap to the very uppermost rank in the pantheon of heroes of the Revolution.

Greene decided to divide his army, "partly from choice and partly from necessity." Besides, what choice did he have? In addition to his desire to maintain a presence west of the Catawba, thereby stiffening the resolve of the Rebels there to continue their resistance, the army had to live off the land, and provisions and forage were too scarce wherever it went for the entire force to survive together. As Mark Boatner pointed out, Greene never heard of Napoleon but used the Napoleonic principle that an army divides to live and unites to fight.

Greene sent the cream of his army west of the Catawba. In command was Daniel Morgan. Greene's orders of 16 December to Morgan were unambiguous. "With these troops you will proceed to the west side of the Catawba river, where you will be joined by a body of volunteer militia under the command of General Sumter." There came the key sentence. "For the present, I give you the entire command in that quarter, and do hereby require all officers and soldiers engaged in the American cause to be subject to your command." Although not deliberately designed to incur Sumter's wrath, it did.

In command of the infantry, Lieutenant Colonel John Eager Howard (1752–1827) of Maryland, well born and well educated, is fittingly memorialized in his state's lovely anthem, *Maryland, My Maryland*. After the war he became a lawyer and politician and served as a delegate to the Continental Congress, Governor of Maryland, and U. S. Senator.

Morgan's cavalry commander was William Washington (1752–1810) of Virginia, a distant kinsman of George Washington. In battle Washington fit Morgan's description of him: "Washington is a Great Officer." On Christmas Day 1780, a band of South Carolina volunteers rode into camp. There were only sixty of them, but the militia colonel who led them—Andrew Pickens—was a godsend for Morgan. He now had to recruit and lead militia a man who lacked Thomas Sumter's charisma but commanded allegiance and deep respect. A very able tactician and brave in battle, and far superior to Sumter in temperament, he would cooperate fully with Daniel Morgan and later with Nathanael Greene.

Andrew Pickens (1739–1817) was the third man in the triumvirate of South Carolina partisan leaders, but he has never commanded the historical press devoted to Thomas Sumter and Francis Marion. Andrew Pickens was a lieutenant Daniel Morgan could count on to the last extremity.

Having done as much as he could for the time being to see to the welfare of the army and having set in motion the machinery that would sustain the coming campaign, Greene chose 16 December as the day when he would lead the main army east to the site chosen by Colonel Thaddeus Kosciuszko. But heavy rains delayed departure until the 20th. It took his 1,100 men, of whom 650 were Continentals, six days to march approximately seventy-five miles to their new camp across the Pee Dee from Cheraw, South Carolina. But it was a very strategic location, blocking the British from the Cross Creek Country of North Carolina, where Tory Highlanders awaited deliverance and denying them, as Greene noted, "command of all the provisions of the lower Country, which is much less exhausted by the enemy and Militia than the upper Country."

The Papers of General Nathanael Greene, edited by Dennis M. Conrad and Richard K. Showman, includes a letter from Greene to Colonel Alexander Hamilton.

> Camp on Pedee River [S.C.]
> January 10th 1781
>
> My dear Colonel
> When I was appointed to this command I expected to meet with many new and singular difficulties; but they infinitely exceed what I apprehended. This is really carrying on a war in an enemy's Country: for you cannot establish the most inconsiderable Magazine or convey the smallest quantity of Stores from one post to another, without being obligd to detach guards for their security. The division among the people is much greater than I imagined, and the Whigs and Tories persecute each other, with little less than savage fury. There is nothing but murders and devastations in every quarter.
>
> This army is in such a wretched condition that I hardly know what to do with it. The Officers have got such a habit of negligence, and the soldiers so loose and disorderly that it is next to impossible to give it a military complexion. Without clothing I am sure I shall never do it. I call no councils of war; and I communicate my intentions to very few.

The states were challenged by the need to support the Continental Army with both funding and men. In *Revolutionaries,* Jack Rakove describes a bill in Virginia's legislature.

> Late in 1780 the Virginia assembly faced the same test that South Carolina had already failed, needing to raise troops to augment Continental forces in the region and to ready itself for an anticipated British invasion. When Congress replaced the discredited Gates with Washington's great protégé, Nathanael Greene, the Continentals finally had a commander who was up to the challenge that the British were mounting.

That development was not certain, however, when the Virginia legislature met for its fall session. To meet its quota of Continental soldiers, the lower house took up a bill to give "a bounty of a Negro not younger than ten or older than 40 years for each recruit." Rather than free slaves in exchange for *their* service, this proposal would convert white soldiers drawn from the lower ranks of the free population into slaveholders. When he learned of this proposal, the young Virginia delegate James Madison wrote home from Congress to propose an obvious alternative. "Would it not be as well to liberate and make soldiers at once of the blacks," Madison asked Joseph Jones, one of his political mentors, "as to make them instruments for enlisting white Soldiers? It would certainly be more consonant to the principles of liberty," he continued, "which ought never to be lost sight of in a contest for liberty."

In late 1780 General Greene sent General Morgan west of the Catawba River and led the main army to camp near Cheraw, South Carolina. In Virginia, Benedict Arnold led a British force up the James River and burned much of Richmond. Washington ordered Major General the Marquis de Lafayette to Virginia with 1,200 men to counter the raids and to capture Arnold.

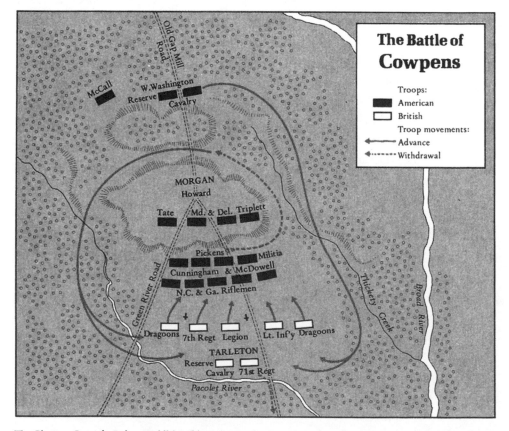

The Glorious Cause by Robert Middlekauff (1982). Map from p. 473. By permission of Oxford University Press, USA.

121. Cowpens, South Carolina

JANUARY 17, 1781

COWPENS NATIONAL BATTLEFIELD
4001 CHESNEE HIGHWAY
GAFFNEY, SOUTH CAROLINA

In early January 1781 General Cornwallis ordered Lieutenant Colonel Tarleton in command of the British Legion, a mobile force of dragoons and mounted infantry, to pursue General Morgan. Morgan ordered his forces to prepare for battle in a South Carolina pastureland known as the Cowpens. The Cowpens National Battlefield Brochure includes this description of the battle.

In September 1780 Morgan rejoined the army after Gates, who had been given command of continental forces in the South, suffered a defeat at Camden, S.C. Promoted to brigadier general, Morgan was commanding a corps of light troops when Maj. Gen. Nathanael Greene replaced Gates in early December and set about recovering American military fortunes. Greene's strategy was to divide his army and force the British to split theirs. He sent Morgan with a detachment called the "Flying Army" into western South Carolina to operate on the British left flank and rear, threatening their outposts and giving "protection to that part of the country and to spirit up the people."

Morgan knew that Tarleton's force outnumbered his own. To help even the odds, he sent for militia units from South Carolina, North Carolina, and Georgia. These were men of courage and experience, but Morgan knew they were no match for British battle tactics. Their rifles would not mount a bayonet, making them defenseless against a bayonet attack or a mounted charge by dragoons. The militia's strength lay in its prowess with rifles—weapons with greater range and, in their hands, deadlier and more accurate than British muskets. Morgan, keeping this in mind, devised a plan of battle to match the strengths of his men and the terrain.

Morgan chose to fight in an open wood on ground that sloped gently southeast, the direction from which the British would approach. The field had three low crests separated by wide swales. A road, later called the Green River Road, curved through the area. Morgan formed his troops in three lines straddling the road. In the front line, sharpshooters stood in small groups. Their job was to slow Tarleton's advance with well-aimed fire, then fall back. The second line, 90 yards behind the sharpshooters, included Andrew Pickens' regional militia. Morgan asked them for two volleys at a "killing distance," then they were to fall behind the Continentals. In the third line, 150 yards behind Pickens and stretching along the forward crest, were John Eager Howard's 600 crack Maryland and Delaware Continentals and veteran Virginia militia. Behind that crest, Morgan stationed 150 cavalry men under the command of William Washington, with orders to protect the militia and be ready to fight.

Just before dawn the British came into full view of the American front line. Tarleton sent cavalry to drive back the American sharpshooters, then he formed and advanced his line of battle—infantry astride the road; on each flank, 50 dragoons; in reserve, a brigade of Highlanders and 200 cavalry. As the British came within range, Pickens' militia line fired, dropping two-thirds of the officers, then withdrew behind the Continental line. The British dragoons on the right pursued the militia but were driven back in a fierce charge by Washington's cavalry.

The British surged onto Howard's line, the fighting pitched. Highlanders threatened to outflank the American right. Then a confused tangle of events brought the fighting to a dramatic conclusion. Howard ordered his right to fall back and form a new front, but his order was misinterpreted—and the entire line began to retreat.

Seeing this Morgan rode up and chose new ground where the Continentals could rally. Reaching that point, the men faced about and fired point-blank at the closing redcoats, then plunged into the staggered ranks with bayonets. As this was happening, Washington's cavalry rode into the swirling fight—while on the British left, Pickens' militia opened a galling fire on the dragoons and Highlanders. British resistance quickly collapsed. A few dragoons rallied to Tarleton, but they were ineffective and followed the British Legion cavalry, which never joined the fight, in a pell-mell dash off the field.

The battle was over in less than an hour. British losses: 110 killed, 229 wounded, and 600 captured or missing. Also captured with the British were a number of slaves. Morgan's losses: 24 killed and 104 wounded. The "Old Waggoner's" unorthodox tactical masterpiece had "spirited up the people," not just those of the backcountry Carolinas but in all the colonies. As Morgan later told a friend, he had given Tarleton and the British a "devil of a whipping."

In *Daniel Morgan: Revolutionary Rifleman,* Don Higginbotham points to the characteristics of Morgan that made him an outstanding field commander.

A teamster and farmer before the Revolution, Morgan also fought in two Indian wars. He was with Braddock in 1755 and was severely beaten for striking a British soldier. Tall and muscular, he was well equipped for the strenuous duties of a combat officer of his day. And as a Revolutionary combat officer Morgan deserves to be remembered most. An excellent tactician, a superb leader of men, an outstanding light infantry commander, Morgan found his background for these accomplishments in his frontier experience. Only a handful of American officers performed on as many battlefields as he. His services ranged from Quebec in Canada to the Cowpens in South Carolina. Leading his famous rifle corps, he played a decisive role in the defeat of General John Burgoyne's Anglo-German army. But Morgan's greatest personal triumph came at the Cowpens, where he gave Banastre Tarleton's hated Tory Legion "a whale of a licking," an action often called the tactical masterpiece of the War for Independence.

Though later serving in the army that put down the Whisky Rebellion and in the United States House of Representatives, Morgan was foremost a Revolutionary soldier.

Morgan's Cowpens triumph and his successful retreat wrought momentous consequences. Two British officers, Charles Stedman and Roderick Mackenzie, asserted that the destruction of Tarleton's Legion was an important factor in accounting for Cornwallis's failure to gain a complete victory at the subsequent battle of Guilford Courthouse and for his eventual downfall in Virginia. In any case, it was Tarleton's defeat that had spurred Cornwallis into a reckless pursuit of Morgan in which he destroyed most of his equipment and abandoned South Carolina, a province Clinton had urged him to hold at all cost. Instead Cornwallis undertook his second North Carolina invasion, which ended in disaster at Yorktown. William Gordon, the future historian of the Revolution, wrote prophetically: "Morgan's success will be more important in its distant consequences, than it was on the day of victory."

Morgan had fulfilled Greene's confidence to the utmost. As the Rhode Islander remarked after Morgan left the Southern army, "Great generals are scarce—there are few Morgans to be found."

Lawrence E. Babits and Joshua B. Howard detail the race to cross the Dan River into Virginia in *Long, Obstinate and Bloody: The Battle of Guilford Courthouse.*

The "Race to the Dan" began shortly after the battle of Cowpens ended. During the early morning of 17 January 1781, Brig. Gen. Daniel Morgan had destroyed a British expeditionary force led by Lt. Col. Banastre Tarleton in less than one hour. Morgan, along with his army and nearly 600 British prisoners, immediately marched north, crossing the Broad River and bivouacking. Convinced that Cornwallis, learning of Tarleton's defeat, would come after him to free the prisoners, Morgan set a furious pace and led by example, despite his deteriorating health. The "Old Wagoner" had his army moving up the road before dawn on 18 January.

That same morning a dejected Tarleton rode into Cornwallis's camp along Turkey Creek, South Carolina, delivering news of the disaster. Nearly one-quarter of Cornwallis's army had been killed or captured. His lordship was in an extremely difficult position, having lost two expeditionary groups from his main force: one, chiefly provincials, to backcountry riflemen at King's Mountain, and the other, his light troops, at Cowpens to Morgan's Continentals and militia. Cornwallis confessed in a letter to Lord Francis Rawdon four days later that "the late affair has almost broke my heart."

On the day Tarleton arrived, Cornwallis wrote his superior, Gen. Sir Henry Clinton, in New York, letting him know that he refused to "give up the important object of this Winter's campaign." That object, he later noted to Lord George Germain, was "to penetrate to North Carolina, leaving South Carolina in security against any probable attack in my absence." Refusing and ignoring orders to remain near Charleston, Cornwallis marched north after Morgan and did not write Clinton for nearly three months.

Late in the evening of 18 January, Cornwallis received some 1,200 reinforcements brought up from Charleston by Maj. Gen. Alexander Leslie. With these men, Cornwallis now fielded an army of nearly 2,500 soldiers, including more than 2,000 regulars. The next morning, he set out after Morgan, who by that time was twenty miles north of Cowpens at Gilbert Town, near present-day Rutherfordton, North Carolina. Cornwallis's later writings indicate that he severely miscalculated not only Morgan's position but also the influence of the numerous fords and rivers in southwestern North Carolina.

122. Cowan's Ford, North Carolina

FEBRUARY 1, 1781

HISTORICAL MARKER ON ROUTE 73 NEAR THE CATAWBA RIVER WEST OF HUNTERSVILLE, NORTH CAROLINA

Even though it was a cold January, General Cornwallis burned his supply wagons so that his army could advance faster in pursuit of Morgan. When General Greene learned of the burning, he began to consolidate his forces to stop Cornwallis. General Morgan crossed the Catawba River and ordered Brigadier General William Lee Davidson, in command of North Carolina militia, to slow Cornwallis's crossing of the Catawba. Greene rode into Morgan's camp on January 30, and the army advanced toward the Yadkin River. Cornwallis led his troops toward Cowan's Ford on the Catawba River. John S. Pancake recounts the crossing in *This Destructive War*.

Shortly before first light, the command reached the crossing. Its appearance was formidable. M'Cowan's was really two fords, a wagon ford that led directly to the opposite bank and a horse ford that angled upstream. The latter, although longer, was much more shallow. The river had fallen somewhat, but it was still far above its normal level, and the horse ford was obviously the best route, especially for the infantry. The British column paused as the men gazed at the "ford"—fully 500 yards wide with the water running in a swift, heavy current. Forbidding as the crossing appeared, delay would only widen the gap between Cornwallis and the Americans. It had begun raining again, ending whatever hope there might be that the river would continue to fall. Cornwallis gave the order. The brigade of the Guards led the way, and all three generals urged their horses into the stream.

Whether the Tory guide did not know about the horse ford or whether he deliberately misled the redcoats, the soldiers headed directly across, "up to their breasts in a rapid stream, their knapsacks on their backs and sixty or seventy rounds of powder and ball in each pouch tied at the pole of their necks, their firelocks with bayonets, fixed on their shoulders." General Leslie's horse was carried downstream, and O'Hara's mount was bowled over by the current. Cornwallis' horse was shot, but all three generals continued the crossing.

General Davidson had been holding a mounted reserve upstream at the horse ford. At the sound of firing, he brought his men downstream and was placing them on a ridge above the bank to check the British advance when it emerged from the river. As he directed his men into their positions, the British delivered their first fire. Davidson was shot in the chest. He fell from his horse, dead before he hit the ground. Without his leadership, his militia command disintegrated.

The battle at Cowan's Ford slowed Cornwallis in his pursuit of the Americans, enabling Greene and Morgan to cross the Yadkin River in boats northeast of Salisbury on February 3. Without boats, Cornwallis had to march twenty-five miles upstream to cross at Shallow Ford on February 8.

Greene and Morgan were reunited with the rest of the southern army on February 9 when General Isaac Huger arrived at Guilford Courthouse. Morgan was in such poor health that Greene granted him leave to go to his farm in the Shenandoah Valley. Greene replaced Morgan with Colonel Otho Holland Williams from Maryland. He led his army toward the Dan River, described by Richard M. Ketchum in *Victory at Yorktown*.

> The march to the Dan was a nightmare—day after day of rain, turning the red clay roads into slippery troughs. To keep from freezing, both armies had to have fires, and the men slept in the open since the only tents were used to keep provisions and powder dry. Greene's soldiers had nothing but rags for clothing; hundreds were without shoes and suffering in agony from lacerated, half-frozen feet. Unhappily, only 200 of the expected reinforcements from Virginia turned up, and as he took stock of his force, Greene could count on a few more than 2,000, of whom 1,426 were reliable Continentals.
>
> Williams and the light troops had turned right and were following Greene's men on a parallel road, ready to swing into action if the British came too close. He kept just far enough ahead of Cornwallis so the latter could not get between him and Greene, and to do so he kept half his men on patrol at night while the others slept, then he got them marching at 3 A.M. to get far enough ahead to cook the meal that had to last until the following morning. Even so, Cornwallis's vanguard was almost always in sight, though never close enough to bring on a fight.

Greene sent Williams in command of a screening force to draw Cornwallis toward the upper fords fifty miles upstream while he marched the army in freezing rain toward the crossings at Boyd's Ferry and Irwin's Ferry. Cornwallis's Tory spies were wrong when they informed him that Greene would not have enough boats to get across the lower Dan River. Greene's quartermaster, Lieutenant Colonel Edward Carrington, had boats ready for the army's crossing, described in *Long, Obstinate and Bloody* by Lawrence E. Babits and Joshua B. Howard.

> Greene's army began crossing the Dan on 13 February. In a letter to Williams written that morning, Greene related that, "The night before last, as soon as I got your letter, I sent off the baggage and stores, with orders to cross as fast as they got to the river." He wrote dejectedly that the "North Carolina militia have all deserted us, except about 80 men. Majors and captains are among the deserters." Greene warned Williams, "You have the flower of the army, don't expose the men too much, lest our situation should grow more critical." Williams replied that evening at 7:00 P.M., stating that he had written Greene that morning from "Harts old Stores" and also from Chamber's Mill imploring his commander to march as hard as possible

for the fords. The tone of Williams's letter is quite dejected and demoralized, evidenced by his statement that "My Dr General at Sun Down the enemy were only 22 miles from you and may be in motion now or will most probably by 3 o[']Clock in the morning." He advised Greene, "Their intelligence is good. They maneuvered us from our Strong position at Chambers Mill and then mov'd with great rapidity." He closed the letter, "I'm confident we may remain in the State but whither it will not be at the risqué of our Light Corps and whither we shall not be wasted by continual fatigue you can determine."

Greene spent the night of 13 February supervising the crossing at Boyd's and Irwin's ferries. At 4:00 A.M., he sent word to Williams to march for the crossings with his light troops. He admitted that he "had not slept four hours" since he last saw Williams on 10 February and was preparing "for the worst." When word arrived at Williams's camp, he roused his men and had them on the road shortly thereafter. At 2:00 P.M., Greene sent a dispatch stating that the "greater part of our wagons are over, and the troops are crossing." Three and a half hours later, Greene sent another letter proclaiming that the army was across and jubilantly stating, "the stage is clear." According to historian William Gordon, as word of Greene's crossing passed along Williams's column, the cheers of the Americans could be heard by Cornwallis's van, led by O'Hara and Tarleton.

As Greene completed crossing, Williams was pushing his men even harder. They were nearly thirty miles from Irwin's and had to set an incredibly fast pace. Cornwallis's advance troops were right on their heels. Williams's infantry and William Washington's dragoons arrived at Irwin's Ferry in the early evening hours. The exhausted men began crossing under torchlight. Greene apparently waited until Williams arrived and then crossed with him. Lee's Legion crossed at Boyd's Ferry, the men in boats and horses swimming. Lee later claimed that the last men to cross were himself and Lt. Col. Edward Carrington, the unsung hero of the river crossing.

Greene's army crossed the Dan River on February 14 and remained in Virginia until February 22, 1781.

123. Wilmington, North Carolina

JANUARY 28, 1781

BURGWIN-WRIGHT HOUSE
224 MARKET STREET
WILMINGTON, NORTH CAROLINA

General Cornwallis needed the port at Wilmington to supply his army and ordered the commandant in Charleston, Lieutenant Colonel Nesbit Balfour, to send a force to capture it. On January 28, 1781, Major James H. Craig, in command of 400 British troops, landed along the Cape Fear River, met little resistance, and occupied the town. In a surprise attack the next day at Heron's Bridge, Craig defeated local militia.

North Carolinians in the countryside were successful in preventing Craig from sending supplies for Cornwallis up the river to the loyalist community of Cross Creek, present-day Fayetteville.

After the battle of Guilford Courthouse on March 15, Cornwallis retreated to Cross Creek, found that there were no provisions for his army, and marched on to Wilmington. He arrived on April 7 and made his headquarters in the Burgwin-Wright House. He left for Virginia on April 25.

Craig evacuated Wilmington on November 18, 1781.

124. Pyle's Defeat, North Carolina

FEBRUARY 25, 1781

HISTORICAL MARKER AT ANTHONY ROAD AND NC 49
SOUTH OF BURLINGTON, NORTH CAROLINA

General Cornwallis, in need of loyalists to reinforce his army, ordered Lieutenant Colonel Tarleton to bring in those who had joined Colonel John Pyle. General Greene sent Lieutenant Colonel Light Horse Harry Lee and Brigadier General Andrew Pickens back across the Dan River with orders to stop Tarleton. John Buchanan recounts the tragic encounter of the loyalists and the dragoons in *The Road to Guilford Courthouse*.

> It began when two young riders from the 400-man Tory band of Colonel John Pyle, while searching for Tarleton, met Lee's van. Seeing the green-jacketed Rebel dragoons, "they were rejoiced in meeting us" and were so deceived that they thought Lee was Tarleton. Lee and Pickens had been carrying out this deception since crossing the Haw. They both reported to Greene that they hoped to pass Pyle's column and attack Tarleton. Lee claimed that he planned to confront Pyle, reveal his identity, and promise no harm if the Tories either went home or united with their countrymen.
>
> Lee reached Pyle at the head of the column and grasped the Colonel's hand, with the intention of unmasking himself and offering Pyle his two choices. Then fighting began in the rear and quickly escalated. Lee said that the Tories recognized the Rebel militia and started it. Captain Graham said that it started when he recognized Pyle's men as Tories and told Captain Joseph Eggleston of Lee's Legion, who asked a Tory, "'To whom do you belong?' The man promptly answered, 'A friend of his Majesty.' Thereupon Captain Eggleston struck him over his head."

What followed was quick and bloody. They sabered to death at least ninety Tories and wounded most of the survivors, who dispersed in all directions. Pyle's Massacre devastated Tory morale. After that, there was little hope of Tory recruits flocking to the King's standard.

After General Greene took command of the Southern Department and General Morgan defeated Lieutenant Colonel Tarleton at Cowpens, South Carolina, in January 1781, the army won the race against General Cornwallis to the Dan River in Virginia. But for America, the future looked bleak because it was in dire straits financially. Walter Isaacson quotes Washington on the problem in *Benjamin Franklin*.

> America's need for more money had indeed become quite desperate by the end of 1780. "Our present situation," Washington wrote Franklin in October of that year, "makes one of two things essential to us: a peace, or the most vigorous aid of our allies, particularly in the article of money."
>
> Franklin thus resorted to all of his wiles—personal pleadings mixed with appeals to idealism and national interests—in his application to Vergennes in February 1781. "I am grown old," he said, adding that his illness made it probable that he would soon retire. "The present conjuncture is critical." If more money did not come soon, the Congress could lose its influence, the new government would be still-born, and England would recover control over America. That, he warned, would tilt the balance of power in a way that "will enable them to become the Terror of Europe and to exercise with impunity that insolence which is so natural to their nation."
>
> His request was audacious: 25 million livres. In the end, France agreed to provide 6 million, which was a great victory for Franklin and enough money to keep American hopes alive.

In *Almost a Miracle*, John Ferling details General Washington's problems with the army, including a mutiny.

> As the last short days of 1780 passed, Washington's spirits continued to sink. He had not only presided over what he called yet another "inactive Campaign," but every ray of hope that had flickered during the year had "prov'd delusory," he sighed. The crowning denouement had been Arnold's treason, and he feared there might be others whose villainy could be purchased by the British. Conditions could not get worse. But they did. On New Years' Day 1781 men in the Pennsylvania Line, in winter quarters near Morristown, mutinied. Washington, who was at West Point, could not even go to New Jersey to deal with the crisis. He dared not leave West Point for fear that in his absence the men there would mutiny, hazarding that crucial post and, with it, the outcome of the war.

125. Independence Hall and Yard, Pennsylvania

MARCH 1, 1781

INDEPENDENCE HALL AND YARD
INDEPENDENCE NATIONAL HISTORICAL PARK
PHILADELPHIA, PENNSYLVANIA

Congress had sent the Articles of Confederation to the states for ratification in November 1777. In January 1781 the last state, Maryland, ratified them. On March 1, 1781, the Articles went into effect. After the Articles of Confederation were ratified, the Confederation Congress met in the State House of the Province of Pennsylvania, now Independence Hall, from March 1, 1781, until June 21, 1783.

John Ferling traces the ratification of the Articles of Confederation in *A Leap in the Dark*.

By the time Charleston fell in May, nearly thirty months had elapsed since Congress had sent the Articles of Confederation to the states for ratification. All save Maryland had acted, but that state refused its assent until the four states with major western land claims surrendered their dominions to the United States. Many Marylanders, including Charles Carroll of Carrollton, who ultimately would be the last surviving signer of the Declaration of Independence, and for whom many towns and counties throughout the United States are now named, had invested in private land companies that purchased "title" to western lands from the Indians. If these speculative interests could compel the "landed states" to relinquish their claims, the land companies faced the prospect of an economic bonanza.

As the years slipped by, three states with royal titles to western lands relinquished their claims, but through most of 1780 Virginia remained intransigent. However, the growing success of Britain's Southern strategy began to change minds in Virginia. On New Year's Eve, a British force, led by Benedict Arnold, penetrated to Richmond, laying waste along the James River and within the new capital. Thereafter, Virginia quickly yielded its western claims, but on one condition. It would cede its claims only if Congress rejected all private claims.

Maryland, the holdout on private claims, was also being squeezed. It was under intense pressure from the new French minister, le Chevalier de la Luzerne, to ratify the Articles. Luzerne told the authorities in Annapolis that the implementation of the Articles of Confederation would be seen in Europe as an impressive demonstration of American solidarity.

David Brion Davis and Steven Mintz detail the Articles of Confederation in *The Boisterous Sea of Liberty*.

In 1781 the thirteen original states ratified the first U.S. constitution, the Articles of Confederation. The Articles served as the new nation's plan of government until the Constitution of the United States was ratified in 1789.

Under the Articles of Confederation, the national government was composed of Congress, which had the power to declare war, appoint military officers, sign treaties, make alliances, appoint foreign ambassadors, and manage relations with Indians. All states were represented equally in Congress, and nine of the thirteen states had to approve a bill before it became law. Amendments required the approval of all the states.

The Articles of Confederation represented an attempt to balance the sovereignty of the states with an effective national government. To protect states' rights, the Articles set strict limits on congressional authority. Under the Articles, the states, not Congress had the power to tax. Congress could raise money only by asking the states for funds, borrowing from foreign governments, or selling western lands. In addition, Congress could not draft soldiers or regulate trade. There was no provision for national courts or a chief executive.

Equally important, the Articles did not establish a genuinely republican government. Members of the Confederation Congress were selected by state governments, not by the people. Further, power was concentrated in a single assembly, rather than being divided, as in the state governments, into separates houses and branches.

Gordon S. Wood points out the problems in the Articles of Confederation in *The Creation of the American Republic, 1776–1787*.

The problem of sovereignty was not solved by the Declaration of Independence. It continued to be the most important theoretical question of politics throughout the following decade, the ultimate abstract principle to which nearly all arguments were sooner or later reduced. Curiously, however, sovereignty was not as explosive and as wide-ranging an issue in the formation of the Americans' confederation as might have been expected from the experience of the debate of the previous decade. The principle of sovereignty was not probed and analyzed by Americans in 1776–77 the way it had been in the sixties, because whatever the limitations the Confederation may have placed in fact on the individual sovereignty of the states, few believed that their union in any theoretical sense contravened that sovereignty.

There were nationalistic sentiments in 1776, brought to the fore by the events of the previous decade—perhaps more of a feeling of oneness among thirteen disparate states than at any time in history. And this sense of union had assumed institutional form. Not only had the Continental Congress since 1774 exercised an extraordinary degree of political, military, and economic power over the colonists—adopting commercial codes, establishing and maintaining an army, issuing a continental currency, erecting a military code of law, defining crimes against the Union, and negotiating abroad. It also through its encouragement and resolves was centrally responsible for the colonies' assumption of new governments and the final break from England. The authority of the Continental Congress and the Continental Army was in fact so great during the critical years of Independence and the war as to provoke a continuing if fruitless debate from the nineteenth century to the present over the priority of the union or the states. Yet for all this exercise of continental authority, for all of the colonists' sense of being "Americans," for all of their talk of choosing between "a sovereign state, or a number of confederated sovereign states," few in 1776 conceived of the thirteen states' becoming a single republic, one community with one pervasive public interest.

The debates that took place in the Continental Congress in 1776–77 over the formation of the Confederation were essentially involved with concrete state interests, the apportionment of taxes and the disposition of western lands. Only the debates over representation, whether the same for each state or proportional to population or wealth, touched on the nature of the union and the problem of sovereignty, and even here the polemics were tied closely to particular state interests: the larger states "threatened they would not confederate at all if their weight in congress should not be equal to the numbers of people they added to the confederacy; while the smaller ones declared against an union if they did not retain an equal vote for the protection of their rights."

The attempts of the centralist-minded to destroy "all Provincial Distinctions" and to make "every thing of the minute kind bend to what they call the good of the whole" bred too many fears of large-state or northern domination and led delegates, like Edward Rutledge of South Carolina, to resolve "to vest the Congress with no more Power than is absolutely necessary."

What is truly remarkable about the Confederation is the degree of union that was achieved. The equality of the citizens of all states in privileges and immunities, the reciprocity of extradition and judicial proceedings among the states (which pointed up their quasi-international relationship), the elimination of travel and discriminatory trade restrictions between states, and the substantial grant of powers to the Congress in Article 9 made the league of states as cohesive and strong as any similar sort of republican confederation in history—stronger in fact than some Americans had expected. Many of the delegates, Samuel Chase told Richard Henry Lee in July 1776, did not even "see the importance, any the necessity, of a Confederacy." If the Articles could not be formed in 1776–77, Roger Sherman feared that a union might never be formed. Some saw the Confederation as only a temporary combination of the states, for the sole purpose of waging war, that with peace should be allowed to lapse. By December 1783 the Congress in Jefferson's opinion had lost much of its usefulness. "The constant session of Congress can not be necessary in time of peace." After clearing up the most urgent business the delegates should "separate and return to our respective states, leaving only a Committee of the states," and thus "destroy the strange idea of their being a permanent body, which has unaccountably taken possession of the heads of their constituents, and occasions jealousies injurious to the public good." Congressional power, which had been substantial during the war years, now began precipitously to disintegrate, and delegates increasingly complained of the difficulty of gathering even a quorum. By the middle eighties Congress had virtually ceased trying to govern.

General Greene had crossed the Dan River into Virginia on February 14, 1781. After he returned to North Carolina with his main army on February 22 and received his reinforcements, Greene waited at Guilford Courthouse, ready to fight General Cornwallis.

Marquis Charles Cornwallis, A Proclamation, February 20, 1781. *(Courtesy of The Gilder Lehrman Institute of American History, GLC00496.023)*

Cornwallis issued his proclamation and marched his army to Hillsborough on February 22 and then west, following Greene.

On February 20, 1781, General Cornwallis issued his proclamation, which included this "wish":

> It is His Majesty's most gracious wish to release his faithful and loyal subjects from the cruel tyranny from which they have groaned for several years.

126. Guilford Courthouse, North Carolina

MARCH 15, 1781

GUILFORD COURTHOUSE NATIONAL MILITARY PARK
2332 NEW GARDEN ROAD
GREENSBORO, NORTH CAROLINA

Robert Middlekauff recounts the battle of Guilford Courthouse in *The Glorious Cause*.

Guilford Court House sat on the edge of a small village clustered on a hill. The ground was Greene's; the tactics were Daniel Morgan's. Greene like Morgan at Cowpens resolved to use a defense that had depth, a defense of three lines. The first that Cornwallis's troops would hit was stretched out along the edge of the woods. To reach it the British would have to go down into the valley and then climb up slopes exposed to American fire. To give that fire Greene deployed the North Carolina militia, 1000 in number, on both sides of the road. Three hundred yards behind, he set up a second line, two brigades, 600 men each of Virginia militia under Brig. Generals Edward Stevens and Robert Lawson. The third and main line occupied the high open ground just below the court house. General Huger commanded the right side composed of almost 800 Virginia Continentals, and Otho Williams, the left, of a little more than 600 Maryland Continentals.

The British began the twelve-mile march to Guilford in the darkness of early morning. They had not eaten, having run out of flour the day before. Altogether the army numbered about 1900 men. The North Carolinian commander facing the British right waited while the enemy marched down the slope, crossed the creek, and moved up the hill. At 150 yards he ordered his men to fire. A captain in the 71st gave a flat description of the sight which is even more telling of the loss of life—"one-half of the Highlanders dropped on that spot." The Highlanders, again on order, then shouted and ran toward the Carolinians with muskets, bayonets attached, thrust forward. The Carolinians seem to have panicked at the sight.

On the extreme edges of the battlefield two separate and savage engagements were fought. Lee's and Campbell's riflemen on the American left had not joined the Carolinians in flight. Rather they had fired down the British line as it came abreast of them. So galling was this enfilade fire, that Leslie committed his support, the 1st Battalion of Guards, to clean the Americans out.

Although the Americans gave ground only slowly, give way they did, and the British left stabilized itself. The Virginians along the second line soon felt the attack of the reconstituted British center. It was Webster's men on the British left, probably of the 33rd, who smashed through first to the third American line.

The third line consisted of American regulars—two regiments of Virginians on the right and next to them the 1st and 2nd Marylanders. The battle along the third line also went through several phases with control of the field shifting back and forth. Greene did not want to risk everything in the battle of surges and surprises—and was satisfied simply to hold his ground.

Simply holding the line soon proved impossible. Greene gave way and ordered a retreat, abandoning his artillery and his wounded. That night the living gave thanks, and the wounded, as always in these eighteenth-century battles, bled and suffered and died.

John Buchanan points to the success of Greene's strategy in *The Road to Guilford Courthouse*.

Cornwallis had to win. But Greene had only to avoid serious defeat while making Cornwallis pay too dearly for victory. He decided that he had accomplished both and at 3:30 P.M. ordered a withdrawal from the battlefield. John Green's 4th Virginia, which had not been committed, was brought up to cover the withdrawal, which was "conducted with order and regularity," wrote Charles Stedman. It bothered Greene that he had to abandon his artillery, but all the draught horses had been killed. What was important, the army was unbowed. Their morale unbroken, the Continentals tramped off, ready to fight another day. Greene's army had suffered seventy-nine killed and 184 wounded, about a mere six percent casualty rate. Of the 1,046 missing, 885 were militia—gone home.

At the main line the fighting ended with Greene's orderly withdrawal from the battlefield. Cornwallis at first ordered a pursuit by the Fusiliers and the Highlanders but quickly recalled them. His army was in no condition to pursue. Behind him, around him, lay hundreds of dead and wounded British soldiers. It was a notable victory he and they had won, as fine as it has been said as any in the long British annals of war. The performance of the rank and file had been magnificent, their officers had conducted themselves with their usual contempt for death. But for what purpose? They had taken over twenty-seven percent casualties: ninety-three killed in action, 413 wounded of whom fifty died during the night, twenty-six missing. The casualty rate of the Guards alone was fifty percent. Cornwallis had set out in January with between 3,200 and 3,300 men. Despite Tarleton's disaster at Cowpens he had pushed on with some 2,550 men. Now his force was reduced to slightly over

1,400 effectives, and they were no longer fit to campaign. Charles 2nd Earl Cornwallis had ruined his army.

Tactically, by a narrow margin, Lord Cornwallis had won the Battle of Guilford Courthouse. Strategically, by a wide margin, Nathanael Greene had set up Cornwallis for an even worse disaster, and laid the firm foundation on which he would proceed to win the campaign for the Carolinas.

In *This Destructive War,* John S. Pancake describes General Cornwallis's decision to invade Virginia.

When the British finally moved from the battlefield at Guilford Court House on March 18, they left seventy of their wounded to be taken care of by the Americans. Cornwallis moved toward Cross Creek (modern Fayetteville), where he hoped that Colonel Balfour, the commandant at Charleston, had provided a store of supplies from Wilmington. His ragged, hungry army looted indiscriminately, killing whatever enthusiasm the appearance of the redcoats might have inspired. "The whole country was struck with terror; almost every man quit his habitation leaving his family and property to the mercy of the merciless enemies."

Cornwallis reached Cross Creek only to find that supplies had not been sent up the river to meet him. His hungry army moved on downriver toward the coast, sweeping up everything in its path. The command finally arrived at Wilmington on April 7.

Cornwallis now revealed the strategy that had been maturing in his mind for some time. Clinton had already become disillusioned with Cornwallis. Realizing this the earl had been corresponding directly with Lord Germain in London. The American Secretary had become increasingly preoccupied with the Chesapeake, and it was in compliance with dispatches from London—and much against his better judgment—that Clinton had been feeding forces into the bay area. First, there had been Arnold's raid in December and then the dispatch of additional regiments under General Philips. The force on the Chesapeake now numbered almost 5,500 men.

The answer to Cornwallis' dilemma was obvious. He had long been obsessed with the "domino strategy." As early as January he had been convinced that the invasion of North Carolina would bring about a collapse of resistance in South Carolina. It followed that an invasion of Virginia would strike at the source of Greene's supplies and reinforcements and that the safety of the Carolinas—the primary concern of Clinton's instructions—would be assured. Cornwallis' own force would be swelled by the troops already in Virginia, and he would then be able to sweep all before him. If this strategy made Clinton unhappy, it would surely find approval in the eyes of Lord Germain. The southern campaign would be brought to a successful conclusion, and, not incidentally, the Earl of Cornwallis would be the hero of the hour.

His decision made, Cornwallis dared not wait for approval from Clinton in New York. On April 25 he left Wilmington, moving north toward Virginia.

Don Higginbotham details the consequences of Cornwallis's decision in *The War of American Independence.*

Cornwallis's decision to abandon the Carolinas, besides conflicting with Clinton's instructions to hold South Carolina at all cost, upended the strategy behind the Southern campaign: to rally and organize the loyalists as a means of holding areas overrun by the British army. In fact, for three months in 1781—from January to April—Clinton was largely in the dark as to the operations of Cornwallis, who finally wrote his superior from Wilmington, announcing his intention of marching to Virginia and urging Clinton to make that rebellious province the strategic focus, "the Seat of war"—even if necessary at the expense of abandoning New York.

The endemic friction in the British councils of war consumed these two generals as it had others. Willful and ambitious, Lord Charles had sought to advance his own cause over that of Clinton with the court and the politicians in London. Clinton knew this, just as he was aware that Germain, who continued to voice senseless optimism on prospects for victory in the South, had lost confidence in him. Consequently, Cornwallis went his own way, leaving Clinton to fuss and fume in New York. Clinton's relationship was as bad or worse with that aging incompetent, Vice Admiral Marriot Arbuthnot, who had commanded the naval contingent in American waters since 1779. At odds with his counterpart in the navy, overridden by his number two officer in the army, and denied the confidence of the chief war minister in London, Clinton was wholly ineffective, though he continued to hold the supreme command.

127. Fort Watson, South Carolina

APRIL 15–23, 1781

SANTEE NATIONAL WILDLIFE REFUGE BLUFF UNIT
OFF I 95 AT EXIT 102 TO U.S.301/15
SOUTH OF SUMMERTON, SOUTH CAROLINA

Between about 1200 and 1450 this was the site of a Mississippian village centered on a large earthen mound. "Mississippian" is a term describing the farming people who flourished in the eastern woodlands beginning about A.D. 1000.

During the American Revolution the British built Fort Watson on top of the mound, known today as the Santee Indian Mound. The fort was one of the British outposts that connected Charleston to the backcountry.

While General Cornwallis was in Wilmington, Lieutenant Colonel Light Horse Harry Lee and Brigadier General Francis Marion invested Fort Watson on April 15, 1781. Since they had no artillery, Colonel Hezekiah Maham of Marion's brigade designed a tower with a protected platform that was tall enough for them to fire into the fort. On the morning of April 23, riflemen on the platform fired, forcing the commander, Lieutenant James McKay, to surrender the 120-man garrison. The Americans lost two killed and six wounded.

Fort Watson was the first of the British forts around Charleston and Savannah to be captured by the Americans during 1781.

128. Hobkirk Hill, South Carolina

APRIL 25, 1781

HISTORIC CAMDEN REVOLUTIONARY WAR SITE
222 BROAD STREET
CAMDEN, SOUTH CAROLINA

In *Almost a Miracle,* John Ferling summarizes General Greene's plan for South Carolina in the spring of 1781 and the battle of Hobkirk Hill between his force of about 1,400 and Lord Rawdon's 800 soldiers.

Finding that Cornwallis opted to go to Virginia, Greene adopted a simple plan of operations. As large British garrisons held Charleston and Savannah, there was little he could do to liberate those cities. But the enemy occupied several backcountry outposts and strategic sites from the coast of South Carolina to the Georgia border. Greene planned piecemeal attacks on each site, and he had about 1,400 Continental and ever changing numbers of militia with which to achieve his ends.

Greene's adversary was Lord Rawdon, whom Cornwallis had left in charge of defending the broad frontier. Though only twenty-seven, Rawdon was an exceptional soldier and an experienced hand. Rawdon faced insuperable obstacles in defending South Carolina. Compelled not only to defend isolated posts, but to keep open the umbilical cords that linked each to supply depots and, eventually, to Charleston, he simply lacked the manpower for his job.

Greene fought only one major battle during the spring. In April he paused at Hobkirk's Hill, about a mile outside Camden, to await reinforcements before attacking that post. Seeing the danger, Rawdon, who was outnumbered, vowed to strike first, hoping to take his adversary by surprise. Rawdon fell on Greene's startled pickets in a sudden attack. Rawdon's surprise failed. The rebel sentries fought well, delaying the enemy until the heart of the American army could take up strong positions on the high ground. The fight that followed was fierce and confused, and before it ended Greene was in the thick of it, helping even with the moving of artillery. The fighting ebbed and flowed for a time, but just when the rebels appeared to have victory in their grasp—Greene later said that he was three minutes away from a triumph—things went awry. Greene, "frantic with vexation," as he later put it, blamed the near miss on an underling's unwise attempt to reposition his Maryland regiment in the heat of battle, a movement that sowed confusion, then terror, among the men. Others believed that the fatal disorder within the Maryland line was sparked by the death of a company commander involved in the drive against Rawdon's center. Whatever the cause, once large numbers of rebels broke and ran, the British won the day, and they might have gained an even greater victory had not Colonel Washington's dragoons belatedly entered the fray and prevented Rawdon from pursuing his scattering foe. While Greene lost the fight, the British losses in the engagement were nearly twice those of the rebels. Not long after the battle, he proclaimed that the "little repulse will make no alteration in our general plan of operation." To this he added one of the more memorable comments to survive this war: "We fight[,] get beat[,] and fight again." A German officer discerned the same dynamic, remarking of Greene: "the more he is beaten, the farther he advances in the end."

129. Ninety Six, South Carolina

MAY 22–JUNE 18, 1781

NINETY SIX NATIONAL HISTORIC SITE
1103 HIGHWAY 248
NINETY SIX, SOUTH CAROLINA

Settlers had been moving into South Carolina's backcountry since the 1730s, and in 1751 Robert Gouedy built a trading post at Ninety Six. In 1759 the settlers built palisades around Gouedy's barn, which protected them from two attacks by Cherokees. During the next decade the population increased to several hundred, and in 1772 the first courthouse in the backcountry was built at Ninety Six.

As tensions between patriots and loyalists increased, both began to organize. On November 19–21, 1775, 1,800 loyalists attacked 600 patriots led by Major Andrew Williamson in the first land battle in the south. It ended in a truce, with twelve patriot and fifty-three loyalist casualties. Private James Birmingham was the first patriot soldier killed in South Carolina.

The British captured Charleston in May 1780 (see #98), and took control of the backcountry, including Ninety Six, 175 miles inland from Charleston. They built the earthen Star Fort about eighty yards east of the newly fortified village and a small stockaded fort on the west side of the village. Ninety Six was one of the half dozen strategic British outposts in the backcountry.

After General Cornwallis marched toward Virginia in April 1781, General Greene began a siege of the Star Fort with 1,000 men. The commander of the 550-man British garrison was Lieutenant Colonel John Harris Cruger, a New York loyalist. Colonel Thaddeus Kosciuszko, the chief engineer of the Continental Army, directed the siege with saps and parallels dug for the Americans to move toward the fort. He also led the construction of the log Maham Tower, which was thirty feet high and thirty yards from the fort. On the night of June 9, ten loyalists attacked the Americans, and Kosciuszko was wounded. On June 18, fifty Americans (known as the Forlorn Hope) staged a final assault on Star Fort. They engaged in hand-to-hand combat with loyalists while Greene's best riflemen in the tower fired into the fort. In the forty-five-minute attack, thirty Americans were killed. On June 19 after Greene learned of the approach of Lord Rawdon's relief column, he ended the twenty-eight-day siege. In early July Rawdon concluded that the fort could not be held. He ordered it evacuated, and burned. The British force and loyalist refugees withdrew to Charleston.

Two months after Cornwallis left for Virginia, the British held only the areas of Wilmington, Savannah, and Charleston. Robert Middlekauff summarizes Greene's success in South Carolina in *The Glorious Cause*.

Thomas Sumter had resisted Greene's urging that he join his force to the main army, deciding instead in favor of independent operations. But he pleased Greene by taking Orangeburg on the North Fork of the Edisto River on May 10. This post and its small garrison provided an important link between Charleston and Camden. Lee and Marion picked off another the following day, Fort Motte on the Congaree River. Motte had not given in easily, and Lee and Marion had been forced to conduct a small-scale siege, running regular approaches, until they came close enough to burn their enemy out. Meanwhile Pickens had darted south to Augusta, which held out until June 5.

Before most of these attacks had even begun, Rawdon had decided to evacuate Camden. His impression was that the backcountry had risen against him—so he wrote Cornwallis on May 24, two weeks after his column heavily laden with sick and wounded began to clear Camden. The slow progress southward along the Santee deepened his discouragement. There, along the river his experiences repeated Cornwallis's in North Carolina, as sullen civilians carefully kept their distance from him and his army. "I had been five Days within the Santee before a single Man of the County came near me," he remarked to Cornwallis. Food, as well as friends, was scarce, and only revolt seemed to be in harvest.

Too late Rawdon ordered Colonel John Cruger to pull his command from Ninety-Six. Greene, with the assistance of Lee's Legion, lay siege to the place on May 22. Its defenses were formidable and Cruger, a Tory from New York, knew how to use them. He had some 500 men against Greene's 1000 regulars. But though outnumbered, he held on and threw back a fierce attack on June 18. Two days later Greene reluctantly ended the siege, for Rawdon with 2000 men, including three regiments fresh from England marching to Cruger's rescue, now threatened to overwhelm him. There was a brief chase, but Greene's head start and the summer heat combined to discourage Rawdon after he reached the Enoree River, thirty miles to the southeast.

Greene did not know it, but he had won the war in the Carolinas.

130. Eutaw Springs, South Carolina

SEPTEMBER 8, 1781

HISTORICAL MARKER AND MONUMENT
EUTAW SPRINGS BATTLE GROUND ON SC 6
EUTAW SPRINGS, SOUTH CAROLINA

By September, Lord Francis Rawdon, unsuccessful in driving General Greene out of South Carolina and in poor health, turned over his command to Lieutenant Colonel Alexander Stewart. Stewart's camp was at Eutaw Springs. Dan L. Morrill describes the battle of Eutaw Springs in *Southern Campaigns of the American Revolution*.

Greene spent July and most of August 1781 in the High Hills of the Santee, a twenty-mile string of sand and clay hills that rise up to 200 feet above the left bank of the Wateree River. Here the Rhode Islander could rest his army and wait for militia to join him. By August 22, having a force of some 2,400 men, about three-fourths of whom were either Continentals or seasoned veterans, Greene felt strong enough to take the offensive against the redcoats. Greene knew that Rawdon's successor as British commander in South Carolina, Colonel Alexander Stewart, had brought an army of some 2,000 men inland from Charleston.

The Battle of Eutaw Springs served no real purpose other than to confirm that the British had no chance of reviving Germain's defunct Tory recruiting strategy. Local support for the king had become so anemic that Stewart and his men had no idea that Nathanael Greene and his army were only a few miles away and closing fast. The main body of Stewart's command, which unlike Ferguson's at Kings Mountain or Cruger's at Ninety Six contained substantial numbers of British regulars, formed a single defensive line across the road in the open woods west of the field where they had pitched their tents. Greene brought his men to the battlefield with the militia in the lead. Just as at Guilford Court House, the Continentals were situated behind the irregulars and were expected to deliver the decisive blow. The battle commenced with the exchange of artillery fire. Much like what had transpired at Cowpens, some of the redcoats eventually broke formation and rushed forward helter-skelter when they saw elements of the patriot militia beginning to fall back after delivering several volleys.

The battlefield was fast becoming a scene of almost total confusion. Riderless horses, terrified by the screaming, yelling, and shooting coming from all around them, galloped through the British camp, knocking over tents and scattering provisions over the blood-stained ground. For almost four hours the two armies tore at one another in savage hand-to-hand combat.

If the patriots had maintained their pace and if the Fighting Quaker had been willing to throw all of his available strength into the fray at this most opportune moment, the victory over Stewart might have been total. But Greene's troops, many of whom were "thirsty, naked, and fatigued," could not resist the temptation of stopping in the British camp and rummaging through the enemy's discarded belongings, including the liquor, with the result that the American officers were "nearly abandoned by their soldiers, and the sole marks for the party who now poured their fire from the windows of the house."

When Greene learned that Major John Majoribanks had succeeded in capturing several artillery pieces that had been brought up to fire into the brick house, the patriot general predictably broke off the engagement and retreated into the woods to the west of the open field. Stewart was too weak to follow, and Greene marched unmolested to his camp in the High Hills of the Santee.

Greene lost almost 25% of his men, and Stewart suffered casualties of about 42%. William Washington was seriously wounded and taken prisoner.

After Eutaw Springs, the only British garrisons in the Carolinas and Georgia were Savannah, Charleston, and Wilmington. "The conquered states were regained, and our exiled countrymen were restored to their deserted homes—sweet rewards of our toil and peril," proclaimed Light Horse Harry Lee.

In *The War of American Independence,* Don Higginbotham summarizes General Greene's campaign.

In his Southern campaign Greene showed signs of true greatness, and not merely because he triumphed: a general may win a battle or a campaign without being primarily responsible for its outcome. Greene's laurels rest upon the "how's" and "why's" of his achievement. The "how's" are easy to enumerate. He won with an army poorly provisioned, shabbily clad, and thin in numbers, reinforced by fiercely independent partisan bands and undisciplined militia. The "why's" are more elusive. The most obvious ones—the failure of the loyalists to turn out as expected and the errors of Cornwallis—were important determinants, but it remained for Greene to capitalize on them with the means at hand. His native intelligence, his selection of subordinates, and his finesse in dealing with partisans and politicians were of a high order. Tactically, he suffered from his own mistakes and bad luck, although every battle that he lost hurt the enemy more than it did him. We have noted that the essential quality of a great captain is what most perceptive students and practitioners of warfare have called "character." That elusive quality, defying easy delineation, involves moral courage, plain nerve, relentless determination, combined with (or producing?) the ability to dominate any situation, to obtain a psychological initiative over one's adversary. In varying degrees Greene revealed these components when he divided his army at Charlotte and made Cornwallis divide his own command; when he fell back into North Carolina and drew the British General on a fruitless, debilitating chase; when he returned to South Carolina leaving His Lordship weak and dispirited near Wilmington; when, one by one, he plucked Rawdon's bases in the Palmetto state; and when he chose the time and place of every major battle—Guilford Courthouse, Hobkirk's Hill, and Eutaw Springs— which cut deeply into British manpower.

In short, Greene made up his own game and compelled Cornwallis and Rawdon to play it largely by his rules. It was predominantly a game of rapid movement highlighted by constant pressure applied to the enemy to keep him off balance. It involved an assortment of methods: hit-and-run raids, assaults on supply lines, sieges, and fixed battles. Greene was always bold but never rash, always flexible, always willing to give up the battlefield in order to return for a better day. "There are few generals," he remarked puckishly, who have "run oftener, or more lustily than I have done. But I have taken care not to run too far, and commonly have run as fast forward as backward, to convince our Enemy that we were like a Crab, that could run either way." To the British, Greene and his partisan allies were a swarm of hornets. Drive them away and back they came, again and again, to sting in a new and often unexpected place. A single sting inflicted a minor wound to the British lion; but when the hornets were through the lion was all but dead.

There is another, lesser known, side of Greene's service in the South. He, with the possible exception of Washington, had a better opportunity than any other American general of the Revolution to make solid contributions in the area of civil government and domestic tranquility. For the lower South was ravaged by the war as no other section of the country. He started the wheels rolling for the restoration of state government in South Carolina, gave sought-after advice, and helped prepare for the convening of the first assembly in many months.

<hr />

The challenges confronting the American Revolution were not just on the battlefields. Gary B. Nash evaluates the grave problems resulting from fiscal reform and the effects on the army in *The Unknown American Revolution*.

Like fellow patriots of ordinary means in southern states, northern commoners felt the sting of drastic fiscal reform beginning in 1780. With the war now centered in the South, fierce debates over ramped-up taxation procedures moved to the center of state politics. The stabilization of the currency was a boon for money and security holders, principally seaboard merchants, but a bane for farmers, especially in the western counties. Complaints of impossible tax burdens reeked of class hostility. Robert Morris enlisted Tom Paine to pen "The Crisis Extraordinary," in which he gamely tried to convince Americans that their tax burden was not heavy and that the war effort would collapse if Congress could not support the army.

But this did not convince farmers standing on the brink of personal collapse. In 1780–82, they threatened tax collectors, refused to sell their land as the only way to pay taxes, and mobbed assessors. The possibility of a new revolution was all too apparent.

Robert A. Gross details America's financial problems and their effects on Americans and the Revolution in *The Minutemen and Their World*.

The darkening military outlook was accompanied by an increasingly desperate financial situation. At the start of the contest in 1775, the Continental Congress faced a dilemma: it had taken charge of the sixteen-thousand-man army outside Boston, but it had no cash to pay the troops and no power to raise any through taxes. The only solution was to turn to the printing press and issue money of its own. Congress took the plunge—again and again and again. Meanwhile, every state government was doing the same. And that was not all. Other forms of currency were added to the flood: the interest-bearing bonds that both Congress and states gave in exchange for private loans; the "I.O.U.'s" that Army commissary officers forced on reluctant farmers for supplies; and the counterfeit bills that British agents spread in order to disrupt the American war effort. Until late 1776 this infusion of money, combined with the Army demand for provisions, pumped new life into the state economies and brought good prices and prosperity to town and country alike. But no one bets on a likely loser without demanding higher and higher odds. As American military fortunes deteriorated, paper money inevitably sank in value, and prices and wages soared. Beef cost $.04 a pound in 1777; three years later, it stood at $1.69 and was still rising. Paper money had become simply that—a piece of paper and "not worth a Continental." In 1780, Congress conceded the obvious: through a drastic devaluation of the dollar, it effectively repudiated its money in which no one believed. Even that didn't work. The new bills it issued sank in value almost as soon as they came off the press.

People in Concord drowned in paper along with everyone else. Runaway inflation disordered the finances of the town and claimed its classic victims: the poor, wage laborers and all who lived on fixed incomes. Common soldiers suffered especially in their country's service. But even ministers of the gospel struggled to stay afloat. Rev. Ezra Ripley, who spent his senior year in Concord as a member of Harvard's class of 1776, returned two years later as William Emerson's successor. Before accepting the call to the ministry, Ripley shrewdly negotiated a contract that would protect him against the ravages of inflation. His annual salary of £100 was pegged to specific commodity prices and so would rise and fall with changes in the cost of grain and meat. But the arrangement failed to work. Despite the good will of his parishioners, they could not collect the ministerial tax fast enough to catch up with the ever-increasing prices. By October 1779, Ripley's salary had already dropped in real value to some £85; when he received it the following May, it was worth but £41. To get by, he had to take in students and do his own manual labor; even so, he weathered the financial crisis only with a long line of credit at deacon John White's store. Concord eventually made good Ripley's loss, but years later he was still lamenting his "loss in ministerial studies and acquirements."

The skyrocketing prices of food and fuel benefited those farmers who could raise large surpluses for market and satisfy many of their own consumer needs. Self-sufficiency, of course, was never fully possible except at the rudest standard of living. But the war stimulated household industries and thereby saved money that had previously been drained away to the country stores and from there to Boston and beyond the sea. Before the Revolution many families had grown accustomed to buying the latest in imported English and European finery. Now that trade with Britain was proscribed, homespun clothing became the patriotic fashion of the day and women at the loom heroines of the Revolution.

Army demands and farming problems led to real scarcities of food, further fueling the raging inflation. The hardships bore with particular severity on women, who often had to run farms while their men were away at war. But even after the men came home, farm families had to make sacrifices. From October 1780 to July 1781, Concord was called upon to furnish 42,779 pounds of beef for the Army—the equivalent of at least a hundred head of mature cattle. Such animals were not quickly replaced. By 1784 Concord's holdings of oxen, cows, and swine were well below prewar levels. To feed the Army, the townspeople had to take food from their own mouths.

Congress finally recognized the need for a Superintendent of Finance and elected Robert Morris. He took office on May 14, 1781. In *The First Salute,* Barbara W. Tuchman points to his importance to the Revolution.

Since the exciting prospect raised at Saratoga, the French, who had put large expectations in the abasement of Britain that American success would cause, had been disappointed by the weakness of the American military effort. Instead of an aggressive ally, they were tied to a dependent client, unable to establish a strong government and requiring transfusions of men-at-arms and money to keep its war effort alive. The war, like all wars, was proving more expensive for the Bourbons than planned. Since the alliance, France had advanced to the Americans over 100 million livres, about $25 million, in loans, supplies and gifts, and before it was over the cost of the American war for France would amount, by some estimates, to 1.5 billion livres, an historic sum that was virtually to bankrupt the French national budget and require the summoning of the Estates General in 1789 that led to the arrest of the King and the sequence of eruptions that became the French Revolution. The Americans were notified that the French government had already spent more than "Congress had a right to expect from the friendship of their ally." Vergennes made it clear that no more troops or ships or infusions of money would be forthcoming after 1781. This time, Washington knew, the Allied reinforcement must be made effective. But to march an army of sufficient strength for a major American role to meet the French in Virginia was not a project to be organized on air. It had to be fed, shod and supported by field guns.

In the American wilderness of want, the first angel to appear to revive offensive capacity was Robert Morris, richest of the merchants who had profiteered from the war and who in 1781 was elected by Congress to the post of Superintendent of Finance. In its abiding fear of centralized power, so like the Dutch, Congress for five years had avoided the submission of finances to a single governor. Only in 1781, when the state was sliding toward a collapse of credit, did it admit the necessity of a financial director. Morris, whose opinion of mankind grew worse "from my experience of them," and who believed that public office exposed an honest man to envy and jealousy and to the "malicious attacks of every dirty scoundrel that deals in the murther of reputations," nevertheless accepted the post and, by virtue of the funds he generated, did as much as anyone at this hour to preserve the fight for independence. The rich have their uses; although assumed to be knaves, they can prove to be pillars of the state like anyone else. Virtue and patriotism are not a prerogative of the humble. Through the influence of his personal credit, Morris obtained contributions from the various states, reduced government spending, laid the foundations for a national bank and persuaded a group of Philadelphia bankers to make a substantial loan in cash. Altogether, he borrowed from Rochambeau and from the Philadelphia businessmen a total of $40,000, which provided the ragged half-fed Continentals with their first touch of hard cash since enlistment, cut down desertions and even brought in recruits. More than that, the money enabled Washington to move to the offensive.

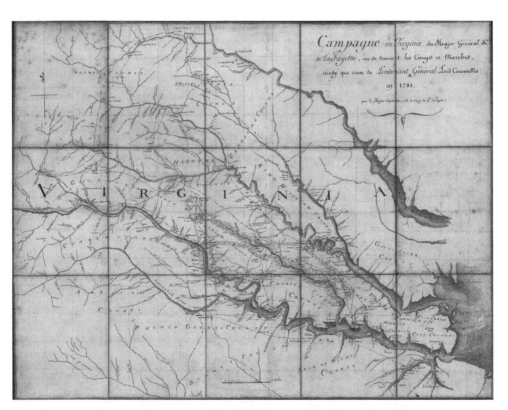

General Lafayette leading the Continental Army toward Yorktown, 1781. Michel Capitaine du Chesnoy 1746–1804. *Campagne en Virginie du Major Général M'is de LaFayette : ou se trouvent les camps et marches, ainsy que ceux du Lieutenant Général Lord Cornwallis en 1781 / par le Major Capitaine, aide de camp du G'l LaFayette* [1781]. *(Courtesy, Library of Congress, Geography and Map Division. http://hdl.loc.gov/loc.gmd/g3881s.ar300600)*

131. Green Spring, Virginia

JULY 6, 1781

HISTORICAL MARKERS ON GREENSPRINGS ROAD NEAR JAMESTOWN ROAD SOUTHWEST OF WILLIAMSBURG, VIRGINIA

General Cornwallis marched from North Carolina, arrived in Virginia the second week of May, and took command of the 7,000-man British force. General Lafayette marched, as the map on page 267 shows, from Richmond to the Yorktown peninsula. In *The Guns of Independence: The Siege of Yorktown, 1781,* Jerome A. Greene describes General Lafayette's strategy.

> Once in command in Virginia, Cornwallis was forced to contend with Lafayette and his 2,000 American soldiers. The zealous French nobleman and experienced soldier—who was but nineteen years old in 1777 when he volunteered his services without pay to the American cause—had received a commission of major general from the Continental Congress. His distinguished service in Pennsylvania and New Jersey thereafter had won Washington's utmost confidence and taken him to Virginia in 1780. In late April 1781, Lafayette arrived at Richmond to protect the new state capital from British incursions. Cornwallis decided his first course of action was to send selected units to protect the British station at Portsmouth. Thereafter, he marched his remaining 5,300 men north toward Richmond to expel Lafayette and to destroy American supplies.
>
> Lafayette fully realized he was too weak to make a stand at the capital and that his prime role while awaiting reinforcements was "that of a terrier baiting a bull." The Frenchman thus retreated generally northward, keeping one step ahead of Cornwallis's command, alternately threatening and withdrawing from his front. Throughout, he was careful to keep his troops situated between the British and the American capital at Philadelphia. Eventually, Lafayette's command was bolstered by the arrival of militia from western Virginia and, on June 25, by about 800 Pennsylvania Continentals sent by Washington under the command of Brigadier General Anthony Wayne. A detachment under Major General Frederick William Augustus, Baron Von Steuben, further augmented Lafayette's command, which now totaled nearly 4,000 soldiers.

On June 4, 1781, General Cornwallis ordered Lieutenant Colonel Tarleton on a raid of Charlottesville, where the members of Virginia's assembly had fled. He captured seven assemblymen. Governor Thomas Jefferson barely escaped on horseback as Tarleton rode up to Monticello.

In *A Battlefield Atlas of the American Revolution,* Craig L. Symonds recounts General Wayne's narrow escape in the battle at Green Spring in July.

> The threat of an imminent junction between Rochambeau's 4,000 men in Newport and Washington's army outside New York convinced Clinton that he was about to be attacked. He therefore

ordered Cornwallis to return 3,000 of his troops from Virginia to New York. In order to comply, Cornwallis left Williamsburg on July 4 to cross the James River en route to Portsmouth where the troops could be embarked. Lafayette determined to strike Cornwallis while the British army was astride the James. On July 6 he sent 500 men under Anthony Wayne against what he believed was Cornwallis's rear guard at Green Spring. But in fact Cornwallis had sent his baggage across the river first, and his entire army was still on the northern bank. When Wayne's men attacked they found themselves in serious danger of being annihilated. Wayne ordered a desperation bayonet attack to extricate his force from the British and, though he did manage to escape with the bulk of his forces, his unit was badly mauled. Cornwallis proceeded to Portsmouth with his army, but Clinton had already countermanded the order to send reinforcements and he now directed Cornwallis to occupy and hold a deep water seaport for the British fleet. Obediently, Cornwallis shipped his army to Yorktown, and Lafayette occupied Williamsburg.

132. Joseph Webb House, Connecticut

WEBB-DEANE-STEVENS MUSEUM
211 MAIN STREET
WETHERSFIELD, CONNECTICUT

The Comte de Rochambeau, in command of the French army in America, had arrived in Narragansett Bay off Newport on July 10, 1780, on the French fleet commanded by Commodore the Chevalier de Ternay. The army wintered in Newport and the cavalry in Lebanon, Connecticut. After the death of de Ternay in December 1780, the Comte de Barras took command of the French fleet at Newport in May 1781.

The Joseph Webb House, built in 1752, was the site of General Washington's May 19–26, 1781, meeting with Rochambeau and Major General the Chevalier de Chastellux, who served as interpreter. Accompanying Washington were General Henry Knox and the French engineer, Louis de Presle Duportail, who had joined the Continental Army in February 1777 and was the Commandant of the Corps of Engineers and Sappers and Miners. Don Higginbotham recounts Washington's conference with Rochambeau in *The War of American Independence*.

For months Washington had contemplated an attack on New York City, a scheme Rochambeau had viewed with scant enthusiasm, although the two leaders agreed that any such endeavor should await French naval superiority. The realization of Washington's ambitions was soon to be in prospect as reports arrived in May, 1781, that Admiral François Joseph Paul, the Comte de Grasse, had sailed from Brest for the West Indies with twenty ships-of-the-line. In conference at Wethersfield, Connecticut, the Virginian was unable to determine from Rochambeau whether de Grasse would consent to joint operations with the Franco-American armies on the continent of North America. At the time plans were broadly outlined for Rochambeau's regiments to join Washington's army for a thrust at New York, which, if less than completely successful, might nonetheless compel Clinton to draw troops away from Cornwallis and consequently ease the pressure on Lafayette in Virginia.

In *Victory at Yorktown,* Richard M. Ketchum details the news about the Comte de Grasse.

On August 14 Washington received what was unquestionably one of the most important letters of the war. Barras wrote from Newport, having heard from de Grasse that he was definitely sailing for the Chesapeake, bringing twenty-nine warships and more than three thousand troops. As Washington now knew, he had barely two months in which to concentrate the allied armies in Virginia, at least six hundred miles from Newport, and he wrote, "Matters having now come to a crisis and a decisive plan to be determined on, I was obliged, from the shortness of Count de Grasse's promised stay on this coast … and the feeble compliance of the States to my requisitions for men … to give up all idea of attacking New York …."

On August 15 the General instructed Lafayette to position his force in such a way as to prevent Cornwallis from returning to North Carolina, and at the same time ordered General William Heath to remain behind with a regiment of artillery, Sheldon's dragoons, and a number of understrength infantry regiments to safeguard the Hudson River posts. It was by no means enough, but it was all he could possibly spare. At the same time, since the crucial need was to convince Clinton that an attack was to be made on New York, rumors were spread that de Grasse was expected imminently, while the allied troops began crossing the Hudson near King's Bridge.

On June 18, 1781, Rochambeau's army headed to Providence from Newport and began to march south to join Washington's Continental Army. The Washington-Rochambeau Revolutionary Route National Historic Trail commemorates the route (as shown on today's maps) taken by Rochambeau's army from Providence, Rhode Island, to Hartford and Danbury, Connecticut, and south to near White Plains, New York, on July 6.

The French met Washington's army near White Plains on August 18 and began marching north, crossing the Hudson River at King's Ferry to Stony Point, and south again to near the intersection of Interstates 87 and 287, west of New York City through New Jersey to Trenton, southwest through Philadelphia, Pennsylvania, on September 2 and 3, through Wilmington, Delaware, and on to Head of Elk (Elkton), Maryland.

Some Continentals embarked there and others marched on to Baltimore, where they boarded vessels, headed down the Chesapeake, and landed at various sites. The French marched to Annapolis and embarked on vessels sent by de Grasse, arriving at College Creek Landing on the James River near Williamsburg on September 23. The two armies reached Yorktown on September 28.

On August 23 the Comte de Barras eluded the British and sailed south from Rhode Island with his nine ships, bringing Rochambeau's artillery. On August 30 the Comte de Grasse sailed into the Chesapeake Bay and landed his soldiers to join General Lafayette, who was holding General Cornwallis.

Washington rode to Mount Vernon and hosted Rochambeau as his guest for two of the three days he was there. They continued south on September 12 and met with de Grasse on his flagship on September 18.

On September 5 in the Atlantic Ocean, the French fleet battled the British fleet commanded by Admiral Thomas Graves. Barbara W. Tuchman recounts the battle and its importance in *The First Salute*.

Which fleet had prevailed?

The outcome was, in fact, to be the turning point of the war and, it might be said, of the 18th century, for it proved to be the enabling factor of the rebels' Yorktown campaign.

Graves saw, instead of the twelve to fourteen ships he had expected de Grasse to bring, the great array of de Grasse's fleet of 28 ships of the line plus some frigates and gunboats. Against this superior force, Graves had, however, the superior position in that he was sailing in regular procession with the wind behind him, while de Grasse, after the knotty business of landing his troops to join Lafayette, was trying to maneuver his ships out of the harbor into the open sea where he would have room to form a battle line. In seeking combat, his purpose was to deny the Bay to the British and prevent the entrance of a force to aid or rescue Cornwallis. Graves's purpose was, of course, the reverse: to keep the sea lanes open to Cornwallis. His opportunity to overwhelm the French was, according to naval critics, ideal. He was running down before the wind in good order, while the enemy in straggling succession was laboring to negotiate the uneasy passage around Cape Henry to the open sea. If he had attacked the disconnected French van one by one, he could have destroyed them. But that was not the tactical formula of Fighting Instructions, and Graves was a conformist to the code, and a product of the Royal Navy's greatest self-inflicted wound, the lost initiative left by the execution of Admiral Byng and the court-martial of Admiral Mathews. He knew that his duty under Fighting Instructions was to form line ahead in a battle line parallel to that of the enemy. Because the enemy had no line, Graves was at a loss. From one o'clock to 3:30 p.m., with the wind in rapid changes of direction, first in favor of the French and then of the English, Graves struggled to fulfill the formula, and by the time he raised the signal to engage, he had lost his advantage. While hoisting the blue-and-white-checkered flag that signaled "bear down," meaning that every captain should turn toward the enemy and attack the nearest individually, he kept the line ahead signal, which supersedes all others, still flying from his mizzenmast. "Bear down" would mean there would be no line, while the superior signal said to stay with it. The puzzled captains obeyed the superior signal. Keeping their line, they were brought up against the French at an angle instead of parallel, with the result that only their lead ships—part of Graves's force, instead of the whole—could engage. Cannon boomed and French gunnery told. Four of Graves's ships were so badly damaged as to be useless to him for renewing action next morning.

For the next two days, September 6 and 7, while carpenters and riggers made what repairs they could at sea, the two fleets watched each other without engaging. They broke contact next day with no clear-cut victory or defeat discernible, yet with import that would place the Battle of the Bay among the decisive sea combats of history. Graves's fleet was damaged and dispersed; de Grasse's fleet held command of the Bay. The old culprit, "misunderstood" signals—the word was Graves's in his subsequent explanation to Parliament—had mangled yet another naval battle, although in fact the signals had been understood only too well.

On September 9, de Grasse precipitated a resolution by sailing his fleet back into the Bay to make it his domain. At the same time, de Barras, the critical addition to the contest, slipped in from Newport with his siege guns and his beef and his eight fresh ships.

133. The Burning of New London, Connecticut

SEPTEMBER 6, 1781

FORT GRISWOLD BATTLEFIELD STATE PARK
PARK AVENUE
GROTON, CONNECTICUT
FORT TRUMBULL STATE PARK
90 WALBACH STREET
NEW LONDON, CONNECTICUT

In March 1776 Congress had legalized privateering, which permitted private owners to arm their ships. Privateers who captured British ships were rewarded with prize money. The deep harbor at New London was a stronghold of privateers.

On September 5 in the Atlantic Ocean off the coast of Virginia, the French fleet battled the British. On September 6, Benedict Arnold commanded an amphibious force of British and loyalist troops that arrived in New London, ordered by General Clinton to destroy the ships and warehouses. The twenty-three men at Fort Trumbull in New London on the west side of the harbor were under orders to retreat to Fort Griswold. Arnold destroyed houses, stores, warehouses with valuable supplies, and public buildings in the thriving seaport and the privateering ships that did not escape up the Thames River.

On the east side of the harbor, Colonel William Ledyard commanded the small garrison that defended Fort Griswold against the attack that included two British regiments. In the short battle, both forces suffered heavy losses. After the battle, the British looted and burned Groton. The wounded were taken to the Ebenezer Avery House.

134. Yorktown, Virginia

SEPTEMBER 28–OCTOBER 19, 1781

COLONIAL NATIONAL HISTORICAL PARK
YORKTOWN BATTLEFIELD VISITOR CENTER
1000 COLONIAL PARKWAY, YORKTOWN, VIRGINIA

General Cornwallis had taken command in Virginia in May, fought General Wayne at Green Spring in July, occupied Yorktown, and waited for reinforcements from General Clinton. In *The Guns of Independence,* Jerome A. Greene summarizes September 1781 at Yorktown.

Events picked up momentum as September passed. During the night of the 17th, American reconnaissance parties harassed and alarmed British outposts. In the early morning darkness of September 22, Cornwallis sent fire ships against the French vessels blocking the mouth of the York River. "The sight was worth the trouble to see!" remembered Captain Johann Ewald, a one-eyed Prussian who had lost his left eye in a duel in 1770. "The [fire] ships were set on fire and illuminated the area so brightly that we could easily detect the French ships at anchor in the very dark night. But since the fire ships had been ablaze too soon, the enemy ships cut their cables and sailed away."

As the days passed, Cornwallis pushed ahead with his fortifications at Gloucester Point and Yorktown. He confidently expected relief at any time. Two days before his experiment with the fire ships, his nominal strength stood at 8,885 men, excluding sailors attached to the armed British ships and the twenty-four transports and smaller vessels anchored off Yorktown. The addition of the seamen, who numbered 840, brought Cornwallis's strength in mid-September to 9,725 men. In addition, some 1,500 to 2,000 slaves were used to help build defenses. The effective strength of his land force, however, was much lower (and was reflected as such in Cornwallis's official strength reports). Without the 840 sailors, the strength of the British army in Virginia fluctuated little over the months and averaged only about 5,500 men.

By September 26, all of Washington's and Rochambeau's soldiers had arrived. Williamsburg teemed with a motley assortment of colors and styles, languages, and dialects. We can safely estimate that some 1,500 Americans and 600 French were absent due to sickness or other reasons at any given time, and that the militia probably numbered no more than 3,500 effectives. Therefore, the reasonable effective strength under Washington at Williamsburg was approximately 18,000 men, compared to Cornwallis's 5,500. Under Washington's supreme command, the Allied armies became a single force capable of acting efficiently against a wily and skilled opponent.

Friday, September 28, broke clear with the promise of another intolerably hot and humid day before the Allied armies of France and the United States reached Yorktown.

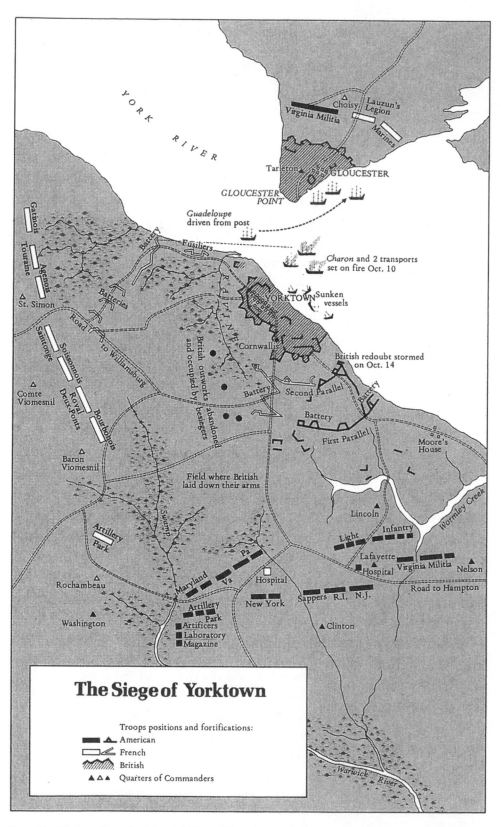

The Siege of Yorktown

Troops positions and fortifications:

- American
- French
- British
- Quarters of Commanders

From: The Glorious Cause *by Robert Middlekauff (1982). Map from p. 565. By permission of Oxford University Press, USA.*

The soldiers struck camp before dawn and set out on the march at daybreak, leaving a detachment of 200 men behind in Williamsburg to mind the hospital and stores.

General Cornwallis continued to strengthen his earthworks while Washington prepared the siege. The allied bombardment began on October 9. General Washington lit the fuse to fire the first American cannon. Jerome A. Greene points out the importance of the two redoubts in *The Guns of Independence.*

While these batteries and those of the French in the first parallel continued to rake the British lines, Washington concentrated on advancing his ordnance closer to finish off Cornwallis's obviously weakening resistance. Most of the American guns, for the moment, would have to remain in the first line until the American sector of the second was prolonged and completed. That, in turn, depended upon the speedy capture of the detached British works that blocked the way and thwarted progress: Redoubts 9 and 10.

Time, however, was not Washington's friend. The Virginian needed to capture the redoubts, finish his second line, and crush Cornwallis before General Clinton arrived with reinforcements or withdrew the Yorktown and Gloucester troops, and before Admiral de Grasse's time expired and he returned to the West Indies. The pair of redoubts, therefore, was the key for concluding the siege and forcing a surrender. By October 13, everyone in the Allied command structure agreed that only a direct assault against these strongholds would accomplish the desired objective. The terrain helped dictate this conclusion, for the ground between the second line and the British redoubts was not well suited to the further erection of batteries. Only by taking the enemy structures, concluded one officer, could American guns "level the way, cut off palisades, and beat down other obstructions."

On October 14 Americans led by Lieutenant Colonel Alexander Hamilton took Redoubt 10, and French soldiers led by Guillaume, Comte de Deux-Ponts captured Redoubt 9. Jerome A. Greene recounts the British surrender on October 19.

In the face of the vigorous new assault from the Allied guns, an enemy drummer, beating a chamade, appeared on the British parapet before Yorktown. "Had we not seen the drummer in his red coat when he first mounted, he might beat away till doomsday," wrote Lieutenant Ebenezer Denny in his diary. "The constant firing was too much for the sound of a single drum; but when the firing ceased, I thought I never heard a drum equal to it—the delightful music to us all." A red-coated officer joined the drummer. He lifted his hand and began waving something: it was a white handkerchief.

When no one shot in their direction, the plain intention of the handkerchief-waving obvious to all, the officer and drummer climbed down the parapet and walked slowly toward the Allied line, all the while the drummer beating his chamade. One by one Allied guns fell silent, whether on order or word of mouth is unknown. An American officer ran out of the works toward the advancing duo and sent the drummer back to his own lines. The white handkerchief was tied over the eyes of the British officer, who was ushered forward to meet Lafayette in the American entrenchments. The officer was then quickly escorted to Washington's headquarters in a nearby house, where he delivered Cornwallis's message: "I propose a Cessation of Hostilities for 24 hours, & that two Officers may be appointed by each side, to meet at Mr. Moore's house to settle terms for the Surrender of the Posts of York & Gloucester."

Washington's terms were harsher than Cornwallis expected. The Allied commander was not about to return home the King's army and bluntly said as much. For Washington it was a matter of avenging the ill-treatment General Clinton had inflicted upon the American garrison at Charleston, South Carolina, in 1780, when he refused to allow it to surrender with the full honors normally extended to a defeated enemy. "The same Honors will be granted to the Surrendering Army [Cornwallis's] as were granted to the Garrison of Charles Town," insisted Washington.

Washington appointed two commissioners to represent Allied interests. One was his aide-de-camp Lieutenant Colonel John Laurens of South Carolina, whose own father was even then imprisoned in the Tower of London. Laurens would represent the Americans. General Rochambeau selected Viscount de Noailles to represent the French. These two plenipotentiaries were authorized to negotiate with officers of equal rank chosen by Cornwallis.

One particular area of dispute concerned the formal surrender ceremony. Cornwallis's agents demanded the same terms accorded General Burgoyne at Saratoga, where the Americans allowed the British Army to march out with colors flying. Laurens and de Noailles adamantly stood their ground and denied these repeated requests. The humiliating and recent capitulation of Lincoln's army at Charleston was fresh in their minds, too.

Another controversial article dealt with the question of the Loyalists, those Americans who had chosen to support the Crown and as a result had earned Washington's undying contempt. The Allied commander rejected Cornwallis's request for immunity for the Loyalists serving with his army—most of whom served with Lieutenant Colonel John Graves Simcoe's "Queen's Rangers." According to Washington, that matter, as well as the persons involved, lay completely within the jurisdiction of the United States government. Washington yielded somewhat, placing the sloop *Bonetta* at Cornwallis's disposal to carry dispatches and private property to General Clinton. The vessel could proceed *without inspection*, subject only to being delivered to de Grasse upon its return. Washington was providing Cornwallis a means to convey the Loyalists under him to New York, which allowed Washington to retreat gracefully from his own previously announced determination to hang all deserters found in Yorktown.

Near the appointed hour, the British general and his naval commander, Captain Thomas Symonds, held the final document before them. In what must have been the most painful signature of his life, Cornwallis dipped his quill into an inkwell and affixed his name to the surrender document; Symonds did the same, and it was sent to the Allied leaders waiting in Redoubt 10B. There, Washington studied the signatures and wrote nine simple words and the date: "Done in the trenches before York Town in Virginia, Oct. 19 1781." He signed the paper

"G. Washington." Rochambeau signed for the Army of France, and Admiral Louis de Barras for the French Navy in place of de Grasse, who could not be present.

With these signatures, the siege of Yorktown formally ended.

Jerome A. Greene also points out the importance of the close cooperation of the two allies.

Contrasted with the British facility for ineptitude and mismanagement, the Allies exhibited a cohesion of purpose paralleled by an admirable ability to coordinate their maneuvers toward the desired objective. Washington's campaign worked because of an interplay of careful design and good fortune. The close cooperation between de Barras's and de Grasse's fleets, St. Simon's volunteers, Rochambeau's French troops, and Washington's American command made victory possible. Cooperation between the French and Americans in the prosecution of a successful siege—itself largely dependent on French weapons, expertise, and enterprise—assured the triumph of the campaign. After many years of misfortune punctuated by large losses and small gains, Washington had at last acquired and utilized the military components of success.

This Glorious Struggle, edited by Edward G. Lengel, includes the letter General Washington wrote to Thomas McKean, the president of Congress, after the surrender.

TO THOMAS MCKEAN
The Articles of Capitulation were signed on the morning of October 19, leaving Cornwallis and his entire garrison prisoners in American hands. Washington describes the British surrender in this letter to the president of Congress.

Head Quarters near York [town] 19th Octo. 1781

Sir

I have the Honor to inform Congress, that a Reduction of the British Army under the Command of Lord Cornwallis, is most happily effected—The unremitting Ardor which actuated every Officer & Soldier in the combined Army on this Occasion, has principally led to this Important Event, at an earlier period than my most sanguine Hopes had induced me to expect.

The singular Spirit of Emulation, which animated the whole Army from the first Commencement of our Operations, has filled my Mind with the highest pleasure & Satisfaction—and had given me the happiest presages of Success.

On the 17th instant, a Letter was received from Lord Cornwallis, proposing a Meeting of Commissioners, to consult on Terms for the Surrender of the Posts of York & Gloucester—This Letter (the first which had passed between us) opened a correspondence, a copy of which I do myself the Honor to inclose. That Correspondence was followed by the Definitive Capitulation, which was agreed to, & Signed on the 19th Copy of which is also herewith transmitted—and which, I hope, will meet the Approbation of Congress.

I should be wanting in the feelings of Gratitude, did I not mention on this Occasion, with the warmest Sense of Acknowlegments, the very chearfull & able Assistance, which

I have received in the Course of our Operations, from his Excellency the Count de Rochambeau, and all his Officers of every Rank, in their respective Capacities. Nothing could equal this Zeal of our Allies, but the emulating Spirit of the American Officers, whose ardor would not suffer their Exertions to be exceeded.

The very uncommon Degree of Duty & Fatigue which the Nature of the Service required from the officers of Engineers & Artillery of both Armies, obliges me particularly to mention the Obligations I am under to the Commanding & other Officers of those Corps.

I wish it was in my Power to express to Congress, how much I feel myself indebted to The Count de Grasse and the Officers of the Fleet under his Command, for the distinguished Aid and Support which has been afforded by them; between whom, & the Army, the most happy Concurrence of Sentiments & Views have subsisted, and from whom, every possible Co-operation has been experienced, which the most harmonious Intercourse could afford.

Returns of the Prisoners, Military Stores, Ordnance, Shipping & other Matters, I shall do myself the Honor to transmit to Congress, as soon as they can be collected by the Heads of Departments, to which they belong.

Colo. Laurens & the Viscount de Noailles, on the Part of the combined Army, were the Gentlemen who acted as Commissioners for forming & setting the Terms of Capitulation & Surrender herewith transmitted—to whom I am particularly obliged for their Readiness & Attention exhibited on the Occasion.

Colo. Tilghman, one of my Aids de Camp, will have the Honor to deliver these dispatches to your Excellency—he will be able to inform you of every minute Circumstance which is not particularly mentioned in my Letter. His Merits, which are too well known to need any Observations at this Time, have gained my particular Attention—& I could wish that they may be honored by the Notice of your Excellency & Congress.

Your Excellency & Congress will be pleased to accept my Congratulations on this happy Event—& believe me to be With the highest Respect & Esteem sir Your Excellencys Most Obedient and most humble Servant

Go: Washington

On October 21, Virginia militia began to march the rank-and-file prisoners to prison camps at Winchester, Virginia, York, Pennsylvania (see #135), and Fort Frederick, Maryland (see #90). The high-ranking officers received paroles, including General Cornwallis, who sailed for New York and then to London.

General Clinton's promised and long-delayed relief force sailed from New York on the day that Cornwallis surrendered. After Clinton received confirmation of the surrender, he ordered the British fleet to return to New York on October 29.

In *Founders,* Ray Raphael details the British land forces in America and the West Indies.

The war was far from over, and Washington understood this better than most. Just to the south, in the West Indies, British and French fleets continued to battle for control of the seas. In addition, British land forces were still formidable: 17,000 troops stationed in New York; 9,000 in

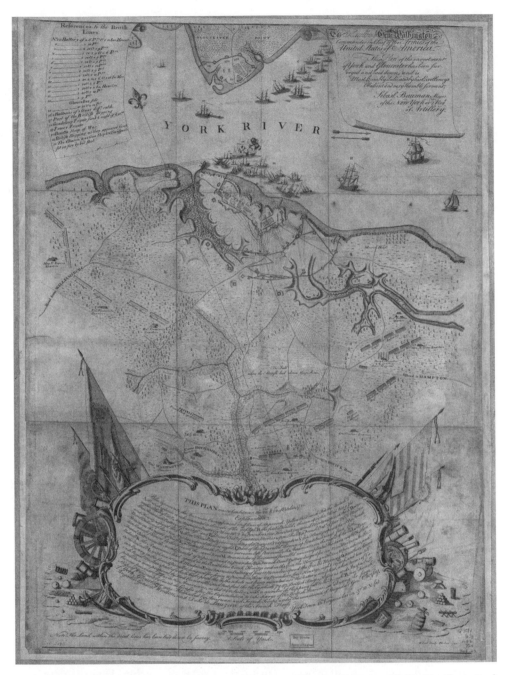

American, French, and British troop positions at Yorktown. Sebastian Baumann. *To His Excellency Genl. Washington, Commander in Chief of the armies of the United States of America, this plan of the investment of York and Gloucester has been surveyed and laid down, and is most humbly dedicated by His Excellency's obedient servant, Sebastn. Bauman, major of the New York or 2nd Regt of Artillery. This plan was taken between the 22nd & 28th of October, 1781. R. Scot, sculp. Philad[elphia]* 1782. *(Courtesy, Library of Congress, Geography and Map Division. http://hdl.loc.gov/loc.gmd/g3884y.ar147100)*

Canada; 11,000 in South Carolina and Georgia; 10,000 in the West Indies—a total of 47,000 men, several times the size of the Continental Army. In this context, the capture of 7,000 fighting men at Yorktown was hardly a crippling blow. Both the British at Saratoga and the Americans at Charleston had suffered comparable defeats, and yet they had continued to fight. The question was not whether the British *could* continue the war, but whether they had the will to do so, and the answer to that was beyond the control of George Washington, the Continental Army, or the Continental Congress. The outcome was likely to be determined by Britain's concurrent struggle with France in the Indies, with France and Spain in the Mediterranean, with the Netherlands in the North Sea, South Africa, and the East Indies, and with anticolonial insurgents in India.

Benjamin H. Irvin describes the presentation of Cornwallis's flags in *Clothed in Robes of Sovereignty: The Continental Congress and the People Out of Doors.*

On November 3, ten days after Congress received word of the French and American victory, Colonel David Humphreys, a second of Washington's aides, carried into Philadelphia twenty-four standards surrendered by the British army at Yorktown. In the rich ceremony of early modern nations, the presentation and exhibition of conquered standards bespoke the glory and might of the triumphant sovereign. Extremely rare in the revolutionary United States, these ceremonies carried extraordinary significance; they bore witness to the strength of continental arms and validated the republic's claim to independence. In 1775, after General Schuyler forwarded the British flags captured at Fort Chambly, the congressional president John Hancock invited local dignitaries to view them hanging in his lodgings. The failure or refusal of Horatio Gates to secure the British and German colors at Saratoga unfortunately deprived Congress of a similar opportunity in 1777.

For the arrival of Cornwallis's flags, Congress and Pennsylvania state officials prepared a spectacle. The Philadelphia light horse met Colonel Humphreys at the Schuylkill River and escorted him into town in an "ever memorable procession" that consisted of music, an advanced party of light dragoons, "[t]he colours of the United States of America and the French nation, displayed…twenty four British and German standards, also displayed," and a detail of light horse. Parading along Market Street, "amid the acclamation of thousands," the procession at last arrived at the State House, where, as the *Maryland Gazette* reported, Col. Humphreys "laid" the standards "at Congress's feet." As the *Gazette's* gallant language suggested, this presentment ceremony not only affirmed the sovereignty of Congress but also signified the subordinacy of military to civil authorities. By dispatching Humphreys to hand over the spoils of war, Washington paid symbolic deference to Congress, his master.

Following the British surrender at Yorktown, the Comte de Grasse's fleet sailed for the Caribbean in early November. The Continental Army began to move north to camps in Pennsylvania, New Jersey, and New York. General Washington was in Philadelphia during the winter.

In *The American Revolution,* Gordon S. Wood compares Britain and America in the Revolutionary War.

On the face of it, a military struggle seemed to promise all the advantage to Great Britain. Britain was the most powerful nation in the world, with a population of about 11 million, compared with only 2.5 million colonists, a fifth of whom were black slaves. The British navy was the largest in the world, with nearly half its ships initially committed to the American struggle. The British army was a well-trained professional force, numbering at one point in 1778 nearly 50,000 troops stationed in North America alone; and more than 30,000 hired German mercenaries were added to this force during the war.

To confront this military might the Americans had to start from scratch. The Continental Army they created numbered usually less than 5,000 troops, supplemented by state militia units of varying sizes. In most cases inexperienced amateur officers served as the American military leaders.

Yet such a contrast of numbers and abilities was deceptive, for the British disadvantages were immense and perhaps overwhelming—even at the beginning when their opportunities to put down the rebellion were greatest. Great Britain had to carry on the war three thousand miles across the Atlantic, with consequent problems of communications and logistics; even supplying the army with food became a problem. The great breadth of territory and the wild nature of the terrain made conventional maneuverings and operations difficult and cumbersome. The fragmented and local character of authority in America inhibited decisive action by the British. There was no nerve center anywhere whose capture would destroy the rebellion. The British generals came to see that engaging Washington's army in battle ought to be their main objective; but, said the British commander in chief, they did not know how to do it, "as the enemy moves with so much more celerity than we possibly can."

The British never clearly understood what they were up against—a revolutionary struggle involving widespread support in the population. Hence they continually underestimated the staying power of the rebels and overestimated the strength of the loyalists. And in the end, independence came to mean more to the Americans than reconquest did to the English.

In *The Great Experiment,* John Rhodehamel describes Washington, the commander.

Washington's army was the soul of the Revolution. The Continental Congress remained little more than a provisional committee until the Articles of Confederation, adopted in 1777, were finally ratified in 1781. As presidents of Congress came and went, as Congress itself dodged from one temporary capital to another, General Washington was more a head of state than any figure in America. He struggled to maintain a coalition, not only the alliance with France, but the alliance among the thirteen states themselves. To succeed in such a command required a statesman of genius.

Washington had seen in the 1750s the destruction wrought by stubbornly disunited colonies striving to wage a common war. He had become an American nationalist before there was an American nation. From the day of his appointment as commander in chief he had labored "to discourage all kinds of local attachments, and distinctions of Country, denominating the whole under the greater name of American." He soon became the symbol of national unity, as well as its advocate. The Revolution was fought in the name of noble ideals, but abstract principles do not always provide the most inspiring standard for rallying a people.

Noble words must be made flesh, and that substance Washington provided. A few republicans feared his immense popularity, but this general did not hunger for power. Indeed, his devotion to republican principles, particularly the scrupulous obedience he gave to popular government, was the quality of Washington's leadership that his contemporaries found most heroic. As a French general wonderingly observed in 1782, "This is the seventh year that he has commanded the army, and that he has obeyed the Congress; more need not be said."

135. Camp Security

HISTORICAL MARKER ON ROUTE 462 AT LOCUST GROVE ROAD YORK, PENNSYLVANIA

Camp Security, a prisoner of war camp, was established in July 1781 to house British prisoners of war. They included those who had been taken prisoner in 1777 when General John Burgoyne surrendered at Saratoga, New York. Known as the Convention Army, they had been marched after the battle first to a camp in Cambridge, Massachusetts, then in 1779 to Charlottesville, Virginia. When the war moved to Virginia in 1781, they were sent to Fort Frederick, Maryland, and to Camp Security. Following the British surrender at Yorktown, Virginia, in October 1781, prisoners from Cornwallis' army were marched to Camp Security. The camp included a stockade, log huts, and a temporary village outside the stockade. Washington ordered the "Cessation of Hostilities" proclaimed on April 19, 1783. The prisoners were released in May.

136. Sharon Springs, New York

JULY 10, 1781

HISTORICAL MARKER ON ROUTE 20 SOUTH OF SHARON SPRINGS, NEW YORK FORT PLAIN MUSEUM AND HISTORICAL PARK FORT PLAIN, NEW YORK

While the American, French, and British armies were at Yorktown, Colonel Marinus Willett's challenge was to protect the settlers on the New York frontier from raids—with only 400 men. The battles began in July and continued through October 1781.

Lieutenant John Doxstader's force of loyalists and Indians had plundered and burned Currytown in the Sharon Springs area and were camped on high ground in a swamp. On July 10, 1781, Colonel Marinus Willett drew Doxstader's force into a trap in a forested area down the ridge. In the short battle, Willett drove them off with heavy fire and bayonets, forcing them to abandon their dead, their camp, and the plunder they had taken at Currytown.

137. Johnstown, New York

OCTOBER 25, 1781

MONUMENT IN SIR WILLIAM JOHNSON PARK
JOHNSON HALL STATE HISTORIC SITE
JOHNSTOWN, NEW YORK

Major John Ross, in command of more than 600 men including 130 Iroquois and British regulars, and Captain Walter Butler, leading 150 Butler's Rangers, moved up the Mohawk Valley, burning fields and homes. Colonel Marinus Willett and his 400 men pursued the British through the night of October 24 and attacked the next day. In the fighting near Johnson Hall, Willett was outnumbered. The battle ended with darkness, and Ross retreated north.

138. West Canada Creek, New York

OCTOBER 30, 1781

ON THE NORTH SIDE OF WEST CANADA CREEK

After the battle of Johnstown, Colonel Willett resumed his pursuit of Major John Ross's force as they retreated toward Canada. They began to fight at Black Creek and continued at West Canada Creek.

In *Forgotten Allies*, Joseph T. Glatthaar and James Kirby Martin describe the fight at West Canada Creek.

The British and their Indian allies retreated at near breakneck speed, yet they could not elude Willett's pursuing force, with the Oneidas leading the way. At West Canada Creek, the British finally offered resistance. By defending a fordable crossing, they tried to delay the rebel pursuers long enough to allow their main column to escape. A bloody firefight ensued. Captain Walter Butler, commanding the British rearguard, held this position as long as possible. After he ordered his detachment to pull out, he turned to taunt his patriot enemies. An Oneida warrior named Anthony raised his weapon and fired from great range. The ball crashed into Butler's head, knocking him to the ground. His comrades instantly dispersed, leaving their stunned captain semiconscious but mortally wounded. According to Willett, another Oneida warrior rushed forward and "finished his business for him and got a Considerable booty," including Butler's scalp and everything he had in his pockets. The scourge of Cherry Valley and one of the most detested Tories of them all lay dead at the hands of two Oneida warriors.

After the engagement at the ford, Willett halted the pursuit. The swift marches had fatigued his command badly, and his supplies were dwindling. The British later indicated that they had suffered thirteen killed, twelve wounded, and forty-nine missing during this campaign. As for Willett, he reported thirteen rebels killed, twenty-three wounded, and five missing. He did not mention any Oneida casualties.

Violence on the frontier continued in 1782 and 1783, including conflicts in Ohio, Kentucky, and Arkansas.

139. Gnadenhutten, Ohio

MARCH 8, 1782

GNADENHUTTEN HISTORICAL PARK AND MUSEUM
352 SOUTH CHERRY STREET
GNADENHUTTEN, OHIO

Gnadenhutten, a mission founded by Moravians for Delawares, was attacked on March 8, 1782, by militia commanded by Colonel David Williamson. They massacred more than ninety Delaware men, women, and children as they prayed at the mission.

140. Crawford's Defeat, Ohio

JUNE 4–5, 1782

HISTORICAL MARKER NEAR THE INTERSECTION OF ROUTES 29 AND 199
NORTH OF UPPER SANDUSKY, OHIO

The conflicts in the Ohio Valley that pitted Americans against the loyalists and their Indian allies were brutal. Colonel William Crawford led 480 militiamen from Pennsylvania and

Virginia in an attack on Shawnees and Wyandots at Sandusky in June of 1782. Major David Williamson, who had led the Gnadenhutten massacre, was with Crawford. They were stopped in the two-day battle by a force led by British Captain William Caldwell that included Simon Girty, Alexander McKee, Mathew Elliot, 100 Butler's Rangers, and 340 Indians, including Delaware and Wyandot chiefs. Caldwell was reinforced the second day by more Rangers with two cannon and more Indians, including Shawnees. The forty-eight American casualties included Crawford, who was captured, tortured, and killed in revenge for the Gnadenhutten massacre.

141. Bryan's Station, Kentucky

AUGUST 15–17, 1782

HISTORICAL MARKER ON BRYAN STATION ROAD NEAR BRIAR HILL ROAD
LEXINGTON, KENTUCKY

Bryan's Station, a fortified settlement of about forty cabins and corner blockhouses, was built on a ridge near the North Elkhorn Creek. It was defended by about forty Kentucky militiamen when Captain William Caldwell with thirty Canadian Rangers and about three hundred Indians from several tribes including two Shawnee chiefs, Black Hoof and Blue Jacket, attacked the settlement on August 15, 1782. The men who rode to Lexington for help returned in the afternoon with reinforcements. They were hit by fire from Caldwell's men; two were killed and four wounded. The militia defended the fort until Caldwell withdrew toward Blue Licks on August 17 after firing flaming arrows into the fort, burning cornfields, and killing livestock.

142. Blue Licks, Kentucky

AUGUST 19, 1782

BLUE LICKS BATTLEFIELD STATE RESORT PARK
10299 MAYSVILLE ROAD
NORTHEAST OF CARLISLE, KENTUCKY

On August 19, 1782, Colonel John Todd led 180 Kentucky militia in pursuit of Captain Caldwell up the Buffalo Trace to Blue Licks on the Licking River. Todd's force included Daniel Boone and his son, Israel. They crossed the river, advanced into Caldwell's ambush, and were defeated in the fifteen-minute battle. The seventy American casualties included Colonel Todd and Israel Boone. Caldwell returned to Ohio, having failed to force the settlers to abandon the Kentucky frontier.

In reprisal, Brigadier General George Rogers Clark returned in the fall and burned five Shawnee villages and their crops.

143. Arkansas Post, Arkansas

APRIL 17, 1783

ARKANSAS POST NATIONAL MEMORIAL
GILLETT, ARKANSAS

In "Colbert's Raid on Arkansas Post: Westernmost Action of the Revolution," on the National Park Service website, Bob Blythe describes the April 1783 raid.

At the time of the American Revolution, the lower Mississippi River Valley had only scattered white settlements, and its control was disputed among the Spanish, the British, and various Indian tribes. At the end of the Seven Years' War (French & Indian War) in 1763, Great Britain had taken over East and West Florida. The boundary of West Florida extended to the Mississippi River, and the province included Pensacola, Mobile, and the Natchez district of present-day Mississippi. The capital of Spanish Louisiana was New Orleans, and Spain largely controlled the traffic up and down the Mississippi. Although white settlement was just beginning, many understood the great potential for agriculture in the Mississippi Valley. Control of the river and its vast hinterlands was one of the prizes up for grabs in the war between American patriots and the British government.

Even before Spain formally entered the war on the patriot side in June 1779, the Spanish in New Orleans had given secret aid to the Americans. The Spanish governor at New Orleans, José de Gálvez, had helped supply George Rogers Clark's 1778–1779 campaign against the British posts in the Northwest. After Spanish entry into the war, the contest for Florida and the lower Mississippi began in earnest.

Gálvez immediately made plans to attack British outposts. With a force composed of regular army troops as well as black and white militias, the Spanish took Baton Rouge and Natchez by early October 1779. Having secured the great river, Gálvez then moved on to the British garrison at Mobile, which fell in May 1780. Alarmed by the Spanish gains, the British commander at Pensacola roused British supporters to retake Fort Panmure at Natchez. A British and Choctaw force under Captain John Blommart held the fort for about six weeks, until the Spanish recaptured it and took Blommart and others captive on June 22. In the meantime, Gálvez had taken Pensacola, capital of West Florida.

British citizens and Chickasaw Indians who had fled Natchez before the Spanish retook it then formed a partisan band under the leadership of James Logan Colbert. Colbert had been a captain in the British army at Pensacola. Instead of surrendering to the Spanish, he sought refuge in the Chickasaw Nation and fought on. From late 1781 through early 1783, Colbert's band raided Spanish and American shipping on the Mississippi. Aiming to get Blommart and other British prisoners released, Colbert took hostages in hopes of arranging a prisoner exchange.

Throughout 1782, Colbert proclaimed an intention to attack the vulnerable Spanish garrison at Arkansas Post. Located about 35 miles up the Arkansas River from its confluence with the Mississippi, this small outpost was protected by 40 Spanish troops in a stockade known as Fort Carlos III. In April 1783, Colbert, with a force of about 100 whites and Indians, made his way up the Arkansas River toward Fort Carlos. In the early morning of April 17, the British force took several prisoners in the village outside the fort's walls, and then went after the fort. For about six hours, the battle raged. The Spanish garrison fired about 300 cannon balls at the attackers, but did little damage because Colbert's men lay protected in a ravine. At about 9:00 am, the Spanish commander, Captain Jacobo Du Breuil, ordered a sortie that sent the British force running for its boats. A pursuit by Du Breuil's Quapaw Indian allies forced Colbert to release his remaining prisoners. Later in 1783, after making a final report to his British superiors in St. Augustine, Colbert was thrown from his horse and killed.

Word of the preliminary peace treaty concluded among France, Spain, and Britain in January 1783 reached the Mississippi Valley shortly after Colbert's Raid. Hostilities ceased, and Spain prepared to reoccupy the Floridas. Spain remained in possession of New Orleans, and the right of the new United States to send cargo down the Mississippi and deposit goods at New Orleans would remain a disputed issue until New Orleans and all of Louisiana was purchased by the U.S. in 1803. By this time, France had forced Spain to return Louisiana to her, and the $15 million sale was arranged between President Thomas Jefferson and France's Napoleon Bonaparte.

Most of the battleground now lies beneath the Post Bend, but the site of Fort Carlos III and the history of Colbert's Raid, the final battle of the Revolutionary War, can be explored through exhibits at Arkansas Post National Memorial.

❦

Changes swept through London after General Cornwallis's surrender. The resignation of Lord George Germain, the American secretary, was announced on February 11, 1782. On February 23, George III had General Clinton recalled and replaced with General Guy Carleton, who arrived in New York on May 5. Lord North resigned as prime minister on March 20. Lord Rockingham succeeded him, serving from March 27 until his death on July 1. The Earl of Shelburne was prime minister from July 4, 1782, until April 2, 1783.

In *The First Salute,* Barbara W. Tuchman details the changes that followed Lord North's resignation.

Agents quickly conveyed news of the Cornwallis catastrophe across the Channel, bringing it first to Lord George Germain, who in turn took it to Lord North in Downing Street. The First Minister flung open his arms "as [if] he would have taken a ball in the breast," crying in what may be the most quoted words of the war, "Oh, God, it is all over!" and repeating the words "wildly" as he strode up and down the room. Not he but Germain brought the news to King George, who, unshaken in his singleness of purpose, ordered Germain to make plans for the most feasible mode of continuing the war. Apart from diehards in the Cabinet surrounding Germain and Sandwich, few in Parliament and the country offered support. Most acknowledged that the war had been ineffectual, and that to continue it by defensive measures as proposed by Germain, with no hope of winning, but merely to hold out against independence and drive a stiff bargain with the Americans, would be no more effective. It would only mean unacceptable cost to raise new levies to replace the army lost by Cornwallis as well as to pay for the past costs of the war.

The City of London, sensitive to the prospect of prolonged and costly expenditure, petitioned the King to end the war. Country meetings echoed the sentiment. Motions in Parliament urging an end were resisted by the government with smaller and smaller majorities. On December 12, a motion by a private member, Sir James Lowther, that "all further attempts to reduce the revolted colonies are contrary to the true interests of this kingdom," was voted down by only forty-one, less than half the former majority. In February, Henry Seymour Conway, a former Secretary of State, moved that the war in America "be no longer pursued for the impracticable purpose of reducing the inhabitants by force," and this was put down by a majority of only one. A week later, a second motion by Conway to the same effect was carried. Implacably, a third time, on March 4, Conway moved to inform the King that "this House will consider as enemies to his Majesty and this country, all those who shall [advise] the farther prosecution of offensive war on the continent of North America." This rather startling proposition was carried without a vote. It put an end to the matter. To refuse Parliament's advice was unconstitutional. No lawless monarch, George III knew only that he must stay within the rules.

On March 20, 1782, in "one of the fullest and most tense Houses...that had ever been seen," with the streets outside equally crowded, the First Minister, who for twelve years had placidly presided over the most turbulent times since the Gunpowder Plot, was relieved at last. Given his long-desired and perhaps now ambivalent wish, Lord North resigned. A government of the Opposition took over, with Rockingham, Shelburne, Fox and the young Pitt. On April 25, the Cabinet agreed to negotiate peace terms with no allowance for a veto of independence.

Change was also under way in America. Even though the British continued to occupy Charleston three months after the surrender of General Cornwallis, the state held elections. In *This Destructive War*, John S. Pancake describes the meeting of the newly elected General Assembly.

Political as well as military considerations lay behind the steady pressure that Greene was exerting on the enemy. He was as anxious as Governor Rutledge to reestablish civil government, not only because of the generally salutary effect that it would have for the Whig cause but because he was increasingly confronted with problems that he felt were outside the province of military authority. General elections were held, and on January 18, 1782, the South Carolina General Assembly convened at Jacksonboro. The town was a scant thirty miles from Charleston. By establishing the seat of government on the enemy's doorstep, Greene was demonstrating that British power in South Carolina was at an end. Among the members of the assembly were Marion, Pickens, and Sumter.

The British slowly began to evacuate the cities they had occupied: Savannah in July, Wilmington in November, Charleston in December, and New York nearly a year later. In *Liberty's Exiles: American Loyalists in the Revolutionary World*, Maya Jasanoff describes the departures of the soldiers, the loyalists, and their slaves from Savannah in July 1782.

Loyalists in Savannah were the first to confront a situation that would be replayed on successively larger stages in the months ahead. Seven thousand white civilians and slaves prepared to depart in less than four weeks' time. How or if loyalists readied themselves psychologically for leaving can never be really known, but there were concrete chores aplenty. The city's neat grid of angles and squares turned into a moving mosaic. Days became busy with selling and packing, transactions and farewells. Soldiers piled up military stores and ordnance below the fort walls to be rowed out to the coast. Slaves hauled furniture and baggage and gathered by the hundreds to ship out with their masters. Ultimately almost all of the five thousand enslaved blacks in Savannah would leave, transported from the city as loyalist property. On July 11, 1782, the garrison trooped into flatboats and rowed around the grassy curves of the river mouth to the sea.

In *A People's History of the American Revolution*, Ray Raphael describes the treatment of the loyalists who remained in America.

Although many patriots displayed vindictive behavior, communities which depended upon loyalists to fill an important economic role tended to show more mercy. New Haven civic leaders solicited wealthy Tory merchants from New York who might want to relocate their businesses. Animosities ran high in New Haven, which had been troubled during the war by its proximity to the British forces on Long Island, and rancor did not disappear at the end, but any desire for vengeance was subordinated to the interests of economic development.

In South Carolina, which was ravaged by civil war, patriots were sharply divided in their attitudes toward the defeated loyalists: most could not abide the enemy in their midst, but a few favored a policy of reconciliation. Judge Aedanus Burke, himself an ardent patriot, argued that "the experience of all countries has shewn, that where a community splits into a faction, and has recourse to arms, and one finally gets the better; a law to bury in oblivion past transactions is absolutely necessary to restore tranquility." Such ideas were not well received by those with personal accounts to settle. Burke wrote that he was warned before holding court "agt. admitting Lawyers to plead for the Tories, and as to myself, that I should be cautious how I adjudged any point in their favor." At some personal risk, Burke disregarded these warnings and endeavored to conduct proper trials. At Ninety-Six, a focal point of the civil war, Aedanus Burke presided over the trial of Matthew Love, accused of participating in "Bloody Bill" Cunningham's massacres. Burke refused to find Love guilty, reasoning that killing during time of war could not be tried as murder. Indeed, Burke was "shocked at the very idea of trying & condemning to death after so singular, so complicated & so suspicious a Revolution."

The spectators at Love's trial, including friends and relatives of the victims, did not take such an enlightened view. Once Burke had left the room, they seized Matthew Love, who was no longer guarded by the court, and hanged him.

The harsh treatment of loyalists during the Revolutionary period was never formally repudiated, but at least some Americans tried to prevent it from happening again. Freedom of speech, trial by jury, the right of cross-examination, prohibition against bills of attainder—these and other civil liberties, once denied to people called Tories, were guaranteed to everyone under the new federal government. American schoolchildren have always been taught that the Bill of Rights was meant to insure against the tyrannical abuses of Old World governments, but the new American states had also been abusive to basic civil liberties. Many of the Revolutionaries, once the war had ended, recoiled at the consequences of popular fury, the "tyranny of the majority" they had witnessed firsthand. The War for Independence had proven that Americans needed protection—not just from kings, but from themselves.

John Adams signed a treaty of commerce with the Dutch Republic in The Hague in early October 1782 and returned to Paris on October 27. Benjamin Franklin, John Jay, and John Adams began formal peace negotiations with Richard Oswald, the chief negotiator for the British, on October 30, 1782.

Gordon S. Wood details the importance of Franklin in Paris in *The Americanization of Benjamin Franklin.*

> Ultimately, Congress in June 1781 decided to assign the peace negotiations to a commission composed of Adams, Thomas Jefferson, John Jay, Henry Laurens, and Franklin. According to Arthur Lee, it was Franklin whom Congress almost left out. The only reason Franklin was included, said Lee, was "because France wills it."
>
> Although Jefferson declined the appointment and Laurens was captured at sea and imprisoned in the Tower of London, the other three commissioners were on hand in Paris by the fall of 1782. Jay and Adams were nearly as suspicious of their colleague's partiality to France as Arthur Lee had been. They also thought their French ally was not to be trusted. According to Franklin, Adams especially thought that Vergennes was "one of the greatest Enemies" of the United States. For Americans "to think of Gratitude to France," said Adams, "is the greatest of Follies," and "to be influenced by it, would ruin us." Franklin told the American foreign secretary, Robert R. Livingston, that Adams was beguiled by conspiratorial notions. Adams believed

that Vergennes and Franklin were "continually plotting against him and employing the News writers of Europe to depreciate his Character, &ca." And worse: Adams said all this publicly, in "extravagant and violent Language," even in front of English officials. What could be done with such a man? Perhaps Franklin was too generous in his famous summary of the man from Massachusetts, when he said that Adams "means well for his Country, is always an honest Man, often a Wise One, but sometimes and in some things, absolutely out of his Senses."

Franklin hoped that "the ravings of a certain mischievous Madman here against France and its Ministers, which I hear every Day will not be regarded in America." But Adams was not alone in his views; many Americans at home shared Adams's suspicions that Franklin was too attached to France. Franklin's "Enemies" in Congress, his friend Robert Morris warned him, were spreading the word "that a sense of Obligation to France seals your Lips when you should ask their Aid."

Franklin was sorry to hear such criticism of America's connection with France. He wanted his critics to know that they were doing America "irreparable harm" by destroying "the good understanding that has hitherto so happily subsisted between this court and ours." America's connection with France was what gave the United States weight with England and the respect of Europe. Therefore Franklin believed that "the true political interest of America consists in observing and fulfilling with the greatest exactitude the engagements of our alliance with France." He was grateful to France for its aid in the Revolution, and he thought all of America ought to be too.

All this American carping about overweening French influence could have eroded the Franco-American alliance. Indeed, without Franklin's presence it is hard to see how the alliance could have held together as it did and without the alliance it is hard to see how the Americans could have sustained their revolution. By the early 1780s Vergennes had become virtual first minister of the French government and the chief supporter of aiding the Americans. He retained the confidence of Louis XVI, and Franklin alone among the American commissioners retained Vergennes's confidence. Probably only Franklin could have persuaded Vergennes to keep on supporting the American cause, and probably only Franklin could have negotiated so many loans from an increasingly impoverished French government. Certainly no one else could have represented America abroad as Franklin did. He was the greatest diplomat America has ever had.

Not only did Franklin hold the Franco-American alliance together, but he also oversaw the initial stages of the successful peace negotiations with Britain. And he did all this with a multitude of demands placed on him. In addition to his duties as minister plenipotentiary, which included dealing with countless persons offering advice, seeking favors, and asking for information, he effectively acted as consul general, director of naval affairs, and judge of admiralty. He handled mercantile matters, commissioned privateers, and served as judge in the condemnation and sale of the prizes captured by the privateersmen; at one point he was even called upon to help plan a prospective French invasion of England.

All the while countless Europeans continually pestered him for letters of recommendation that they hoped would be passports to prosperity in America. But these difficulties in

France with supplicants and would-be emigrants were nothing compared with the problems Franklin faced having to raise and spend money for the United States abroad. He had to request loan after loan from France, and time after time Vergennes came through for him. At times it seemed as if it was Vergennes's trust in Franklin alone that made the many French loans and subsidies possible. By 1783 France had granted more than twenty-five million livres in loans and subsidies to the United States in a war that eventually cost France over one billion livres. Without this French financial aid the Americans could scarcely have continued their fight.

Franklin was increasingly embarrassed to keep asking Vergennes for money. His fellow Americans back home seemed to think "that France has Money enough for all her Occasions and all ours besides; and that if she does not supply us, it is owing to her Want of Will, or to my Negligence." It was especially mortifying that the American states could not even agree on "a most reasonable proposition" of granting the Confederation the power to levy a 5 percent impost on imported goods. "Our People certainly ought to do more for themselves," he complained. "It is absurd the Pretending to be Lovers of Liberty while they grudge Paying for the Defence of it."

In *The Glorious Cause* Robert Middlekauff summarizes the peace negotiations with the British that began in September 1782 and ended with the agreement on November 29. The provisional treaty was signed the next day and the definitive peace treaty on September 3, 1783.

In September, Jay and Franklin agreed to proceed with negotiations if Oswald's commission was altered to permit him to treat with them as representatives of the United States. The formula adopted was ambiguous—Congress took it as recognition of American independence; the Shelburne ministry did not and, had negotiations broken off, would doubtless have denied that Britain had recognized the United States.

What happened in the next three months may have taken place on diplomatic quicksand, but the results were solid enough and preliminary articles of peace were signed on November 30 by the Americans and the British commissioners. A few hours before the signing, Franklin sent Vergennes word that agreement had been reached. He did not admit of course that, in negotiating, the American delegation had violated its instructions from Congress to consult the French and to follow their advice. The Americans had not, however, violated the treaty obligations to France, for the agreement with Britain was not to go into effect until France and Britain concluded peace.

The first article of the treaty stated that "His Britannic Majesty acknowledges the said United States...to be free Sovereign and independent States...." After this supremely important article, boundaries were taken care of: in the north, a line close to the present-day line; in the south, the thirty-first parallel; in the west, the Mississippi River. The old American fishing rights off Newfoundland and the St. Lawrence were guaranteed along with "the Liberty" to dry and cure fish in the unsettled bays, harbors, and creeks of Nova Scotia, the Magdalen

Islands, and Labrador. Creditors "on either side" were to meet "no lawful Impediment" in collecting debts "of the full value in Sterling Money" "heretofore contracted"; and Congress was to recommend earnestly to the state legislatures to return confiscated property of British subjects. This article, which has to be read in full to be appreciated, dealt with the tricky issue of loyalist property. The article slid over the question of how much a recommendation by Congress would be worth. If loyalists believed that Congress could force the states to act on their behalf, they were soon to change their minds.

The treaty also provided that there would be no further confiscations of property or prosecutions of persons for actions taken in the war; that the British would withdraw their forces "with all convenient speed"; that the Mississippi River would be open to navigation by citizens of both Britain and the United States, and that any conquests of territory made before the articles of peace arrived in America would be returned.

Agreement between the Americans and the British stimulated the French, who wanted to end the drain on their treasury the war created, and on January 20, 1783, they and their ancient enemy signed preliminary articles of peace. Spain and Britain agreed on peace at the same time, and orders went out to suspend all military operations. The way to agreement had been eased by events—the great Spanish attack on Gibraltar had failed in September and, of course, the Americans had settled. Spain did not receive Gibraltar, but Britain did cede Minorca, which had fallen in the war to the Spanish, and east and west Florida.

All parties signed the definitive articles of peace on September 3, 1783. In America, General Carleton who had replaced Henry Clinton performed the melancholy tasks of packing up the army and evacuating America. By the end of 1783, the United States was free of British troops except for the detachments still occupying posts in the Northwest.

In *Benjamin Franklin,* Walter Isaacson describes Franklin's meeting with Vergennes.

To Franklin fell the difficult duty of explaining to Vergennes why the Americans had breached their obligations to France, and their instructions from the Congress, by agreeing to a treaty without consulting him. After sending Vergennes a copy of the signed accord, which he stressed was provisional, Franklin called on him at Versailles the following week. The French minister remarked, coolly but politely, that "proceeding in this abrupt signature of the articles" was not "agreeable to the [French] King" and that the Americans "had not been particularly civil." Nevertheless, Vergennes did allow that the Americans had done well by themselves, and he noted that "our conversation was amicable."

Only when Franklin followed up with a brash request for yet another French loan, along with the information that he was transmitting the peace accord to the Congress, did Vergennes take the opportunity to protest officially. It was lacking in propriety, he wrote Franklin, for him "to hold out a certain hope of peace to America without even informing yourself on the state of negotiation on our part." America was under an obligation not to consider ratifying any peace until France had also come to terms with Britain. "You have all your life performed your duties,"

Vergennes continued. "I pray you to consider how you propose to fulfill those which are due to the King."

Franklin's response, which has been called "a diplomatic masterpiece" and "one of the most famous of all diplomatic letters," combined a few dignified expressions of contrition with appeals to France's national interest. "Nothing has been agreed in the preliminaries contrary to the interests of France," he noted, not entirely correctly, "and no peace is to take place between us and England until you have concluded yours." Using a French word that roughly translates as "propriety," Franklin sought to minimize the American transgression:

> In not consulting you before they were signed, we have been guilty of neglecting a point of *bienséance*. But, as this was not from want of respect for the King, whom we all love and honor, we hope it will be excused, and that the great work, which has hitherto been so happily conducted, is so nearly brought to perfection, and is so glorious to his reign, will not be ruined by a single indiscretion of ours.

He went on, undaunted, to press his case for another loan. "Certainly the whole edifice sinks to the ground immediately if you refuse on that account to give us any further assistance." With that came both a plea and an implied threat: making a public issue of the transgression, he warned, could hurt the mutual interests of both countries. "The English, I just now learn, flatter themselves they have already divided us. I hope this little misunderstanding will therefore be kept a secret, and that they will find themselves totally mistaken."

Vergennes was stunned by Franklin's letter, a copy of which he sent to his ambassador in Philadelphia. "You may imagine my astonishment," he wrote. "I think it proper that the most influential members of Congress should be informed of the very irregular conduct of their commissioners in regard to us." He did not blame Franklin personally, except to say that "he has yielded too easily to the bias of his colleagues." Vergennes went on to lament, correctly, that the new nation was not one that would enter into entangling alliances. "We shall be but poorly paid for all that we have done for the United States," he complained, "and for securing to them a national existence."

There was little Vergennes could do. Forcing a showdown, as Franklin had subtly warned, would drive the Americans into an even faster and closer alliance with Britain. So, reluctantly, he let the matter drop, instructed his envoy not to file an official protest with the Congress, and even agreed to supply yet another French loan.

Franklin had been instrumental in shaping the three great documents of the war: the Declaration of Independence, the alliance with France, and the treaty with England. Now he turned his thoughts to peace. "All wars are follies, very expensive, and very mischievous ones," he wrote Polly Stevenson. "When will mankind be convinced of this, and agree to settle their differences by arbitration? Were they to do it, even by the cast of a die, it would be better than by fighting and destroying each other." To Joseph Banks, one of the many old friends from England he wrote in celebration, he asserted yet again his famous, albeit somewhat misleading, credo: "There never was a good war or a bad peace."

In *Revolutionaries,* Jack Rakove points out the challenges the negotiators had to confront and the results of the treaty.

To allow loyalists to return to America and regain property, Adams warned, would be to admit a discontented, subversive force into the republic, ripe for future manipulation by Britain or even, somehow, France. (Adams suspected that French agents, such as Rayneval, were somehow culpable for whipping "the Tories to set up their Demands" upon the king and his ministers.) But for all his anxieties, Adams ran second to Franklin in resisting the British claims for compensation. This became clear after Henry Strachey, having returned to London for fresh instructions, came back to Paris with a revised treaty still seeking restitution of loyalist property. After it was read on November 25, an irritated Franklin spent the night drafting a response, which he shared with his colleagues over breakfast at Jay's rooms the next day. If Britain clung to this point, he argued, the Americans should respond by compiling accounts of the wanton damage wreaked by British arms during a war "brought on and encouraged" by the "Falshoods and Misrepresentations" of the very people Britain sought to protect. Franklin was "more decided" on this matter than Jay or Adams, and they agreed he should read his letter as a statement of "his private Sentiments." But then, having agreed on that strategy, the three men spent some time conversing about "the Conduct, Crimes and Demerits of those People." That they would do so suggests that their feelings on this point were genuine. Here was an emotional bond that united the American negotiators—a way of recalling the circumstances that had turned them from loyal subjects into active and committed revolutionaries.

With the Americans adamant, the most Richard Oswald and Strachey could gain was a weak concession that Congress would merely *urge* the states to allow loyalists to seek restitution of their property.

In late June Congress abandoned its original capital at Philadelphia for nearby Princeton after mutinous unpaid soldiers staged a threatening protest outside the State House and the Pennsylvania government refused to call out the militia in its defense. The ferrying of delegates over the Delaware was rather less heroic than Washington's famous crossings, which had saved the revolutionary cause just after Franklin's arrival in Paris in December 1776. Not only did Americans lack a permanent capital of any kind—much less a metropolis akin to London or Paris. Their national government was little more than a rotating pool of officeholders who served more for reasons of conscience and duty than from any deep ambition to wield power or make epochal decisions. With such a Congress to answer to, historians generally agree that the American peacemakers did right to bypass their formal instructions and negotiate separately. The results justify their decision. Perhaps Jay, Franklin, and Adams could have fared better on particular points. But a treaty that ended the war, recognized independence, secured a Mississippi boundary, and pledged Britain to abandon territory it still occupied was a peace worth having.

The French army left Williamsburg, Virginia, in June, continued its march north, and sailed from Boston in December 1782. Rochambeau sailed from the Chesapeake in January 1783. *This Glorious Struggle,* edited by Edward G. Lengel, includes General Washington's letter to General Rochambeau.

The time had come for farewells to Washington's departing French allies.

DECEMBER 14

TO LIEUTENANT GENERAL ROCHAMBEAU

Newburgh Decr 14th 1782

I cannot, my dear Genl, permit you to depart from this Country without repeating to you the high sense I entertain of the Services you have rendered America, by the constant attention which you have paid to the Interests of it. By the exact order and discipline of the Corps under your command—and your readiness, at all times, to give facility to every measure which the force of the combined Armies was competent to.

To this testimony of your Public character, I should be wanting to the feelings of my heart, was I not to add expressions of the happiness I have enjoyed in your private friendship—The remembrance of which will be one of the most pleasing, circumstances of my life.

My best wishes will accompany you to France, where I have no doubt of your meeting the Smiles & rewards of a generous Prince—and the warmest embraces of affectionate friends. I have the honor to be with great personal attachment, respect & regard, Yr Most Obedt & Most Hble Servant

Go: Washington

144. New Windsor Cantonment, New York

NEW WINDSOR CANTONMENT STATE HISTORIC SITE
NATIONAL PURPLE HEART HALL OF HONOR
374 TEMPLE HILL ROAD
NEW WINDSOR, NEW YORK

General Cornwallis had surrendered in October 1781, but since there was no peace treaty, the Continental Army had to remain in the field.

The site for the 1782–1783 winter quarters near Newburgh was chosen for its location on the east-west transportation routes and on the Hudson River. It was also near forests that could provide wood for huts for the 6,000–8,000 troops, women and children, and for buildings on the hilltop, including the Temple of Virtue (or Honor), where the army held both social events and religious services. The Temple was also the site of General Washington's March 15 meeting with his officers.

Gary B. Nash describes the event known as the Newburgh Conspiracy in *The Unknown American Revolution.*

Just two days before the dispatches from Congress's peace commissioners arrived on March 12, 1783 (having taken fourteen weeks to cross the Atlantic in stormy seas), with the glad tidings that a preliminary treaty had been hammered out, officers in the main part of Washington's army, huddled in winter quarters at Newburgh, New York, addressed their commanding officer with bitter words born of exhausted patience. If Congress failed to rectify their grievances, they would refuse to disband and "retire to some unsettled country," presumably the western frontier. In this event, Congress would lose its army, the nation would be disgraced, and the mutineers would retire with their weapons as a disaffected thorn in the side of the shaky new nation.

Washington's sympathy for his men was real, for he knew intimately about their starvation, the rags that substituted for uniforms, the insufferable arrears in pay, the plunging value of the paper money they intermittently received, Congress's dallying on the promised lifetime half-pay pension for officers, and the uncertainty of the promised land bounties. He remembered well how he had warned Congress on at least seven occasions the previous autumn about the dark mood of the officers "about to be turned into the world soured by penury and what they call the ingratitude of the public, involved in debts, without one farthing of money to carry them home, after having spent the flower of their days and many of them their patrimonies in establishing the freedom and independence of their country, and suffered everything human nature is capable of enduring on this side of death." He also knew that a delegation of officers, headed by New York's Major General Alexander McDougall, had presented the same grievances to Congress two months before to no avail. He probably did not know that Major John Armstrong, Jr., aide-de-camp to General Horatio Gates, had composed the address. But Washington had never wavered in the conviction that the military must always subordinate itself to civil authority. Yet this time, it was his officers who had promised mutiny and withdrawal from the nation, with the inference that the enlisted men under them would follow.

Although the so-called Newburgh Conspiracy seemed to unite the officers with their bedraggled enlisted men, the officers were mostly tending to their own interests. They knew that state and congressional support of the army, limited and insufficient from the beginning, had wavered even more as the fighting drew to a close and everyone awaited the peace treaty. They also knew about the public displeasure with the promised lifetime half-pay pensions for officers, first offered by Congress in 1778 for those who pledged to serve for the duration of the war.

Sizing up the situation with plenty of advice from Henry Knox, Washington defused the powder keg masterfully. Rather than trying to ferret out the precipitators of the officers' revolt and execute them on the spot, he called their bluff and turned an ugly situation to his advantage. Gathering together officer representatives of each regiment on March 15, he read an address he had labored over for nearly five days. "Gentlemen," he began, "by an anonymous summons, an attempt has been made to convene you together; how inconsistent with the rules of propriety! How unmilitary! And how subversive of all order and discipline, let the good sense of the army decide." Here he drew on eight years of leadership and the fund of reverence he had built up for his unwavering service to the nation. In a stroke of genius, he then pulled a letter from his pocket from a member of Congress promising that the officers would not be left in the lurch. Taking his glasses from his uniform to read the letter, he told the men "that he had grown grey in their service and now found himself growing blind." One of the officers present remembered later that "there was something so natural, so unaffected, in this appeal," "as rendered it superior to the most studied oratory. It forces its way to the heart, and you might see sensibility moisten every eye." Washington then made his plea—rather more of an order—that the men desist, trust him to promote the interests of his army with Congress, and condemn in their own way Major Armstrong's threatening address. The shamefaced officers withdrew, patriotism won the day, and Washington prevailed.

Samuel Shaw had joined the army in 1775 and was an aide to General Henry Knox in April of 1783 when he wrote a letter to the Reverend Eliot about Washington at Newburgh. The following, the last paragraph, is in *The American Revolution: Writings from the War of Independence,* edited by John Rhodehamel.

I cannot dismiss this subject without observing, that it is happy for America that she has a *patriot army*, and equally so that a *Washington* is its leader. I rejoice in the opportunities I have had of seeing this great man in a variety of situations;—calm and intrepid where the battle raged, patient and persevering under the pressure of misfortune, moderate and possessing himself in the full career of victory. Great as these qualifications deservedly render him, he never appeared to me more truly so, than at the assembly we have been speaking of. On other occasions he has been supported by the exertions of an army and the countenance of his friends; but in this he stood single and alone. There was no saying where the passions of an army, which were not a little inflamed, might lead; but it was generally allowed that longer forbearance was dangerous, and moderation had ceased to be a virtue. Under these circumstances he appeared, not at the head of his troops, but as it were in opposition to them; and for a dreadful moment the interests of the army and its General seemed to be in competition! He spoke,—every doubt was dispelled, and the tide of patriotism rolled again in its wonted course. Illustrious man! What he says of the army may with equal justice be applied to his own character. "Had this day been wanting, the world had never seen the last stage of perfection to which human nature is capable of attaining."

145. John Ellison House, New York

KNOX'S HEADQUARTERS STATE HISTORIC SITE
ROUTE 94 AND FORGE HILL ROAD
VAILS GATE, NEW YORK

The Ellison house, built in 1754, was the headquarters for General Henry Knox and other officers during the Revolution. It was General Horatio Gates's headquarters in 1782–1783 when he was commander of the nearby New Windsor Cantonment. The gristmill provided flour for the army.

146. Hasbrouck House, New York

WASHINGTON HEADQUARTERS STATE HISTORIC SITE
84 LIBERTY STREET
NEWBURGH, NEW YORK

Hasbrouck House was General Washington's headquarters from April 1, 1782, until August 19, 1783. During that time Washington made important decisions. In his General Orders of the Day, August 7, 1782, he established the military award, the Badge of Military Merit, now the Order of the Purple Heart. On March 15, 1783, he quelled the so-called Newburgh Conspiracy (see #144). On April 9, 1783, he issued orders suspending "all Acts of Hostilities." On April 18 he ordered the "Cessation of Hostilities" to be proclaimed on April 19, 1783, the eighth anniversary of the battles at Lexington and Concord.

In *The Ascent of George Washington,* John Ferling quotes Washington, urging Congress and the states to act.

Washington quickly and candidly told Congress that the officers could no longer be mollified "upon the string of forbearance." Congress must act, he added. The officers will not "grow old in poverty wretchedness and contempt." It was *"indispensable,"* he added, "that every soldier, men and officers, be fully paid prior to demobilization." Within the month, Congress acted. It sent to the states another impost amendment that, as Hamilton had wanted, was identical to the unsuccessful emendation of 1781. Congress, badly frightened by the show staged at Newburgh, also approved the commutation plan advocated by the officers.

Washington pitched in further by dispatching a circular letter to the states as they considered the proposed amendment. While the war had been won, he said, the question of whether the Union would be preserved remained undecided. The survival of the Union hinged on giving "a tone to our Federal Government." The national government must have greater power, he insisted for the first time to a national audience, nothing less than the "Supreme Power" to overcome "local prejudices and policies" when the national well-being was at stake. Congress must have the means through which it could pay the "Soldier…his Stipend, and the Public Creditor his due." Unless the states ratified the impost, he warned obliquely, the Union might not survive and in its place the states would "become the sport of European politics, which may play one State against another to prevent their growing importance, and to serve their own interested purposes." The American Revolution hung in the balance, he asserted. It remained to be determined whether it would be "a blessing... not to the present age alone," but to "unborn Millions" in succeeding generations.

Washington's stirring appeal was unavailing. With peace assured, the impost amendment narrowly failed once again. The army simmered, and in Pennsylvania a mutiny flared among troops who demanded their back pay, leading Congress to flee Philadelphia for the greater security offered by bucolic Princeton. Once there, Congress ordered the virtual dissolution of the army. Almost overnight in the early summer of 1783, the army was reduced from about eleven thousand men to some two thousand. Those still in the army, moreover, were scattered about to reduce the likelihood of a grand mutiny. In lieu of their commuted pension, the officers were given certificates that could be redeemed whenever they chose to do so. The men who were mustered out were paid with what Congress knew to be worthless certificates that the soldiers called "Morris notes," as each was signed by Superintendent Morris. These "final settlement certificates," as they were officially called, could not be redeemed for six months. As the certificates had no immediate value, and few believed they would be worth the paper they were printed on in six months, most of the soldiers sold their Morris notes to speculators for a fraction of their supposed value. Many soldiers had to do this to find the money necessary to pay for their journey home. Others took jobs, working for weeks or months before they had sufficient cash to make the trip home (some enlisted men drifted to New York City and found work in businesses that served the British army, which was awaiting Parliament's ratification of the peace accord prior to evacuating America). One of the soldiers, left in what he described as a "pitiful, forlorn condition," raged that the government that had been "rigorous in exacting my compliance to my engagements" had been "careless in performing her contracts with me." Most of the officers fared no better. They had been given their five years' full-pay pension in the form of interest-bearing bonds, but when the second stab at an impost amendment failed, they believed the bonds were worthless, at least for the foreseeable future. Within three years, according to Rufus King, a Massachusetts congressman, most of the officers had sold their bonds to speculators.

In *Almost a Miracle,* John Ferling describes General Washington and his officers.

In the end, Washington became the symbol of virtue, courage, steadfastness, accomplishment, and endurance. His lofty stature was earned to be sure, but it was also carefully crafted by Congress, by those about Washington who saw him as their aegis to success, and by Washington himself. His eminence was crucial for holding together the army and a war-weary nation until, at last, the decisive victory was secured. But victory was not due to Washington alone. Several general officers—notably Ward in 1775, Schuyler, Gates, and Arnold in 1777; Greene and Lafayette in 1780–1781; and Morgan and Knox all through the war—performed with commendable merit in their great hours of trial. Numerous junior officers, such as John Glover, William Washington, and Henry Lee, excelled, outshining their counterparts in the enemy army. Largely devoid of military experience, civilians through and through, they emerged from the pack through their innate talents, drawing on lessons they had learned before the war, but honing their skills as leaders in the course of their cruel experiences under fire in this war. But no commander played a greater role than Nathanael Greene in securing American independence, for it was his daring campaign in 1781 that thwarted Cornwallis and sent him on his fateful errand into Virginia, and it was rebel forces under Greene that liberated South Carolina and Georgia while the allies gathered at Yorktown. John Adams understood that, and nearly his first words on learning of Yorktown were: "General Greenes last Action...is quite as glorious for the American Arms as the Capture of Cornwallis."

General Washington's Circular to State Governments, in which he sets out four essentials for the future of the United States, is included in *George Washington: Writings*, edited by John Rhodehamel.

Head Quarters, Newburgh, June 8, 1783

Sir: The great object for which I had the honor to hold an appointment in the Service of my Country, being accomplished, I am now preparing to resign it into the hands of Congress, and to return to that domestic retirement, which, it is well known, I left with the greatest reluctance, a Retirement, for which I have never ceased to sigh through a long and painful absence, and in which (remote from the noise and trouble of the World) I meditate to pass the remainder of life in a state of undisturbed repose;...

There are four things, which I humbly conceive, are essential to the well being, I may even venture to say, to the existence of the United States as an Independent Power:

1st.   An indissoluble Union of the States under one Federal Head.

2dly.   A Sacred regard to Public Justice.

3dly.   The adoption of a proper Peace Establishment, and

4thly. The prevalence of that pacific and friendly Disposition, among the People of the United States, which will induce them to forget their local prejudices and policies, to make those mutual concessions which are requisite to the general prosperity, and in some instances, to sacrifice their individual advantages to the interest of the Community.

These are the Pillars on which the glorious Fabrick of our Independency and National Character must be supported; Liberty is the Basis, and whoever would dare to sap the foundation, or overturn the Structure, under whatever specious pretexts he may attempt it, will merit the bitterest execration, and the severest punishment which can be inflicted by his injured Country.

In *His Excellency: George Washington,* Joseph J. Ellis quotes Washington on the war.

How, then, did the improbable become the inevitable? Washington's fullest answer, composed soon after victory was assured, suggested that historians would have a difficult time explaining the triumph.

If Historiographers should be hardy enough to fill the page of History with the advantages that have been gained with unequal numbers (on the part of America) in the cause of this contest, and attempt to relate the distressing circumstances under which they have been obtained, it is more than probable that Posterity will bestow on their labors the epithet and marks of fiction; for it will not be believed that such a force as Great Britain has employed for eight years in Country could be baffled…by numbers infinitely less, composed of Men oftentimes half starved; always in Rags, without pay, and experiencing, at times, every species of distress which human nature is capable of undergoing. More succinctly, Washington also observed that the war was won "by a concatenation of causes" which had never occurred before in human history, and which "in all probability at no time, or under any Circumstance, will combine again." In the midst of the bedeviling concatenations, he called attention to one abiding core of perseverance, the officers and soldiers of the Continental army, whose sacrifices would never be fully understood or appreciated. He did not mention the other abiding presence—modesty forbade it.

On September 3, 1783, the Treaty of Paris was signed in Paris by John Adams, Benjamin Franklin, and John Jay, representing the United States of America and by David Hartley, a member of Parliament representing King George III, ending the Revolutionary War.

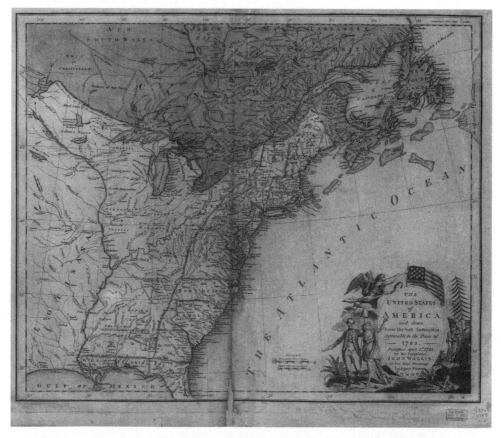

Map of the United States of America following the Treaty of Paris, 1783. John Wallis. *The United States of America laid down from the best authorities, agreeable to the Peace of 1783.* **London, 1783.** *(Courtesy, Library of Congress, Geography and Map Division. http://hdl.loc.gov/loc.gmd/g3700.ct000080)*

Published in London shortly after the Treaty of Paris, this map is one of the first European commercially published maps recognizing the United States of America.

In *The American Revolution,* Gordon S. Wood describes the Treaty of Paris.

The long war was costly for the new country: more than 25,000 American military deaths—nearly 1 percent of the population, second only to the Civil War in deaths relative to population.

Despite the end of the war, the peace still had to be won. The main objective of the new nation—independence from Great Britain—was clear and straightforward. But this objective and others concerning America's territorial boundaries and its rights to the Newfoundland fisheries had to be reconciled with the aims of America's ally, France, and with the aims of France's ally, Spain, which had been at war with Great Britain since 1779. The United States and France had pledged in 1778 not to make a separate peace with Britain. But since France was bound to Spain against Britain until Gibraltar was recovered, there was great danger of American interests getting lost in the machinations of the European powers. Despite the desire of France and Spain to humiliate Britain, neither Bourbon monarchy really wanted a strong and independent American republic. Spain in particular feared the spread of republicanism among its South American colonies and sought to protect its interest in the Mississippi Valley.

Although Franklin, John Adams, and John Jay, the American negotiators in Europe, were only, in Adams's words, "militia diplomats," they wound their way through the intricate corridors of international politics with professional diplomatic skill. Despite instructions from the Congress to do nothing without consulting the French, the American diplomats decided to negotiate with Britain alone. By hinting at the possibility of weakening the Franco-American alliance, they persuaded Great Britain to recognize the independence of the United States and to agree to much more generous boundaries for the new country than the French and particularly the Spanish were willing to support. On the west, the United States reached to the Mississippi River; on the south, to the thirty-first parallel; and on the north, to roughly the present boundary with Canada. The American negotiators then presented this preliminary Anglo-American treaty to France and persuaded the French to accept it by suggesting that allies must conceal their differences from their enemies. The prospect of American peace with Britain now compelled Spain to abandon its demands for Gibraltar and to settle for the return of East and West Florida. In the final treaty signed by September 3, 1783, the United States, by shrewdly playing off the mutual fears of the European powers, gained both independence and concessions that stunned the French and indeed all of Europe. It was the greatest achievement in the history of American diplomacy.

The peace treaty was a blow to the loyalists in East Florida, described by Maya Jasanoff in *Liberty's Exiles.*

The news of the peace treaty hit East Florida loyalists like a hurricane. Article V of the peace with the United States, which neutered the possibility of receiving compensation from the states, paled for them next to Article V of Britain's peace treaty with Spain and France, by which Britain agreed to cede East and West Florida to Spain, with no strings attached. It had seemed like a reasonable arrangement to British diplomats, who were more committed to keeping the strategically valuable Gibraltar than the economically disappointing Floridas. But the treaty yanked the ground from beneath the refugees' feet. They had already undergone the ordeal of leaving their homes under duress, often more than once, and accepted the challenge of starting over in an underdeveloped land. Now even this hard-won asylum was denied them—and by their own government at that. Unless loyalists were prepared to swear allegiance to the king of Spain and practice Catholicism, they had eighteen months to gather up their possessions and go.

Maya Jasanoff also details the departures of the loyalists from New York following the Treaty of Paris.

By late summer 1783, New York City witnessed a continuous parade of loyalist departures, and some patriot returns. It must have been an eerie thing to watch one of the largest cities in America turning inside out. "No News here but that of Evacuation," one bemused (undoubtedly patriot) commentator wrote, "This…occasions a Variety of physiognomic, laughable Appearances.—Some look smiling, others melancholy, a third Class mad. To hear their Conversation would make you feel merry: Some…represent the cold Regions of Nova-Scotia as a new-created Paradise, others as a Country unfit for any human Being to inhabit. Tories are vexed with Tories; they curse the Powers to whom they owe Allegiance, and thus render themselves *rebellious*." Advertisements crowded the columns of the *Royal Gazette* announcing sales and business closures, and informing loyalists when and at which wharf to board their ships. British regulars and Hessians packed their gear and began to leave by the regiment-load. Cannon came down from the ramparts, munitions were crated up. The commissary's office sold off its surplus stock: 63,596 pairs of shoes and 68,093 pairs of worsted stockings, 10,100 shoe buckles, 21,000 needles. On summer Wednesdays and Saturdays, the Wagon Office auctioned its draught and saddle horses, carts, and equipage.

   Colonel Beverley Robinson had an especially close look at the loyalist plight during these last hectic months of British occupation. As one of three inspectors of refugees, he and his colleagues visited and assessed the needs of hundreds of "distressed Loyalists" who had poured into the city from as far away as Florida. The inspectors distributed nearly £9,000 (New York currency) to 529 refugees for the first quarter of 1783 alone. He surely knew personally some of the 312 New Yorkers on that list, reduced to destitution from positions of perfect comfort.

It was not just loyalists who fled after the end of hostilities. In *Epic Journeys of Freedom,* Cassandra Pybus estimates the number of slaves who ran away to freedom in Britain and in northern cities.

It was a war-weary General Washington who finally laid claim to all of the United States of America on November 25, 1783. His satisfaction at victory was somewhat diminished by the magnitude of the Loyalist defection by which as many as sixty thousand Americans took their leave. Just how many fugitive slaves had also gone he had no way of knowing, but he was correct to assume that it was greater than the three thousand listed in the documentation British commissioners later sent to Congress. Taking into account the people who had left from the southern ports, as well as from Boston and other northern ports, plus those in the army and navy, the number of runaways who had left America as free people must have been close to nine thousand.

An unknown number of the black allies of the British who found freedom in the revolutionary period chose to stay. Washington was well aware that runaways had "many doors" through which they could escape within the newly created United States, recognizing the extreme difficulty of recovering people whose names could be so readily changed and whose physical appearance could no longer be recalled after years of absence. Washington chose not to further pursue his own runaways, even though six from Mount Vernon were never accounted for. These were young men with skilled trades who could readily have found a niche for themselves as artisans in the cities of New York, Philadelphia, Baltimore, or Boston. It is highly possibly that they, together with thousands like them, successfully forged a free life in the new republic.

In his letter to General Knox (see page 306), General Washington wrote that the arrival of the peace treaty and the British evacuation of New York had been so delayed that it would be best to defer the "Celebration of Peace" until after the British evacuated the city.

The British sailed from New York on November 25, 1783.

John Ferling describes Washington's celebrated return to New York City and his departure in *The Ascent of George Washington.*

At the beginning of the last week in November, the Continental army set foot on Manhattan Island for the first time since November 1776. On November 23, the day appointed for the British army's departure, Washington brought his army to the periphery of New York City. Fittingly for an army that had so often been slow to act during the war, the British were running behind schedule. Two days passed before their last soldier left Manhattan. When the final redcoat exited the city, Washington ordered his men to march in. Under a flawless blue sky, with a chill November wind blowing briskly off the Hudson River, the army set off on the last leg of this trek and of the war. Knox, with a select corps, rode at the head of the army. A martial band, with drums beating and fifes playing, followed. Soldiers carrying flags and banners that stood straight out in the strong breeze came next, followed on foot by civilian authorities, eight abreast. Washington, immaculate in his uniform and majestic astride his powerful white charger, was next, heading up a line of the highest-ranking officers and their staffs. The soldiers, many in threadbare, makeshift uniforms, brought up the rear. The army proceeded down Broadway, lined this day with cheering residents who were anxious for a glimpse of Washington, hailed far and wide as the conqueror of the vaunted British and Hessians. Washington spent nearly a week in town, attending an array of formal dinners. In his final ceremony, Washington took leave of his officers at a noon repast at Fraunces Tavern.

Rocky hill 23 Oct. 1783

Dear Sir

The arrival of the definitive Treaty, and the evacuation of New York has been so long delayed as to interfere very much really with our arrangements for the Celebration of Peace; at this Season no use can be made of the Bower, the only possible means of accomodation, besides, the dissolution of the Army at so short a period totally defeats the object in view, for if we were even determined not to wait the events on which the Celebration has hitherto depended, it would now be impossible either to make the necessary preparations or to give timely notice to the Officers, before the Army would be dissolved — I think therefore that it will be best to defer it until the British leave the City, and then to have it at that place, where all who chuse to attend can find accomodation —

Sir Guy Carleton some time since informed me, thro' Mr. Parker, that he should leave New York in all next month, probably by the 20th, and that when the Transports which were gone to Nova Scotia returned, he should be able to fix the day; this notice may be short, and as it is best to be prepared, I wish you to confer on the subject with Governor Clinton and have every necessary arrangement made

Maj Genl. Knox

George Washington to Henry Knox, October 23, 1783. *(Courtesy of The Gilder Lehrman Institute of American History, GLC02437.09394)*

Tables were set with cold meats and fruit, bottles of wine and brandy. But little was consumed, and no speeches were given. After all these years and all the tensions of this year, there was not much to be said. Washington did not know many of the men who were present. Most of those who had served the longest with him had been furloughed against their will six months earlier. Only Generals Knox, Steuben, McDougall, and Timothy Pickering—who once had been Washington's aide—had been with the commander in chief over the long haul. Not every officer still in the army bothered to attend, nor did any who were out of the army but living nearby. Colonel Hamilton, for instance, who now practiced law in Manhattan and lived just a couple of blocks from Fraunces Tavern, chose not to attend. As the good-byes were said and Washington embraced each man, tears were shed as men were moved both by affection for one another and by the realization that an epoch in their lives—perhaps the most exciting and meaningful period they would ever experience—was ending this day. When all the farewells were said, Washington hurried out the door and rode for Annapolis, where the footloose Congress had moved.

147. Fraunces Tavern, New York

FRAUNCES TAVERN MUSEUM
54 PEARL STREET
NEW YORK, NEW YORK

The home of Stephan Delancey and his family was built in 1719. In 1762 Samuel Fraunces bought the home and made it into a popular tavern.

On December 4, 1783, General Washington's officers gathered at the Tavern. He toasted them, and they said their farewells.

After the Revolution when New York was the nation's capital, the government rented the tavern for offices. In 1904 the Sons of the Revolution in the State of New York bought the tavern, restored it, and opened it in 1907 to the public as the Fraunces Tavern Museum.

On December 23, 1783, General Washington resigned his commission before Congress in Annapolis. His address is included in *The American Revolution: Writings from the War of Independence*, edited by John Rhodehamel.

December 23, 1783

According to order, his Excellency the Commander in Chief was admitted to a public audience, and being seated, the President, after a pause, informed him, that the United States in Congress assembled, were prepared to receive his communications; Whereupon he arose and addressed Congress as follows:

Mr. President: The great events on which my resignation depended, having at length taken place, I have now the honor of offering my sincere congratulations to Congress, and of presenting myself before them, to surrender into their hands the trust committed to me, and to claim the indulgence of retiring from the service of my country.

Happy in the confirmation of our independence and sovereignty, and pleased with the opportunity afforded the United States, of becoming a respectable nation, I resign with satisfaction the appointment I accepted with diffidence; a diffidence in my abilities to accomplish so arduous a task; which however was superseded by a confidence in the rectitude of our cause, the support of the supreme power of the Union, and the patronage of Heaven.

The successful termination of the war has verified the most sanguine expectations; and my gratitude for the interposition of Providence, and the assistance I have received from my countrymen, increases with every review of the momentous contest.

While I repeat my obligations to the army in general, I should do injustice to my own feelings not to acknowledge, in this place, the peculiar services and distinguished merits of the gentlemen who have been attached to my person during the war. It was impossible the choice of confidential officers to compose my family should have been more fortunate. Permit me, sir, to recommend in particular, those who have continued in the service to the present moment, as worthy of the favorable notice and patronage of Congress.

I consider it an indispensable duty to close this last act of my official life by commending the interests of our dearest country to the protection of Almighty God, and those who have the superintendence of them to his holy keeping.

Having now finished the work assigned me, I retire from the great theatre of action, and bidding an affectionate farewell to this august body, under whose orders I have so long acted, I here offer my commission, and take my leave of all the employments of public life.

The Treaty of Paris and the Constitution

On January 14, 1784, Congress, meeting temporarily in Annapolis, Maryland, ratified the 1783 Treaty of Paris.

The many challenges the United States of America faced included the problem of sovereignty, the continuing crisis in governance, the prevailing anxiety about the lack of order, and the public debt. The Confederation could not regulate commerce. It could not impose taxes, and its currency and certificates had little value. Soldiers and other settlers who wanted to move west encountered jurisdictional conflicts among the states, problems with securing titles, and resistance from American Indians whose homelands were being taken illegally by settlers. The crisis in legitimate authority at all levels of government and the struggles for control within governments revealed the inadequacies of the Articles of Confederation. Congress concluded that the Articles of Confederation should be amended.

In May 1787 the delegates to the Constitutional Convention met in Philadelphia in the same building in which the delegates had signed the Declaration of Independence in 1776. Instead of amending the Articles, they drafted a new Constitution. On September 17, 1787, thirty-nine of the fifty-five delegates signed the Constitution. After eleven state conventions ratified it, the first Congress convened in New York on March 4, 1789. On April 30, 1789, George Washington was inaugurated the first president of the United States of America. Rhode Island's convention was the last one to ratify the Constitution: May 29, 1790.

The Preamble to the Constitution:
We the People of the United States, in Order to form a more perfect Union, establish Justice, insure domestic Tranquility, provide for the common defence, promote the general Welfare, and secure the Blessings of Liberty to ourselves and our Posterity, do ordain and establish this Constitution for the United States of America.

In *The American Revolution,* Gordon S. Wood points to the principle of sovereignty in the Constitution.

The new Constitution provided for a strong government with an extraordinary amount of power given to the president and the Senate. It also created a single republican state that would span the continent and encompass all the diverse and scattered interests of the whole of American society—an impossibility for a republic according to the best political science of the day. During the debates over ratification in the fall and winter of 1787–88, the Anti-Federalists focused on these Federalist violations of the earlier Revolutionary assumptions about the nature of power and the need for a small homogeneous society in a republican state.

Despite these formidable Anti-Federalist arguments, the Federalists did not believe that the Constitution repudiated the Revolution and the principles of 1776. They answered the Anti-Federalists not by denying the principle of sovereignty but by relocating it in the people at large. In doing so they forged an entirely new way of thinking about the relation of government to society. It marked one of the most creative moments in the history of political thought.

The Anti-Federalists may have lost the contest over the Constitution, but by 1800 they and their Jeffersonian-Republican successors eventually won the larger struggle over what kind of society and culture America was to have, at least for a good part of the nineteenth century. Not only as president in 1801 did Jefferson reduce the power of the national government, but those who had been Anti-Federalists—narrow-minded middling men with interests to promote—soon came to dominate American politics, especially in the North, to a degree that Federalist gentry had never imagined possible.

In the 1780s the arch-Anti-Federalist William Findley had pointed the way. In a debate in the Pennsylvania assembly over the role of interest in public affairs, Findley set forth a rationale for modern democratic interest-group politics that has scarcely been bettered. Unlike his patrician opponents, who continued to hold out a vision of disinterested leadership, Findley argued that since everyone had interests to promote, self-made middling men like himself, who had no lineage, possessed no great wealth, and had never been to college, had as much right to political office as wealthy gentry who had gone to Harvard or Princeton. This was what American equality meant, he said. Furthermore, since everyone did have interests to promote, it was now quite legitimate for candidates for public office to campaign for election on behalf of the interests of their constituents. This was a radical departure from customary practice, for none of the Founders ever thought it was proper for a political leader to campaign for office. In this debate Findley anticipated all of the popular political developments of the next generation—the increased electioneering and competitive politics; the open promotion of interests in legislation, including the proliferation of chartered banks and other private corporations; the emergence of political parties; the extension of the actual and direct representation in government of particular groups, including ethnic and religious groups; and the eventual weakening, if not the repudiation, of the classical republican ideal that legislators were supposed to be disinterested umpires standing above the play of interests. This was democracy as Americans came to know it.

As the Federalists of the 1790s eventually discovered to their dismay, this democracy was no longer a technical term of political science describing the people's representation in the lower houses of representation. And it was no longer a simple form of government that could be skeptically challenged and contested as it had been since the ancient Greeks. Instead, it became the civic faith of the United States to which all Americans must unquestionably adhere. The emergence of this rambunctious middling democracy was the most significant consequence of the American Revolution.

By December 15, 1791, the first ten amendments to the Constitution, the Bill of Rights, had been ratified by three-fourths of the states.

The Achievements of the American Revolution

The descriptions of the 147 places, the events, and the people in this *Historical Guidebook* add to an understanding of the American Revolution and its significance today. In the following excerpts, the authors describe the achievements of the Revolutionaries and the challenges they met in founding the United States of America. Their achievements and their challenges continue to guide us in the twenty-first century.

In *1776*, David McCullough details the importance of the Continental Army, and its commander, in winning the Revolutionary War.

Financial support from France and the Netherlands, and military support from the French army and navy, would play a large part in the outcome. But in the last analysis it was Washington and the army that won the war for American independence. The fate of the war and the revolution rested on the army. The Continental Army—not the Hudson River or the possession of New York or Philadelphia—was the key to victory. And it was Washington who held the army together and gave it "spirit" through the most desperate of times.

He was not a brilliant strategist or tactician, not a gifted orator, not an intellectual. At several crucial moments he had shown marked indecisiveness. He had made serious mistakes in judgment. But experience had been his great teacher from boyhood, and in this his greatest test, he learned steadily from experience. Above all, Washington never forgot what was at stake and he never gave up.

Again and again, in letters to Congress and to his officers, and in his general orders, he had called for perseverance—for "perseverance and spirit," for "patience and perseverance," for "unremitting courage and perseverance." Soon after the victories of Trenton and Princeton, he had written: "A people unused to restraint must be led, they will not be drove." Without Washington's leadership and unrelenting perseverance, the revolution almost certainly would have failed. As Nathanael Greene foresaw as the war went on, "He will be the deliverer of his own country."

The war was a longer, far more arduous, and more painful struggle than later generations would understand or sufficiently appreciate. By the time it ended, it had taken the lives of an estimated 25,000 Americans, or roughly 1 percent of the population. In percentage of lives lost, it was the most costly war in American history, except for the Civil War.

The year 1776, celebrated as the birth year of the nation and for the signing of the Declaration of Independence, was for those who carried the fight for independence forward a year of all-too-few victories, of sustained suffering, disease, hunger, desertion, cowardice, disillusionment, defeat, terrible discouragement, and fear, as they would never forget, but also of phenomenal courage and bedrock devotion to country, and that, too, they would never forget.

Especially for those who had been with Washington and who knew what a close call it was at the beginning—how often circumstance, storms, contrary winds, the oddities or strengths of individual character had made the difference—the outcome seemed little short of a miracle.

In *The Creation of the American Republic, 1776–1787,* Gordon S. Wood quotes Edmund Randolph on the role of reason in the great American Revolution.

The American Revolution has always seemed to be an extraordinary kind of revolution and no more so than to the Revolutionaries themselves. To those who took stock at the end of three decades of revolutionary activity, the Revolution was not "one of those events which strikes the public eye in the subversions of laws which have usually attended the revolutions of governments." Because it did not seem to have been a usual revolution, the sources of its force and its momentum appeared strangely unaccountable. "In other revolutions, the sword has been drawn by the arm of offended freedom, under an oppression that threatened the vital powers of society." But this seemed hardly true of the American Revolution. There was none of the legendary tyranny of history that had so often driven desperate people into rebellion. The Americans were not an oppressed people; they had no crushing imperial shackles to throw off. In fact, the Americans knew they were probably freer and less burdened with cumbersome feudal and hierarchical restraints than any part of mankind in the eighteenth century. To its victims, the Tories, the Revolution was truly incomprehensible. Never in history, said Daniel Leonard, had there been so much rebellion with so "little real cause." It was, wrote Peter Oliver, "the most wanton and unnatural rebellion that ever existed." The Americans' response was out of all proportion to the stimuli: "The Annals of no Country can produce an Instance of so virulent a Rebellion, of such implacable madness and Fury, originating from such trivial Causes, as those alledged by these unhappy People." The objective social reality scarcely seemed capable of explaining a revolution.

Yet no American doubted that there had been a revolution. How then was it to be justified and explained? If the American Revolution, lacking "those mad, tumultuous actions which disgraced many of the great revolutions of antiquity," was not a typical revolution, what kind of revolution was it? If the origin of the American Revolution lay not in the usual passions and interests of men, wherein did it lie? Those Americans who looked back at what they had been through could only marvel at the rationality and moderation, "supported by the energies of well-weighed choice," involved in their separation from Britain, a revolution remarkably "without violence or convulsion." It was, said Edmund Randolph, a revolution "without an immediate oppression, without a cause depending so much on hasty feeling as theoretic reasoning." It seemed in fact to be peculiarly "the result of reason." The Americans were fortunate in being born at a time when the principles of government and freedom were better known than at any time in history. By "reading and reasoning" on politics they had learned "how to define the rights of nature,—how to search into, to distinguish, and to comprehend, the principles of physical, moral, religious, and civil liberty," how, in short, to discover and resist the forces of tyranny before they could be applied. "Justly it may be said, 'the present is an age of philosophy, and America the empire of reason.' "

The result was phenomenal: an outpouring of political writings—pamphlets, letters, articles, sermons—that has never been equaled in the nation's history. It was as if "every order and degree among the people" had heeded John Adams's urgent appeal to "become attentive to the grounds and principles of government." To those who watched the flood of Whig literature with increasing apprehension it seemed that "ALMOST EVERY AMERICAN PEN" was at work. Even "peasants and their housewives in every part of the land" had begun "to dispute on politics and positively to determine upon our liberties." True Whigs, however, were hardly surprised at the prevalence of political interest, for they were coming to see that the stakes were high indeed. If the principles of politics could be comprehended by the people, if "the science of man and society, being the most extended in its nature, and the most important in its consequences, of any in the circle of erudition," were made the "object of universal attention and study," then, wrote Josiah Quincy in 1774, the rights and happiness of man would no longer remain buried "under systems of civil and priestly hierarchy."

In *Faces of Revolution,* Bernard Bailyn presents the beliefs held by Americans that led to the Revolution.

In its origins, the Revolution, I believe, was no product of social or economic forces developing inexorably toward an explosion; it was not a product of social conflict. Shaping circumstances, of course there were, as well as important social struggles that accompanied the revolt and that played into it in complicated ways. And the Revolution had profound social consequences. But social conflict did not determine the outbreak of the Revolution, which in its essence was

> a response to acts of imperial power deemed arbitrary, degrading, and uncontrollable— a response that was inflamed to the point of explosion by ideological currents generating fears everywhere in America that irresponsible and self-seeking adventurers—what the twentieth century would call political gangsters—had gained the power of the British government and were turning first to the colonies.

Some great events have indeed arisen from social discontent: explosions of the long-smoldering anger of the dispossessed. But the American Revolution was not one of them, however much it expressed the failure of public institutions to adjust to social and economic change, however much it evoked the aspirations of ordinary people, drew into public roles new men unaccustomed to power, freed certain American businessmen from the constraints of overseas control, and produced a wave of social and political reform. These were consequences, not causes. What accounts for the outbreak of the Revolution, which proved in the end to be a radically transforming event, was the interaction of events with a set of beliefs and ideals that were deeply and widely disseminated through the population and were comprehended with various degrees of detail and precision and with various emphases at different levels of society, beliefs bearing mainly on the uses of power and the meaning of political liberty.

The familiar descriptions of the British actions that led to the Revolution include taxation without representation and the battles at Lexington and Concord. In *The Challenge of the American Revolution,* Edmund S. Morgan points to the role of imagination in the Revolution.

The Revolution was not merely a protest against British taxation. It was not merely the movement for independence that followed that protest. It was much more. It meant different things to different men—and different things to the same men at different times. It was a revolution because it upset men and made them think as they never thought before, made them see things that they never saw before, made possible what had seemed impossible before. It was a revolution because it challenged the human imagination and because Americans responded to the challenge as they have never responded to any subsequent challenge in our history.

But before I go any further, let me explain what I mean by imagination, when I say that the Revolution challenged it. Imagination is a quality on which all thinking persons set a high value but which is not easy to define. Sometimes we call it originality, an ability to see a problem in a new way or to offer a new solution to it. I like to think of it as an awareness that something need not be the way it is, that it might be different, or in the immortal words of *Porgy and Bess* that "it ain't necessarily so." Few of us have the imagination to pronounce those words in most situations. We tend to take things for granted. We tend to see what we expect to see, and we often see it even when it isn't there simply because we expect it must be there. We sometimes see crime where there is no criminal and peace where there is no peace. Our limited vision, our lack of imagination helps to perpetuate the world as we find it. Perhaps it is just as well that our imaginations are seldom very active, for we gain a certain stability by taking things for granted. But revolutions are made by not taking things for granted. When a whole people suddenly stop taking for granted the institutions under which they have been brought up and begin to think about how else things might be, a revolution is under way and there is no telling where it will stop.

In the American colonies the first protests against British taxation required no use of the imagination. The colonists objected to the stamp tax and the Townshend duties precisely because they were not what Americans had hitherto taken for granted—their exclusive right to tax themselves. The new taxes were innovations, produced by imaginative finance ministers in England, to whom it had occurred that the colonies might offer a fresh source of revenue to the hard-pressed British treasury. The colonists insisted that they merely wanted to keep things the way they were.

It was only as the quarrel progressed and finally came to a showdown that Americans turned to novelty, to independence; and even independence may at first have seemed to many simply a last, desperate means of averting the mother country's innovative attempts to tax them. But once embraced, the idea of independence excited the imagination, and made Americans realize that things they had taken for granted were not necessarily so. From a population of scarcely three million, the challenge of independence generated a galaxy of leaders unmatched in the previous or subsequent history of the country: Franklin, Washington, Adams, Hamilton, Jefferson, Madison, not to mention a host of lesser lights who in any other period would have stood out as giants. By almost any standard that can be devised to measure greatness, the American Revolution produced more great men in public life than all the rest of American history put together. They were great because they had imagination to respond to the challenge of the Revolution.

In *Setting the World Ablaze,* John Ferling notes the crucial role of leadership in the success of the Revolution.

The American Revolution had been secured by the War of Independence, a terrible eight-year ordeal that was won by a people's struggle and sacrifice. Almost every free man of military age soldiered in some capacity in the course of the war. More than 25,000 in the Continental army, roughly ten percent of those eligible to have borne arms, died. Countless others died in the course of militia service. Nor were young men the only ones who sacrificed to win this war. Many older men served on local committees and boards that pertained to the war effort. Every family paid higher taxes. Many women made bullets, sewed shirts and uniforms for the soldiers, worked in clothing drives to secure blankets and uniforms for the men at the front, and acted as spies and gathered intelligence. Perhaps as many as 20,000 women accompanied the army, cooking, washing, nursing the men, and helping to keep the camps clean. Furthermore, it would have been difficult to find a family that was untouched by the conflict, whether through the long absences of one of its own, the death of a loved one, or economic and emotional travail induced by the war. Even civilians sometimes made the supreme sacrifice. In the South many fell victim in the raging civil war after 1779. In the North many found themselves in harm's way when the British conducted military raids, especially on coastal areas. Civilians everywhere succumbed to disease spread by nearby armies or brought home by the soldiers on leave.

However, as Abigail Adams remarked in the course of the war, "Great necessities…wake into Life, and form the Character of the Hero and the Statesman" who would lead. The thousands who struggled in the American Revolution required direction. John Adams had never doubted this. In the first days of the war he had declared that leadership was imperative if thirteen disparate colonies that constituted such "a vast, unwieldy Machine" were to gain victory. General Washington, with his mettle, management, acumen, enterprise, and sacrificial example, came closer than any other participant to providing the indispensable leadership that was crucial to the success of the American Revolution. No congressman played a more important role than Adams in 1775 and 1776 in seeing to it, as he later remarked, that "Thirteen clocks were made to strike together." Leadership was crucial to unify the provinces, rally them when despair set in, direct them through the brightest days and darkest nights of the long struggle, and to brazenly face every danger, whether posed by foreign soldiers or America's powerful ally.

The leaders of the Revolution shared certain ideas about conduct, including the attributes of a gentleman, which Gordon S. Wood details in *Revolutionary Characters*.

As aspiring gentlemen the leaders of the revolutionary generation shared these assumptions about work, politeness, and civilization. They were primed to receive all these new enlightened ideas about civility and gentility. Because America, as the future governor of New Jersey William Livingston declared, was "just emerging from the rude unpolished Condition of an Infant country," it was especially eager to move along the spectrum of social development toward greater refinement and civilization, more so perhaps than England itself. Indeed, all the talk of acquiring the enlightened attributes of a gentleman had a special appeal for all the outlying underdeveloped provinces of the greater British world, Scotland as well as North America.

All the founders would have heartily endorsed William Livingston's injunctions for becoming truly enlightened gentlemen: "Let us abhor Superstition and Bigotry, which are the Parents of Sloth and Slavery. Let us make War upon Ignorance and Barbarity of Manners. Let us invite the Arts and Sciences to reside amongst us. Let us encourage every thing which tends to exalt and embellish our Characters. And in fine, let the Love of our Country be manifested by that which is the only true Manifestation of it, a patriotic soul and a public Spirit." They struggled to internalize the new liberal man-made standards that had come to define what it meant to be truly civilized—politeness, taste, sociability, learning, compassion, and benevolence—and what it meant to be good political leaders: virtue, disinterestedness, and an aversion to corruption and courtierlike behavior. Once internalized, these enlightened and classically republican ideals, values, and standards came to circumscribe and control their behavior. They talked obsessively about earning a character, which, as Dr. Johnson defined it, was "a representation of any man as to his personal qualities."

In *George Washington: Man and Monument,* Marcus Cunliffe describes the extraordinary leader.

Wealthy gentleman, impeccable generalissimo, guerilla warrior: Congress sought all these in the person of George Washington. In addition, Congress required such a paragon to think as a civilian. This putative commander, a dignified brigand capable of imposing his authority over forces, regular and militia, from thirteen different and semiautonomous states, must yet submit cheerfully to the supreme authority of Congress.

The marvel is that, demanding the impossible, Congress nearly got it in George Washington. As a bonus, they found in him a man of quite extraordinary persistence. Fitzpatrick's huge edition of Washington's writings is unlikely to be read by many in its entirety. There are some ten thousand for the war years alone, and the documents in them are too minutely detailed and far too repetitive to whet one's appetite. Yet the repetition is vital to an understanding of the nature of the man. We watch him hammering away, in plain, workman-like prose, neither witty nor pompous, neither blustering nor apologetic, until he either gets his way or concludes that he has come to an absolute impasse. Particularly is this true when he writes of the means, however remote, of bringing the war to a close. Victory was the goal he kept in sight; unlike the British commanders, he never hopelessly confused the secondary advantage with the primary aim. Grand strategy was not his forte (and, perhaps he believed, not his business but that of Congress); after the failure of the Canada invasion in 1775–1776 he did not encourage ambitious projects of that kind. Instead, he concentrated upon what must be: a larger army, better ways of maintaining it, more prompt and more generous contributions from the states, the support of a navy that could, at least for a space, wrest naval supremacy from the British. His long-deferred reward came at Yorktown.

David Ramsay of South Carolina, who published a *History of the American Revolution* in 1789, said, "It seemed as if the war not only required, but created talents." The remark well fits George Washington. He was never the "little paltry Colonel of Militia" that Lord Howe's secretary, Ambrose Serle, sneered at in 1776. His critics in America argued that he had not so much grown in stature as in public esteem. Yet even they, by the end of the war, had to admit that he wore his honors becomingly—and unassumingly. We can trace the process by working through those ten thousand crowded pages of his wartime writings. In them, little by little, we can detect the signs of greater assurance, wisdom and equanimity. The comments of the French officers who met him in the later stages of the conflict (when he had mellowed a good deal) tell the same story. They speak of a man respected by nearly all, revered by some; capable of geniality if not of gaiety; keeping a good table but not a sot; well mounted and well tailored but not a dandy; proud but not vainglorious—"His Excellency" in fact as well as in title.

In *Revolutionary Characters,* Gordon S. Wood considers George Washington's great legacy.

In 1783 Washington, consummate actor that he was, made his most theatrical gesture, his most moral mark, and the results were monumental. The greatest act of his life, the one that made him internationally famous, was his resignation as commander in chief of the American forces. This act, together with his circular letter to the states in which he promised his retirement, was what he called his legacy to his countrymen. No American leader has ever left a more important legacy.

Following the signing of the peace treaty and British recognition of American independence, Washington stunned the world when he surrendered his sword to the Congress on December 23, 1783, and retired to his farm at Mount Vernon. As Garry Wills has shown, this was a highly symbolic act, a very self-conscious and unconditional withdrawal from the world of politics. In order to enhance the disinterestedness of the political advice he offered in the circular letter to the states he wrote six months before his actual retirement, he promised not to take "any share in public business hereafter." He even resigned from his local vestry in order to make his separation from the political world complete.

His retirement from power had a profound effect everywhere in the Western world. It was extraordinary; a victorious general's surrendering his arms and returning to his farm was unprecedented in modern times. Cromwell, William of Orange, Marlborough—all had sought political rewards commensurate with their military achievements. Though it was widely believed that Washington could have become king or dictator, he wanted nothing of the kind. He was sincere in his desire for all his soldiers "to return to our Private Stations in the bosom of a free, peaceful and happy Country," and everyone recognized his sincerity. It filled them with awe. Jefferson was not exaggerating when he declared in 1784 that "the moderation and virtue of a single character…probably prevented this revolution from being closed, as most others have been, by a subversion of that liberty it was intended to establish."

Benjamin Franklin was the only American who signed the Declaration of Independence, the 1778 treaties of alliance and commerce with France, the 1783 Treaty of Paris, and the Constitution. In *The Americanization of Benjamin Franklin,* Gordon S. Wood considers how Americans remember Franklin.

Among the peoples of the world only Americans of the early republic, as their great observer Alexis de Tocqueville pointed out, celebrated work as "the necessary, natural, and honest condition of all men." What most astonished Tocqueville was that Americans thought not only that work itself was "honorable," but that "work specifically to gain money" was "honorable," By contrast, European society not only possessed proportionally fewer middling people than America, but was still dominated by aristocrats who scorned working for profit.

With everyone working for pay, everyone became alike. Even "servants do not feel degraded because they work," Tocqueville wrote, "for everyone around them is working. There is nothing humiliating about the idea of receiving a salary, for the President of the United States works for a salary." Of course, as Tocqueville explained, the "Americans" he described were those "who live in the parts of the country where there is no slavery. It is they alone who provide a complete picture of a democratic society." It was the northern working people of 1830 who created America's dominant sense of nationhood, not the cavalier South.

At the time of the Revolution in 1776, Virginia had thought itself to be the undisputed leader of the nation, with good reason. It was by far the most populous state, with a population of well over 600,000 people, 40 percent of whom were black slaves. It was over twice the size of its nearest competitor, Pennsylvania. It supplied much of the Revolutionary leadership and dominated the Constitutional Convention with its Virginia plan. In 1776 it had the strongest claim to the bulk of the western territory comprising most of the present-day Midwest. It is not surprising that four of the first five presidents and the longest-serving chief justice of the United States should have been Virginians. But by 1830 Virginia's day in the sun had passed, its population outstripped by both New York and Pennsylvania. Its economy had become largely engaged in the export of slaves to the burgeoning regions of the Deep South.

Virginia and the South always claimed that they had remained closer to the eighteenth-century beginnings of the nation, and they were right. It was the North that had changed and changed dramatically. Because northern Americans came to celebrate work so emphatically—with Franklin as their most representative figure—the leisured slaveholding aristocracy of Virginia and the rest of the South became a bewildered and beleaguered minority out of touch with the enterprise and egalitarianism that had come to dominate the country. As long as work had been held in contempt, as it had for millennia, slavery could never have been wholeheartedly condemned. But to a society that came to honor work as fully as the North did, a leisured aristocracy and the institution of slavery that supported it had to become abominations.

This dynamic, democratic, and enterprising world that Tocqueville described created the modern image of Franklin as the bourgeois moralist obsessed with the making of money and getting ahead. Although this image was the one that D. H. Lawrence and other imaginative writers have so much scorned, Franklin might not have been unhappy to learn that this powerful entrepreneurial symbol would be the way most people in the world would come to know him.

In some ways his career had come full circle. Near the end of his life he glimpsed that some people were coming to see him once again as the tradesman printer who had made it, and he seemed to welcome this view of himself. It is the image of the hardworking self-made businessman that has most endured. Franklin was one of the greatest of the Founders; indeed, his crucial diplomacy in the Revolution makes him second only to Washington in importance. But that importance is not what we most remember about Franklin. It is instead the symbolic Franklin of the bumptious capitalism of the early republic—the man who personifies the American dream—who stays with us. And as long as America is seen as the land of opportunity, where you can get ahead if you work hard, this image of Franklin will likely be the one that continues to dominate American culture.

In "To Begin the World Over Again" in *Revolutionary Founders: Rebels, Radicals, and Reformers in the Making of the Nation*, edited by Alfred F. Young, Gary B. Nash, and Ray Raphael, the editors consider the founders and their accomplishments.

Our protagonists in this book wanted to extend the lofty principles expressed in the Declaration of Independence to areas of life that the traditional founders never intended. These people *did* have a sense of the promise of the Revolution, and they wanted to fulfill it in their own time. Sharing no single agenda, they acted in the spirit of the words of Thomas Paine: "We have it in our power to begin the world over again." The new nation was "a blank sheet to write upon," Paine wrote, and on that sheet they placed their marks. Their actions were many and varied:

- Common farmers, artisans, and laborers often led the resistance to imperial policies, moving the colonies toward independence while reshaping the character of political life in North America.

- Slaves emancipated themselves by fleeing to freedom, then established their own viable communities.

- Women staked claims to "equality of the sexes" and to retain rights to their own property in marriage.

- Persecuted religious dissenters pushed for, and obtained, "the free exercise of religion."

- Resisting the inequities of rank, soldiers carried democratic values into the military.

- Native Americans claimed sovereignty and fought to defend it, with a spirit of independence that paralleled that of colonists.

- Farmers threatened with the loss of their land resorted to collective action, including taking up arms.

- Printers published what they wanted, overriding attempts to repress them.

- Self-proclaimed democrats, turning that term of derision on its head, won the right of ordinary people to vote, hold public office, and pass judgment on their rulers.

Most of these "Revolutionary founders" were *radicals* in the literal sense of the word: they promoted root changes in the very structure of social or political systems. One of those fundamental changes, of course, was independence from Britain, a goal they shared with the traditional founders, but often they pushed for others. Many of these people can also be considered *rebels*, either because they forcibly challenged British authority or because they confronted old or new hierarchies. Finally, some might best be described as *reformers* who sought to change a particular feature of society while leaving others intact.

Each of these rebels, radicals, and reformers moved the American Revolution in some direction the traditional founders did not want to take, extending it farther and deeper than a separation from the British Empire. They made the Revolution more revolutionary.

In *Clothed in Robes of Sovereignty,* Benjamin H. Irvin describes the symbols and traditions that Congress created to encourage independence.

The invented traditions by which Congress endeavored to fortify the resistance movement and to make meaning of American independence were patriotic and hortatory in nature. Congress's inventions consisted of a wide variety of things: behavioral codes, such as proscriptions against horseracing, cockfighting, and theatergoing; holidays, such as fast days, thanksgivings, and anniversaries of independence; iconography, such as emblems and mottoes printed on the continental currency; ceremonies of state, such as public audiences granted to foreign ministers; and commemorative artifacts, such as swords and medals awarded to distinguished army officers and monuments erected to their memory. By crafting rituals, celebrations, and objets d'art, Congress appealed not merely to reason, but to emotion, passion, faith, morality, sensibility, and aesthetics. This was not a volitional model of governance, but rather an affective one.

Perhaps most significantly, Congress formulated symbols and rituals to inspire the people's love for the United States. To achieve independence, American patriots destroyed the Britannic mementos that once adorned their lives. They pulled down statues of King George

III; they trampled on the British lion; they tore the Hanoverian arms from their state house walls; and they let pass uncelebrated the anniversaries of royal births and accessions. The Continental Congress worked concertedly to supplant the tokens and habits of the British nation with fresh ones devoted to the United States. It implemented codes of conduct by which patriotic Americans could distinguish those who belonged to their imagined community from those who did not. It offered emblematic assurances, during the bleakest moments of the war, that the United States would persevere. It seized opportunities, slowly though they came at first, to embarrass the British enemy and to celebrate American triumph. By crafting monuments, insignia, and civic traditions, Congress aimed at nothing less than a revolution in Americans' national identity.

How, then, did the American public react to Congress's vision of the infant republic? How did ordinary laborers, women, loyalists, and other marginalized persons receive a body of works that bore all the social and political prejudices of its elite patriot makers? Eighteenth-century Britons used the descriptive phrase "out of doors" to distinguish popular political action and discourse—that which took place in taverns, in coffeehouses, and out in the streets—from official proceedings that unfolded within the halls of government. In recent decades, social and political historians have adapted the phrase "out of doors" to signify early American mobs, or crowds, and to evoke the public spaces in which they gathered for demonstration. Such crowds performed a unique function in Anglo-American society.

At the war's end, the Continental Congress faltered in its efforts to manufacture a material and ceremonial identity for the United States. Bereft of credit, plagued by absenteeism, enfeebled by the constitutional limitations and procedural constraints of the Articles of Confederation, and censured for its failure to clothe and feed the Continental Army, Congress declined in both stature and authority. Meanwhile, rival institutions—particularly the French embassy and the Society of the Cincinnati—rose to fill the festive and commemorative void. By that time, however, the Continental Congress and its successor, the Confederation Congress, had made enduring impressions on the material and ceremonial culture of the Revolution and on the national identity of the United States. By manufacturing new emblems and rituals, Congress provided the people out of doors with a vocabulary by which to articulate their own vision of national identity. The Continental Congress could not stabilize the meanings of its inventions. In their very mutability lay power for the people out of doors. Rather than passively adopting Congress's creations, the American people embraced, rejected, reworked, ridiculed, or simply ignored them as they saw fit.

Change for American Indians began before the Revolution as settlers took over their homelands and violence increased. In *The American Revolution in Indian Country*, Colin G. Calloway summarizes the tragic consequences of the Revolution for Indian people.

For Indian people in eastern North America, the entire century was an age of revolution, a pivotal era in which, as James Merrell wrote, "the balance tipped irrevocably away from the Indian." In some ways the Revolution only intensified familiar pressures on Indian lives and lands. The Indians' "War of Independence" was well under way before 1775, was waged on many fronts—economic, cultural, political, and military—and continued long after 1783.

War was nothing new in Indian country in the eighteenth century, but the Revolution generated new sources of conflict and new levels of violence that destroyed much of the world Indians and non-Indians had created there. As elsewhere in North America, old structures, traditional patterns of behavior, and long-standing alliances broke down in a climate of tumult and change. Religious ferment and dissension split Indian congregations and communities as well as white ones. Dissident groups challenged established authority in Indian country as well as in colonial society. Refugees from war and hunger choked forts and villages.

In the end, white Americans excluded Indians from the republican society that the Revolution created. Despite their absence from much of the historical literature, Indian people were everywhere in colonial America. In 1775, Indian nations, despite intrusive and disruptive pressures unleashed by European contact, still controlled most of America west of the Appalachians. In 1783, when Britain transferred that territory to the new United States, most of it was still in Indian hands, but a new era had begun. The American revolutionaries who fought for freedom from the British Empire in the East also fought to create an empire of their own in the West. Contention over Indian land was an old story by 1775, but the Revolution elevated acquisition of Indian lands into a national policy. The new nation, born of a bloody revolution and committed to expansion, could not tolerate America as Indian country. Increasingly, Americans viewed the future as one without Indians. The Revolution both created a new society and provided justification for excluding Indians from it.

The agony of the American Revolution for American Indians was lost as the winners constructed a national mythology that simplified what had been a complex contest in Indian Country, blamed Indians for the bloodletting, and justified subsequent assaults on Indian lands and cultures. In the aftermath of the Revolution, new social orders were created and new ideologies developed to explain which groups of people were included and excluded, and why. In the long run, the legacy the war produced in the minds of non-Indians proved almost as devastating to Indian peoples as the burned towns, fractured communities, and shattered lives of the war itself.

The Declaration of Independence depicted Indians as savage allies of a tyrannical monarch, who "endeavored to bring on the inhabitants of our frontiers, the merciless Indian savages, whose known rule of warfare is an undistinguished destruction of all ages, sexes, and conditions." Embodied in the document that marked the nation's birth, the image of Indians as vicious enemies of liberty became entrenched in the minds of generations of white Americans.

The vicious border warfare of the Revolution produced atrocities and lasting impressions on both sides. Benjamin Franklin admitted in 1787 that "almost every War between the Indians and Whites has been occasion'd by some Injustice of the latter towards the former."

Pequot William Apess bitterly understood that "the Revolution which enshrined republican principles in the American commonwealth, also excluded African Americans and Native Americans from their reach." Referring to the guardian system reinstituted by Massachusetts, placing Indian settlements under the authority of state-appointed overseers, he wrote, "The whites were no sooner free themselves, than they enslaved the poor Indians." The new republic needed African labor, and it excluded African Americans from its definition of "free and equal" on the basis of supposed racial inferiority. The new republic needed Indian land and excluded Native Americans on the basis of supposed savagery.

American Indians could not expect to be accepted in a nation that denied the fruits of an egalitarian revolution to so many of its citizens and that lived with the contradiction of slavery in a society built on principles of freedom. Native Americans had been heavily dependent on, and interdependent with, colonial society and economy before the Revolution. But as Indian land became the key to national, state, and individual wealth, the new republic was less interested in their dependence than in their absence.

The United States looked forward to a future without Indians. The Indians' participation in the Revolution guaranteed their exclusion from the new world born out of the Revolution; their determination to survive as Indians guaranteed their ultimate extinction. Artistic depictions of Indian people showed them retreating westward, suffused in the heavy imagery of setting suns, as they faded from history.

Fortunately for us all, Indian people had other ideas.

In *Revolutionary Backlash: Women and Politics in the Early American Republic,* Rosemarie Zagarri points to the importance of women to the Revolution and the many ways in which they supported it.

The American Revolution marked a watershed in the popular perceptions of women's relationship to the state. Almost as soon as the controversy began in the 1760s, Whig leaders realized that the effectiveness of their resistance to Britain depended on their ability to mobilize popular support.

What was different about the American Revolution was the nature and extent of the appeals to women. The more extensive use of print media made this change possible. Newspapers, magazines, and broadsides reached out to women in a direct, wide-spread, and public fashion. Using poems, essays, plays, and orations, male political leaders urged women to join in the effort. The two most prominent women to take advantage of this expanding print culture were Mercy Otis Warren and Judith Sargent Murray. Both were born in Massachusetts; both started their writing careers during the ferment of the revolutionary era. Warren's husband, James, and brother, James Otis, were leaders in the Massachusetts resistance movement. Over time John Adams, a family friend, recognized that although she was a woman, Mercy had a gift for writing. He urged her to use her gift to support the patriot cause. During the 1760s and 1770s Warren wrote political poems and satirical plays, published anonymously, that attacked British tyranny and rallied support for the American cause. In particular, *The Adulateur* and *The Group,* attacked the corruption of royal government in Massachusetts and called on the colonists to resist infringements on their liberties. Adams praised her contributions to the revolutionary movement, commenting, "[Her] poetical pen has no equal that

I know of in this country." Despite Warren's official anonymity, in the close-knit world of patriot leaders she was known and celebrated.

During the 1760s political leaders asked women to boycott imported luxury goods, produce homemade textiles and clothing, and give up drinking British tea. Once armed resistance began, they asked them to sacrifice the conveniences of life, take over their husbands' duties at home in their absence, and, if necessary, be willing to offer their men's lives for their country on the field of battle. Printed appeals drew women to the cause.

Women responded with a widespread outpouring of support. During the 1760s women in Boston, Massachusetts, and Edenton, North Carolina, signed formal agreements to abide by the boycotts forbidding the importation of British goods.

It is undeniably true that at the beginning of the war for independence, most American leaders would never have dreamed that their struggle against Britain would turn into an attack on the gender status quo. Yet, like all revolutions, the American Revolution produced its share of unintended consequences. No single person or group could control the direction of events or the flow of ideas. This was especially true with regard to ideas about women's relationship to the state, their involvement with politics, and their political rights and privileges.

By 1776 many Americans believed that Britain had violated not only their rights as Englishmen but also their God-given natural rights, inscribed in nature. The Declaration of Independence justified independence by asserting men's natural equality and by invoking the "Laws of Nature and of Nature's God." Natural rights commanded assent because they were said to be inalienable, immutable, and universal—possessed by virtue of one's personhood rather than as a result of citizenship, parentage, or wealth. Such claims were hard to refute.

Yet unbeknownst to the revolutionaries, these concepts could take on a life of their own. Equality and natural rights had an elastic quality, capable of almost infinite expansion and extension. Once the Revolution began, the very existence of property qualifications for voting started to bother some members of society. As states began to write their first constitutions, agitation for lowering or eliminating property qualifications became a subject of debate. Some commentators pointed out the inconsistency in allowing men to fight and die for their country but not allowing them to vote. Others pointed out that by expanding the franchise, state governments would broaden their base of popular support. Still others noted that if Americans believed that those who paid taxes should be represented, then all tax-payers, not just owners of real property, should be enfranchised. The most powerful argument, however, was that if all men were truly created equal and shared the same natural rights, then all men should be entitled to vote.

Before the Revolution, questions had seldom arisen about whether women could or should be able to vote. Because of the legal doctrine of coverture, married women, under the guardianship of their husbands, could not own property. Although widows and single women could own property, they constituted just a small fraction of the population. Hence the question of women voting did not often arise. Even so, it is significant that women were not alone in their disfranchisement. Substantial numbers of white males (from 20 percent to 50 percent) and in most colonies all free black males also did not meet the property qualifications and thus were excluded from the franchise. Thus, while it is true that women did not have the right to vote, neither did a lot of men. Class, not sex, represented the primary basis for inclusion or exclusion.

The American Revolution opened up a brief window of opportunity for women. New venues arose in which women might participate informally in politics. Some women embraced politics with a vigor that earned them the designation "female politicians." The triumph of equality and natural rights as foundational principles of American society and government also changed women's status. Women gained recognition as the possessors of rights that put them in certain respects, on an equal footing with men. A lively popular debate erupted over the precise nature of women's rights, including whether women had the right to vote and hold public office. Within a few decades, however, a backlash ensued, resulting in the closing of many of the political opportunities that the Revolution had opened up. The specter of Mary Wollstonecraft, the experience of women voting in New Jersey, and the visibility of female politicians provoked fears of a larger transformation in gender roles and relations. Although most women were not yet demanding political rights for themselves, it was clear that they might one day do so.

In *Liberty's Daughters: The Revolutionary Experience of American Women, 1750–1800,* Mary Beth Norton considers the effects of the Revolution on women.

The war necessarily broke down the barrier which seemed to insulate women from the realm of politics, for they, no less than men, were caught up in the turmoil that enveloped the entire populace. Most understood that the old notions had to be discarded. Abigail Adams is a case in point. In June 1776, she still adhered to the conventional formula, telling John, "I can serve my partner, my family and myself, and injoy the Satisfaction of your serving your Country," thereby indicating that she believed her contributions to the patriots' cause had to be filtered through the medium of her husband. But less than two years later, in February 1778, she described her "satisfaction in the Consciousness of having discharged *my* duty to the publick." Like others of her contemporaries, she no longer drew a sharp dividing line between the feminine sphere and the masculine realm of public responsibilities.

But to recognize that women had a role to fulfill in the wider society was not to declare that male and female roles were, or should be, the same. Not even Judith Sargeant Murray conceived of an androgynous world; men's and women's functions were to be equal and complementary, not identical. And so the citizens of the republic set out to discover and define woman's public role. They found it not in the notion that women should directly participate in politics, New Jersey's brief experiment with woman's suffrage to the contrary. Rather, they located woman's public role in her domestic responsibilities, in her obligation to create a supportive home life for her husband and particularly in her duty to raise republican sons who would love their country and preserve its virtuous character.

The ironies of this formulation were manifest. On the one hand, society had at last formally recognized women's work as valuable. No longer was domesticity denigrated; no longer was the feminine sphere subordinated to the masculine, nor were women regarded as inferior. The white women of nineteenth-century America could take pride in their sex in a way their female ancestors could not. The importance of motherhood was admitted by all, and women could glory in the special role laid out for them in the copious literature that rhapsodized about beneficent feminine influences both inside and outside the home.

But, on the other hand, the republican definition of womanhood, which began as a marked step forward, grew ever more restrictive as the decades passed. Woman's domestic and maternal role came to be seen as so important that it was believed women sacrificed their femininity if they attempted to be more (or other) than wives and mothers. Accordingly, the women who were most successful in winning society's acceptance of their extradomestic activities were those who—like teachers, missionaries, or charitable workers—managed to conceal their flouting of convention by subsuming their actions within the confines of an orthodox, if somewhat broadened, conception of womanhood and its proper functions.

In the prerevolutionary world, no one had bothered to define domesticity: the private realm seemed unimportant, and besides, women could not escape their inevitable destiny. In the postrevolutionary world, the social significance of household and family was recognized, and simultaneously women began to be able to choose different ways of conducting their lives. As a direct result, a definition of domesticity was at last required. The process of defining woman's proper role may well have stiffened the constraints that had always encircled female lives, but that definition also—by its very existence—signaled American society's growing comprehension of woman's importance within a sphere far wider than a private household or a marital relationship.

The legacy of the American Revolution for women was thus ambiguous. Republican womanhood eventually became Victorian womanhood, but at the same time the egalitarian rhetoric of the Revolution provided the women' rights movement with its earliest vocabulary, and the republican academies produced its first leaders. Few historical events can ever be assessed in absolute terms. With respect to its impact on women, the American Revolution is no exception.

In *Slavery and the Making of America,* James Oliver Horton and Lois E. Horton describe slavery during and as a result of the Revolution.

In 1770, on the eve of the American Revolution, Africans and African Americans were a significant part of the population in the colonies of British North America. By 1750 there were almost a quarter million slaves in the mainland colonies of British North America, all but 30,000 held in the southern colonies. Their numbers continued to grow in the last half of the century, so that the black proportion of the population in the colonies had grown from 4 percent in 1700 to nearly 40 percent by 1770, doubling between mid-century and the Revolution.

The major slave-produced crops in British North America were tobacco in the Chesapeake region and rice in South Carolina, but slavery also provided the labor needs of colonies farther north without large cash crops. There, both the slaveholdings and the black populations were smaller. This was especially true in New England, where great profits were more often made in slave trading than in slaveholding.

By the end of the war, more than five thousand African Americans had served in the American forces, and more than a thousand black men and women had served with the British armed forces. The end of the war brought freedom to thousands of slaves, most of those who fought with the Americans, some who left with America's French allies, and many more who left with the withdrawing British troops or with the Tories who fled to Canada.

Probably more slaves gained their freedom through their association with the British than by fighting with the Americans. In all, more than fourteen thousand blacks went with the British troops when they withdrew, but not all of these people were freed. Some who had sought asylum with the British but had not actually served in the British armed forces remained slaves. Moreover, during the next ten years, British slavers continued a brisk trade, sailing more than eight hundred slave-trading ships out of Liverpool alone. Between 1783 and 1793, Liverpool traders transported at least three hundred thousand slaves worth more than fifteen million pounds sterling.

Vermont outlawed human bondage in its state constitution in 1777, echoing the Declaration of Independence in declaring "all men are created equally free and independent." In the United States, by 1804 all states north of Maryland had either abolished slavery outright or had enacted plans for gradual emancipation. Although the Revolution had not begun as an anti-slavery crusade, it had nonetheless brought freedom to vast numbers of slaves.

In the "Foreword" in *Epic Journeys of Freedom* by Cassandra Pybus, Ira Berlin details how black men and women used the Revolution to challenge slavery.

Revolutions generally benefit those who have the least to lose and the most to gain. In the middle of the eighteenth century, few had less to lose and more to gain than the black men and women held as slaves in the American colonies. Black men and women understood this, and when the simmering dispute between imperial Britain and its American colonies flared into open warfare and that war began to unravel the fabric of colonial life, they seized the moment. The result was a massive transformation that propelled thousands of black people from slavery to freedom, introduced a new ideology that presumed universal equality, and began the reconstruction of African American life as black people married, established families, secured waged employment, built churches and schools, and organized societies and associations. The spectacular increase in the number of free blacks dissolved the easy equation of slavery and blackness.

Revolutions that go forward can also go backward, and the men and women who seize the moment often have it wrestled from their grasp. Black men and women, much to their horror, also learned of the force of counterrevolution. If some black people gained their freedom during the American Revolution, many more were consigned to a dismal captivity, as slave masters consolidated their power atop the new state and initiated a massive expansion of the plantation system. There would be more black people enslaved at the end of the Revolution than at the beginning. Even as the Republic wrapped itself in the cloak of equality, new ideologies emerged that excluded black people from its democratic promise. Finally, as former slaves began to reconstruct their society, they found themselves excluded from all but the most menial employment, barred from established churches, denied access to education, and deprived of many of the rights of citizens.

But whether the Revolution smashed the shackles of slavery or tightened the manacles, it transformed black life in the eighteenth century as fully as the Civil War would in the nineteenth and the civil rights movement would in the twentieth. Indeed, the Civil War and the civil rights movement could not have taken place without the changes in black life initiated by the Revolution. The American Revolution divided the nation into free and slave. It unleashed the radical egalitarianism upon which the abolitionist movement, the wartime emancipation, the promise of Reconstruction, and the long struggle against Jim Crow rested. The contest between civil nationalism—which demanded the extension of the Declaration's principles to all—and racial nationalism—which sequestered those principles for a chosen few—had its beginnings in the Revolutionary settlement. That dispute continues to resonate in American life.

None of this would have been possible had not black men and women seized the Revolutionary moment to challenge slavery.

Gordon S. Wood considers slavery after the Revolution in *The Radicalism of the American Revolution.*

For a century or more the colonists had taken slavery more or less for granted as the most base and dependent status in a hierarchy of dependencies and a world of laborers. Rarely had they felt the need either to criticize black slavery or to defend it. Now, however, the republican attack on dependency compelled Americans to see the deviant character of slavery and to confront the institution as they never had to before. It was no accident that Americans in Philadelphia in 1775 formed the first anti-slave society in the world. As long as most people had to work merely out of poverty and the need to provide for a living, slavery and other forms of enforced labor did not seem all that different from free labor. But the growing recognition that labor was not simply a common necessity of the poor but was in fact a source of increased wealth and prosperity for ordinary workers made slavery seem more and more anomalous. Americans now recognized that slavery in a republic of workers was an aberration, "a peculiar institution," and that if any Americans were to retain it, as southern Americans eventually did, they would have to explain and justify it in new racial and anthropological ways that their former monarchical society had never needed. The Revolution in effect set in motion ideological and social forces that doomed the institution of slavery in the North and led inexorably to the Civil War.

In *American Creation*, Joseph J. Ellis points out that while the success of the Revolution was the result of the leaders' creative responses to many challenges, they failed to assure equality for all Americans.

First, Adams was essentially correct in insisting that the major political decisions that shaped the founding were usually improvisational occasions. While there were a few cerebral epiphanies based on intense thinking, most creative choices were pragmatic responses to rapidly moving events beyond human control, on-the-run adaptations of classical texts to shifting contexts. The founders were, in fact, making it up as they went along, and any historical interpretation that emphasizes their otherworldly serenity or uncommon prescience in grasping how it would all turn out is a fundamental distortion of the way history happened.

Second, Washington was also correct in claiming that space was a priceless American asset. While that asset was an unsolicited geographic gift for which the founders could take no credit, recognizing its advantages provided the occasion for several of the most creative moments in the founding era. The scale of the American theater was unprecedented, especially when compared to tidier European spaces, and the most original political contributions made by the founders were offered in response to that unique condition.

Third, in terms of creativity, the control of pace was almost as impressive as the control of space. The founders opted for an evolutionary rather than revolutionary version of political and social change, preferring to delay delivery on the full promise of the American Revolution rather than risk implosion in the mode of the French Revolution. Although it is difficult for many modern-day critics to acknowledge the point, this deferral strategy, far from being a moral failure, was in fact a profound insight rooted in a realistic appraisal of how enduring social change best happens. But the exception to this rule, removing slavery from the political agenda on the grounds that it would die a natural death, proved a massive miscalculation.

Fourth, the successful management of space and pace was not matched when it came to race, which proved impervious to any imaginative response whatsoever. In the end, it was psychologically impossible for the founders to imagine the peaceful coexistence of whites and free African Americans in the same nation-state. (The same was not true for Native Americans.) Without any historical precedents to guide them, the founders could imagine a secular state and a large-scale republic, but they could not imagine a biracial society. As a result, whenever race entered the founding conversation, tragedy prevailed.

In *The Scratch of a Pen*, Colin G. Calloway assesses the impact of the two Paris peace treaties on the United States of America.

As the roots of the Second World War can be found in the Versailles Peace Settlement of 1918, so in the 1763 Peace of Paris can be found the roots of the American Revolution, the Peace of Paris in 1783, and the American national empire that followed. Looking back, the road from victory in 1763 to revolution in 1775 seems clear, and the British government's missteps and misjudgments with regard to taxing the colonists seem obvious. But Britons, on whichever side of the Atlantic they lived, did not see things so clearly in 1763. They were entering uncharted territory, sometimes literally. Never before had Britons enjoyed such power, imagined such possibilities, or confronted such challenges. The path to revolution was only one of many stories unfolding that year.

At the Peace of Paris in 1763, France handed over to Great Britain all its North American territories east of the Mississippi. It transferred Louisiana to Spain, and Spain transferred Florida to Britain. Twenty years later, at another Peace of Paris, Britain recognized the independence of thirteen former colonies and transferred to the new United States all its territory south of the Great Lakes, north of the Floridas, and east of the Mississippi. It returned Florida to Spain, and the British inhabitants of St. Augustine packed up and left, just as the Spanish inhabitants had done in 1763. In 1783 as in 1763, the ministry that concluded the Peace of Paris was not the same ministry that had conducted the war.

During the debates in England over whether to give up Canada or Guadeloupe at the 1763 peace settlement, William Burke, a relative of the renowned statesman Edmund Burke, had argued that Canada should be left in French hands as a way of binding the North American colonies to Britain: "A neighbor that keeps us in some awe is not always the worst of neighbors," he explained; removing French Canada would free the original thirteen colonies to separate from the mother country. "By eagerly grasping at extensive territory," he warned, "we may run the risqué, and that perhaps in no very distant period, of losing what we now possess." As Canadian historian William Eccles pointed out, the Duc de Choiseul not only predicted the American Revolution, but "was counting on it." For Choiseul, 1763 gave France the peace it needed to rebuild for war. He started rebuilding the navy even before the treaty was signed, and the ink was barely dry before the French were surveying the English coasts to formulate revised invasion plans. France restored its overseas trade, implemented reforms in its army and navy, and strengthened its economy, while at the same time keeping Britain diplomatically isolated in Europe. When, as Choiseul knew they would, the American colonies revolted, France had the power to make the difference. During the War of Independence Britain found itself in the same position France had been during the Seven Years' War—bogged down in a protracted land war while the enemy took full advantage of its renewed sea power. The British navy momentarily lost command of the seas to France, and Lord Cornwallis lost his army. Louis-Antoine de Bougainville, who had carried the articles of Montreal's surrender to the British in 1760, was present when the British surrendered at Yorktown in 1781.

Looking back over the course of events from 1763 to 1783, Henry Ellis explained the connection between the two treaties. "What did Britain gain by the most glorious and successful war on which she ever engaged?" he asked. "A height of Glory which excited the Envy of the surrounding nations and united them in the late unnatural contest with our revolted colonies—an extent of empire we were equally unable to maintain, defend or govern—the final independence of those colonies which the dispossession of the French from Canada necessarily tended to promote and accelerate, and the enormous debt of two hundred and fifty millions." Faced with a huge new territorial empire in North America in 1763, the British tried to defend it, administer it, and finance it. Instead they lost it. They turned to the kind of empire they did best—an ocean-based commercial empire.

France exacted revenge for the humiliation of 1763 but achieved little else. American negotiators signed the preliminary articles of peace with Britain in 1783 without informing the French. France did not replace Britain as America's trading partner and was unable to shape the direction of American expansion. The French minister, Vergennes, wanted the old Proclamation Line of 1763 to mark the western territorial limits of the new United States, with the lands between the Appalachians and the Mississippi reserved as Indian country. The Earl of Shelburne, now Secretary of State, recognized that American settlements in the West would gravitate to British trade and envisaged joint British participation in the commercial development of the Mississippi Valley. Britain sold out its Indian allies and handed their lands to the United States. "It is rather ironic," notes William Eccles, "that the British government here insisted on giving away what France had once sought to deny to Britain but now desperately wanted Britain to retain."

Neither the Peace of 1763 nor the Peace of 1783 made any mention of the Indian peoples who inhabited the territories being transferred. In both cases, Indian interests were sacrificed to imperial agendas. As in 1763, Indians in 1783 were "thunderstruck" by the terms of a treaty that did not include them. As in 1763, they complained that a foreign king had no right to transfer lands and rights they had never given up, let alone breach treaties previously made in solemn council. No such cession could "be binding without their Express Concurrence & Consent." A Cherokee chief, Little Turkey, said "the peacemakers and our Enemies have talked away our lands at a Rum Drinking." As in 1763, the victors looked west across vast territories transferred to them in Paris and wondered how to make them into an empire. As in 1763, they believed for a time that they could dispense with the protocols of doing business in Indian country and could dictate to the Indians from a position of strength. As in 1763, they learned their mistake.

Pontiac's war was not the last Indian war for independence. States and nation encroached on Indian lands and life even more aggressively than had colonies and empire. Multi-tribal coalitions resisted American occupation of the lands ceded by Britain in 1783 just as they had resisted British occupation of the lands ceded by France in 1763. During the 1780s and 1790s, and again in the first decade of the nineteenth century, multi-tribal coalitions stalled American advance into the West and mounted formidable opposition to American expansion that sought to gobble up tribal lands piecemeal.

The United States learned from some of Britain's mistakes. It bound its new territories to it by interest rather than by imperial administration. In the Northwest Ordinance of 1787, the Confederation Congress laid out the provisions by which western territories could enter the union as equal states. In so doing it established a blueprint for perpetual nation-building rather than eventual separation. In Jefferson's "empire of liberty," the citizens of the nation shared the fruits of its expansion.

Napoleon Bonaparte had dreams of a revived French empire in America, certainly of a revived French sugar empire in the Caribbean. "I know the full value of Louisiana," he said, "and I have been desirous of repairing the fault of the French negotiator who abandoned it in 1763." On October 1, 1800, at the Treaty of San Ildefonso, Spain secretly ceded Louisiana back to France. Thomas Jefferson understood the value of Louisiana too. The threat of an aggressive (rather than a weak) European power having a stranglehold on New Orleans sent a chill down his spine. It looked as if France was to be the United States' "natural enemy." But a French Caribbean empire was not viable so long as British sea power remained intact and the slave revolt of Toussaint l'Ouverture remained defiant in Saint Domingue. Napoleon had to defeat them both. He could do neither. Yellow fever decimated his army in Saint Domingue and Horatio Nelson destroyed his fleet at Trafalgar. The French emperor needed money to wage war against England. He decided to cut his American losses and unload Louisiana. Louisiana, ceded to Spain in 1763, was French again for less than three years. In the spring of 1803, Robert Livingston and James Monroe, special ministers to Paris, concluded negotiations with Charles Maurice de Talleyrand. For $15 million (80 million francs), the 900,000 square miles of Louisiana became American territory. Passed back and forth like an unwanted stepchild since the Peace of Paris in 1763, Louisiana changed hands one more time in Paris in 1803. The events initiated in 1763 finally played themselves out. The empire in the West would not be French, Spanish, or British; it would be American.

Western lands—those between the Appalachians and the Mississippi that passed from French to British hands in 1763 and then from British to American hands in 1783, and those between the Mississippi and the Rockies that passed from French to Spanish hands in 1763, briefly back to France, and then to the United States in 1803—allowed an empire of slavery as well as an empire of liberty to expand. Should the western territories and the new states formed from them be slave or free? The question proved to be volatile and, despite repeated attempts at compromise, defied resolution. The West split the British Empire after 1763. Less than a century later it split the United States. The Revolution severed the relationship between the thirteen colonies and the empire, but it took another revolution to settle the relationship between the states and the union. The relationship between the people who were the citizens of the new nation and peoples who were not continued to contradict the ideals expressed to justify the nation's birth.

The Peace of 1763 transferred huge stretches of territory and transformed America. The contest for North American dominance that had raged between France and Britain for close to 100 years was settled once and, with the exception of a brief Napoleonic dream, for all. But the Peace brought little peace and much turmoil to North America. In wrapping up one round of conflicts, it ushered in others. One peace led to another. Territories that had changed hands in Paris in 1763 changed hands again in Paris in 1783. Twenty years later Louisiana changed hands, again in Paris. A new American nation emerged and built a single empire on the lands of numerous Indian nations transferred among three European nations in 1763.

Like King Midas, eighteenth-century Britons perhaps had wished for something too much in America. As happened in 1861, 1914, and 2003, people in 1763 responded to problems whose consequences they could see but not accept by initiating actions whose consequences they could not clearly foresee. In doing so, they set in motion events that changed forever the America they had known.

In *From Resistance to Revolution*, Pauline Maier traces the movement in America from the war for independence to constitutional governments in the states and the nation.

The colonists' constitutional arguments, their consistent respect for traditional procedures, even their efforts to contain violence have given later generations an impression that the American Revolution was hardly revolutionary at all. The colonists did not seek change; they set out to defend a constitutional system which had been established, they believed, with the Glorious Revolution of 1688. Here, however, they resembled many other revolutionaries of the seventeenth and eighteenth centuries, who also set out to restore an uncorrupted past. Only when that goal proved unobtainable did contenders establish new regimes that differed profoundly from the past, transforming their own land and sometimes shifting a wider civilization as well.

The colonists sought a past that could not be rewon, if indeed it had ever existed. Hence, to protect liberty as they understood it, the Americans broke off from their Mother Country and undertook one of the earliest modern colonial wars for independence. The movement toward independence constituted the negative phase of the Revolution, a rejection of old and once-revered institutions and ties, which for contemporaries constituted a major upheaval in its own right. It, moreover, opened a second phase of more wide-spread influence: a revolution in constitutional forms. The achievement of profound political change in the state and federal constitutions of the 1770's and 1780's grew logically out of the popular agitation of the years before independence. The American leaders' concern with peace and good order, their technique of curtailing individual violence by organizing, in effect institutionalizing, mass force— which continued beyond the extra-legal institutions of the 1760's into the committees, conventions, and congresses of the mid-1770's—led naturally toward the re-establishment of regular government. The overall form of these new institutions had also been largely determined by July 1776. Disillusionment with the English constitution and with contemporary British rulers had proceeded simultaneously until it became clear that the new-founded American state should not be modeled after that of England. Instead, it would be what the colonists came to call "republican." This conversion to republicanism transformed "a petty rebellion within the Empire into a symbol for the liberation of all mankind"; it meant that Americans helped open what R. R. Palmer has called the "Age of the Democratic Revolution."

In *The Radicalism of the American Revolution,* Gordon S. Wood summarizes the fundamental changes that resulted from the American Revolution.

In 1760 America was only a collection of disparate colonies huddled along a narrow strip of the Atlantic coast—economically underdeveloped outposts existing on the very edges of the civilized world. The less than two million monarchical subjects who lived in these colonies still took for granted that society was and ought to be a hierarchy of ranks and degrees of dependency and that most people were bound together by personal ties of one sort or another. Yet scarcely fifty years later these insignificant borderland provinces had become a giant, almost continent-wide republic of nearly ten million egalitarian-minded bustling citizens who not only had thrust themselves into the vanguard of history but had fundamentally altered their society and their social relationships. Far from remaining monarchical, hierarchy-ridden subjects on the margin of civilization, Americans had become, almost overnight, the most liberal, the most democratic, the most commercially minded, and the most modern people in the world.

The American Revolution was integral to the changes occurring in American society, politics, and culture at the end of the eighteenth century. These changes were radical, and they were extensive. To focus, as we are today apt to do, on what the Revolution did not accomplish—highlighting and lamenting its failure to abolish slavery and change fundamentally the lot of women—is to miss the great significance of what it did accomplish; indeed, the Revolution made possible the anti-slavery and women's rights movements of the nineteenth century and in fact all our current egalitarian thinking. The Revolution not only radically changed the personal and social relationships of people, including the position of women, but also destroyed aristocracy as it had been understood in the Western world for at least two millennia. The Revolution brought respectability and even dominance to ordinary people long held in contempt and gave dignity to their menial labor in a manner unprecedented in history and to a degree not equaled elsewhere in the world. The Revolution did not just eliminate monarchy and create republics; it actually reconstituted what Americans meant by public or state power and brought about an entirely new kind of popular politics and a new kind of democratic officeholder. The Revolution not only changed the culture of Americans—making over their art, architecture, and iconography—but even altered their understanding of history, knowledge, and truth. Most important, it made the interests and prosperity of ordinary people—their pursuits of happiness—the goal of society and government. The Revolution did not merely create a political and legal environment conducive to economic expansion; it also released powerful popular entrepreneurial and commercial energies that few realized existed and transformed the economic landscape of the country. In short, the Revolution was the most radical and most far-reaching event in American history.

In *Faces of Revolution,* Bernard Bailyn considers the enduring meaning of the Revolution for Americans.

The American Revolution not only created the American political nation but molded permanent characteristics of the culture that would develop within it. The Revolution is an event, consequently, whose meaning cannot be confined to the past. Whether we recognize it or not, the sense we make of the history of our national origins helps to define for us, as it has for generations before us, the values, purposes, and acceptable characteristics of public institutions. The questions must repeatedly be asked, therefore, what the nature of the event was, and what bearing it should have on our lives.

APPENDIX A

In celebration of the American Revolution, *The American Revolution: A Historical Guidebook* concludes with the transcript of the Declaration of Independence.

THE DECLARATION OF INDEPENDENCE

The Declaration of Independence: A Transcription

The National Archives: http://www.archives.gov/exhibits/charters/declaration_transcript.html

IN CONGRESS, July 4, 1776.

The unanimous Declaration of the thirteen united States of America,

When in the Course of human events, it becomes necessary for one people to dissolve the political bands which have connected them with another, and to assume among the powers of the earth, the separate and equal station to which the Laws of Nature and of Nature's God entitle them, a decent respect to the opinions of mankind requires that they should declare the causes which impel them to the separation.

We hold these truths to be self-evident, that all men are created equal, that they are endowed by their Creator with certain unalienable Rights, that among these are Life, Liberty and the pursuit of Happiness.—That to secure these rights, Governments are instituted among Men, deriving their just powers from the consent of the governed,—That whenever any Form of Government becomes destructive of these ends, it is the Right of the People to alter or to abolish it, and to institute new Government, laying its foundation on such principles and organizing its powers in such form, as to them shall seem most likely to effect their Safety and Happiness. Prudence, indeed, will dictate that Governments long established should not be changed for light and transient causes; and accordingly all experience hath shewn, that mankind are more disposed to suffer, while evils are sufferable, than to right themselves by abolishing the forms to which they are accustomed. But when a long train of abuses and usurpations, pursuing invariably the same Object evinces a design to reduce them under absolute Despotism, it is their right, it is their duty, to throw off such Government, and to provide new Guards for their future security.—Such has been the patient sufferance of these Colonies; and such is now the necessity which constrains them to alter their former Systems of Government. The history of the present King of Great Britain is a history of repeated injuries and usurpations, all having in direct object the establishment of an absolute Tyranny over these States. To prove this, let Facts be submitted to a candid world.

He has refused his Assent to Laws, the most wholesome and necessary for the public good.

He has forbidden his Governors to pass Laws of immediate and pressing importance, unless suspended in their operation till his Assent should be obtained; and when so suspended, he has utterly neglected to attend to them.

He has refused to pass other Laws for the accommodation of large districts of people, unless those people would relinquish the right of Representation in the Legislature, a right inestimable to them and formidable to tyrants only.

He has called together legislative bodies at places unusual, uncomfortable, and distant from the depository of their public Records, for the sole purpose of fatiguing them into compliance with his measures.

He has dissolved Representative Houses repeatedly, for opposing with manly firmness his invasions on the rights of the people.

He has refused for a long time, after such dissolutions, to cause others to be elected; whereby the Legislative powers, incapable of Annihilation, have returned to the People at large for their exercise; the State remaining in the mean time exposed to all the dangers of invasion from without, and convulsions within.

He has endeavoured to prevent the population of these States; for that purpose obstructing the Laws for Naturalization of Foreigners; refusing to pass others to encourage their migrations hither, and raising the conditions of new Appropriations of Lands.

He has obstructed the Administration of Justice, by refusing his Assent to Laws for establishing Judiciary powers.

He has made Judges dependent on his Will alone, for the tenure of their offices, and the amount and payment of their salaries.

He has erected a multitude of New Offices, and sent hither swarms of Officers to harrass our people, and eat out their substance.

He has kept among us, in times of peace, Standing Armies without the Consent of our legislatures.

He has affected to render the Military independent of and superior to the Civil power.

He has combined with others to subject us to a jurisdiction foreign to our constitution, and unacknowledged by our laws; giving his Assent to their Acts of pretended Legislation:

For Quartering large bodies of armed troops among us:

For protecting them, by a mock Trial, from punishment for any Murders which they should commit on the Inhabitants of these States:

For cutting off our Trade with all parts of the world:

For imposing Taxes on us without our Consent:

For depriving us in many cases, of the benefits of Trial by Jury:

For transporting us beyond Seas to be tried for pretended offences:

For abolishing the free System of English Laws in a neighbouring Province, establishing therein an Arbitrary government, and enlarging its Boundaries so as to render it at once an example and fit instrument for introducing the same absolute rule into these Colonies:

For taking away our Charters, abolishing our most valuable Laws, and altering fundamentally the Forms of our Governments:

For suspending our own Legislatures, and declaring themselves invested with power to legislate for us in all cases whatsoever.

He has abdicated Government here, by declaring us out of his Protection and waging War against us.

He has plundered our seas, ravaged our Coasts, burnt our towns, and destroyed the lives of our people.

He is at this time transporting large Armies of foreign Mercenaries to compleat the works of death, desolation and tyranny, already begun with circumstances of Cruelty & perfidy scarcely paralleled in the most barbarous ages, and totally unworthy the Head of a civilized nation.

He has constrained our fellow Citizens taken Captive on the high Seas to bear Arms against their Country, to become the executioners of their friends and Brethren, or to fall themselves by their Hands.

He has excited domestic insurrections amongst us, and has endeavoured to bring on the inhabitants of our frontiers, the merciless Indian Savages, whose known rule of warfare, is an undistinguished destruction of all ages, sexes and conditions.

In every stage of these Oppressions We have Petitioned for Redress in the most humble terms: Our repeated Petitions have been answered only by repeated injury. A Prince whose character is thus marked by every act which may define a Tyrant, is unfit to be the ruler of a free people.

Nor have We been wanting in attentions to our Brittish brethren. We have warned them from time to time of attempts by their legislature to extend an unwarrantable jurisdiction over us. We have reminded them of the circumstances of our emigration and settlement here. We have appealed to their native justice and magnanimity, and we have conjured them by the ties of our common kindred to disavow these usurpations, which, would inevitably interrupt our connections and correspondence. They too have been deaf to the voice of justice and of consanguinity. We must, therefore, acquiesce in the necessity, which denounces our Separation, and hold them, as we hold the rest of mankind, Enemies in War, in Peace Friends.

We, therefore, the Representatives of the united States of America, in General Congress, Assembled, appealing to the Supreme Judge of the world for the rectitude of our intentions, do, in the Name, and by Authority of the good People of these Colonies, solemnly publish and declare, That these United Colonies are, and of Right ought to be Free and Independent States; that they are Absolved from all Allegiance to the British Crown, and that all political connection between them and the State of Great Britain, is and ought to be totally dissolved; and that as Free and Independent States, they have full Power to levy War, conclude Peace, contract Alliances, establish Commerce, and to do all other Acts and Things which Independent States may of right do. And for the support of this Declaration, with a firm reliance on the protection of divine Providence, we mutually pledge to each other our Lives, our Fortunes and our sacred Honor.

APPENDIX B

"REPORT TO CONGRESS ON THE HISTORIC PRESERVATION OF REVOLUTIONARY WAR AND WAR OF 1812 SITES IN THE UNITED STATES"

The following is an excerpt from page 9 of the report.

This report reflects the results of the Revolutionary War and War of 1812 Historic Preservation Study. The Congress of the United States of America authorized this study because it found, in the late 1990s, that:

- Revolutionary War sites and War of 1812 sites provide a means for Americans to understand and interpret the periods in American history during which the Revolutionary War and War of 1812 were fought;
- the historical integrity of many Revolutionary War sites and War of 1812 sites is at risk because many of the sites are located in regions that are undergoing rapid urban or suburban development; and
- it is important for the benefit of the United States, to obtain current information on the significance of, threats to the integrity of, and alternatives of the preservation and interpretation of Revolutionary War sites and War of 1812 sites.

The charge from Congress for this study was the same as for a Civil War sites study of the early 1990s: study the sites associated with significant events of the wars. However, while the Civil War Sites Advisory Commission limited itself to sites of battle, the National Park Service chose in this case to include additional sites associated with significant events other than battles. The result is a much more thorough survey that represents twice the field effort undertaken for the Civil War study.

TIMELINE: 1763–1791

1763

February 10	The Treaty of Paris ends the Seven Years' War.
October 7	Parliament establishes the Proclamation Line, which prohibits settlement west of the Appalachian Mountains.
Spring–Fall 1763	Ottawa war leader, Pontiac, leads a rebellion against the British that began at Detroit.

1764

April 5	Parliament passes the Sugar Act.

1765

March 22	Parliament passes the Stamp Act.
May 15	Parliament passes the Quartering Act.
May 30	The Virginia House of Burgesses passes the Virginia Resolves.
October	The Stamp Act Congress meets in New York City.

1766

March 18	Parliament repeals the Stamp Act and passes the Declaratory Act.

1767

June 29	Parliament passes the Townshend Acts.
December 2	The first of John Dickinson's *Letters from a Farmer in Pennsylvania* is published.

1768

October 1	The British standing army arrives in Boston to enforce duties and protect the Commissioners.

1770

March 5	British soldiers kill 5 civilians in the Boston Massacre.
mid-March	The British standing army is removed to Castle Island.
April 12	Parliament repeals all of the Townshend duties except the duty on tea.

1772

November	*The Votes and Proceedings* of the Boston town meeting lists the American rights violated by the British.

1773

May 10	Parliament passes the Tea Act.
December 16	Colonists in Indian disguise dump chests of tea in the Boston harbor: the Boston Tea Party.

1774

March	Parliament passes the four Coercive Acts, called the Intolerable Acts by the colonists.
July 18	Fairfax County, led by Washington, adopts the Fairfax Resolves.
September 5– October 26	The First Continental Congress meets in Philadelphia: 56 delegates from 12 colonies.
October 20	Delegates to the Congress sign the Continental Association, which authorizes trade restrictions against Britain.

1775

April 18	Paul Revere and others ride to warn communities of the British advance by sea.
April 19	The British fire on the militia at Lexington, MA, and kill 8.
April 19	The British fire the "shot heard 'round the world" at Concord, MA; the militia return fire and drive the British back toward Boston.
April 20	The royal governor of Virginia removes the gunpowder from the Williamsburg Powder Magazine to the HMS *Fowey*.
May 10	Americans capture Fort Ticonderoga, NY.
May 12	Americans capture Crown Point, NY.
May 10– December	The Second Continental Congress meets in Philadelphia.
June 8	Lord Dunmore, the royal governor of Virginia, flees to HMS *Fowey*.
June 14	Congress establishes the Continental Army.
June 15	Congress appoints George Washington commander in chief.
June 17	The British attack and seize Bunker Hill, MA.
July 3	George Washington assumes command of the Continental Army.
July 5	Congress approves the "Olive Branch Petition" to King George III.
August 23	King George III declares the colonies to be in rebellion.
October 13	Congress establishes the Continental Navy and buys the first ships the following month.
October 18	Admiral Graves burns Falmouth (now Portland), ME, to stop American privateers.
November 14	Lord Dunmore, the royal governor of Virginia, issues a proclamation freeing the slaves who joined his force.
November 19–21	Loyalists attacked Ninety Six, SC.
December 3	The flag, the Grand Union, is flown on the *Alfred*.

December 9	Patriots defeat the British force at Great Bridge, VA.
December 22	King George III approves the Prohibitory Act which bans all commerce with the colonies and allows impressment of the officers and crews of captured vessels.
December 30	With the approval of Congress, Washington opens the Continental Army to free black men.
December 31	The Americans' attack on Quebec fails.

1776

January 9	Thomas Paine's *Common Sense* is published.
February 27	Militia defeat loyalists at Moores Creek, NC.
March 2	The British capture rice boats at Savannah and sail away, ending royal authority in Savannah until December 1778.
March	Congress votes to permit privateering.
March 2–16	Washington fortifies Dorchester Heights, MA, with artillery Colonel Knox has hauled from Fort Ticonderoga.
March 17	The British and loyalists evacuate Boston, MA.
April 6	Congress declares all ports open to all nations except Great Britain.
April 12	The North Carolina Provincial Congress adopts the "Halifax Resolves."
April	The Continental Army leaves its winter encampment in Cambridge, marches to New York, and begins to build defenses.
May 10	Congress passes John Adams's resolution that the colonies create new governments.
June 28–29	The British attack on Sullivan's Island at Charleston, SC, fails. Cherokees attack along the southern frontier.
July 4	The Continental Congress approves the Declaration of Independence in Philadelphia, PA.
Mid-July	General William Howe, in command of a 32,000-man army, occupies New York harbor.
August 22-29	The battle on Long Island, NY.
August 29–30	Defeated on Long Island, NY, the Americans retreat to Manhattan.
September 11	John Adams, Benjamin Franklin, and Edward Rutledge meet with Admiral Richard Howe on Staten Island.
September	Militia burn Cherokee towns, including Nikwasi, NC. Washington's generals vote not to defend Manhattan.
September 16	The Americans win the skirmish at Harlem Heights, NY.
October 11–13	Brigadier General Benedict Arnold's naval defeat at Valcour Island, NY, delays the British advance south on Lake Champlain until July 1777.
October 18	Colonel John Glover's Continentals slow the British advance at Pell's Point, NY.
October 28	The British and Hessians win the battle at White Plains, NY.
November 16	The British and Hessians capture Fort Washington, NY.
November 20	The British and Hessians take Fort Lee, NJ; General Nathanael Greene and the garrison escape.

December 8	General Clinton takes Newport, RI, without a battle.
December 19	Thomas Paine's *The American Crisis* is published.
December 21–24	Militia and Hessians skirmish at Mount Holly, NJ.
December 25–26	Washington crosses the Delaware River.
December 26	Washington's Continentals defeat the Hessians at Trenton, NJ.

1777

January 1–2	General Charles Cornwallis's attack on Washington at Trenton, NJ, is unsuccessful.
January 3	The Americans defeat the British at Princeton, NJ.
January 6–May 28	The Continental Army's winter encampment is at Morristown, NJ.
April 26–28	The British raid along the Atlantic coast: Ridgefield and Compo Hill, CT.
May 17	Georgia militia are defeated at Thomas Creek, FL.
May 30–June 1	Indians attack Logan's Fort, KY.
Summer	In two treaties, the Cherokees cede 5 million acres.
July 5–6	After the Americans evacuate Fort Ticonderoga, NY, and Mount Independence, VT, British forces led by General John Burgoyne occupy them.
July 7	The British win the battle at Hubbardton, VT.
July 8	The Vermont Constitution is adopted in Windsor, VT.
July 8	The Americans burn and abandon Fort Ann, NY.
July 30	The Americans evacuate Fort Edward, NY.
August 2–23	The British siege of Fort Stanwix, NY, fails.
August 6	A British and Indian force defeats a militia and Indian force in the battle at Oriskany, NY.
August 16	The Americans defeat the Hessians in the battle at Bennington, NY.
August 19	Congress relieves General Philip Schuyler of his command; General Horatio Gates assumes command.
August 25	British forces sail south from New York, up the Chesapeake Bay, and land at Head of Elk, MD.
September 11	General Howe defeats General Washington in the battle at Brandywine, PA.
September 18	Militia attack Fort Ticonderoga, NY (Lake George).
September 19	The British and Hessians win the battle at Freeman's Farm, Saratoga, NY.
September 19	Congress leaves Philadelphia and meets for one day in Lancaster, PA, and in York during the British occupation.
September 21	The British defeat General Anthony Wayne's Continentals in a surprise night attack at Paoli, PA.
September 26	The British occupy Philadelphia.
October 4	General Washington attacks the British at Germantown, PA.
October 6	General Henry Clinton takes Forts Clinton and Montgomery, NY.
October 7	The American attack at Bemis Heights, Saratoga, NY, is successful.
October 16	The British burn Kingston, NY.

October 9–17	The American siege of Saratoga, NY, forces the surrender of General Burgoyne.
October 22	The Hessians' attack on Fort Mercer, NJ, is unsuccessful.
November 10–16	The British naval bombardment forces the evacuation of Fort Mifflin, PA.
November 21	The loss of Fort Mifflin forces the evacuation of Fort Mercer.
November 15	The Continental Congress approves the Articles of Confederation and sends them to the states for ratification.
October–November	Americans murder Shawnees at Fort Randolph, WV.
December 19– June 19, 1778	The Continental Army's winter encampment is at Valley Forge, PA.

1778

February 6	The United States signs two treaties with France in Paris.
February 23	Friedrich Wilhelm von Steuben arrives at Valley Forge to train the army.
March 2	General Nathanael Greene is appointed quartermaster general.
March 13	The French ambassador informs King George III that France has recognized the United States of America.
April 19	The Americans capture the *Hinchinbrooke* and *Rebecca* in the Frederica River, GA.
May 4	Congress ratifies the treaties with France.
May 8	General Clinton takes over command from General Howe.
June 18	The British evacuate Philadelphia, PA.
June 19	The Continental Army marches out of Valley Forge.
June 28	The Continentals fight effectively at Monmouth, NJ.
June 30	The Americans fail for the third time to take control of East Florida: Fort Tonyn and Alligator Creek Bridge, FL.
July	Colonel George Rogers Clark captures Kaskaskia and Vincennes.
August 5–31	The French fleet and the Americans fail to retake Newport, RI.
September 6–15	General Charles Grey raids along the coast of Massachusetts.
September 7–18	Shawnees put Fort Boonesborough, KY, under siege.
September 28	General Grey defeats the Continentals at Old Tappan, NJ.
November 6–9	The British raid Vermont near Lake Champlain.
November 11	A British and Indian force raids Cherry Valley, NY.
November 25	Fort Morris refuses to surrender to the British.
December 17	The British retake Vincennes, IN.
December 29	The British capture Savannah, GA.
November 1778– June 1779	General Washington divides the army among winter encampments in and near Danbury, CT, West Point, NY, and Middlebrook, NJ.

1779

January 9	The British capture Fort Morris, GA.
February 14	Militia defeats loyalists at Kettle Creek, GA.
February–March	A British and Indian force holds Fort Laurens, OH, under siege.
February 23–25	Colonel Clark retakes Vincennes, IN.

May 11–13	The Americans refuse to surrender Charleston, SC.
May 30–June 1	The British capture two forts at King's Ferry: Fort Lafayette on Verplanck's Point and Stony Point, NY.
June	Spain enters the war as an ally of France.
July 15–16	General Wayne recaptures Stony Point, NY.
July 21–August 13	Commodore Dudley Saltonstall fails to attack the British at Penobscot Bay, ME, and abandons his ships.
August 29	The Continental Army's destruction of Iroquois villages begins with the skirmish at Newtown, NY.
September 23	Captain John Paul Jones captures the HMS *Serapis*.
October 9	The French and American attack on Savannah, GA, fails.
October	The British evacuate Newport, RI.
December 1– June 22, 1780	The Continental Army's winter encampment is at Morristown, NJ.

1780

February 11–May 12	The siege of Charleston, SC, by General Clinton; General Benjamin Lincoln surrenders the city and the army.
May 29	Lieutenant Colonel Banastre Tarleton defeats Colonel Abraham Buford at Waxhaws, SC.
June 5	General Cornwallis assumes command of the British Army in the South.
June 20	Militia defeat loyalists at Ramsour's Mill, NC.
June 22	The Continental Army leaves the Morristown encampment.
June 24	A British and Indian force captures Ruddell's Station, KY.
June 26	A British and Indian force captures Martin's Station, KY.
July 12	Partisans defeat Christian Huck at Williamson's Plantation, SC.
July 10	The Comte de Rochambeau arrives off Newport, RI, on the French fleet with more than 5,000 troops.
July 25	General Horatio Gates assumes Southern Department command.
August 1–2	Joseph Brant leads raids by loyalists and Indians in the Canajoharie District, NY.
August 8	Colonel Clark leads the militia attack on the Shawnee village, Piqua, OH.
August 6	Brigadier General Thomas Sumter defeats loyalists at Hanging Rock, SC.
August 16	The British defeat General Gates at Camden, SC.
August 18	Militia defeat loyalists at Musgrove's Mill, SC.
September 20	General Washington meets with the Comte de Rochambeau in Hartford, CT.
September 25	General Washington learns that General Benedict Arnold has defected.
October 7	Americans defeat loyalists at Kings Mountain, SC.
October 19	A force led by Sir John Johnson and Joseph Brant raids Stone Arabia, NY.

October 19	Militia attack Johnson's force at Klock's Field, NY.
November 20	Brigadier General Sumter stops Colonel Tarleton at Blackstock's Plantation, SC.
November 23	Major BenjaminTallmadge defeats the British at Fort St. George, NY.
December 2	General Greene assumes command of the Southern Department.

1781

January 17	General Daniel Morgan defeats the British at Cowpens, SC.
January 28	The British occupy Wilmington, NC.
February 1	General Cornwallis's victory at Cowan's Ford, NC, slows his pursuit of General Greene on the march to the Dan River.
February 25	Loyalists are defeated at Pyle's Defeat, NC.
March 1	Ratified by all of the states, the Articles of Confederation go into effect.
March 15	General Cornwallis wins a costly victory over General Greene at Guilford Court House, NC.
April 15–23	Americans capture Fort Watson, SC.
April 25	Lord Francis Rawdon wins a costly victory over General Greene at Hobkirk Hill, SC.
April 25	General Cornwallis leads the British out of Wilmington, NC, and marches north toward Virginia.
May 14	Robert Morris takes office as Superintendent of Finance.
May 22–June 19	Americans hold Ninety Six, SC, under siege.
July 6	General Wayne's attack on General Cornwallis fails at Green Spring, VA.
July 10	Colonel Marinus Willett's militia win the short battle at Sharon Springs, NY.
August 18–19	The Continental and French armies begin their march to Virginia.
September 5	The French fleet defeats the British fleet off Virginia.
September 6	Benedict Arnold's command burns New London, CT.
September 8	In the battle at Eutaw Springs, SC, both forces suffer heavy casualties.
September 28–October 19	General Washington and the Comte de Rochambeau hold the British under siege at Yorktown, VA.
October 19	Cornwallis surrenders the British army at Yorktown.
October 25	Colonel Marinus Willett's militia battle British raiders at Johnstown, NY.
October 30	Colonel Willett's militia battle British raiders at West Canada Creek, NY.
November 18	The British evacuate Wilmington, NC.

1782

January 18	The South Carolina General Assembly convenes.
February 11	Lord George Germain resigns as American secretary.
February 23	King George III has General Clinton recalled.
March 8	Americans massacre Delawares at Gnadenhutten, OH.

March 20	Lord North resigns as prime minister.
March 27–July 1	Lord Rockingham is prime minister until his death.
July 4–April 2	The Earl of Shelburne is prime minister.
June 4–5	Loyalists and Indians win the battle of Crawford's Defeat, OH.
July 11	The British evacuate Savannah, GA.
August	The French army begins to march north from Yorktown.
August 15	Canadian Rangers and Indians raid Bryan's Station, KY.
August 19	Rangers and Indians ambush militia at Blue Licks, KY.
October– June 1783	The winter encampment of the Continental Army is at New Windsor Cantonment, NY.
October 30	Formal peace negotiations begin in Paris.
November 29	The provisional peace treaty is signed in Paris.
December 14	The British evacuate Charleston, SC.

1783

March 15	General Washington quells the so-called Newburgh Conspiracy.
April 17	A British and Indian force attacks the Spanish garrison at Arkansas Post, AR.
April 19	General Washington orders the "Cessation of Hostilities" to be proclaimed on the eighth anniversary of the battles at Lexington and Concord.
September 3	The Treaty of Paris is signed by John Adams, Benjamin Franklin, and John Jay.
November 25	The British evacuate New York City and Brooklyn, NY.
December 23	General Washington resigns his command.

1784

January 14	The Treaty of Paris is ratified by Congress in Annapolis, MD.

1787

May 25–September 17	The Constitutional Convention meets in Philadelphia.
September 17	The Constitutional Convention approves the Constitution.

1789

March 4	After the Constitution is ratified by eleven state conventions, the first Congress convenes in New York.
April 30	George Washington is inaugurated the first president of the United States of America.
May 29	The Rhode Island state convention ratifies the Constitution.
November 21	The North Carolina state convention ratifies the Constitution.

1791

December	The first ten amendments to the Constitution, the Bill of Rights, are ratified by three-fourths of the states.

ABOUT THE AUTHORS

Thomas Allen is the author of *Tories: Fighting for the King in America's First Civil War*. Other works include *George Washington, Spymaster; Mr. Lincoln's High-Tech War* (co-author with Roger MacBride Allen); *The First Mormon Candidate; The Bonus Army: An American Epic;* and *Possessed: The True Story of an Exorcism*.

Fred Anderson is professor of history at the University of Colorado and the author of *Crucible of War*, which won the Francis Parkman Prize and the Mark Lynton History Prize. With Andrew Cayton, he is the author of *The Dominion of War: Empire and Liberty in North America, 1500–2000*.

Richard Archer is professor of history emeritus at Whittier College and author of *As If an Enemy's Country* and *Fissures in the Rock: New England in the Seventeenth Century*.

Paul Aron is director of publications for the Colonial Williamsburg Foundation and the author of, among other books, *Unsolved Mysteries of American History, We Hold These Truths*, and *Why the Turkey Didn't Fly*.

Lawrence E. Babits is a maritime and battlefield archaeologist. His specialties include Revolutionary War Southern Campaigns and eastern theater Civil War topics. He authored a study of the Battle of Cowpens and is the co-author (with Joshua B. Howard) of *Long, Obstinate and Bloody: The Battle of Guilford Courthouse*.

Bernard Bailyn is the Adams University Professor and James Duncan Phillips Professor of Early American History, emeritus, at Harvard University. His books, beside *Faces of Revolution*, include *The Ideological Origins of the American Revolution, To Begin the World Anew*, and *The Ordeal of Thomas Hutchinson*.

Carol Berkin is Presidential Professor Emerita of Baruch College of the City University of New York. Her books include *First Generations: Women in Colonial America; A Brilliant Solution: Inventing the American Constitution; Revolutionary Mothers; Civil War Wives; Wondrous Beauty: The Extraordinary Life of Elizabeth Patterson Bonaparte*.

Ira Berlin is Distinguished University Professor at the University of Maryland and the founding director of the Freedmen and Southern Society Project. He is author of *Many*

Thousands Gone: The First Two Centuries of Slavery in North America and *Slaves without Masters: The Free Negro in the Antebellum South.*

Robert W. Blythe is an independent scholar and former chief of history in the Southeast Region of the National Park Service. He is writing two park histories, including the first comprehensive history of Everglades National Park.

Carl P. Borick is the assistant director of the Charleston Museum in Charleston, South Carolina. He is the author of *A Gallant Defense: The Siege of Charleston, 1780* and *Relieve Us of this Burthen: American Prisoners of War in the Revolutionary South.*

T. H. Breen is the James Marsh Professor at large at the University of Vermont and author of *American Insurgents, American Patriots: The Revolution of the People* and *The Marketplace of Revolution: How Consumer Politics Shaped American Independence.*

John Buchanan was chief registrar of The Metropolitan Museum of Art in charge of worldwide art movements. His books include *The Road to Guilford Courthouse: The American Revolution in the Carolina,* and *The Road to Valley Forge: How Washington Built the Army That Won the Revolution.*

Jon Butler is Lamar Professor Emeritus at Yale University and author of "Freedom of Religion" in *Revolutionary Founders: Rebels, Radicals, and Reformers in the Making of the Nation,* edited by Alfred F. Young, Gary B. Nash, and Ray Raphael. His books include *Becoming America* and *Awash in a Sea of Faith.*

Colin G. Calloway is professor of history and professor of Native American Studies at Dartmouth College. He is author of *The Scratch of a Pen, The Shawnees and the War for America, The American Revolution in Indian Country, One Vast Winter Count,* and *Pen and Ink Witchcraft.*

Benjamin L. Carp is associate professor of history at Tufts University and author of *Defiance of the Patriots: The Boston Tea Party and the Making of America* and *Rebels Rising: Cities and the American Revolution.*

Edward J. Cashin was professor emeritus of history and director of the Center for the Study of Georgia History at Augusta State University and author of "Revolutionary War in Georgia" in www.georgiaencyclopedia.org and *William Bartram and the American Revolution on the Southern Frontier.*

Edward Countryman is University Distinguished Professor of History at Southern Methodist University and author of *A People in Revolution: The American Revolution and Political Society in New York, 1760–1790; The American Revolution;* and *Enjoy the Same Liberty: Black Americans and the Revolutionary Era.*

Marcus Cunliffe was University Professor at The George Washington University and author of *George Washington: Man and Monument; The Literature of the United States, The Nation Takes Shape, 1789–1837; Soldiers and Civilians: The Martial Spirit in America, 1775–1865;* and *Chattel Slavery and Wage Slavery: The Anglo-American Context, 1830–1860.*

David Brion Davis is Sterling Professor of History Emeritus at Yale. He is the author of *Inhuman Bondage: The Rise and Fall of Slavery in the New World* and co-author (with Steven Mintz) of *The Boisterous Sea of Liberty.*

Jonathan R. Dull is author of *A Diplomatic History of the American Revolution* and *Benjamin Franklin and the American Revolution.*

Barbara R. Duncan is education director of the Museum of the Cherokee Indian in Cherokee, North Carolina. Her publications include *Cherokee Heritage Trails Guidebook* and *Living Stories of the Cherokee*. In 2008 she received the Brown Hudson Folklore Award.

Christian Y. Dupont, an independent historian and library management consultant, is former director of the Albert and Shirley Small Special Collections Library at the University of Virginia. He is co-editor, with Peter S. Onuf, of *Declaring Independence: The Origin and Influence of America's Founding Document*.

Walter Edgar is Distinguished Professor Emeritus of History and Neuffer Professor of Southern Studies at the University of South Carolina. He is author of *Partisans and Redcoats: The Southern Conflict that Turned the Tide of the American Revolution* and *South Carolina: A History*. He was editor-in-chief of *The South Carolina Encyclopedia*.

R. David Edmunds is Watson Professor of American History at the University of Texas at Dallas. He is author of *The People* (with Frederick E. Hoxie and Neal Salisbury), *The Shawnee Prophet,* and *Tecumseh and the Quest for Indian Leadership*.

Joseph J. Ellis is author of *American Creation: Triumphs and Tragedies at the Founding of the Republic, Founding Brothers,* and *His Excellency: George Washington*.

John Ferling is professor emeritus at the University of West Georgia and author of *A Leap in the Dark, Almost a Miracle, Independence, John Adams, Setting the World Ablaze, The Loyalist Mind, The Ascent of George Washington*, and *Jefferson and Hamilton*.

David Hackett Fischer teaches at Brandeis and is the author of *Albion's Seed, Paul Revere's Ride*, and *Washington's Crossing*.

Thomas Fleming, author of *Washington's Secret War,* has written twenty nonfiction books, many with a focus on the American Revolution, and twenty-three novels about America, from the 1730s to today. His latest book is *A Disease in the Public Mind: A New Understanding of Why We Fought the Civil War*.

Eric Foner is DeWitt Clinton Professor of American History at Columbia University and the author of many books on American history, including *Tom Paine and Revolutionary America*.

Joseph T. Glatthaar is the Stephenson Distinguished Professor of History at the University of North Carolina at Chapel Hill. He is co-author (with James Kirby Martin) of *Forgotten Allies: The Oneida Indians and the American Revolution* and numerous other books on American military history.

John W. Gordon is professor of National Security Affairs, Marine Corps University Command and Staff College, and author of *South Carolina and the American Revolution*. Previously a professor, faculty fellow, and dean of undergraduate studies at The Citadel, he served also as a visiting professor, US Military Academy, West Point.

Jerome A. Greene is retired from the National Park Service. Besides *The Guns of Independence*, he is author of *Beyond Bear's Paw: The Nez Perce Indians in Canada* and *American Carnage: Wounded Knee 1890—The Reality and Denial of the Last Frontier Massacre*, forthcoming from the University of Oklahoma Press.

Robert A. Gross is James L. and Shirley A. Draper Professor of Early American History at the University of Connecticut. He is author of *The Minutemen and Their World* (25th anniversary edition) and editor of *In Debt to Shays: The Bicentennial of an Agrarian Rebellion*.

Ira D. Gruber is Harris Masterson, Jr. Professor Emeritus of History at Rice University and author of *The Howe Brothers and the American Revolution.*

Don Higginbotham was Dowd Distinguished Professor at the University of North Carolina at Chapel Hill and author of *Daniel Morgan: Revolutionary Rifleman, The War of American Independence,* and *George Washington and the American Military Tradition.*

Woody Holton is McCausland Professor of History at the University of South Carolina and the author of four books on the American Revolution, including *Forced Founders: Indians, Debtors, Slaves, and the Making of the American Revolution in Virginia.*

James Oliver Horton is the Benjamin Banneker Professor Emeritus of American Studies and History at The George Washington University, co-author of *Hard Road to Freedom: The Story of African America* and co-editor of *Slavery and Public History* (with Lois E. Horton), and author of *Landmarks of African American History.*

Lois E. Horton is professor of history emerita at George Mason University, co-author of *Slavery and the Making of America* and *In Hope of Liberty: Culture, Community and Protest among Northern Free Blacks, 1700–1860* (with James Oliver Horton), and author of *Harriet Tubman and the Fight for Freedom.*

Joshua Howard is a Revolutionary War historian and co-author (with Lawrence E. Babits) of *Long, Obstinate and Bloody: The Battle of Guilford Courthouse.*

Frederick E. Hoxie is Swanlund Professor of History at the University of Illinois, Urbana/Champaign. He is author of several books, including *This Indian Country* and *The People: A History of Native America* (with Neal Salisbury and David Edmunds).

Benjamin H. Irvin is associate professor of history at the University of Arizona and author of *Clothed in Robes of Sovereignty: The Continental Congress and the People Out of Doors* and *Samuel Adams: Son of Liberty, Father of Revolution.*

Walter Isaacson is the president and CEO of the Aspen Institute and author of *Steve Jobs, Benjamin Franklin: An American Life, Einstein: His Life and Universe, Kissinger: A Biography,* and *American Sketches: Great Leaders, Creative Thinkers, and Heroes of a Hurricane.*

Maya Jasanoff is a professor of history at Harvard and author of *Liberty's Exiles: American Loyalists in the Revolutionary World.*

Richard Ketchum was an author and editor. His books include *Saratoga: Turning Point of America's Revolutionary War, Decisive Day: The Battle for Bunker Hill,* and *Victory at Yorktown: The Campaign that Won the Revolution.*

Michael Kranish is Washington Bureau deputy chief of *The Boston Globe* and author of *Flight from Monticello: Jefferson at War.*

Edward G. Lengel is editor in chief of the Papers of George Washington. He is author of *General George Washington: A Military Life* and editor of *This Glorious Struggle, George Washington's Revolutionary War Letters.*

W. David Lewis was a Distinguished University Professor at Auburn University and author of "The Iron Plantations" in *Hopewell Furnace: Official National Park Handbook* and *Eddie Rickenbacker: An American Hero in the Twentieth Century.*

Piers Mackesy is Emeritus Fellow of Pembroke College, University of Oxford, and a Fellow of the British Academy. He is author of *The War for America, 1775–1783.*

Pauline Maier was the William Rand Kenan, Jr., Professor of American History at MIT. Her books include *From Resistance to Revolution: Colonial Radicals and the Development of American Opposition to Britain, 1765–1776,* and *American Scripture: Making the Declaration of Independence,* and *Ratification: The People Debate the Constitution, 1787–1788.*

James Kirby Martin is the Hugh Roy and Lillie Cranz Cullen University Professor of History at the University of Houston and author of *Benedict Arnold, Revolutionary Hero: An American Warrior Reconsidered* and co-author (with Joseph T. Glatthaar) of *Forgotten Allies: The Oneida Indians and the American* Revolution, among other volumes.

Christian M. McBurney is a partner at the law firm of Nixon Peabody LLP and author of *The Rhode Island Campaign: The First French and American Operation in the Revolutionary War.*

David McCullough is the author of *Truman, Brave Companions, Mornings on Horseback, The Path between the Seas, The Great Bridge, The Johnstown Flood, John Adams, 1776,* and *The Greater Journey.* He is twice winner of the Pulitzer Prize, twice winner of the National Book Award.

Robert M. S. McDonald, associate professor of history at the United States Military Academy, is editor of *Sons of the Father: George Washington and His Protégés* and author of "Thomas Jefferson's Strange Career as Author of Independence" in *Declaring Independence,* Christian Y. Dupont and Peter S. Onuf, editors.

Robert Middlekauff is Preston Hotchkis Professor Emeritus of History at the University of California, Berkeley, and author of *The Glorious Cause: The American Revolution, 1763–1789; The Mathers,* which won the Bancroft Prize; and *Benjamin Franklin and His Enemies.*

Steven Mintz is professor of history at the University of Texas at Austin and director of the Institute for Transformational Learning. His books include *Huck's Raft: A History of American Childhood* and *The Boisterous Sea of Liberty,* co-authored with David Brion Davis.

Edmund S. Morgan was Sterling Professor Emeritus of History at Yale University and recipient of the Pulitzer Prize and the National Humanities Medal. His books include *The Challenge of the American Revolution, The Puritan Dilemma, Benjamin Franklin, American Heroes, The Genius of George Washington,* and *American Slavery, American Freedom.*

Dan L. Morrill is professor of history at the University of North Carolina at Charlotte and author of *Southern Campaigns of the American Revolution, Civil War in the Carolinas,* and *Historic Charlotte, an Illustrated History.* He has also produced numerous documentaries, including "Rural Mecklenburg: A Vanishing Way of Life."

Gary B. Nash is professor of history emeritus and director of the National Center for History in the Schools at UCLA. He is editor (with Alfred F. Young and Ray Raphael) of *Revolutionary Founders: Rebels, Radicals, and Reformers in the Making of the Nation* and author of *The Liberty Bell.*

Mary Beth Norton is Mary Donlon Alger Professor of American History at Cornell University and author of *Liberty's Daughters: The Revolutionary Experience of American Women, 1750–1800,* along with other books on Early American history.

Peter S. Onuf is Thomas Jefferson Foundation Professor Emeritus, University of Virginia, and Senior Research Fellow at the Robert H. Smith International Center for Jefferson Studies, Monticello. Co-editor (with Christian Y. Dupont) and author of the Introduction to

Declaring Independence, Onuf's works include *Jefferson's Empire* and *The Mind of Thomas Jefferson*.

John S. Pancake was professor of history, the University of Alabama from 1949 until his death in 1986 and author of *1777: The Year of the Hangman* and *This Destructive War: The British Campaign in the Carolinas, 1780–1782*.

Cassandra Pybus is Australian Research Council Professor of History at Sydney University and currently Leverhulme Visiting Professor at Kings College London. She is the author of eleven books including *Epic Journeys of Freedom: Runaway Slaves of the American Revolution and Their Global Quest for Liberty*.

Jack Rakove is the William Robertson Coe Professor of History and American Studies at Stanford University and the author of *Original Meanings: Politics and Ideas in the Making of the Constitution* and *Revolutionaries: A New History of the Invention of America*.

Ray Raphael is Senior Research Fellow at Humboldt State University, California. His seventeen books include *Founders, A People's History of the American Revolution, Founding Myths, Constitutional Myths*, and *Mr. President: How and Why the Founders Created a Chief Executive*. With Gary Nash and Alfred Young, he edited *Revolutionary Founders*.

John Rhodehamel, former Norris Foundation Curator of American Historical Manuscripts at the Huntington Library, is the author of *The Great Experiment: George Washington and the American Republic* and editor of *George Washington: Writings*, and *The American Revolution: Writings from the War of Independence*.

Neal Salisbury is Barbara Richmond 1940 Professor Emeritus in the Social Sciences (History) at Smith College. He is author of *Manitou and Providence: Indians, Europeans, and the Making of New England, 1500–1643* and *The People: A History of Native Americans* (with R. David Edmunds and Frederick E. Hoxie).

Barbara Clark Smith is curator of political history at the National Museum of American History, Smithsonian Institution. Her publications include *The Freedoms We Lost: Consent and Resistance in Revolutionary America* and "A Revolutionary Era" in *Boston and the American Revolution*, edited by Raymond Baker.

Craig L. Symonds is professor emeritus at the United States Naval Academy. He is the author or editor of twenty-six books, including *A Battlefield Atlas of the American Revolution, The Battle of Midway*, and *Neptune: The Allied Invasion of Europe and the D-Day Landings*.

Alan Taylor is the Thomas Jefferson Chair in American History at the University of Virginia. He is the author of *The Divided Ground: Indians, Settlers, and the Northern Borderland of the American Revolution* and *The Internal Enemy: Slavery and War in Virginia, 1772–1832*.

Barbara W. Tuchman was awarded the Pulitzer Prize for *The Guns of August* and *Stilwell and the American Experience in China, 1911–45*. Her books include *The Zimmermann Telegram, The Proud Tower, A Distant Mirror, Practicing History, The March of Folly*, and *The First Salute*.

David K. Wilson holds an M.A. in history from the University of Texas at Arlington. He is author of *The Southern Strategy: Britain's Conquest of South Carolina and Georgia, 1775–1780*, and many articles on the American Revolution.

Gordon S. Wood is Alva O. Way University Professor and professor of history emeritus at Brown University. He is author of *The Radicalism of the American Revolution; The Creation of the*

American Republic 1776–1787; Revolutionary Characters: What Made the Founders Different; The American Revolution; and *The Americanization of Benjamin Franklin*.

W. J. Wood was an instructor and research officer at the US Field Artillery School and author of *Battles of the Revolutionary War 1775–1781*.

Alfred F. Young was professor emeritus of history at Northern Illinois University, editor (with Gary B. Nash and Ray Raphael) of *Revolutionary Founders: Rebels, Radicals, and Reformers in the Making of the Nation,* and author of *The Shoemaker and the Tea Party: Memory and the American Revolution*.

Rosemarie Zagarri is a University Professor at George Mason University. She is the author of *The Politics of Size: Representation in the United States, 1776–1850; A Woman's Dilemma: Mercy Otis Warren and the American Revolution*; and *Revolutionary Backlash: Women and Politics in the Early American Republic*.

ADDITIONAL RESOURCES

The following is a list of additional historic places. Also in the list are the paintings and the websites referred to in the text.

Historic Places

Adams National Historical Park at 135 Adams Street in Quincy, Massachusetts, includes the John Adams and John Quincy Adams birthplaces and the residence of the Adams family for four generations.

Benjamin Franklin National Memorial is in Memorial Hall in the Franklin Institute, Independence National Historical Park, in Philadelphia, Pennsylvania.

Bennington Battle Monument is on the site of the supply depot in Bennington, Vermont, north of Route 9.

George Washington Birthplace National Monument is at 1732 Popes Creek Road in Colonial Beach, Virginia.

Gunston Hall, home of George Mason, is at 10709 Gunston Road in Lorton, Virginia.

Hunter House at 54 Washington Street in Newport, Rhode Island, was the headquarters of the commander of the French fleet, Commodore Charles-Louis d'Arsac, Chevalier de Ternay.

Monticello, home of Thomas Jefferson, is on Thomas Jefferson Parkway in Charlottesville, Virginia.

Montpelier, home of James Madison, is at 11407 Constitution Highway in Montpelier Station, Virginia.

Mount Vernon, home of George Washington, is at 3200 Mt. Vernon Memorial Highway in Alexandria, Virginia.

Thaddeus Kosciuszko National Memorial, the home of Thaddeus Kosciuszko, is at Third and Pine Streets in Philadelphia, Pennsylvania.

The Prizery, the arts and cultural center on Bruce Street in South Boston, Virginia, has the exhibit "The Crossing of the Dan."

Touro Synagogue National Historic Site, on Touro Street in Newport, Rhode Island, became a hospital and assembly hall during the British occupation.

Online Resources

The transcript of the Lee Resolution is on the National Archives website: http://www.archives.gov/exhibits/charters/declaration_timeline.html.

The map of the routes of George Rogers Clark and British Lieutenant Governor Henry Hamilton Hamilton are on the National Park Service website: http://www.nps.gov/common/commonspot/customcf/apps/maps/showmap.cfm?alphacode=gero&parkname=George%20Rogers%20Clark.

The Knox Trail website includes maps and information about the route of Colonel Henry Knox's artillery train from Fort Ticonderoga to Boston in 1775–1776: http://www.nysm.nysed.gov/services/KnoxTrail/index.html.

The Crossroads of the American Revolution National Heritage Area website includes maps and information about the American Revolution in New Jersey: http://www.revolutionarynj.org.

Following are the National Park Service websites for the national battlefields, historic sites, historic trails, historical parks, memorials, and monuments included in this book:

Arkansas Post National Memorial:www.nps.gov/arpo/

Boston National Historical Park: www.nps.gov/bost/

Castillo De San Marcos National Monument: www.nps.gov/casa/

Colonial National Historical Park: www.nps.gov/jame/

Cowpens National Battlefield: www.nps.gov/cowp/

Fort Stanwix National Monument: www.nps.gov/fost/

Fort Sumter National Monument: www.nps.gov/fosu/

George Rogers Clark National Historical Park: www.nps.gov/gero/

Guilford Courthouse National Military Park: www.nps.gov/guco/

Hopewell Furnace National Historic Site: www.nps.gov/hofu/

Independence National Historical Park: www.nps.gov/inde/

Kings Mountain National Military Park: www.nps.gov/kimo/

Longfellow House–Washington's Headquarters National Historic Site: www.nps.gov/long/

Minute Man National Historical Park: www.nps.gov/mima/

Morristown National Historical Park: www.nps.gov/morr/

Moores Creek National Battlefield: www.nps.gov/mocr/

Ninety Six National Historic Site: www.nps.gov/nisi/

Overmountain Victory National Historic Trail: http://www.nps.gov/common/commonspot/customcf/apps/maps/showmap.cfm?alphacode=ovvi&parkname=Overmountain%20Victory.

Saratoga National Historical Park: www.nps.gov/sara/

Valley Forge National Historical Park: www.nps.gov/vafo/

Washington-Rochambeau Revolutionary Route National Historic Trail: http://www.nps.gov/waro/index.htm.

Paintings

These two paintings by John Trumbull are of the presentation of Thomas Jefferson's draft of the Declaration of Independence to the Continental Congress.

Declaration of Independence, 4 July 1776. Painting by John Trumball. 1786–1820. 20-7/8 × 31 inches is in the Yale University Art Gallery, New Haven, Connecticut. http://artgallery. yale.edu/collections/objects/declaration-independence-july-4-1776.

Declaration of Independence. Painting by John Trumball. 12 × 18 feet is in the United States Capitol Rotunda. It is one of four commissioned by the US Congress from Trumbull in 1817. http://www.aoc.gov/capitol-hill/historic-rotunda-paintings/declaration-independence.

Emanuel Leutze's painting, *Washington Crossing the Delaware,* 1851, is in The Metropolitan Museum of Art in New York. It depicts Washington crossing the Delaware River on December 25, 1776, in his attack on the Hessian soldiers in Trenton, New Jersey. http://www.met-museum.org/collections/search-the-collections/11417.

BIBLIOGRAPHY, PERMISSIONS, AND COPYRIGHT INFORMATION

The American Revolution: A Historical Guidebook includes excerpts from the following books, handbooks, and websites alphabetized by title. The page numbers of the excerpts are listed in the order in which they appear in this book.

Albion's Seed: Four British Folkways in America by David Hackett Fischer. Copyright © 1989 by David Hackett Fischer. By permission of Oxford University Press, USA. 808–10

Almost a Miracle: The American Victory in the War of Independence by John Ferling. Copyright © 2007 by John Ferling. By permission of Oxford University Press, USA. 54–59, 127, 9–11, 289–90, 302, 412–13, 428–32, 434–35, 466–67, 517–19, 574

American Creation: Triumphs and Tragedies at the Founding of the Republic by Joseph J. Ellis, copyright © 2007 by Joseph J. Ellis. Used by permission of Alfred A. Knopf, a division of Random House LLC. Any third party use of this material, outside of this publication, is prohibited. Interested parties must apply directly to Random House LLC for permission. 18–19, 73–77

American Indian Places: A Historical Guidebook, Frances H. Kennedy, editor. Copyright © 2008 by Frances H. Kennedy. Reprinted by permission of Houghton Mifflin Harcourt Publishing Company. All rights reserved. 112

American Insurgents, American Patriots: The Revolution of the People by T. H. Breen. Copyright © 2010 by T. H. Breen. Reprinted by permission of Hill and Wang, a division of Farrar, Straus and Giroux, LLC. 242, 52–53, 66, 3–4, 279–80, 284, 286

The Americanization of Benjamin Franklin by Gordon S. Wood, copyright © 2004 by Gordon S. Wood. Used by permission of The Penguin Press, a division of Penguin Group (USA) Inc. 195–98, 244–46

The American Revolution. "Colbert's Raid on Arkansas Post: Westernmost Action of the Revolution" by Bob Blythe. http://www.nps.gov/revwar/about_the_revolution/colberts_raid.html.

The American Revolution. Revised Edition by Edward Countryman. Copyright © 1985, 2003 by Edward Countryman. Reprinted by permission of Hill and Wang, a division of Farrar, Straus and Giroux, LLC. 41–44, 57–58, 46–47

The American Revolution by Gordon S. Wood, copyright © 2002 by Gordon S. Wood. Used by permission of Modern Library, a division of Random House LLC. Any third party use of this material, outside of this publication, is prohibited. Interested parties must apply directly to Random House LLC for permission. 35–36, 38–39, 42–44, 57, 80–81, 84, 76–78, 86–88, 158, 159, 165, 166

The American Revolution in Indian Country: Crisis and Diversity in Native American Communities by Colin G. Calloway. Copyright © 1995 Cambridge University Press. Reprinted with the permission of Cambridge University Press. 200–201, xiii, xv, 293, 300–301

The American Revolution: Writings from the War of Independence. John Rhodehamel, editor. Copyright © 2001 Literary Classics of the United States, Inc. From: Josiah Quincy, *The Journals of Major Samuel Shaw, the first American Consul at Canton, with a Life of the Author* (Boston: Wm. Crosby and H.P. Nichols, 1847), 99–105. Used by permission of The Library of America. 788–89

The American Revolution: Writings from the War of Independence. John Rhodehamel, editor. Copyright © 2001 Literary Classics of the United States, Inc. From *Journals of the Continental Congress 1774–1789*, vol. 25, ed. Gaillard Hunt (Washington, DC: Government Printing Office, 1922), 837–39. Used by permission of The Library of America. 793–94

American Scripture: Making the Declaration of Independence by Pauline Maier, copyright © 1997 by Pauline Maier. Used by permission of Alfred A. Knopf, a division of Random House LLC. Any third party use of this material, outside of this publication, is prohibited. Interested parties must apply directly to Random House LLC for permission. 7, 11, 14, 16–17, 21, 25–26, xvii, 27, 34–35, 40–41, 43–44, 46, 130–31, 142, 150

The Ascent of George Washington by John Ferling. Copyright © 2009 by John Ferling. Courtesy of Bloomsbury Press. 85–87, 235–37, 241–42

As If an Enemy's Country by Richard Archer. Copyright © 2010 by Richard Archer. By permission of Oxford University Press, USA. xvi–xvii, 228, 229

A Battlefield Atlas of the American Revolution by Craig L. Symonds, cartography by William J. Clipson, 12th prtg. Copyright ©1986 by The Nautical & Aviation Publishing Co. of America, Inc. Courtesy of The Nautical & Aviation Publishing Co. of America, Inc. 27, 29, 33, 55, 65, 85, 99

Battles of the Revolutionary War by W. J. Wood. © 2003 by W. J. Wood. Reprinted by permission of Algonquin Books of Chapel Hill. All rights reserved. 147–49

Benedict Arnold, Revolutionary Hero: An American Warrior Reconsidered by James Kirby Martin. Copyright © 1997 New York University Press. Courtesy of New York University Press. 79, 5, 426, 429–30, 338

Benjamin Franklin: An American Life by Walter Isaacson. Copyright © 2003 by Walter Isaacson. Reprinted with the permission of Simon & Schuster, Inc. All rights reserved.102–3, 285, 287–89, 319–20, 344–46, 395–96, 415–17

Benjamin Franklin and the American Revolution by Jonathan R. Dull. Copyright © 2010 by the Board of Regents of the University of Nebraska. Reproduced by permission of the University of Nebraska Press. 43–46

Benjamin Franklin: Autobiography, Poor Richard, and Later Writings. J. A. Leo Lemay, editor. Copyright © 1987 Literary Classics of the United States, Inc. From: Benjamin Franklin. *Political, Miscellaneous, and Philosophical Pieces.* Ed. Benjamin Vaughan. London: J. Johnson, 1779. Pages 552–54. Used by permission of The Library of America. 165–66

The Boisterous Sea of Liberty by David Brion Davis & Steven Mintz. Copyright © 1998 by The Gilder Lehrman Institute of American History. By permission of Oxford University Press, USA. 142–43, 156–57, 197–98, 208

Boston and the American Revolution. "A Revolutionary Era" by Barbara Clark Smith. 1998, Official National Park Handbook. National Park Service, Division of Publications. 44

The Challenge of the American Revolution by Edmund S. Morgan. Copyright © 1976 by W. W. Norton & Company, Inc. Used by permission of W. W. Norton & Company, Inc. 199–201

Clothed in Robes of Sovereignty: The Continental Congress and the People Out of Doors by Benjamin H. Irvin. Copyright © 2011 by Oxford University Press, Inc. By permission of Oxford University Press, USA. 261–62, 5, 10, 3, 18

"Cowpens National Battlefield Brochure." National Park Service, U. S. Department of the Interior.

The Creation of the American Republic, 1776–1787 by Gordon S. Wood. Published for the Omohundro Institute of Early American History and Culture. Copyright © 1970 by the University of North Carolina Press, new preface copyright © 1998 by the University of North Carolina Press. Used by permission of the publisher. www.uncpress.unc.edu. 354–59, 3, 4, 6

Crucible of War by Fred Anderson, copyright © 2000 by Fred Anderson. Used by permission of Alfred A. Knopf, a division of Random House LLC. Any third party use of this material, outside of this publication, is prohibited. Interested parties must apply directly to Random House LLC for permission. xxi–xxiii

Daniel Morgan: Revolutionary Rifleman by Don Higginbotham. Copyright © 1961 by the University of North Carolina Press, renewed 1989 by Don Higginbotham. Used by permission of the publisher. www.uncpress. unc.edu. viii–ix, 154–55

Declaring Independence: The Origin and Influence of America's Founding Document. Christian Y. Dupont and Peter S. Onuf, editors. "Thomas Jefferson's Strange Career as Author of Independence" by Robert M. S. McDonald. Copyright © 2008 by Robert M. S. McDonald. Used by permission of the author. "Introduction" by Peter S. Onuf. Copyright © 2008 by Peter S. Onuf. Used by permission of the author. "Preface" by David McCullough. Copyright © 2008 by David McCullough. Used by permission of the author. Published by the University of Virginia Library. ix, xii, vii, 21

Defiance of the Patriots: The Boston Tea Party and the Making of America by Benjamin L. Carp. Copyright © 2010 by Benjamin L. Carp. Courtesy of Yale University Press. 1–3, 145–46

A Diplomatic History of the American Revolution by Jonathan R. Dull. Copyright © 1985 by Yale University. Courtesy of Yale University Press. 14–16

The Divided Ground: Indians, Settlers, and the Northern Borderland of the American Revolution by Alan Taylor, copyright © 2006 by Alan Taylor. Used by permission of Alfred A. Knopf, a division of Random House LLC. Any third party use of this material, outside of this publication, is prohibited. Interested parties must apply directly to Random House LLC for permission. 97–98, 107–8

The Divided Ground: Indians, Settlers, and the Northern Borderland of the American Revolution by Alan Taylor, copyright © 2006 by Alan Taylor, used by permission of The Wylie Agency LLC. 97–98, 107–8

Enjoy the Same Liberty: Black Americans and the Revolutionary Era by Edward Countryman. Copyright © 2012 by Rowman & Littlefield Publishers, Inc. Courtesy of Rowman & Littlefield Publishers, Inc. 64

Epic Journeys of Freedom: Runaway Slaves of the American Revolution and Their Global Quest for Liberty by Cassandra Pybus. Copyright © 2006 by Cassandra Pybus. Reprinted by permission of Beacon Press, Boston. 7, 71, ix–x

Faces of Revolution by Bernard Bailyn, copyright © 1990 by Bernard Bailyn. Used by permission of Alfred A. Knopf, a division of Random House LLC. Any third party use of this material, outside of this publication, is prohibited. Interested parties must apply directly to Random House LLC for permission. xi–xii, 200

The First Salute by Barbara W. Tuchman, copyright © 1988 by Barbara W. Tuchman. Used by permission of Compass, a division of Random House LLC. Any third party use of this material, outside of this publication, is prohibited. Interested parties must apply directly to Random House LLC for permission. 44–47, 47–48, 20, 5–6, 241–42, 260–62, 296–98

Flight from Monticello: Jefferson at War by Michael Kranish. Copyright © 2010 by Michael Kranish. By permission of Oxford University Press, USA. 77–79

Forced Founders: Indians, Debtors, Slaves, and the Making of the American Revolution in Virginia by Woody Holton. Published for the Omohundro Institute of Early American History and Culture. Copyright © 1999 by the University of North Carolina Press. Used by permission of the publisher. www.uncpress.unc. edu. 206–7

Forgotten Allies: The Oneida Indians and the American Revolution by Joseph T. Glatthaar and James Kirby Martin. Copyright © 2006 by Joseph T. Glatthaar and James Kirby Martin. Reprinted by permission of Hill and Wang, a division of Farrar, Straus and Giroux, LLC. 138, 149–50, 159–61, 163–64, 166–69, 230–31, 270–71, 275–76, 281

Founders: The People Who Brought You a Nation by Ray Raphael. Copyright © 2009 by Ray Raphael. Reprinted by permission of The New Press. www.thenewpress.com. 171–72, 234–36, 219, 299–300, 321–22, 390

From Resistance to Revolution: Colonial Radicals and the Development of American Opposition to Britain, 1765–1776 by Pauline Maier, copyright © 1972 by Pauline Maier. Used by permission of Alfred A. Knopf, a division of Random House LLC. Any third party use of this material, outside of this publication, is prohibited. Interested parties must apply directly to Random House LLC for permission. 27–28, 157–58, 48, 267, 271–72

A Gallant Defense: The Siege of Charleston, 1780 by Carl P. Borick. Copyright © 2003 University of South Carolina. Courtesy of the University of South Carolina Press. 222–23

General George Washington: A Military Life by Edward G. Lengel, copyright © 2005 by Edward G. Lengel. Used by permission of Random House LLC. Any third party use of this material, outside of this publication, is prohibited. Interested parties must apply directly to Random House LLC for permission. 82, 84, 89, 157, 345

George Rogers Clark National Historical Park website. National Park Service, US Department of the Interior.http://www.nps.gov/gero/historyculture/index.htm.

George Washington: Man and Monument by Marcus Cunliffe, copyright © 1958, 1982 by Marcus Cunliffe. Used by permission of Dutton Signet, a division of Penguin Group (USA), Inc. 71, 111–12

George Washington: Writings. John Rhodehamel, editor. Copyright © 1997 Literary Classics of the United States, Inc. From: vol. 11, 284–93 of *The Writings of George Washington from the Original Manuscript Sources, 1745–1799*, edited by John C. Fitzpatrick (39 vols., Washington. DC: United States Government Printing Office, 1931–44). Used by permission of The Library of America. 299–300

George Washington: Writings. John Rhodehamel, editor. Copyright © 1997 Literary Classics of the United States, Inc. From: vol. 18, 452–54 of *The Writings of George Washington from the Original Manuscript Sources, 1745–1799*, edited by John C. Fitzpatrick (39 vols., Washington, DC: United States Government Printing Office, 1931–44). Used by permission of The Library of America. 378

George Washington: Writings. John Rhodehamel, editor. Copyright © 1997 Literary Classics of the United States, Inc. From: vol. 26, 483–96 of *The Writings of George Washington from the Original Manuscript Sources, 1745–1799,* edited by John C. Fitzpatrick (39 vols., Washington: United States Government Printing Office, 1931–44). 516, 518–19

The Glorious Cause: The American Revolution, 1763–1789 by Robert Middlekauff. Copyright © 1982 Oxford University Press, Inc. By permission of Oxford University Press, USA. 234–35, 239, 243, 247–49, 345, 3, 345, 375, 379, 379, 383, 391–92, 439, 435, 473, 473, 481–87, 490–99, 565, 573–75

The Great Experiment: George Washington and the American Republic by John Rhodehamel. Copyright © 1998 by Henry E. Huntington Library and Art Gallery and Yale University. Courtesy of Henry E. Huntington Library Press and Yale University Press. 42–44, 68–69

The Guns of Independence: The Siege of Yorktown, 1781 by Jerome A. Greene. Copyright © 2005 by Savas Beatie LLC. Courtesy of Savas Beatie LLC. 9–10, 33, 76, 79, 91, 229–30, 283–89, 323

His Excellency: George Washington by Joseph J. Ellis, copyright © 2004 by Joseph J. Ellis. Used by permission of Alfred A. Knopf, a division of Random House LLC. Any third party use of this material, outside of this publication, is prohibited. Interested parties must apply directly to Random House LLC for permission. 100–101, 125–27, 111–12

Hopewell Furnace. "The Iron Plantations" by W. David Lewis. 1983. Official National Park Handbook. National Park Service, Division of Publications. 7–8

The Howe Brothers and the American Revolution by Ira D. Gruber. Published for the Omohundro Institute of Early American History and Culture. Copyright © 1973 by the University of North Carolina Press. Used by permission of the publisher. 45, 47, 56–57, 362–65

Independence: The Struggle to Set America Free by John Ferling. Copyright © 2011 by John Ferling. Courtesy of Bloomsbury Press. 8–11

"James Ireland, John Leland, John 'Swearing Jack' Waller, and the Baptist Campaign for Religious Freedom in Revolutionary Virginia" by Jon Butler, in *Revolutionary Founders: Rebels, Radicals, and Reformers in the Making of the Nation*, edited by Alfred F. Young, Gary B. Nash, and Ray Raphael, copyright © 2011 by Jon Butler. Used by permission of the author. 169–71, 173–76

John Adams by David McCullough. Copyright © 2001 by David McCullough. Reprinted with the permission of Simon & Schuster, Inc. All rights reserved. 67–68, 131, 101–3, 18–19, 108–10, 129–30

John Adams: A Life by John Ferling. Copyright © 1992 by The University of Tennessee Press. Courtesy of The University of Tennessee Press. 92–93, 187

A Leap in the Dark: The Struggle to Create the American Republic by John Ferling. Copyright © 2003 by John Ferling. By permission of Oxford University Press, USA. 1, 40, 145–46, 182, 230–32

Liberty's Daughters: The Revolutionary Experience of American Women, 1750–1800 by Mary Beth Norton. Copyright © 1980 by Mary Beth Norton. Used by permission of the publisher, Cornell University Press. 297–99

Revolutionary Founders: Rebels, Radicals, and Reformers in the Making of the Nation, edited by Alfred F. Young, Gary B. Nash, and Ray Raphael. Used by permission of Alfred A. Knopf, a division of Random House LLC. Any third party use of this material, outside of this publication, is prohibited. Interested parties must apply directly to Random House LLC for permission. "Introduction," copyright © 2011 by Alfred F. Young, Ray Raphael, and Gary B. Nash. 4–5; "Ebenezer Mackintosh: Boston's Captain General of the Liberty Tree," copyright © 2011 by Alfred F. Young. 30–32.

Revolutionary Founders: Rebels, Radicals, and Reformers in the Making of the Nation, edited by Alfred F. Young, Gary B. Nash, and Ray Raphael, copyright © 2011 by Alfred F. Young, Ray Raphael, and Gary B. Nash. Reprinted by permission of the editors and the Sandra Dijkstra Literary Agency.

Revolutionary Mothers: Women in the Struggle for America's Independence by Carol Berkin, copyright © 2005 by Carol Berkin. Used by permission of Alfred A. Knopf, a division of Random House LLC. Any third party use of this material, outside of this publication, is prohibited. Interested parties must apply directly to Random House LLC for permission. 42–43

The Rhode Island Campaign: The First French and American Operation in the Revolutionary War by Christian M. McBurney. Copyright © 2011 Christian M. McBurney. Courtesy of Westholme Publishing. viii, 193–94

The Rising Glory of America, 1760–1820 edited by Gordon S. Wood. Copyright © 1971, 1990 by Gordon S. Wood. Courtesy University Press of New England. 5–7

The Road to Guilford Courthouse: The American Revolution in the Carolinas by John Buchanan. Copyright © 1997 by John Buchanan. This material is reproduced with permission of John Wiley & Sons, Inc. 108–10, 135–36, 178–79, 139–40, 275–77, 288, 292–94, 296–99, 363–64, 379–81

The Road to Valley Forge: How Washington Built the Army That Won the Revolution by John Buchanan. Copyright © 2004 by John Buchanan. This material is reproduced with permission of John Wiley & Sons, Inc. 68–69, 71–72, 213–14, 216, 261–62, 286–88

Saratoga: Turning Point of America's Revolutionary War by Richard M. Ketchum. Copyright © 1997 by Richard M. Ketchum. Reprinted by arrangement with Henry Holt and Company, LLC. 208, 248, 242–44, 378–79, 383, 429–31, 448

"Saratoga National Historical Park Brochure." National Park Service, U. S. Department of the Interior.

The Scratch of a Pen: 1763 and the Transformation of North America by Colin G. Calloway. Copyright © 2006 by Colin G. Calloway. By permission of Oxford University Press, USA. 63–64, 165–71

Setting the World Ablaze: Washington, Adams, Jefferson and the American Revolution by John Ferling. Copyright © 2000 by John Ferling. By permission of Oxford University Press, USA. 158–59, 305–6

1776 by David McCullough. Copyright © 2005 by David McCullough. Reprinted with the permission of Simon & Schuster, Inc. All rights reserved. 25, 58–59, 62–63, 69, 70–71, 78–79, 81–82, 85, 88, 90, 93–94, 96, 99, 104–5, 111, 293–94

1777: The Year of the Hangman by John S. Pancake. Copyright © 1977 by The University of Alabama Press. Courtesy of The University of Alabama Press. 1–2, 119–23, 124–27, 167

The Shawnees and the War for America by Colin G. Calloway. Copyright © 2007 by Colin G. Calloway. Used by permission of Viking Penguin, a division of Penguin Group (USA) Inc. xxii, xxiv–xxviii, xxxv, 64–65, 70, 70–72, 67–68

Slavery and the Making of America by James Oliver Horton and Lois E. Horton. Copyright © 2005 by Oxford University Press, Inc. By permission of Oxford University Press, USA. 59–60, 33, 41, 64–67

South Carolina and the American Revolution by John W. Gordon. Copyright © 2003 University of South Carolina. Courtesy of the University of South Carolina Press. 112–17, 121–23

Southern Campaigns of the American Revolution by Dan L. Morrill. Copyright © 1993 by The Nautical & Aviation Publishing Co. of America, Inc. Courtesy of The Nautical & Aviation Publishing Co. of America, Inc. 12–13, 165–69

The Southern Strategy: Britain's Conquest of South Carolina and Georgia, 1775–1780 by David K. Wilson. Copyright © 2005 University of South Carolina. Courtesy of the University of South Carolina Press. 257–59

This Destructive War: The British Campaign in the Carolinas, 1780–1782 by John S. Pancake. Copyright © 1985, 2003 by The University of Alabama Press. Courtesy of The University of Alabama Press. 70–71, 148–49, 163–64, 188–90, 238

GENERAL INDEX

Note: Page numbers in *italics* indicate illustrations and maps.

INDEX OF AUTHORS
AND PUBLICATIONS

Note: Page numbers in *italics* indicate illustrations and maps.

DISCARD